PLANNI
ACT 2011

Other titles available from Law Society Publishing:

Conveyancing Handbook (19th edn) (forthcoming, 2012)
Frances Silverman (ed)

Environmental Law Handbook (7th edn)
Valerie Fogleman, Trevor Hellawell and Andrew Wiseman

Environmental Information Regulations
Susan Wolf

Planning and the Compulsory Purchase Act 2004
Stephen Tromans, Martin Edwards, Richard Harwood and Justine Thornton

Property Development
Gavin Le Chat

Titles from Law Society Publishing can be ordered from all good bookshops or direct (telephone 0870 850 1422, email **lawsociety@prolog.uk.com** or visit our online shop at **www.lawsociety.org.uk/bookshop**).

PLANNING AND THE LOCALISM ACT 2011

A Guide to the New Law

Dr Paul Stookes and Pat Thomas OBE

The Law Society

ISBN-13: 978-1-907698-28-6

Published in 2012 by the Law Society
113 Chancery Lane, London WC2A 1PL

Typeset by Columns Design XML Ltd, Reading
Printed by CPI Group (UK) Ltd, Croydon, CR0 4YY

The paper used for the text pages of this book is FSC certified. FSC (the Forest Stewardship Council) is an international network to promote responsible management of the world's forests.

CONTENTS

ABOUT THE AUTHORS

Paul Stookes PhD, MSc, LLB, CEnv, MIEMA is a solicitor-advocate and partner at specialist law firm Richard Buxton Environmental & Public Law and an accredited mediator. He has been involved in law reform as a specialist adviser to the government on the clean neighbourhood provisions, by progressing prominent cases in planning and environmental impact assessment, and as a member of the Law Society's Planning and Environment Committee. Paul regularly lectures on planning and environmental law and was senior lecturer at the School of Law, University of Hertfordshire between 2005 and 2011. He is author of *A Practical Approach to Environmental Law (2nd edn)* (OUP, 2009), co-author of *People Power* (Lawpack, 2008) and editor of *Costing the Earth (2nd edn)* (Magistrates' Association, 2009). His developing mediation practice is wide-ranging, covering civil and public law and community disputes.

Pat Thomas OBE, MA, LARTPI is a planning law consultant and a solicitor admitted in 1974. She was formerly a partner at SJ Berwin where she established their planning law practice, and before that was a partner at Denton Hall (as it then was). She has been a member and chair of the Law Society's Planning and Environment Committee, and for many years was a member of the Oxford Joint Planning Law Conference Organising Committee as one of the Law Society's representatives. Pat is a vice-chair and trustee of the Town and Country Planning Association and, since January 2012, the Honorary Solicitor and Secretary to the Royal Town Planning Institute. She sits on the British Property Federation Planning Committee, and holds various other trusteeships. She received an OBE in 2006 for services to town and country planning.

FOREWORD

The land use planning system in England and Wales is perhaps necessarily complex. It seeks to resolve a range of competing interests through detailed regulatory provisions, within a structure of democratic decision-making at all levels of government and full public involvement. Over time this regulation of town and country planning through legislation, case law and policy has grown into an extensive body of documentation. The reforms brought about by the Localism Act 2011 and the National Planning Policy Framework (NPPF) seek to simplify this system and make it more accessible to its users and benefactors through the focus on community involvement, with a substantial reduction in policy statements and the correction of abuses of the system, seen particularly in relation to enforcement. I welcome the objectives of the new Act and the NPPF. This guide provides a useful summary of the planning provisions of the Act and the NPPF, and will provide valuable help through the new system for practitioners and laypeople alike. I commend the authors and publishers for having responded so promptly and expertly to this need.

Lord Carnwath
May 2012

TABLE OF CASES

TABLE OF STATUTES

TABLE OF STATUTORY INSTRUMENTS

TABLE OF EUROPEAN LEGISLATION

LIST OF ABBREVIATIONS

the Act	Localism Act 2011
CIL	Community Infrastructure Levy
CIL Regulations	Community Infrastructure Levy (Amendment) Regulations 2011, SI 2011/987
CJEU	Court of Justice of the European Union
CLEUD	certificate of lawfulness for existing use and development
CRBO	community right to build order
EC	European Commission
EIA Directive	Environmental Impact Assessment Directive (2011/92/EU)
EU	European Union
GLA	Greater London Authority
GLA 1999	Greater London Authority Act 1999
HRA 2008	Housing and Regeneration Act 2008
IPC	Infrastructure Planning Commission
LCA 1961	Land Compensation Act 1961
LDA	London Development Agency
LDEDCA 2009	Local Democracy, Economic Development and Construction Act 2009
LDO	local development order
LGA 1972	Local Government Act 1972
LGA 2000	Local Government Act 2000
Local Development Regulations 2004	Town and Country Planning (Local Development) (England) Regulations 2004, SI 2004/2204
LPA	local planning authority
MDC	Mayoral development corporation

MPG	Minerals Planning Guidance
MTAN	Mineral Technical Advice Note
NDO	neighbourhood development order
NDP	neighbourhood development plan
NPPF	National Planning Policy Framework
NPS	national policy statement
NSIP	nationally significant infrastructure project
PA 2008	Planning Act 2008
PAS	Planning Advisory Service
PCPA 2004	Planning and Compulsory Purchase Act 2004
PINS	Planning Inspectorate
PPG	Planning Policy Guidance
PPS	Planning Policy Statement
RIA	regulatory impact assessment
RPB	regional planning body
RPG	regional planning guidance
RSS	regional spatial strategy
RTPI	Royal Town Planning Institute
SEA Directive	Strategic Environment Assessment Directive (2001/42/EC)
TAN	Technical Advice Notice
TCPA 1990	Town and Country Planning Act 1990
TFEU	Treaty on the Functioning of the European Union

PART A INTRODUCTION AND GENERAL MATTERS INFLUENCING PLANNING

1 INTRODUCTION

The primary purpose of this book is to explain, clarify and provide commentary on elements of the Localism Act 2011 (the Act) that relate directly and indirectly to land use planning. This chapter provides a general introduction to the Act. It describes the progression through Parliament of the Localism Bill and sets out some of the key terms used. It also aims to explain how the Act will work and enter into force.

1.1 STRUCTURE OF THIS BOOK

The structure of this book follows the structure of the Act in as much as the Parts, Chapters and sections are followed consecutively where consistency and sense permits. The book is divided into three main parts:

- Part A focuses on the rights and responsibilities following decentralisation, including clarification of the general powers of local authorities, their liability for EU fines, and the opportunities for community involvement. While the Act is not expressly part of the town and country planning legislative regime, these parts of the Act will apply to planning matters alongside other aspects of local governance.
- Part B covers the specific planning provisions within the Act including the abolition of regional spatial strategies, the duty to co-operate in relation to planning of sustainable development, the use of the Community Infrastructure Levy, neighbourhood planning, enforcement and infrastructure projects.
- Part C summarises specific planning reform measures, such as matters in relation to London and compulsory purchase. It also discusses the provisions in the National Planning Policy Framework.

1.2 THE DEVELOPING IDEA OF LOCALISM AND REFORM OF THE PLANNING PROCESS

1.2.1 The emerging localism agenda

The political will to place localism at the heart of government came to the fore during the 2010 parliamentary elections. The coalition agreement of May 2010 stated that: 'The time has come to disperse power more widely in Britain today'. Yet defining localism has not proved easy.

The Communities and Local Government Committee set up to examine the expenditure, administration, and policy of the Department for Communities and Local Government was one of a number of select committees appointed by the House of Commons that has recently considered localism and took evidence from a range of interested parties. The *Communities and Local Government Committee – Third Report: Localism* (9 May 2011) (**www.parliament.gov.uk**) stated:

> 12. On the surface, localism is an uncontroversial concept. The large majority of our witnesses were, with some caveats, appreciative of the Government's intentions, enthused by the prospect of more powers being made available to local authorities, communities, and third sector organisations, and welcoming of more opportunities for citizens to influence how their services are designed and delivered. We took evidence at the outset of our inquiry from local government leaders from all three major parties, who emphasised that there is considerable cross-party consensus on the need for decentralisation. Cllr Richard Kemp, leader of the LGA Liberal Democrats, defined localism as:
>
> '*involving people, wherever possible, in the decisions that affect their life, and devolving to officers, members and civil society – that's probably the easiest way to describe it – power to make those decisions at the lowest possible level, so we meet the real needs of local communities and individuals, not the perceived needs of people in Whitehall and town halls.*'
>
> Cllr Steve Reed, Leader of Labour-controlled Lambeth Council, said
>
> '*I think we're looking at equalising the power relationship between the citizen and the state, or between public services and the people who use public services, so that citizens are able to become active shapers, rather than just passive recipients, of services. Localism is about putting in place the mechanisms that allow that transfer of power to happen and have meaning in terms of the services that people receive.*'
>
> 13. Cllr Colin Barrow, Conservative Leader of Westminster City Council, summed up their agreement: 'I think we all believe that decisions should be taken as close to the people who are affected by them as possible'. This sits comfortably alongside the Department's own declaration that 'Our guiding principle is that power should be held at the lowest possible level, whether this is individuals, communities, neighbourhoods, local institutions or local government'. These statements reflect the general thrust of the principle of 'subsidiarity'; that decisions should be taken and power exercised at the lowest appropriate level. Decisions affecting a particular area should wherever possible be taken within that area, without interference from higher tiers of government.
>
> 14. We asked the Minister for Decentralisation, Greg Clark, what international examples the Government had in mind as models for the sort of localism it is seeking to promote. He did not cite a particular country, emphasising instead that the English system is 'one of the most centralised' in the world. Mr Clark talked about the greater involvement of communities at local level in planning in the Netherlands, greater community ownership of rewards for development in Denmark, and the freedom of states in the United States; 'Wherever you look you come to the ineluctable conclusion that we are very centralised to a dysfunctional extent.'
>
> 15. We welcome the Government's commitment to localism and decentralisation. We agree with the Government that power in England is currently too centralised, that each community should be able to influence what happens in its locality to a

> much greater extent, that there has been in the past too much central government interference in the affairs of local authorities, and that public services have been insufficiently accountable to their local populations. In these respects we concur with the conclusions of our predecessors in their report on the balance of power between central and local government.
>
> 16. Barnsley Council, however, identified why localism can in fact prove a contentious concept:
>
> *'the problem with "localism" is that like sunshine, no one can be against it, which means that everyone is a "localist". But the concept is sufficiently broad so as to invite a number of varying interpretations from a range of people and political parties. Often, this ensures that there is a perpetual sea of uncertainty and structural and functional change, some of which is genuinely supportive of localism, some of which, despite the stated claims, is profoundly not.'*

The Act does not define localism and, given the range of views above, the authors make no attempt to define localism. The legislation now requires account to be taken of local interests and needs through, for example, the community right to challenge and neighbourhood planning. It will not, however, be possible to avoid the European and international obligations that also influence our local communities.

Whatever comment the new legislation may prompt, the Localism Act 2011 does take a bold step towards a more decentralised system of governance. It remains to be seen whether this will be positive or problematic for society.

1.2.2 The planning reforms

Land use planning is one of the most important responsibilities of local government. It is essentially a predictive process whereby society and local communities can be shaped by strategic planning decisions and individual development control decisions (now referred to as 'development management decisions').

There has long been a desire to simplify and reform planning in order to create a less bureaucratic but nevertheless democratically accountable system.

By the early 1990s the government had consolidated and revised the town and country planning legislation and was looking forward to improving the system and other rules that govern land and its use. Land use and the planning system were, for instance, critical elements of the White Paper, *This Common Inheritance: Britain's Environmental Strategy* (HMSO, 1990).

Ten years on and it was suggested that it was time for change. In the Labour Party's Green Paper, *Planning: delivering a fundamental change* (2001), the Secretary of State for Transport, Local Government and the Regions explained:

> Getting planning right means that our goals for society are easier to achieve. Good planning can have a huge beneficial effect on the way we live our lives. It must have a vision of how physical development can improve a community. But, some fifty years after it was first put in place, the planning system is showing its age. What was once an innovative emphasis on consultation has now become a set of inflexible, legalistic and bureaucratic procedures. A system that was intended to promote development

> now blocks it. Business complains that the speed of decision is undermining productivity and competitiveness. People feel they are not sufficiently involved in decisions that affect their lives. So it is time for change. We need good planning to deliver sustainable development, to harness growth to build a better future.

In February 2010 the Conservative Party published its Green Paper *Open Source Planning* in which it stated that: 'The planning system is vital for a strong economy, for an attractive and sustainable environment, and for a successful democracy. At present, the planning system in England achieves none of these goals. It is broken.' It explained that 'Open Source' was a concept which originated in the software industry that aims to make computer programming open to all in a highly flexible and adaptable way. The Green Paper proposed that this was the approach that the planning system required.

The White Paper *Local growth: realising every place's potential* (28 October 2010) set the scene for localism and planning reform. The government was explicit in its aims. At page 23 it explained that:

> Both businesses and communities need to feel that investment will be rewarded and they can work together to produce an economically, socially and environmentally sustainable future. Government is committed to reforming the planning system, so that it actively encourages growth. Reforms will ensure that people have greater ownership of the planning system. Actions proposed include:
>
> - introducing a national presumption in favour of sustainable development, which will apply to decisions on all planning applications;
> - giving local communities ... new Right-to-Build powers;
> - fundamentally reforming and streamlining national planning policy and guidance, presenting to Parliament a simple national planning framework; and
> - placing a new statutory duty to cooperate on local authorities, public bodies and private bodies that are critical to plan-making, such as infrastructure providers.

Within two months the Localism Bill had been published enacting many of the proposed reforms alongside other measures to transform local governance.

1.2.3 Progression of the Bill through Parliament

Discussion as to how the particular elements of the Localism Bill became statute is left, where relevant, to specific sections. Generally, the Bill expanded and contracted as it wove its way through the Houses of Commons and Lords, particularly in relation to the arrangements for local referendums, and was largely unopposed by the Lords. Contentious aspects such as concerns over concealment and planning enforcement remained. The impact of other apparently modest sections may yet materialise as associated planning policy unfolds: in particular, the application of the National Planning Policy Framework (discussed in **Chapter 14**).

1.3 PURPOSE AND STRUCTURE OF THE ACT

1.3.1 Purpose of the Act

The preamble to the Localism Act 2011 states that it is:

> An Act to make provision about the functions and procedures of local and certain other authorities; to make provision about the functions of the Commission for Local Administration in England; to enable the recovery of financial sanctions imposed by the Court of Justice of the European Union on the United Kingdom from local and public authorities; to make provision about local government finance; to make provision about town and country planning, the Community Infrastructure Levy and the authorisation of nationally significant infrastructure projects; to make provision about social and other housing; to make provision about regeneration in London; and for connected purposes.
>
> [15th November 2011]

This is helpful in understanding the extent and scope of the Act. It covers local authority functions, associated financial matters, planning, housing and regeneration in London. Its purpose is further explained in government guidance first published in December 2010 to support progress of the Localism Bill through Parliament and twice updated. In his foreword to *A plain English guide to the Localism Act update* (DCLG, November 2011) (*the Guide*), the Rt. Hon Greg Clark MP, Minister of State for Decentralisation explains that:

> ... The Localism Act sets out a series of measures with the potential to achieve a substantial and lasting shift in power away from central government and towards local people. They include: new freedoms and flexibilities for local government; new rights and powers for communities and individuals; reform to make the planning system more democratic and more effective, and reform to ensure that decisions about housing are taken locally.

1.3.2 Structure of the Act

The Act runs to some 483 pages comprising 241 sections and 25 Schedules and, while there is frequent reference to guidance and regulations to be enacted, the Act itself is not framework in style or nature. Many of its provisions are highly specific and detailed. There is also frequent cross-referencing to other legislation including numerous insertions into the Town and Country Planning Act (TCPA) 1990 (e.g. s.123 on enforcement) and the Planning and Compulsory Purchase Act (PCPA) 2004 (e.g. s.110 on sustainable development). Although the elements of the Local Democracy, Economic Development and Construction Act (LDEDCA) 2009 relating to regional strategies are repealed (s.109), on balance, it is estimated that there is now more legislation than less in an effort to streamline the planning system.

1.3.3 Terms, definitions and acronyms

There is frequent reference to the Localism Act 2011 throughout this book. Any reference to 'the Act' is assumed to be to the Localism Act 2011. Similarly any reference to 'planning' is assumed to mean the town and country planning system, also known as land use planning. There are numerous acronyms in the Act. These are set out in full when first used in the book but not otherwise repeated. There is a list of abbreviations at the beginning of this book covering the acronyms used.

Other general points: at the present time the 'Secretary of State' means the Secretary of State for Communities and Local Government. There is frequent reference throughout the Act to 'relevant authority' and 'local authority' although the scope of the terms varies from section to section. A common definition of local authority is, for example, found in s.106 in Part 5, Chapter 3, 'Assets of Community Value'. This defines local authority in relation to England as:

(a) a district council,
(b) a county council for an area in England for which there are no district councils,
(c) a London borough council,
(d) the Common Council of the City of London, or
(e) the Council of the Isles of Scilly.

For Wales, local authority means:

(a) a county council in Wales, or
(b) a county borough council.

Contrast this with the scope of 'relevant authority' in Part 5, Chapter 7 on Standards, which includes 16 distinct authorities in England alone. It is important therefore to check the particular meaning of 'relevant authority' as it applies to any particular part of the Act. To avoid repetition in this book, reference is often made to a particular section of the Act relevant to the Part or section under discussion but without reciting the complete text of that section. Reference should then be made to extracts from the Act itself set out in **Appendix A**.

1.3.4 Interpretation

Many Chapters and sections in the Act have their own interpretation provisions as opposed to an overall interpretation section at the beginning or the end of the legislation. While adding to the length of the Act, it makes sense where different terms apply depending on the particular provision being considered (see the discussion of local authority above). There are, however, gaps in interpretation where the legislation is simply seeking to limit the use of a term or phrase (see e.g. 'relevant service' in s.81(5) relating to the community right to challenge) rather than to assist a broad understanding of the provisions. There is also frequent reference to the Interpretation Act 1978 to explain, for instance, the meaning of 'enactment'.

1.4 ENTRY INTO FORCE AND COMMENCEMENT

Section 240 sets out the commencement provisions for the Act.

1.4.1 General statement: commencement by statutory instrument

Section 240(2) of the Act provides a general statement that 'subject to subsections (1) and (3) to (6), provisions of this Act come into force on such day as the Secretary of State may by order appoint'. Section 235(1) provides that any power to make an order or regulations under the Act is exercisable by statutory instrument. Thus, the starting point is that many provisions in the Act only come into force once the government has published a statutory instrument providing a specific date that the relevant sections may enter into force; see e.g. the Localism Act (Commencement No. 1 and Transitional Provisions) Order 2011, SI 2011/2896, enacted on 2 December 2011. It will therefore be necessary to be alert to emerging statutory instruments to find out when particular sections are brought into effect.

Section 240 also provides exceptions to the general rule that the provisions will be enacted by order including specific dates for particular elements of the Act.

1.4.2 Exceptions to the rule that provisions are enacted by order

Section 240(5) of the Act lists a range of provisions that came into force on the day the Act was passed (15 November 2011). These include, for instance, s.110 on the duty to co-operate in relation to planning of sustainable development and s.116 so far as it enables the Secretary of State to make regulations about neighbourhood planning; while s.240(6) brought the provisions on Community Infrastructure Levy (s.114) into force on 16 November 2011.

Under s.240(1) of the Act, certain provisions came into force at the end of two months beginning with the date on which the Act was passed (i.e. in force on 15 January 2012): for instance, ss.111–113 relating to local development schemes and s.143 on local finance considerations for planning permissions.

1.4.3 Commencement

A full list of the dates that each section and Schedule came into force (as at 20 April 2012) appears in **Appendix D** with references to the relevant commencement orders. The list also indicates those provisions not yet in force as at 20 April 2012.

1.4.4 The repeal of earlier legislation

Section 237 of and Sched.25 to the Act make provision for the repeal of a range of legislative provisions as part of the implementation of the planning and localism reforms.

1.5 ASSOCIATED SECONDARY LEGISLATION AND GOVERNMENT GUIDANCE

1.5.1 Secondary legislation

As at 20 April 2012 various pieces of secondary legislation have already entered into force. These are listed in **Appendix C** and include, e.g.:

- the Localism Act 2011 (Infrastructure Planning) (Consequential Amendments) Regulations 2012, SI 2012/635 – in force 1 April 2012; and
- the Neighbourhood Planning (General) Regulations 2012, SI 2012/637 – in force 6 April 2012.

The government is maintaining an updated list of secondary legislation relating to the Act that is now in force at **www.communities.gov.uk**.

1.5.2 Government guidance

Despite (or perhaps because of) the brief transition between White Paper and the publication of the Bill, the government published a considerable amount of guidance as the Localism Bill progressed through Parliament. There were three revisions to the 'plain English' *Guide* and numerous specific briefing papers and guidance such as *Decentralism and the Localism Bill: an essential guide* (December 2010). Also, and consistent with almost all modern primary legislative texts, there are helpful supporting Explanatory Notes to the Act which run to some 100 pages alone (the 'Explanatory Notes').

There are also a number of select committee reports published on matters relating to the Act including e.g. *Localism*; the *Abolition of Regional Spatial Strategies*; *Regeneration*; the *National Planning Policy Framework*; and the *General Power of Competence*. These reports are all available at **www.parliament.gov.uk**.

1.6 AN OVERVIEW OF THE ACT

This book focuses on planning and the Localism Act 2011. However, in order to get a sense of the scale of the legislative text, its breadth of application and implications, a summary of the whole Act is provided below.

Part 1: Local government

Part 1 of the Act (ss.1–47) covers local government. It clarifies the general powers of authorities, covers the transfer of functions to permitted authorities and makes new arrangements in relation to governance, including providing for directly elected mayors in England's largest cities by making substantial amendment to the Local Government Act 2000. Part 1 also clarifies the position on predetermination by decision-makers, and revises the rules on standards in public office abolishing the Standards Board for England. It makes certain provision for pay accountability for local authorities and revises arrangements for the provision of services and discharge of functions for the Commission for Local Administration in England.

Parts 2 and 3: EU financial sanctions

The government creates a new power in Parts 2 and 3 of the Act (ss.48–67) to require public authorities to make payments in respect of certain EU fines imposed by the Court of Justice of the European Union. Part 2 applies to England, Part 3 to Wales.

Part 4: Non-domestic rates

Part 4 of the Act (ss.68–71) revises rules relating to non-domestic rates by amendment of the Business Rate Supplements Act 2009 requiring approval by ballot of all persons eligible to vote in relation to proposals for the imposition of a business rate supplement. It also amends the Local Government Finance Act 1988 by:

1. replacing the limited circumstances in which local authorities can give discretionary relief for non-domestic rates and enabling the Secretary of State to make guidance;
2. enabling the Secretary of State to make provision for a new small business rate relief scheme which does not require ratepayers to apply for small business rate relief in some or all cases; and
3. cancelling liability to backdated non-domestic rates.

Part 5: Community empowerment

Central to the concept of localism, Part 5 of the Act (ss.72–108) creates a number of provisions relating to community empowerment. It enables referendums to be held in relation to council tax increases in England and provides Welsh Ministers with the power to revise the timing of council tax revaluations, currently set for 2015. It provides for a new community right to challenge the way local services may be provided and run by enabling local community groups to make an expression of interest to run a service. It also enhances the opportunity for local community groups to bid for land and assets of community value.

Part 6: Planning

There are wide-ranging changes to the planning system under Part 6 of the Act (ss.109–144) primarily by amendments to the pre-existing planning legislation including TCPA 1990, PCPA 2004 and the Planning Act 2008. The new measures include the abolition of regional strategies, a new duty on planning authorities to co-operate in relation to sustainable development, and revision to the provision of local development plan documents.

The Act amends legislation relating to the charging and use of the Community Infrastructure Levy. It also develops the principles of neighbourhood planning by enabling planning permission to be granted by neighbourhood development orders. It amends the consultation provisions requiring developers to consult with local communities prior to submitting planning applications in certain circumstances. Part 6 also amends the rules on enforcement and, in particular, revises the rules on time limits for enforcement in instances of concealment, while raising the maximum penalties for certain offences. It abolishes the Infrastructure Planning Commission and makes express provision for the need to consider local finance considerations when determining a planning application.

Part 7: Housing

Legislation relating to public and private sector housing is amended under Part 7 of the Act (ss.145–185). This includes revision of the rules relating to the allocation of housing accommodation and homelessness under the Housing Act 1996, tenure reform in relation to social housing including revision of the Housing Act 1985 and a new system of social housing finance with the introduction of the Housing Revenue Account scheme. The Act also revises the way in which social housing tenants may complain about service provision to a housing ombudsman. Finally, s.183 repeals Part 5 of the Housing Act 2004 and the duty on home sellers to provide a home information pack to prospective home buyers.

Part 8: London

Certain matters relating to London are covered under Part 8 of the Act. These include the removal of limitation on the power of the Greater London Authority (GLA) to promote the primary purposes of economic, social and environmental development and improvement of Greater London as well as creating new housing and regeneration functions. It empowers the Mayor to create Mayoral development corporations and reforms certain aspects of GLA governance.

Parts 9 and 10: Compensation for compulsory acquisition and tax

There is amendment of the Land Compensation Act 1961 under Part 9 of the Act (s.232) in relation to the assumptions as to planning permission when assessing compensation for compulsory acquisition. Finally, s.233 (in Part 10) and Sched.24 make certain tax provisions relating specifically to transfers of property, rights and liabilities by the Office for Tenants and Social Landlords, the Homes and Communities Agency and the London Development Agency.

For clarity, reference in this book to the masculine includes reference to the feminine as appropriate. Any views expressed are the authors' personal views rather than those of any organisation that they may represent. Nevertheless, it is hoped that it does provide a helpful guide to the new law.

2 LOCAL GOVERNMENT

There are a number of Chapters in Part 1 of the Localism Act 2011 that are relevant to land use planning including:

- Chapter 1: General powers of authorities (ss.1–8);
- Chapter 4: Transfer and delegation of functions to certain authorities (ss.15–20);
- Chapter 5: Governance (ss.21–24);
- Chapter 6: Predetermination (s.25); and
- Chapter 7: Standards (ss.26–37).

Each of the above Chapters is considered below.

2.1 GENERAL POWERS OF AUTHORITIES

The modern regime of local administration, including local planning authorities (LPAs), was put in place by the Local Government Act (LGA) 1972 which consolidated, revised and generally overhauled earlier legislation. Local authorities were required to operate the duties laid down by statute and were conferred express and subsidiary powers. The Local Government Act (LGA) 2000 sought to widen the scope of local authority functions to provide more flexible working arrangements. Section 4 of LGA 2000 required local authorities to publish strategies to promote well-being in their areas and LGA 2000, s.2(1) provided local authorities with the power to do anything which they considered was likely to achieve any one or more of the following objects: to promote or improve the economic, social and environmental well-being of their area. While some innovative authorities sought to test the boundaries of well-being: see e.g. the Torbay Development Agency and Greenwich Gateway Employment (cf. *Practical Use of the Well-Being Power* (DCLG, 2008)), Parliament felt local authorities continued to be constrained. For instance, the well-being powers were limited to ensuring that the local authorities did not do anything that they were unable to do by virtue of any prohibition, restriction or limitation contained in legislation and they were not able to raise money.

The *Guide* explains that the Localism Act 2011 has turned the assumption that local authorities can only act where the law says they can 'upside down' and that they will now be free to do anything. It explains that:

> The Localism Act includes a 'general power of competence'. It gives local authorities the legal capacity to do anything that an individual can do that is not specifically prohibited; they will not, for example, be able to impose new taxes, as an individual has no power to tax.

This chapter considers Part 1 of the Act and the legislation relating to local government. It considers the new general powers for authorities and other functions of governance that will be relevant to LPAs. Section 240(2) of the Act provides that almost all of the Part 1 provisions will come into force by further statutory instrument.

Chapter 1, Part 1 of the Act (ss.1–8) provides new powers for local authorities to operate. It confers a general power and then places boundaries and limits on that power. It defines what legislative provision does, and does not, still apply. Importantly, while general powers are provided, the structures and arrangements for the discharge of functions (e.g. delegated decision making and contracting out) remain in place. Section 8 provides an interpretation section.

2.1.1 Local authority's general power of competence

Section 1(1) of the Localism Act 2011 provides that:

> A local authority has power to do anything that individuals generally may do.

The s.1(1) power is referred to as 'the general power' in ss.1(5) and 8(1). It appears novel, yet it is unclear how much has actually changed. Since at least the introduction of LGA 1972, s.111, a local authority has always had a subsidiary power to do anything which is 'calculated to facilitate, or is conducive or incidental to, the discharge of any of their functions.' This power has not been repealed. Further, government guidance on LGA 2000, s.2 stated that the purpose of the well-being power was to reverse the 'traditionally cautious approach' taken by local authorities to improve the quality of life of their communities (*Power to promote or improve economic, social or environmental well-being*, DETR, 2000, paras.5–6). It seems then that the general power of competence now really does intend to address this 'assumption' that local authorities did not have wide powers to act.

The remainder of s.1 refines and reinforces the diversity of the general power. Section 1(2) explains that the general power applies to things that an individual may do even though they are in nature, extent or otherwise unlike anything an authority or other public bodies may do, while s.1(3) provides that 'individual' means an individual with full capacity. Section 1(4) notes that the general power can be used:

(a) anywhere in the UK;
(b) for a commercial purpose or not, with or without charge; and
(c) for the benefit of the authority and persons in its area – or not.

According to s.1(5)–(6), the general power is not limited by the existence of any other power which may overlap, and any other power is similarly not constrained by the general power subject to s.5(2) (discussed below). In effect, s.1(5) of the Act amplifies any pre-existing powers and, if there is an overlap with a pre-existing power and potential conflict, the Secretary of State can resolve this.

A simple example that appears to fit the general power criteria is where (subject to the limitations discussed below) a local authority in England invests in a zero-carbon, non-fossil-fuel energy plant in Northern Ireland in order to help reduce global greenhouse gas emissions.

2.1.2 Boundaries of the general power

The general power is not unlimited. Section 2(1)–(2) of the Act provides that existing restrictions and limitations on a pre-commencement power still apply and any post-commencement limitation will apply providing that limitation is expressed to apply (s.2(2)(b)):

(i) to the general power,
(ii) to all of the authority's powers, or
(iii) to all of the authority's powers but with exceptions that do not include the general power.

Also, s.2(3) provides that the general power does not confer power to make or alter:

(a) arrangements of a kind under Part 6 of LGA 1972 (e.g. discharging functions by committees, officers, etc. (delegated decision making);
(b) arrangements of a kind under Part 1A of LGA 2000 (relating to local governance in England); or
(c) any contracting-out or other arrangements, that authorise a person to exercise a function of a local authority.

The practical application of s.2 is that the general power will not disapply any obligation to comply with European Union law, e.g. the requirement under art.2(1) of the Environmental Impact Assessment (EIA) Directive 2011/92/EU that projects likely to have significant effects on the environment are subject to environmental impact assessment. Further, LPA schemes of delegation for certain planning decisions, e.g. relating to enforcement under Part 7 of TCPA 1990, continue as before.

2.1.3 Limits on charging and on 'things for commercial purpose'

Sections 3 and 4 of the Act place limits on the general power in relation to charging for services and carrying on 'things' for a commercial purpose. The limits include the following:

- ss.3(2) and 4(3) prohibit a local authority from charging for a service or doing something for a commercial purpose where it is required under a statutory provision to carry out that service or function;
- by s.3(3) the general power is subject to a duty to secure that the income from charges allowed in s.3 does not exceed the costs of provision, i.e. the local authority must make a profit or 'break even' when charging for services under the general power;

- s.4(1) confers the power to do things for a commercial purpose only if they are things which the authority may do otherwise than for a commercial purpose under the general power, i.e. if an authority could not do something under the general power, carrying out that thing for a commercial purpose does not then mean it can be brought within the general power; or
- by s.4(2), anything done for a commercial purpose must be done through a company (within the meaning of the Companies Act 2006) or a society registered under the Co-operative and Community Benefit Societies and Credit Unions Act 1965 or the Industrial and Provident Societies Act (Northern Ireland) 1969.

2.1.4 Secretary of State's powers to make supplemental provisions

While decentralisation is said to be critical to the Localism Act 2011, the Secretary of State retains an overarching competence as to the application and use of the general power through the implementation of secondary legislation. Section 5 of the Act provides that if the Secretary of State thinks that a statutory provision (whenever passed or made) either prevents or restricts local authorities from exercising the general power (s.5(1)), or that the general power is overlapped by another power (s.5(2)), then the Secretary of State may by order amend, repeal, revoke or disapply that provision.

The power to amend or disapply can be for a particular period (s.5(6)). Significantly, s.5(3) provides that the Secretary of State may also prevent local authorities from using the general power in any way by making an order to that effect. The Secretary of State may also, under s.5(4), provide that the exercise of the general power be subject to conditions. Section 5(5) provides that the Secretary of State's power under s.5(1)–(4) may be exercised in relation to:

- all local authorities;
- particular local authorities; or
- particular descriptions of local authority.

However, s.5(7) requires that before making any order under s.5 the Secretary of State must consult with local authorities, representatives of local government and any other persons as he considers appropriate. Further, before making an order under s.5(1) that relates to Wales, the Secretary of State must consult the Welsh Ministers.

As well as the need to consult, ss.6–7 of the Act provide that the Secretary of State's ability under s.5(1) to amend, repeal, revoke or disapply legislation for the good of the general power must be proportionate, fair and subject to due process. Section 6(1) provides that the Secretary of State may not make an order under s.5(1) (referred to as a 'provision') unless he considers that conditions in s.6(2), where relevant, are satisfied. The conditions in s.6(2) are that the provision:

(a) is proportionate to the policy objective intended by the order;

(b) taken as a whole, strikes a fair balance between the public interest and the interests of any person adversely affected;
(c) does not remove any necessary protection;
(d) does not prevent any person from continuing to exercise any right or freedom which that person might reasonably expect to continue to exercise; and
(e) is not of constitutional significance.

Further, the s.5(1) provision may not delegate or transfer legislative functions (s.6(3)), nor abolish or vary any tax (s.6(5)).

Section 7 of the Act sets out the procedure for making either a s.5(1) or s.5(2) order. This requires the Secretary of State, following any relevant consultation, to lay before Parliament a draft order and an explanatory document.

2.1.5 General powers of competence relevant to planning

The general power of competence does not cross-refer to Part 6 of the Act relating to planning. However, the scope and extent of LPA powers under previous legislation highlight how the general power is likely to interact with the planning system. In *R (on the application of Millgate Developments Ltd)* v. *Wokingham BC* [2011] EWHC 6 (Admin), HHJ Pearl held that it was lawful for the LPA to rely upon LGA 1972, s.111 in order to reimburse surplus sums paid to it by a developer pursuant to a unilateral undertaking under TCPA 1990, s.106. He noted at 56–59 that:

> The Defendant submits that it is within the powers of the Council under s.111 to refund any surplus. Mr Williams argues that a payment to the Claimant, after it has exercised its function of mitigating the effects of the development, is incidental to its planning functions, and therefore covered by s.111. It is not a modification of the s.106 undertaking.
>
> 57 I have to say that I am in entire agreement with Mr Williams. The cases cited by Mr Pugh-Smith in support of his approach, *Hazell* v. *Hammersmith & Fulham LBC* [1992] 2 AC 1 and *R* v. *Richmond upon Thames LBC ex p. McCarthy & Stone (Developments) Ltd* [1992] 2 AC 48, in so far as they are both concerned with swap transactions in the former case and charging for pre-application planning advice in the latter case both deal with very different factual situations to the present set of circumstances.
>
> 58 Lord Lowry said in *ex parte McCarthy and Stone*:
>
> '*There is yet a further point, to which I have already adverted. As the Court of Appeal have said (p. 1302H), the power to give pre-application advice is neither a duty nor a discretionary express power, but is a subsidiary power arising by virtue of section 111(1) (which has codified the common law), because it is calculated to facilitate, or is conducive or incidental to, the discharge of one of the Council's functions. To charge for the exercise of that power is, at best, incidental to the incidental and not incidental to the discharge of the functions.*'
>
> 59 I have no doubt but that the power to refund part of a s.106 undertaking is 'calculated to facilitate, or is conducive or incidental to, the discharge of their functions'. It is a subsidiary power arising by virtue of s.111(1).

The Court of Appeal dismissed the claimant's appeal: *R (on the application of Millgate)* v. *Wokingham BC* [2011] EWCA Civ 1062. This seems sensible. The use of the general power in this context is consistent with the principle of *functus officio* and that once planning permission has been granted by an LPA its duties and functions have been completed.

2.1.6 Entry into force and repeal of earlier provisions

Repeal provisions under s.237 of and Sched.25 to the Act that are relevant to the general power are the repeal of LGA 2000, ss.2(3) and (3A), 3(7), 4A(2) and(3).

The general power provisions enter into force by order. See **Appendix D** for a list of commencement dates as well as provisions that are not in force as at 20 April 2012.

2.2 TRANSFER AND DELEGATION OF FUNCTIONS TO CERTAIN AUTHORITIES (SECTIONS 15–20)

The provisions for the transfer and delegation of functions were a consequence of an amendment by the Lords in October 2011. The justification for this was to provide the opportunity to local authorities, comparable to that provided to the Mayor of London and to the major cities, to change their governance arrangements to a leader and cabinet executive model of governance (*Hansard*, HL debate, 2.9.11, c558). The purpose, according to the *Guide*, is to 'improve local accountability or promote economic growth' whereby 'authorities will be encouraged to come forward with innovative proposals'.

Under s.15 of the Act the Secretary of State may by order transfer a local public function from the public authority whose function it is to a permitted authority. A permitted authority includes a county council in England, a district council and an economic prosperity board (s.20). A 'local public function' means a public function that relates to:

(a) a permitted authority's area, or
(b) persons living, working or carrying on activities in the area;

but does not include the power to make regulations or other instruments of a legislative character (s.20).

The transfer may not be made unless it is considered that the order would promote economic development or wealth creation, or increase local accountability in relation to each local public function. The Secretary of State must be satisfied that the permitted authority can exercise the function appropriately and has consented to the transfer. Similarly, a Minister may delegate to a permitted authority any of the Minister's eligible functions, providing it is not conferring a power to make regulations and that the Minister considers that the permitted authority can exercise the power appropriately (s.16).

In order to facilitate the transfer of functions under s.15, the Secretary of State may make a scheme for the transfer of property, rights and liability to the permitted authority from the person or body which, but for the transfer, would have had a local public function (s.17(1)). A similar scheme may be made by the Minister in relation to a s.16 delegation (s.17(2)). Before making a s.15 transfer order, the Secretary of State must a lay a draft order before each House of Parliament and have regard to any representations, resolutions from either House, and any committee recommendations made on the draft order.

The transfer and delegation provisions enter into force by order with ss.15 and 19 being enacted on 3 December 2011 by the Localism Act 2011 (Commencement No. 1 and Transitional Provisions) Order 2011, SI 2011/2896.

2.3 GOVERNANCE (SECTIONS 21–24)

The Localism Act 2011 introduces extensive new governance arrangements for English local authorities.

2.3.1 Executive functions

Section 21 refers to, and gives effect to, Sched.2 which, in turn, inserts a new Part 1A into LGA 2000. This provides for certain permitted forms of governance for English authorities under LGA 2000, s.9B, which are:

(a) executive arrangements;
(b) a committee system; or
(c) arrangements that may be prescribed by the Secretary of State in further regulations.

New LGA 2000, s.9C provides that an executive of an English authority must take the form of either:

- an elected mayor of the authority and two or more councillors of the authority appointed to the executive by the elected mayor (s.9C(2)); or
- a councillor elected as the leader of an executive and two or more councillors appointed to the executive by the executive leader (s.9C(3)).

The new provisions provide that the number of members of a local authority executive must not exceed 10 or such other number that the Secretary of State may specify. The new Part 1A of LGA 2000 also makes provision for the discharge of functions and the operation of overview and scrutiny committees. These committees have a range of functions including, among other things, reporting on the duties of certain partner authorities, flood risk management and information provision.

2.3.2 Directly elected mayors

Another significant change in local governance brought about by the introduction of LGA 2000, Part 1A (via s.21 of and Sched.2 to the Act) is the opportunity for areas to vote for a directly elected mayor, as currently happens in London. Where a local authority wishes to change its governance arrangements to provide for a mayor and cabinet, such wish will be subject to approval through a local referendum. These provisions are subject to regulations being made by the Secretary of State. The regulations will specify the particular authorities that will be permitted to hold a referendum.

The government consultation paper: *What can a mayor do for your city?* (DCLG, November 2011) suggested that directly elected mayors can encourage decentralisation and also that public authorities can be more accountable:

> 14. Mayors being directly elected are thereby directly accountable to the city as a whole. They have a mandate from the city's people who will pass judgement at the ballot box on the job they are doing as leader of the city. This gives mayors a mandate which has 'provided a basis for a stronger, more proactive and individualised style of leadership than other models [of local government leadership]' ([*Local Political Leadership in England and Wales*,] JRF, 2005).

Secondary legislation, including individual mayoral referendum orders and rules setting out the conduct and governance of referendums, were laid before Parliament on 5 December 2011. There is presently a commitment to hold a referendum in 11 of the largest English cities: Birmingham, Bradford, Bristol, Coventry, Leeds, Liverpool, Manchester, Newcastle upon Tyne, Nottingham, Sheffield and Wakefield. Leicester has already elected a mayor. Many of the referendums will be held on 3 May 2012. Any city voting in favour of a mayor in its referendum may then proceed to hold formal elections for the post. Mayors would be elected to hold office for a four-year term.

2.4 PREDETERMINATION (SECTION 25)

The issue of predetermination has been a prominent and contentious element of planning decision making for many years. Wade and Forsyth in *Administrative Law (10th edn)* (OUP, 2009) explain that:

> Predetermination consists in 'the surrender by a decision-making body of its judgment' [*Per* Sedley J in *R* v. *Secretary of State for the Environment ex p. Kirkstall Valley Campaign Ltd* [1996] 3 All ER 304], for instance, by failing to apply his mind properly to the task at hand or by adopting an over-rigid policy. The decision is unlawful but not because it may appear biased (although in many cases it will). (pp. 389–390).

Wade and Forsyth regard the appearance of bias and predetermination as distinct concepts adding that:

> The significance of the conceptual distinction between predetermination and the apprehension of bias lies in the fact that administrative decision-makers, unlike judicial decision-makers, will often, quite rightly, be influenced, formally or informally, in their decision by policy considerations. They will naturally approach their task with a legitimate predisposition to decide in accordance with their previously articulated views or policies.

This approach was approved in *R (on the application of Persimmon Homes Ltd)* v. *Vale of Glamorgan Council* [2010] EWHC 535 (Admin), in which the developer unsuccessfully challenged the Council's endorsement of a 'draft preferred strategy' alleging, among other things, that officers preparing the report were illegitimately predisposed towards one option and biased against alternatives. However, the courts have found occasions when predetermination and the appearance of bias converge; see e.g. *Condron* v. *National Assembly for Wales* [2006] EWCA Civ 1573. They have also found that in terms of the appearance of bias the same approach should be adopted to both administrative and judicial decisions; see e.g. *R* v. *Secretary of State for the Environment, ex p. Kirkstall Valley Campaign Ltd* [1996] 3 All ER 304. However, more recently the Court of Appeal held in *R (on the application of Lewis)* v. *Redcar and Cleveland BC* [2008] EWCA Civ 746 that:

> 71. It is for the court to assess whether Committee members did make the decision with closed minds or that the circumstances give rise to such a real risk of closed minds that the decision ought not in the public interest be upheld. The importance of appearances is, in my judgment, generally more limited in this context than in a judicial context. The appearance created by a member of a judicial tribunal also appearing as an advocate before that tribunal (*Lawal* v. *Northern Spirit Ltd* [2003] ICR 856) may make his judicial decisions unacceptable but the appearance created by a Councillor voting for a planning project he has long supported is, on analysis, to be viewed in a very different way.

2.4.1 Decision-maker's previous action no indication of a closed mind

The Localism Act 2011 attempts to clarify the position on predetermination. Section 25(2) states that:

> A decision-maker is not to be taken to have had, or to have appeared to have had, a closed mind when making the decision just because –
>
> (a) the decision-maker had previously done anything that directly or indirectly indicated what view the decision-maker took, or would or might take, in relation to a matter, and
> (b) the matter was relevant to the decision.

Section 25(1) of the Act provides that subsection (2) only applies if:

(a) there is an allegation of bias or predetermination or otherwise there is an issue about the validity of a relevant authority's decision; and
(b) it is relevant to that issue whether the decision-maker, or any of the decision-makers, had or appeared to have a closed mind, to any extent, when making the decision.

Subsection (2) only applies if the decision-maker is a member (whether elected or not) of the relevant authority, or is a co-opted member of that authority.

The section refers to a 'relevant authority' which according to the definition in s.25(4) is wider than the definition in, say, the general power provisions under s.8 of the Act. It includes, for instance, parish and community councils, the Greater

London Authority, National Park authorities and the Broads Authority, none of which are cited in the general power provisions.

The predetermination provision does not appear to extend to officers of a relevant authority who may be taking decisions under delegated powers. It only refers to decision-makers who are members or co-opted members of the relevant authority. The definitions of member or co-opted member under s.25 are inclusive rather than exhaustive in nature. For example, a 'co-opted member' includes any committee member and a 'member' includes a council's elected mayor (s.25(4)).

However, s.25(4) states that the 'decision' referred to in s.25 means:

> ... a decision made in discharging functions of the authority, functions of the authority's executive, functions of a committee of the authority or functions of an officer of the authority (including decisions made in the discharge of any of those functions otherwise than by the person to whom the function was originally given);
> ...

2.4.2 Scope and purpose of the predetermination provision

With an extremely wide and diverse range of decisions in planning (e.g. *Persimmon Homes* above), and a considerable number of those taken by officers under delegated powers, the issue of predetermination is not academic. The government notes at p.5 of the *Guide* that it has used the Localism Act to clarify the rules on predetermination:

> These rules were developed to ensure that councillors came to council discussions – on, for example, planning applications – with an open mind. In practice, however, these rules had been interpreted in such a way as to reduce the quality of local debate and stifle valid discussion. In some cases councillors were warned off doing such things as campaigning, talking with constituents, or publicly expressing views on local issues, for fear of being accused of bias or facing legal challenge.
>
> The Localism Act makes it clear that it is proper for councillors to play an active part in local discussions, and that they should not be liable to legal challenge as a result. This will help them better represent their constituents and enrich local democratic debate. People can elect their councillor confident in the knowledge that they will be able to act on the issues they care about and have campaigned on.

The government's intended purpose of the predetermination provision was evident early in the Localism Bill process: 'The Bill will end the absurd situation where councillors are prevented from acting on local issues because of the risk of challenge that they are biased.' (p.6, *Decentralisim and the Localism Bill, an essential guide* (DCLG, December 2010)).

Thus, the government seems clear in the purpose of the provision: it relates to campaigning, elections and the democratic process, rather than officer functions.

2.4.3 Entry into force and conclusion on predetermination

Drawing the various threads together it is apparent that the new s.25 provision on predetermination tends to affirm the present judicial position rather than extend it.

It focuses on encouraging and promoting the democratic process rather than applying across the board to all aspects of administrative decision making. Section 25 applies to elected council members rather than officers or civil servants. It does not shift the present state of the law on bias or the appearance of bias explained, for instance, in *Lewis* v. *Redcar*, albeit that if such an allegation of bias is made in relation to a decision, an elected member will not be taken to have had, or to have appeared to have had, a closed mind because of anything the member had previously said or done.

The provision came into force on 15 January 2012 (s.240(1)(a)). It is helpful but unlikely to be the final word. It is anticipated that there will be yet further intervention by the courts; see e.g. *R (on the application of Berky)* v. *Newport City Council* [2012] EWCA Civ 378.

2.5 STANDARDS (SECTIONS 26–37)

Part 1, Chapter 7 of the Act revises the statutory provisions relating to standards in local government. The overriding purpose is to promote and maintain high standards of conduct. The Act abolishes the Standards Board for England and replaces this with a requirement to publish a code of conduct for councillors and the creation of new offences of failing to comply with requirements in the Act relating to disclosure of a pecuniary interest; and providing false or misleading information about a pecuniary interest. The Act also removes the obligation on local authorities to maintain a standards committee and replaces this with a permissive right to maintain one if a local authority so wishes.

2.5.1 Amendments to existing provisions

Section 26 of and Sched.4 to the Act amend existing provisions relating to the conduct of local government members and employees in England.

2.5.2 Duty to promote and maintain high standards of conduct

Section 27(1) of the Act states that:

> A relevant authority must promote and maintain high standards of conduct by members and co-opted members of the authority.

A 'relevant authority' is defined in s.27(6) and includes the range of planning authorities such as: (a) county councils; (b) district councils; (c) London borough councils; (e) the Greater London Authority; (h) the Common Council of the City of London; (l) a joint authority established under Part 4 of the Local Government Act 1985; (n) a combined authority established under s.103 of the Local Democracy, Economic Development and Construction Act 2009; (o) the Broads Authority; and (p) a National Park authority.

To assist an authority in discharging its duty to promote and maintain high standards of conduct, s.27(2) requires a relevant authority to adopt a code of conduct explaining what is expected of its members and co-opted members. The Act does not define the term 'member' but explains at s.27(4) that a 'co-opted member' is someone who is not a member of the authority but is a member of a committee who is also entitled to vote.

2.5.3 Codes of conduct

Section 28(1) states that a relevant authority must ensure that its code of conduct as required by s.27(2) is consistent with principles of:

(a) selflessness;
(b) integrity;
(c) objectivity;
(d) accountability;
(e) openness;
(f) honesty;
(g) leadership.

Section 28(1) adopts the seven principles developed and promoted by the Committee on Standards in Public Life (the Nolan Committee), an independent advisory body that monitors, reports and make recommendations on all issues relating to standards in public life: see **www.public-standards.gov.uk** for more details on the principles.

In addition to the seven principles, the code of conduct must include appropriate provisions relating to the register of members' interests under s.29 of the Act including:

(a) pecuniary interests; and
(b) interests other than pecuniary interests (s.28(2)).

The current Model Code of Conduct is found in the Local Authorities (Model Code of Conduct) Order 2007, SI 2007/1159.

2.5.4 Pecuniary and sensitive interests and register of interests

The monitoring officer of a relevant authority must establish and maintain a public register of interests of members and co-opted members of the authority (s.29(1)) and it is for the authority to determine what is to be entered in that register (s.29(2)). In compliance with s.30(1) a member or co-opted member of a relevant authority must, within 28 days of becoming a member, notify the authority's monitoring officer of any disclosable pecuniary interests which that person has at the time when the notification is given.

Section 31 of the Act sets out the requirements and obligations if a member or co-opted member has a disclosable pecuniary interest in a matter being considered at any relevant authority committee meeting that person attends. These include that if the interest is not entered on the authority's register the member must disclose the interest to the meeting (s.31(2)) and notify the monitoring officer within 28 days of the meeting (s.31(3)). Further, under s.31(4), the member or co-opted member may not participate in:

(a) any discussion; or
(b) any vote on the matter,

nor must the member take any steps in relation to that matter (s.31(8)).

Section 33 enables the authority to grant a dispensation of the prohibitions in s.31(4), having taking into account all the relevant circumstances. Also, if disclosure of the details of an interest placed on the register could lead to the member or someone connected to the member being subject to violence or intimidation, then in accordance with s.32 copies of the register either published or made available for inspection must not include details of the interest.

2.5.5 Offences relating to disclosable pecuniary interests

Section 34(1) provides that a person commits an offence if, without reasonable excuse, the person:

(a) fails to comply with an obligation imposed by ss.30(1), 31(2), (3) or (7) relating to notification of disclosable interests;
(b) participates in any discussion or vote in contravention of s.31(4); or
(c) takes any steps in contravention of s.31(8).

Section 34(2) states that a person commits an offence if the person provides information under ss.30(1), 31(2), (3) or (7) that is false or misleading information and the person either:

(a) knows that the information is false or misleading; or
(b) is reckless as to whether the information is true and not misleading.

A person found guilty under s.34(1) or (2) is liable on summary conviction to a fine not exceeding level 5 on the standard scale (currently £5,000) and, further, may be disqualified by the court for being, or becoming, a member or co-opted member of a relevant authority. A prosecution must be brought within 12 months of the date on which sufficient evidence came to the prosecutor's knowledge.

2.5.6 Entry into force, transitional provisions and repeal

Section 237 of and Sched.25, Part 5 to the Localism Act 2011 abolish the Standards Board for England previously established under LGA 2000, s.57. Further, Parts 1 and 2 of Sched.4 provide for amendments to existing provisions such as deleting reference to the Standards Board in a range of parliamentary Acts and providing for the cessation of any code of conduct adopted under LGA 2000. The relevant provisions come into force by order on a date to be appointed. See **Appendix D** for a list of commencement dates as well as provisions that are not in force as at 20 April 2012.

2.5.7 Standards and the planning system

The financial advantages and other consequences of planning decisions at both strategic and development control level need not be rehearsed. A number of planning related cases came before the Standards Board and the First-tier Tribunal prior to abolition. Some of these may still be reviewed on the tribunals website (**www.justice.gov.uk/guidance/courts-and-tribunals/tribunals/local-government-standards/decisions.htm**). These were primarily about a failure to disclose. It will remain to be seen how many cases come before the magistrates' courts.

3 EU FINANCIAL SANCTIONS

Parts 2 and 3 of the Localism Act 2011 confer powers on Ministers to make regulations requiring public authorities to pay all or part of any financial sanctions imposed by the Court of Justice of the European Union (CJEU) for a breach of European Union (EU) rules. The UK government has been liable to pay all fines for sanctions relating to actions by public bodies throughout England, Wales, Scotland and Northern Ireland. Until now, there have been no powers for central government to recover any fine from a public authority whose actions caused or contributed to the financial sanction being imposed.

The underlying purpose appears to be to make public authorities responsible for their actions and could reasonably be seen as another aspect of the rights and responsibilities of localism. In simple terms, it is saying to public bodies: 'if the UK is fined by the CJEU following infraction proceedings as a consequence of your actions you can pay for, or at least contribute to the fine'.

Part 2 of the Act (ss.48–57) relates to public bodies in England; Part 3 (ss.58–67) covers Wales. The text of each Part is substantially the same although there is reference to Secretary of State in Part 2, and to Welsh Ministers in Part 3. To avoid repetition, this chapter focuses on Part 2.

3.1 POWER TO REQUIRE PUBLIC AUTHORITIES TO PAY CERTAIN EU FINANCIAL SANCTIONS

Section 48(1) of the Act confers power on a Minister (e.g. the Secretary of State for Communities and Local Government) to require a public body to pay some, or all, of a financial sanction (e.g. a fine) imposed by the CJEU on the UK. A payment may only be imposed if: (i) the authority has been designated under s.52; (ii) the EU sanction is one to which the designation applies; and (iii) a final notice issued under s.56 has been given to the authority (s.48(2)).

Section 51 defines 'public authority'. The Act aims to ensure that devolved functions by Scottish and Welsh Ministers as well as the relevant Northern Ireland departments are liable for EU sanctions, although the text appears unduly complicated. It is clear that LPAs, as either county, district or London councils, are expressly included within the provisions (s.51(3)). All other planning authorities (e.g. the Broads Authority, unitary councils, and the Planning Inspectorate) are covered by the broad scope of the term 'public authority', which includes under s.51(2)(b) 'any other person or body which has any non-devolved functions'.

3.2 WHEN AND IN WHAT CIRCUMSTANCES WILL EU FINANCIAL SANCTIONS APPLY?

3.2.1 When does Part 2 apply?

The payment provisions under Part 2 apply to any EU financial sanctions imposed on the UK after commencement of Part 2 of the Act (s.50), unless the relevant Minister provides a certificate that specifies a part or parts of an EU financial sanction does/do not apply (s.50(2)). Part 2 comes into force by order (s.240(2)). Section 48(5) provides that:

> (a) 'EU financial sanction' means a sanction consisting of a lump sum or penalty payment (or both) imposed by the Court of Justice in Article 260(2) proceedings for an infraction of EU law; [and]
> (b) 'infraction of EU law', in relation to an EU financial sanction, means the failure to comply with a judgment of the Court of Justice given in proceedings under Article 258 or 259 of the Treaty on the Functioning of the European Union [(TFEU)]; and
> (c) 'Article 260(2) proceedings' means proceedings under Article 260(2) of [the TFEU].

3.2.2 Article 260 of the TFEU

The Act does not elaborate on the judicial process and obligations under the TFEU. Article 258 of the TFEU provides that if the European Commission (EC) considers that a Member State has failed to fulfil an obligation under the TFEU or another Treaty it must deliver a Reasoned Opinion on the matter after giving the State concerned the opportunity to submit its observations. If the State concerned does not comply with the Opinion, the Commission may bring the matter before the CJEU. Article 260 of the TFEU states that:

> (1) If the [CJEU] finds that a Member State has failed to fulfil an obligation under the Treaties, the State shall be required to take the necessary measures to comply with the judgment of the Court.
> (2) If the Commission considers that the Member State concerned has not taken the necessary measures to comply with the judgment of the Court, it may bring the case before the Court after giving that State the opportunity to submit its observations. It shall specify the amount of the lump sum or penalty payment to be paid by the Member State concerned which it considers appropriate in the circumstances.
>
> If the Court finds that the Member State concerned has not complied with its judgment it may impose a lump sum or penalty payment on it. …

According to the government's regulatory impact assessment (RIA) for EU infraction fines (DCLG, January 2011), the specified financial sum recommended by the

EC will be calculated according to EC Communications SEC (2005) 1658 and SEC (2010) 9233. The level of fine will be based upon the UK's gross domestic product with a minimum lump sum of €9.666m. The government believes that this sum could be increased according to the seriousness of the breach, with a possible substantial daily fine of thousands of pounds for continuing non-compliance.

3.3 PROCEDURE FOR REQUIRING PAYMENT

A Minister of the Crown is the person who may seek a payment under Part 2. The procedure for securing funds from a public authority is provided for in ss.49–56 and requires the relevant Minister to designate a public authority as one to which Part 2 applies. Part 2 refers to 'acts' of a public authority which are those acts within a description of activities covered by a designation by a Minister (s.52(8)), and further, 'act' includes an omission (s.57).

3.3.1 Publication of a policy statement

The Secretary of State is required to publish a policy statement concerning the application of Part 2 of the Act (s.49). He is also required to consult with any persons he considers appropriate before publishing the statement. The policy statement may be revised and republished. Any Minister exercising functions under Part 2 must have regard to the policy statement when exercising functions under the Act. While it is not explicit in the Act, it would be reasonable to conclude that the s.49 policy statement should be published prior to any Minister requiring payment.

3.3.2 Designation of public authorities

To secure a payment under Part 2, s.52 of the Act provides that a Minister is required to designate one or more public authorities by order. Section 235(6) and (7) requires that a Minister may not make an order under s.52 unless a draft of the statutory instrument containing the order 'has been laid before, and approved by a resolution of, each House of Parliament'. In accordance with s.52(2), the order must:

(a) specify the public authority by name;
(b) identify any EU financial sanction to which the designation applies; and
(c) describe the activities of the authority which are covered by the designation.

The order may further identify the EU sanction by specifying:

(a) the sanction imposed;
(b) any art.260(2) proceedings;
(c) a judgment of the CJEU finding that the UK has failed to comply with an EU obligation; or
(d) any proceedings under art.258 or art.259 of the TFEU (s.52(3)).

It may also describe any:

(i) Reasoned Opinion addressed to the UK; or
(ii) any other document sent by the EC (s.52(4)).

Section 52(7) requires that, before making an order designating a public authority, a Minister must consult with (a) the public authority concerned, and (b) if it is a public authority with mixed functions, the appropriate national authority.

3.3.3 The independent advisory panel

The Act requires that once a public authority has been designated the relevant Minister must 'establish a panel for the purpose of carrying out any functions it may be given by or under any provision of this Part in relation to that EU financial sanction' (s.53(2)). And further, that the panel must be established before any warning notice is served on the public authority (s.53(3)). The heading to s.53 states that it is an 'independent' panel, while para.151 of the Explanatory Notes to the Act explains that:

> The [independent advisory] panel will have a number of functions under Part 2, including dealing with representations following the giving of a warning notice to a designated public authority.

3.3.4 Warning notices

Before a public authority is required to make any payment under Part 2, the authority designated under Part 2 must be given a warning notice (under s.54) and a final notice (s.55) by the Minister. Section 54 provides the procedure to be followed in serving a warning notice. The notice must, for instance, include a statement that the relevant Minister believes:

> (a) that acts [or omissions] of the authority may have caused or contributed to the infraction of EU law for which the EU financial sanction was imposed, and
> (b) that, if acts of the authority did cause or contribute to that infraction of EU law, it would be appropriate to consider requiring the authority to make payments under this Part (which may be or include ongoing payments) in respect of the EU financial sanction [s.54(2)].

Section 54(3) provides that the warning notice must also, among other things:

(a) identify the sanction;
(b) specify the total amount of the sanction;
(c) specify the amount of any periodic payments;
(d) set out the reasons for making the statement under s.54(2);
(e) set out procedures for the Minister to determine matters under s.55(4);
(f) provide a timetable for those procedures; and
(g) invite the authority to make representations.

The Minister must also determine matters set out in s.55(4) before a final notice is given. These include:

(i) whether any acts of the authority did cause or contribute to the infraction of EU law or the obligation to make periodic payments;

(ii) the proportion of:

  (a) the total amount of the sanction; and
  (b) any periodic payments to be paid

  that is to be regarded as reflecting the authority's share of the responsibility;

(iii) whether the authority should be required to make any payment; if so
(iv) what payment(s) the authority should make; and
(v) when any payment(s) should be made.

3.3.5 Final notices

Section 56(1) of the Act states that a Minister may only give a final notice to a public authority if he or she has decided, in accordance with s.55, to impose a requirement for payment on the authority. The final notice must:

(a) identify the EU sanction;
(b) specify the total amount due;
(c) describe the acts that a Minister has determined have caused or contributed to the infraction of EU law and set out the reasons for that determination;
(d) summarise other determinations;
(e) specify the amount to be paid towards the total amount of the sanction;
(f) specify the amount to be paid towards any future periodic payments; and
(g) specify how and to whom payments are to be made.

Under s.56 the authority is required to continue making periodic payments for as long as the UK is required to make payments to the EU. However, under s.56(5) the Minister may vary or terminate the requirement to make any periodic payments that may continue to be due if there is a change in circumstances. A variation or termination notice under s.56(5) may be given either on the application of the authority or where the Minister considers it appropriate. Any sums paid by a public authority under Part 2 are paid into the Consolidated Fund (s.48(4)).

The UK has never had a financial sanction imposed by the CJEU, although the RIA for EU infraction fines (DCLG, January 2011) noted that the UK has come close on more than one occasion, adding that:

> Following significant amendments to the infraction process made by the Lisbon Treaty, financial sanctions could be imposed on the UK in shorter timescales. … [and also that] within the UK there are thought to be a number of cases where there is a pressing need to ensure compliance with EU law in order to minimise the risk of infraction proceedings and subsequent fines imposed by the European Court of Justice. … The Government is giving local authorities more powers and freedoms to conduct their business and deliver services to the public. This includes a major reduction in the 'oversight' role of central government. Local authorities must, therefore, accept responsibility for the consequences of their actions or inaction. (pp.5–6)

3.4 ENTRY INTO FORCE

Parts 2 and 3 of the Localism Act come into force by order on a date to be appointed (s.240(2)). See **Appendix D** for a list of commencement dates as well as provisions that are not in force as at 20 April 2012.

4 COMMUNITY EMPOWERMENT

The central thrust of the Localism Act 2011 is the concept of handing power back to the people. The coalition agreement of May 2010 included the statement by the Prime Minister and Deputy Prime Minister that: 'The time has come to disperse power more widely in Britain today'. The principle of 'people power' comes to the fore in Part 5 of the Act: Community Empowerment. Chapter 1 focuses on a review of council tax including referendums on tax increases, while Chapter 2 provides a right to certain organisations to challenge local public service provision. Chapter 3 provides a regime of selling off public land and property.

The *Guide* states that the Act: 'passes significant new rights direct to communities and individuals, making it easier for them to get things done and achieve their ambitions for the place where they live' (p.8).

4.1 COUNCIL TAX

Section 72 of and Scheds.5 and 6 to the Localism Act 2011 provide quite complex rules for amending the council tax provisions in England and Wales primarily by inserting entire new chapters into the Local Government Finance Act 1992. All local authorities responsible for collecting council tax are required to decide whether the basic council tax they collect or any proposed increase is excessive. The new provisions then set out what a council must do if it concludes that taxes are excessive, including holding a referendum. The new provisions provide arrangements for holding a referendum, the effect of any outcomes and the circumstances if there is a failure to hold a referendum. Sections 73–79 then provide for council tax calculations.

The provisions were brought into force on 3 December 2011 by the Localism Act 2011 (Commencement No. 1 and Transitional Provisions) Order 2011, SI 2011/2896.

4.2 COMMUNITY RIGHT TO CHALLENGE

Chapter 2, Part 5 of the Localism Act 2011 (ss.81–86) confers on voluntary and community groups, parish councils and, in some instances, local authority employees, the right to express an interest in running a local authority service (i.e.

challenging the way a service is provided). The right to challenge only applies to England, unless the Secretary of State specifies otherwise by regulations.

4.2.1 Duty to consider an expression of interest (section 81(1))

Section 81 of the Act places a duty on relevant authorities to consider an expression of interest in running a service under the right to challenge. It states that:

> (1) A relevant authority must consider an expression of interest in accordance with this Chapter if–
>
> (a) it is submitted to the authority by a relevant body, and
> (b) it is made in writing and complies with such other requirements for expressions of interest as the Secretary of State may specify by regulations.

Two initial points to consider are: (i) that the expression of interest in running a service must be in writing; and (ii) that the time when an expression of interest may be made is limited. Section 82(2) permits an authority to provide certain time periods for submitting an expression of interest by publishing details of the service and the time periods that apply and, if it is submitted outside a specified period, the authority may refuse to consider the submission. Absent a published time period an expression of interest may be submitted at any time (s.82(1)).

4.2.2 Defining the right to challenge (section 81)

As well as placing a duty on relevant authorities to consider an expression of interest, s.81 of the Act also sets the scope of the right to challenge by defining, to some extent, who may exercise the right, who the relevant authority is, and what the relevant service may be. As with the overarching duty, further detail is to be provided by secondary legislation published by the Secretary of State.

In summary, Part 5, Chapter 2 of the Act provides that: a 'relevant body' may challenge the way in which a 'relevant authority' provides a 'relevant service' by submitting an 'expression of interest'.

This is relatively straightforward as a concept but does require further definition. For this s.81 sets out critical terms relating to the community right to challenge. In particular:

- 'relevant authority' (s.81(2)) means:

  (a) a county council in England,
  (b) a district council,
  (c) a London borough council, or
  (d) such other person or body carrying on functions of a public nature as [specified by regulations]

- 'relevant body' (s.81(6)) means:

  (a) a voluntary or community body,

(b) a body of persons or a trust which is established for charitable purposes only,
(c) a parish council,
(d) in relation to a relevant authority, two or more employees of that authority, or
(e) such other person or body as [specified by regulations]

- 'voluntary body' (s.81(7)) means:

  a body, other than a public or local authority, the activities of which are not carried on for profit

- 'community body' (s.81(9)) means:

  a body, other than a public or local authority, that carries on activities primarily for the benefit of the community

- 'expression of interest' (s.81(4)) means:

  an expression of interest in providing or assisting in providing a relevant service on behalf of the authority

- 'relevant service' (s.81(5)) means:

  a service provided by or on behalf of [the relevant authority] in the exercise of any of its functions in relation to England, other than a service of a kind specified in regulations ...

Section 81(8) of the Act states that the fact that a body's activities generate a surplus, which is assumed to mean a financial profit, does not prevent it from being a voluntary body for the purposes of the Act, so long as that surplus is used for the purposes of those activities or invested in the community. However, a warning on the statutory terms and scope of the rights: s.81(10) enables the Secretary of State to amend or repeal by regulations many of the s.81 provisions and so, while the above provides a good working legislative basis for pursuing the right to challenge, be aware of regulatory revision as the rights unfold.

The statutory definitions as to what is a 'relevant authority' and 'relevant body' are relatively clear. Guidance on what is a function of a local authority, which is not subject to this right to challenge, and what is a service provided by a local authority, which is subject to this right to challenge, can be found in the consultation paper 'Proposals to introduce a Community Right to Challenge' (DCLG, February 2011, available at **www.communities.gov.uk/documents/localgovernment/pdf/1835810.pdf**).

What constitutes an 'expression of interest' under the Act is clarified in ss.83 and 84 (discussed below).

4.2.3 Consideration of expressions of interest to run a service (sections 83 and 84)

If a relevant body submits an expression of interest to run a service, the authority must either accept or reject that expression of interest (s.83(1)) or, under s.84(1), modify the proposal. Section 84(2) provides that an authority may only exercise its power to modify under s.84(1) if:

> (a) the authority thinks that the expression of interest would not otherwise be capable of acceptance, and
> (b) the relevant body agrees to the modification.

A relevant authority must specify in writing the maximum period that will elapse between the date it receives an expression of interest and the date it will notify the relevant body of its decision in relation to the submission (s.84(3) and (6)). The authority must also publish details of the time periods set in relation to the expression of interest under s.84(3) and also, one assumes, details of the submission (s.84(5)).

Section 84(8) of the Act requires the relevant authority to:

(a) notify the relevant body of its determination of the expression of interest; and
(b) give reasons for any decision to reject or modify the expression of interest.

The authority must then publish its decision (s.84(9)). It may only reject the expression of interest on one or more grounds that are to be specified in regulations (s.83(11)). A relevant body may withdraw an expression of interest (either before or after a determination by the authority) (s.84(10)). However, s.84(11) provides that any withdrawal of an expression of interest, or refusal of a relevant body to modify an expression of interest, does not prevent the relevant authority from proceeding with the procurement exercise required by s.83(2) following acceptance of an expression of interest if the authority thinks that it is appropriate to do so.

Section 83(3)–(10) provides some indication of what the s.83(2) procurement exercise involves. It includes, for instance, that it is appropriate to have regard to the value and nature of the contract that may be awarded as a result of the procurement exercise (s.83(3)). It includes the requirement for the authority to specify and publish a timetable for completing the exercise (s.83(4)–(6)). Under s.83(8), a relevant authority must also consider:

> whether acceptance of the expression of interest would promote or improve the social, economic or environmental well-being of the authority's area.

Consideration of the well-being principles also extends to the procurement exercise itself.

4.2.4 Guidance, advice and assistance and entry into force of the right to challenge

It is anticipated that the Secretary of State is highly likely to publish further guidance as to the nature, extent and operation of the s.83(2) procurement exercise. This is permitted under s.85. If so, the relevant authority will have to have regard to such guidance when exercising its functions under this part of the Act. Further, the Secretary of State may provide advice and assistance about the operation of the Chapter. The Explanatory Notes to the Act state that:

> 223. Section 86 authorises the Secretary of State to provide advice and assistance in relation to the community right to challenge, either directly or through others.

> This could include financial assistance to a relevant body, such as a grant or loan, or education and training.

The power conferred on the Secretary of State to make regulations and also to provide advice and assistance under s.86 came into force with the passing of the Act (s.240(5)). Other sections of this Chapter come into force by order. See **Appendix D** for a list of commencement dates as well as provisions that are not in force as at 20 April 2012.

4.3 COMMUNITY RIGHT TO BID FOR ASSETS OF COMMUNITY VALUE

Chapter 3, Part 5 of the Localism Act 2011 (ss.87–108) confers upon local communities in England and Wales the right to bid for land and other assets of community value to prevent such assets being lost to the community. The *Guide* explains the rationale behind the new provisions:

> In many places across the country, when local amenities have been threatened with sale or closure, community groups have taken them over. In some cases, however, community groups who have attempted to take assets over have faced significant challenges. They often need more time to organise a bid and raise money than the private enterprises bidding against them.
>
> The Localism Act requires local authorities to maintain a list of assets of community value which have been nominated by the local community. When listed assets come up for sale or change of ownership, the Act then gives community groups the time to develop a bid and raise the money to bid to buy the asset when it comes on the open market. This will help local communities keep much-loved sites in public use and part of local life. (p.9)

In outline, Chapter 3 creates the community right to bid for assets by requiring the local authority to maintain a list of assets of community value, permitting community nominations to be added to that list, by requiring a moratorium on disposing of listed land and by providing compensation, land charge and enforcement mechanisms for the scheme.

4.3.1 Meanings in relation to the right to bid for assets of community value

'Land of community value' is described in s.88(1) as, subject to subsection (3):

> a building or other land in a local authority's area . . . if in the opinion of the authority–
>
> (a) an actual current use of the building or other land that is not an ancillary use furthers the social wellbeing or social interests of the local community, and
> (b) it is realistic to think that there can continue to be non-ancillary use of the building or other land which will further (whether or not in the same way) the social wellbeing or social interests of the local community.

Subsection (3) enables the appropriate authority to make regulations to provide that a building or land is not of community value. 'Social interests' include cultural, recreational and sporting interests (s.88(6)).

Section 106(1) of the Act provides that a 'local authority' means: (a) a district council; (b) a county council for areas in England where there are no district councils; (c) a London borough council; (d) the Common Council of the City of London; and (e) the Council of the Isles of Scilly. In Wales a 'local authority' means: (i) a county council; or (ii) a county borough council (s.106(3)). The Secretary of State and Welsh Ministers may amend the meaning of 'local authority' by order (s.106(2) and (4)).

The meaning of 'owner' of listed land includes the freeholder or a qualifying leaseholder who is the most distant (in terms of the number of intervening leasehold estates) from the freeholder (s.107(1)–(4)). A qualifying leasehold estate means a lease for a term which, when granted, had at least 25 years to run (s.107(5)). The appropriate authority may amend the meaning of 'owner' by order.

Section 108 provides a general interpretation section and, for example, provides that the meaning of 'land' includes: (a) part of a building; (b) part of any other structure; and (c) mines and minerals, whether or not held with the surface. There are further interpretation and definition provisions in the specific sections. An 'appropriate authority' means: (a) in relation to England, the Secretary of State; and (b) in relation to Wales, the Welsh Ministers.

4.3.2 List of assets of community value (sections 87–90)

Under s.87(1) of the Act a local authority must maintain a list of land in its area that is land of community value, to be known as its 'list of assets of community value' (s.87(2)). Any land entered on a local authority list remains there for five years unless removed beforehand. After five years the land is removed from the list (s.87(3)). The appropriate authority may, through regulations, provide some other period than five years (s.87(4)).

Section 87(6) provides that it is for the local authority to decide the form and contents of its list of assets of community value. However, s.87(5) enables the appropriate authority to intervene and that regulations may be made to make provision about a local authority's list of assets including:

(a) its form;
(b) the contents of an entry in the list;
(c) modification of an entry;
(d) removal of an entry;
(e) matters relating to land in multiple ownership; and
(f) the inter-relationship with the list of unsuccessful nominations (discussed below).

A local authority must publish and make available for free inspection and copy its list of:

(i) assets of community value; and
(ii) land determined to be unsuccessful community nominations to be maintained under s.93.

4.3.3 Procedure for including land in a list of assets

Land may only be included in a local authority list of assets of community value: (a) in response to a community nomination; or (b) where permitted by regulations (s.89(1)). A community nomination is one made by: (i) a parish council in England; (ii) a community council in Wales; (iii) a person that is a voluntary or community body with a local connection (s.89(2)), or by regulations (s.89(3)).

A local authority must accept a community nomination if the land:

(a) is in the authority's area; and
(b) is of community value (s.90(3)).

The local authority will have to assess the nomination against the criteria in s.88(1) (see above). Section 90(4) provides that if the land satisfies (a) and (b) above the authority must cause the land to be included in the authority's list of assets of community value. If not, the nomination will be regarded as unsuccessful and the land must be placed on the list of unsuccessful community nominations (s.90(5)). The authority must give written reasons to the person who made the nomination as to why the land could not be included in its list of assets (s.90(6)).

4.3.4 Notice of inclusion or removal of land in list of assets

If land is included in, or removed from, an authority's list of assets of community value, the authority must, where reasonably practicable, give written notice of this action to:

(a) the land owner;
(b) the occupier;
(c) the person who made a nomination (if this prompted the inclusion); and
(d) any person specified in regulations (s.91(1) and (2)).

A notice under s.91 must draw attention to the consequences of listing and that there is a right to ask for review under s.92 of the Act. Section 92 enables a land owner to review the authority's decision to include the land in the list. It also permits regulations to be made in relation to procedures and time limits for any review.

4.3.5 Moratorium on disposing of land and potential bidders

The moratorium on disposing of land is a critical element of the community right to bid. Section 95(1) of the Act provides that a person who is an owner of land included in a local authority's list of assets of community value must not enter into a relevant disposal of the land unless each of three conditions (A–C) is met. A 'relevant disposal of the land' is either a disposal of a freehold estate with vacant possession or a grant or assignment of a qualifying leasehold estate (s.96(2) and (3)). The three conditions are:

A that the owner has notified the local authority in writing of his wish to enter into a relevant disposal (s.95(2));

B that an interim moratorium period (i.e. six weeks (s.95(6)) has ended without the local authority having received a written request from a community interest group to be treated as a potential bidder, or that the full moratorium period (i.e. six months (s.95(6)) has ended (s.95(3)); and

C that the protected period has not ended (i.e. the maximum five-year period) (s.95(4)).

Section 95(5) provides an extensive list of disposals which are not to be regarded as a 'relevant disposal' of land including, among others:

(a) a disposal by way of gift; or
(b) a disposal by personal representatives of a deceased person.

When a local authority receives a request under s.95(2) that an owner wishes to enter into a relevant disposal of land within its list of assets, s.97 requires the authority to publish a notice to that effect. The local authority must also give written notice to the person who made the nomination. If the local authority then receives a written request from a community interest group, to be treated as a potential bidder, in relation to the land within the interim moratorium period the authority must as soon as practicable either pass on the request to the land owner or inform the owner of the details of the request.

4.3.6 Compensation, enforcement and co-operation

Under s.99 the appropriate authority may, by regulations, make provision for the payment of compensation in connection with the operation of this part of the Act. Similarly, the appropriate authority may, by regulations, make provision for the contravention of s.95(1), i.e. entering into a relevant disposal of land without meeting conditions A–C. The authors anticipate that the nature of any enforcement provisions will need to include some form of prohibition or stop mechanism preventing the disposal of land or, if land has been disposed of, enable reference to the court to set aside any land disposal. There may also be criminal sanctions akin to the planning enforcement mechanisms under TCPA 1990, Part VII.

If different parts of any land are in different local authority areas, the authorities concerned must co-operate with each other in carrying out functions under this Chapter in relation to the land or any part of it (s.102).

Finally, s.100 provides that if land is included in a local authority's list of assets of community value:

(a) inclusion in the list is a local land charge; and
(b) that authority is the originating authority for the purposes of the Local Land Charges Act 1975.

4.3.7 Guidance, advice and assistance and entry into force

Sections 103 and 104 permit the Secretary of State and Welsh Ministers to provide advice and assistance to anyone in relation to the community right to bid for land of community value including, in particular, advice and assistance to a community interest group in relation to a wide range of matters on bidding for, or acquiring land. This extends to the provision of education and training as well as financial assistance by any means including providing a loan and the giving of a guarantee or indemnity (ss.103(2), (3) and 104(2), (3)).

The power conferred on the Secretary of State and Welsh Ministers to make regulations and also to provide advice and assistance under ss.103 and 104 came into force with the passing of the Act on 15 November 2011 (s.240(5)(g)). Other sections of this Chapter come into force by order (s.240(2)). See **Appendix D** for a list of commencement dates as well as provisions that are not in force as at 20 April 2012.

PART B PLANNING REFORM

5 PLANNING: PLANS AND STRATEGIES

A key purpose of the Localism Act 2011 is to reform the land use planning system to 'make [it] clearer, more democratic, and more effective' (the *Guide*, p.11). It seeks to achieve this by revision to the strategic planning process and the provisions as to how land may be used and designated over the medium to long term. It also revises elements of the development management process and the control or regulation of development through the process of applying for and granting planning permission for site-specific development, operations and activities.

5.1 ABOLITION OF REGIONAL STRATEGIES

Rather than reforming the entire strategic planning system, Chapter 1, Part 6 of the Act revises specific aspects of regional spatial planning, sustainable development and local development schemes. The concept of regional spatial strategies is not new. It can be found in the European Spatial Development Perspective adopted in May 1999 and articulated in terms of local spatial planning in former PPS12 (2008). The Greater London Authority Act 1999 was the first legislative basis for spatial planning in England, with the introduction of the London Plan, although arguably the Greater London Development Plan (1976) prepared by the Greater London Council, under the London Government Act 1963, amounted to a spatial plan for Greater London, albeit not described in those terms.

The concept of regional spatial planning was placed upon a statutory footing, outside London, by Part 1 of the Planning and Compulsory Purchase Act (PCPA) 2004 with the introduction of regional spatial strategies (RSSs). These were to be prepared by the regional planning bodies (RPBs), usually non-elected regional assemblies appointed by the Secretary of State. The structure plans first prepared under the Town and Country Planning Act 1968 by county councils or joint authorities were to be gradually replaced by the RSSs. The transitional arrangements provided for certain structure plan policies to be 'saved' until an RSS for the region had been adopted. The initial RSSs were effectively updates to the regional planning guidance (RPG). Prior to the RSSs, there was RPG which set out broad strategic policies at regional level in England, as drafted by the government offices. Following devolution, Wales has relied upon an overarching policy document,

Planning Policy Wales (2002) (now in its 4th edition February 2011) which has been supplemented over time by Technical Advice Notes.

The procedures for formulating regional strategy were further refined by Part 5 of the Local Democracy, Economic Development and Construction Act (LDEDCA) 2009 where s.70 provided that there should be a regional strategy for each region in addition to London and that the strategy for each region should set out policies in relation to:

(a) sustainable growth for the region; and
(b) the development and use of land in that region.

The regional strategy was to consist of the RSS for the region which was in existence when the provision came into force on 1 April 2010, and the regional economic strategy for the region also subsisting when the provision came into force, also on 1 April 2010. LDEDCA 2009 also provided for 'Leaders' Boards' under s.71, and the 'responsible regional authorities' which were charged with preparing the regional strategies were to be the regional development agency and the Leaders Board for the relevant region (s.72). LDEDCA 2009, ss.73–80 provided for the revision of the regional strategies. The revised RSSs, submitted to the Secretary of State, all provoked large numbers of objections, primarily directed at the housing numbers, followed by some judicial reviews. For example, the West Midlands RSS Phase Two revision that underwent an Examination in Public in summer 2009 had not been adopted by May 2010, when the new government sought to abolish immediately the regional strategies, as described below.

The life of regional spatial planning in England has been brief and formal abolition of the regional tier of planning is achieved by s.109 of the Localism Act 2011. On 27 May 2010, Eric Pickles, as the recently appointed Secretary of State in the coalition government, wrote to local authorities confirming the commitment in the Conservative Green Paper: *Open Source Planning* (2010) to abolish regional strategies. The government then sought to use the power in LDEDCA 2009, s.79(6) to revoke the adopted regional strategies. This use of power was challenged by the developer Cala Homes (South) Ltd who was concerned that the Secretary of State had exceeded his discretion and not properly complied with his obligations under the Strategic Environment Assessment Directive (2001/42/EC) ('the SEA Directive'). Sales J. in *R (on the application of Cala Homes (South) Ltd)* v. *Secretary of State for Communities and Local Government* [2010] EWHC 2866 (Admin) (*Cala Homes No. 1*) found that the Secretary of State was not entitled to use the discretionary power under s.79(6) effectively to repeal legislation and that this could only be done through primary legislation, as now appears in the Localism Act 2011.

Following the *Cala Homes No. 1* decision, the Chief Planner wrote on 10 November 2010 to advise local planning authorities that the intention to abolish the regional strategies remained a material consideration as stated in the Secretary of State's letter of 27 May 2010 and that it should be taken into account. Cala Homes then sought to challenge this letter, consent for which was refused by Lindblom J. and whose decision was subsequently upheld in *R (on the application of Cala Homes*

(South) Ltd) v. *Secretary of State for Communities and Local Government (No. 2)* [2011] EWCA Civ 639.

Various legislative provisions are repealed by s.109(1)(a) and (b) of the Act, including ss.70(5), 82(1) and the remaining parts of s.83 of LDEDCA 2009, which with Sched.5 of LDEDCA 2009 had amended PCPA 2004, Part 1: Regional functions by introducing RSSs. Section 109(2) provides that the repeals in s.109(1)(b) do not apply to consequential amendments made when the regional strategy provisions in PCPA 2004 were amended to take account of the LDEDCA 2009 provisions. The repeal of references to RSSs in other legislation is covered by the list of consequential repeals set out in Part 16 of Sched.25 to the Act. Further, the Secretary of State is granted power under s.109(3) and (4) to revoke by order the whole or part of a regional strategy or all strategies made under LDEDCA 2009, Part 5.

Section 109(5) and (6) also provide the Secretary of State with the power to make orders to revoke all or part of a direction preserving development plan policies relating to structure plan policies made under PCPA 2004, Sched.8. This represents the final abolition of structure plans and such orders will remove any direction as to 'saved' structure plan policies. These consequential amendments are referred to in s.109(7) of the Act and relate to removing references in other related legislation to 'regional strategy', 'region', 'regional planning body' and so on. Whilst every effort has been taken to expunge the term 'regional' from the planning legislation, it is worth noting that certain references in the Town and Country Planning Act 1990, previously amended to read 'the responsible regional authorities' are now replaced with 'the county planning authority', and the reference to 'regional strategy' in the heading to PCPA 2004, s.24 is replaced with 'spatial development strategy', thereby demonstrating that there remains a need for some term to describe the tier between national and local.

Certain enabling provisions of s.109 came into force on the date that the Localism Act 2011 received Royal Assent (15 November 2011), including s.109(1)(b), and (2)–(6) and aspects of s.109(7), as well as paras.1, 13(1), 18 and 19 of Sched.8 (s.240(5)(h)). A series of orders formally and finally abolishing the adopted regional strategies are expected once the appropriate strategic environmental assessments have been carried out, the need for which was a finding in *Cala Homes No. 1*.

5.2 DUTY TO CO-OPERATE IN RELATION TO SUSTAINABLE DEVELOPMENT

A new 'duty to co-operate in relation to planning of sustainable development' (the duty to co-operate) was enacted by s.110 of the Act inserting a new s.33A into Part 2 of PCPA 2004. This Part of the 2004 Act has the sub-heading 'Local development' and sets out the procedures for the preparation of local development documents. The new s.33A has no particular connection with the sections immediately preceding or following it: e.g. s.33 relates to urban development corporations and s.34

requires an LPA to take account of any guidance issued by the Secretary of State in the preparation of local development documents.

5.2.1 Who must comply with the duty to co-operate?

The duty to co-operate applies to the persons and bodies defined in s.33A(1) of PCPA 2004 including: (a) an LPA; (b) a county council in England, that is not an LPA; or (c) a body or other person, that is prescribed or of a prescribed description. The Explanatory Notes to the Act state that the nature and extent of the bodies in s.33A(1)(c) will be prescribed in regulations.

5.2.2 Requirements of the duty to co-operate

Section 33A(2) of PCPA 2004 provides that the duty to co-operate under s.33A(1) requires the relevant person (as explained above) to 'engage constructively, actively and on an ongoing basis' in one or more of the activities set out in PCPA 2004, s.33A(3). These include:

> (a) the preparation of development plan documents,
> (b) the preparation of other local development documents,
> (c) the preparation of marine plans under the Marine and Coastal Access Act 2009 [for the English inshore and relevant offshore regions],
> (d) activities that can reasonably be considered to prepare the way for activities within any of paragraphs (a) to (c) that are, or could be, contemplated, and
> (e) activities that support activities within any of paragraphs (a) to (c),
>
> so far as relating to a strategic matter.

A 'strategic matter' is defined in PCPA 2004, s.33A(4) as:

> (a) sustainable development or use of land that has or would have a significant impact on at least two planning areas, including (in particular) sustainable development or use of land for or in connection with infrastructure that is strategic and has or would have a significant impact on at least two planning areas, and
> (b) sustainable development or use of land in a two-tier area if the development or use–
>
> (i) is a county matter, or
> (ii) has or would have a significant impact on a county matter.

The meaning of a two-tier area does not, however, include an area which is covered by a National Park (PCPA 2004, s.33A(5)).

The *Guide* explains that:

> In many cases there are very strong reasons for neighbouring local authorities, or groups of authorities, to work together on planning issues in the interests of all their local residents. This might include working together on environmental issues (like flooding), public transport networks (such as trams), or major new retail parks. (p.11)

This duty to co-operate requires the relevant persons to consider whether they should enter into a formal agreement on their joint approach to the preparation of the relevant plan or document. Such agreement should be publicly available (PCPA 2004, s.33A(6)). In the case of LPAs, this can be an agreement under PCPA 2004, s.28 (Joint local development documents) which enables two or more LPAs to agree upon the preparation of one or more local development document(s).

As well as inserting the new s.33A into PCPA 2004, s.110(3) of the Localism Act 2011 also amends PCPA 2004, s.20(5) requiring LPAs to provide evidence at independent examination of their development plan documents that they have complied with the duty to co-operate in order to ensure that their plans are not rejected by an examiner.

It seems clear that the extent and scope of the duty to co-operate in relation to sustainable development only applies to strategic matters covering two or more planning areas; this could mean, for example, the areas of two district councils, or the area of a district council and a county council. However, given that the duty only extends to the preparation of development plans rather than, say, determining planning applications, it is difficult to see when the duty would not be engaged during the plan-making process.

5.2.3 Defining sustainable development

There is no definition of sustainable development in either PCPA 2004 or the Localism Act, despite the efforts made by various parties during the passage of the Bill to introduce some definition. Indeed, the House of Commons Environmental Audit Committee published a short report entitled 'Sustainable Development in the Localism Bill' in March 2011 urging the government *inter alia* to define the term 'sustainable development' in the land use planning context. This is discussed further in **Chapter 14** in relation to the introduction of the National Planning Policy Framework (NPPF).

5.2.4 Guidance, advice and assistance and entry into force

Section 33A(7) of PCPA 2004 requires a person subject to the duty to co-operate in relation to sustainable development to have regard to any guidance issued by the Secretary of State about how the duty is to be complied with. The new sustainable development duty came into force on 15 November 2011 (s.240(5)(i)).

5.3 LOCAL DEVELOPMENT SCHEMES

Part 2 of PCPA 2004 introduced a requirement to prepare local development schemes, which set out the framework for the development plan documents to be prepared as part of the overall development plan. Section 111 of the Localism Act 2011 has revised certain elements of PCPA 2004, Part 2 relating to the preparation, revision and promulgation of local development schemes. The amendments are directed towards achieving the overall objective of the Act to reduce national or top-down intervention in plan-making. In particular, an LPA will no longer have to submit its local development scheme to the Secretary of State or, for London, to the Mayor. The Secretary of State and Mayor of London will retain powers to direct changes, but only in order to ensure effective plan coverage.

The original s.15(7) of PCPA 2004 made provision for the Secretary of State to make regulations relating to publicity, inspection and bringing schemes into effect. These were set out in the Town and Country Planning (Local Development) (England) Regulations 2004, SI 2004/2204, as amended ('Local Development Regulations 2004'). Section 111 of the Act provides for a replacement s.15(7) which simplifies the process and provides that the LPA need now only 'resolve that the scheme is to have effect and in the resolution specify the date from which the scheme is to have effect'.

The LPA must ensure that the public is provided with information on the local development scheme, including the up-to-date text of the scheme, any amendments, and up-to-date information on the LPA's compliance with the timetable for the preparation or revision of the development plan documents, set out in the scheme. This is achieved by inserting a new s.15(9A) into PCPA 2004 (s.111(7)).

The revised provisions came into force on 15 January 2012 under s.240(1)(h). The Local Development Regulations 2004 will need to be further amended.

5.4 ADOPTION AND WITHDRAWAL OF DEVELOPMENT PLAN DOCUMENTS

The procedure for the independent examination of a development plan document by a person appointed by the Secretary of State (i.e. the planning inspector) is set out in PCPA 2004, s.20. This provides that the planning inspector checks compliance with the procedure set out in the regulations and checks whether the development plan document satisfies the tests for soundness. Under PCPA 2004, s.23, the LPA was bound to adopt the report of the inspector, including any recommended modifications. Section 112 of the Localism Act 2011 has amended PCPA 2004, ss.20–23 so that the inspector's report and any recommended modifications are no longer binding upon the LPA. Notably, under a new s.20(7) inserted into PCPA 2004 (substituted by s.112(2) of the Act) the inspector still carries out the independent examination and may still find that the procedure for the preparation of the plan has been correctly followed, that the plan is sound and may recommend that it should be adopted. However, under the new provisions the LPA may adopt the plan but also may make its own modifications, provided that these do not materially affect the policies in the plan (substituted s.23(2) of PCPA 2004).

Under new s.20(7A), where the inspector is not satisfied, he must recommend non-adoption of the plan and must give his reasons (inserted by s.112(2)). If the inspector concludes that, in all the circumstances, the plan is not sound, but the LPA has complied with the duty under s.33A to co-operate in relation to sustainable development (see above), the LPA may ask the inspector to recommend the modifications that would make the plan compliant with the regulations and/or make it sound (PCPA 2004, new ss.20(7B) and (7C)).

The LPA may adopt the plan with the main modifications recommended by the planning inspector, and may make additional modifications provided that, taken together, the modifications do not materially affect the policies in the plan.

A new power conferred upon the Secretary of State to direct the withdrawal of a development plan, after the independent examination and before its adoption, has been inserted into PCPA 2004. Intervention by the Secretary of State is via a new s.21(9A). The prohibition in PCPA 2004, s.22(2), on the withdrawal by the LPA of a local development plan once it has been submitted for independent examination unless the inspector or the Secretary of State directs that it be withdrawn, no longer applies.

As with local development schemes the revised adoption and withdrawal provisions came into force on 15 January 2012 under s.240(1)(h).

5.5 LOCAL DEVELOPMENT: MONITORING REPORTS

The final aspect of this Chapter of the Localism Act on plans and strategies relates to the monitoring and the progress by LPAs as to their local development documents.

First, the heading to PCPA 2004, s.35 is changed from 'Annual monitoring report' to 'Authorities' monitoring reports'. Next, the duty imposed upon an LPA by PCPA 2004, s.35(1) to make an annual report to the Secretary of State on its local development scheme, and how far the policies set out in the local development documents are being achieved, is removed. Next, PCPA 2004, s.35(2) and (3) is amended to remove the emphasis on prescription. The requirement to prepare reports containing information on the implementation of the local development scheme and the extent to which the policies are being achieved remains with an obligation to publish the information direct to the public at least annually in the interests of transparency. This may be regarded as a further example of decentralisation, shifting the requirement of LPAs to report on the progress of their strategic planning progress to local communities rather than to central government.

The monitoring report provisions came into force on 15 January 2012 further to s.240(1)(h) of the Act. The Local Development Regulations 2004 will need to be further amended or replaced to take account of the new monitoring regime.

6 COMMUNITY INFRASTRUCTURE LEVY

The Community Infrastructure Levy (CIL) was introduced by the Planning Act (PA) 2008. Chapter 2 of Part 5 of the Localism Act 2011 amends elements of the CIL legislation by revision to PA 2008.

6.1 BACKGROUND

The Planning Advisory Service (PAS), which helps councillors and local authority officers understand and respond to planning reform, explains on its website (**www.pas.gov.uk**) that CIL is a new levy that local authorities can choose to charge on new developments in their area and that '[t]he money can be used to support development by funding infrastructure that the council, local community and neighbourhoods want'. In 'An introduction to the community infrastructure levy', PAS further explains that:

> The levy will help pay for the infrastructure required to support new development. This includes development that does not require planning permission. The levy should not be used to remedy pre-existing deficiencies unless the new development makes the deficiency more severe.
>
> The levy can be charged by local authorities in England and Wales – but they do not have to. Authorities that wish to charge a levy need to develop and adopt a CIL charging schedule.
>
> Councils must spend income from the levy on infrastructure to support the development of the area but they can decide what infrastructure to spend it on and it can be different to that for which it was originally set. Authorities should set out on their website what they will use CIL for.

CIL may be charged by a 'charging authority' (which is usually the LPA) in accordance with a charging schedule. The detailed provisions for the imposition of CIL, the preparation of charging schedules, and the collection and use of the CIL receipts are set out in the Community Infrastructure Levy Regulations 2010, SI 2010/948, as amended by the Community Infrastructure Levy (Amendment) Regulations 2011, SI 2011/987 ('the CIL Regulations'). Before approving a charging schedule the charging authority is required to appoint an independent person to examine the draft charging schedule. When submitting the draft schedule for examination the charging authority must give a declaration that it has complied with the drafting requirements of PA 2008, Part 11 and the requirements of the CIL Regulations.

6.2 AMENDING PROVISIONS UNDER THE ACT

The amendments introduced by ss.114 and 115 of the Localism Act 2011 are intended to make CIL more flexible. The *Guide* notes that:

> It will give local authorities greater freedom in setting the rate that developers should pay. And crucially, the Act gives the Government the power to require that some of the money raised from the levy go directly to the neighbourhoods where development takes place. This will help ensure that the people who say 'yes' to new development feel the benefit of that decision. (p.13)

6.2.1 Approval of CIL charging schedules

Section 114 of the Act revises what constitutes appropriate available evidence to be defined in the CIL Regulations (or subsequent revised regulations). This is achieved by amending PA 2008, ss.211–213.

The amount of levy under PA 2008, s.211 is amended by the insertion of new s.211(7A) and (7B); although new s.211(7A) requires the charging authority to use appropriate evidence to inform the preparation of its charging schedule. The new PA 2008, s.211(7B) provides that what constitutes appropriate or inappropriate evidence, or available or unavailable evidence, and how evidence is to be used or not to be used, is to be set out in further amendment to the CIL Regulations. How and whether the charging authority has done this properly will be reviewed by the independent examiner, who is required by PA 2008, s.212(7) to consider such matters, to make recommendations and give his reasons for such recommendations.

A new PA 2008, s.212A entitled 'Charging schedule: examiner's recommendations' has been inserted to deal with the options open to the examiner on consideration of a draft charging schedule. If the examiner considers that the drafting of the charging schedule has not been done properly, and that such non-compliance cannot be remedied by making modifications then the examiner must recommend that the draft be rejected (s.212A(2)). If the examiner considers that non-compliance can be remedied by making modifications, he must recommend what modifications need to be made to remedy the non-compliance in the drafting, and recommend approval of the draft charging schedule with these modifications, or others that achieve the same purpose of remedying the non-compliance (s.212A(3)–(7)). Subject to s.212A(2)–(4), the examiner must recommend approval of the draft schedule (PA 2008, s.212A(5)).

PA 2008, s.213 deals with the approval of the CIL charging schedule. Amendments are made to the procedure for approving a charging schedule to take account of the implications of new PA 2008, s.212A. A charging authority may only approve a charging schedule if it has taken account of any recommendations made by the examiner, and his reasons for making them. If the examiner recommends that the draft charging schedule be rejected, then the charging authority cannot approve it. Where the examiner recommends that modifications can be made to the draft charging schedule to make it compliant, then the charging authority may approve it if the modifications recommended by the examiner have been made, or may approve it with other modifications that are sufficient and necessary to deal with the inadequacies identified by the examiner (ss.213(1) and (1A)–(1D)).

Where the charging authority approves the charging schedule with modifications it must publish a report explaining how the charging schedule as approved has been amended to remedy the inadequacies so that it is now compliant with the CIL Regulations. The form or contents of such report may be specified in a further amendment to the CIL Regulations (s.213(3A)–(3C)).

The Explanatory Notes neatly summarise the consequences of s.114 of the Act:

> 255. The effect of this section is to change the relationship between the charging authority and the examiner. The charging authority will no longer be required to submit a declaration to the examiner with the draft charging schedule. The examiner will now consider whether the charging authority has complied with the relevant requirements within Part 11 of [PA 2008] and the [CIL Regulations], which will now be referred to as 'drafting requirements'. Any recommended modifications to the draft charging schedule made by the examiner will no longer be binding on the charging authority.

6.2.2 Use of CIL

Section 115 of the Act inserts new ss.216A and 216B into PA 2008 relating to the application of CIL receipts and by whom. Section 115 makes changes to various sections of PA 2008 to clarify the general purpose of CIL by confirming that it may be spent on the ongoing costs of providing infrastructure and should not be operated so as to render a development unviable. The words in PA 2008, s.205(2) are amended to read:

> In making the regulations the Secretary of State shall aim to ensure that the overall purpose of CIL is to ensure that costs incurred in *supporting* the development of an area can be funded (wholly or partly) by owners or developers of land *in a way that does not make development of the area economically unviable*. (s.115(2)) [emphasis added to new text]

The Table in s.205(3) which lists the provisions of PA 2008, Part 11 is amended by including a reference to the new ss.216A and 216B of PA 2008 (s.115(3)).

Section 211(4) of PA 2008 relates to the preparation of the charging schedules, including the rates at which CIL is to be charged. The matters in PA 2008, s.211(2) to which the charging authority should have regard when setting rates or other criteria, as specified in the CIL Regulations, are widened by the insertion of new subsections (aa) and (ab) into s.211(4). Thus the charging authority must now not only take account of:

(a) the actual and expected costs of infrastructure;

(b) the matters specified in the CIL Regulations relating to the economic viability of development; and
(c) other actual and expected sources of funding for infrastructure,

but also is required:

> (aa) to have regard, to the extent and in the manner specified by the regulations, to actual and expected costs of anything other than infrastructure that is concerned with addressing demands that development places on an area (whether by reference to lists prepared by virtue of section 216(5)(a) or otherwise);
> (ab) to have regard, to the extent and in the manner specified by the regulations, to other actual and expected sources of funding for anything other than infrastructure that is concerned with addressing demands that development places on an area;

The use of the levy to fund infrastructure is expanded by amendments to PA 2008, s.216. The amendments make clear that CIL is not restricted to funding new infrastructure. Section 216(1) as amended now provides that the CIL Regulations should require the charging authority to apply CIL to 'supporting development by funding the provision, improvement, replacement, operation or maintenance of infrastructure', instead of merely 'funding infrastructure'.

The matters to be specified in the CIL Regulations that are to be, or not to be, funded by CIL are expanded by the addition of maintenance and operational activities (including operational activities of a promotional kind), and things that may be carried out by another body other than the charging authority, as provided in the new s.216A of PA 2008. There are also various consequential drafting amendments.

The new s.216A introduces a new duty to pass CIL receipts to other bodies. How the duty is to operate will be set out in the CIL Regulations and will cover the area in which it will apply; the bodies to which it will apply; the amount and timings of payments; monitoring; accounting and reporting responsibilities of the charging authorities; and when the funding is to be returned to the charging authority.

The new s.216B of PA 2008 deals with use of CIL in an area to which the duty in s.216A does not apply, described as 'the uncovered area'. When and where in the uncovered area CIL may be used will be set out in revised CIL Regulations.

Again, the Explanatory Notes to the Act helpfully summarise key effects of s.115:

> 259. . . . The section extends the permitted uses of levy receipts, in specified situations, so that they may be applied to any matter that supports development by addressing the demands that it places on the areas that host it.
> 260. The section also amends the purpose of the [CIL] to explicitly require that regulations must aim to ensure that the imposition of a levy charge in an area will not make the development of the area economically unviable. . . .

6.3 REGULATIONS, GUIDANCE AND ENTRY INTO FORCE

The amendments to the CIL provisions in PA 2008 brought about by ss.114 and 115 of the Localism Act 2011 will also require amendment to the CIL Regulations.

Section 114 came into force on 16 November 2011 (s.240(6)). Section 115 came into force by order on 15 January 2012 (Localism Act 2011 (Commencement No. 2 and Transitional and Saving Provision) Order 2012, SI 2012/57).

7 NEIGHBOURHOOD PLANNING

As will have been seen from **Chapter 5** on plans and strategies, the Localism Act 2011 alters the decision-making hierarchy in planning by removing the regional planning tier throughout England outside London and also the residue of the 'saved' structure plan policies. However, while the Act simplifies regional planning to some extent, it introduces neighbourhood planning as a new tier of strategic planning at a very local level. Neighbourhood planning, as with the new community rights to bid for and own assets, is central to the localism political agenda. The government's aims are set out on p.12 of the *Guide*:

> Neighbourhood planning will allow communities, both residents, employees and business, to come together through a local parish council or neighbourhood forum and say where they think new houses, businesses and shops should go – and what they should look like.
>
> These plans can be very simple and concise, or go into considerable detail where people want. Local communities will be able to use neighbourhood planning to grant full or outline planning permission in areas where they most want to see new homes and businesses, making it easier and quicker for development to go ahead.
>
> Provided a neighbourhood development plan or order is in line with national planning policy, with the strategic vision for the wider area set by the local authority, and with other legal requirements, local people will be able to vote on it in a referendum. If the plan is approved by a majority of those who vote, then the local authority will bring it into force.
>
> Local planning authorities will be required to provide technical advice and support as neighbourhoods draw up their proposals. The Government is funding sources of help and advice for communities. This will help people take advantage of the opportunity to exercise influence over decisions that make a big difference to their lives.

The government's short guide *An introduction to neighbourhood planning* (DCLG, October 2011, available at **www.communities.gov.uk/documents/planningand building/pdf/1985896.pdf**) explains that there will be five key stages to neighbourhood planning. These are summarised below.

- **Stage 1: Defining the neighbourhood**
  This will involve local people deciding how they would like to work together. In areas with a parish or town council, they will take the lead; in other areas an existing or new group may co-ordinate the debate. It is the LPA's role to consider

requests to progress neighbourhood planning in its area. If the LPA decides that a community group meets the right standards, the group will be able to call itself a 'neighbourhood forum'.

- **Stage 2: Preparing the plan**
  Local people will begin collecting their ideas together and drawing up their plans to establish general planning policies for the development and use of land in a neighbourhood. Local people can choose to draw up either a plan, or a development order, or both. Both must follow some ground rules:
  - They must generally be in line with local and national planning policies.
  - They must be in line with other laws.
  - If the LPA says that an area needs to grow, then communities cannot use neighbourhood planning to block the building of new homes and businesses.
- **Stage 3: Independent check**
  Once a neighbourhood plan or order has been prepared an independent examiner will check that it meets the right basic standards.
- **Stage 4: Community referendum**
  The local council will organise a referendum on any plan or order that meets the basic standards. This will ensure that the community has the final say on whether a plan or order comes into force.
- **Stage 5: Legal force**
  Once a neighbourhood plan is in force, it carries real legal weight. Decision-makers will be obliged, by law, to take what it says into account when they consider proposals for development in the neighbourhood. A neighbourhood order will grant planning permission for development that complies with the order. Where people have made it clear that they want development of a particular type, it will be easier for that development to go ahead.

There are then two new rungs on the planning ladder:

(a) neighbourhood development plans (NDPs), which set the local planning context; and
(b) neighbourhood development orders (NDOs) which effectively act as the grant of planning permission and therefore provide the development management mechanism.

These are brought into being by revision to TCPA 1990 (for NDOs) and to PCPA 2004 (for NDPs) with a series of regulations intended to support their implementation.

The primary legislative revisions are made by s.116 of the Act, an enabling section. Section 116(1) gives effect to Sched.9 which then inserts new ss.61E to 61Q into TCPA 1990. Schedule 9 also amends s.38 of PCPA 2004 and thereafter inserts new ss.38A–38C into PCPA 2004. Section 116(2) gives effect to Sched.10 which inserts a new Sched.4B into TCPA 1990. Sections 117–121 of the Act give further enactment to neighbourhood planning by providing for charging, costs and consequential amendments. Neighbourhood planning applies in England alone.

This chapter covers the following parts of the Act:

- Sections 116–121;
- Schedule 9, Part 2 relating to NDPs which inserts new provisions into PCPA 2004;
- Schedule 9, Part 1 relating to NDOs which inserts new provisions into TCPA 1990;
- Schedule 10 relating to the process for making NDOs;
- Schedule 11 relating to community right to build orders which inserts new provisions into TCPA 1990;
- Schedule 12 which makes consequential amendments.

7.1 NEIGHBOURHOOD DEVELOPMENT PLANS

A new subsection (10) of PCPA 2004, s.38 provides that an NDP must be construed in accordance with s.38A of the same Act. New s.38A(2) of PCPA 2004 explains that:

> A 'neighbourhood development plan' is a plan which sets out policies (however expressed) in relation to the development and use of land in the whole or any part of a particular neighbourhood area specified in the plan.

7.1.1 'Qualifying body'

Any 'qualifying body' may initiate a process for requiring an LPA in England to make an NDP (PCPA 2004, s.38A(1)). Further, PCPA 2004, s.38A(3) with Sched.4B provides for the making of NDOs, including:

(a) the provision for independent examination of orders proposed by qualifying bodies; and
(b) the holding of referendums on orders proposed by qualifying bodies,

as apply to the making of NDPs (subject to the modifications in PCPA 2004, s.38C(5)).

A critical element of neighbourhood planning is therefore who can act as a 'qualifying body' and utilise the new neighbourhood planning provisions. A 'qualifying body' means:

> a parish council, or an organisation or body designated as a neighbourhood forum, authorised for the purposes of [an NDP] to act in relation to a neighbourhood area as a result of section 61F of the principal Act [i.e. TCPA 1990], as applied by section 38C of this Act. (PCPA 2004, s.38A(12))

A new s.61F inserted into TCPA 1990 helps to clarify the position. The provision for a parish council to be a 'qualifying body' is reasonably clear with s.61F(1) and (2) providing the precise scope for parish councils in relation to their boundaries. Who may be 'designated as a neighbourhood forum' is more complex.

The LPA may designate an organisation or body as a neighbourhood forum providing there is not a parish council within the neighbourhood area.

New s.61F(5) of TCPA 1990 provides that the LPA may designate a neighbourhood forum if it is satisfied that it meets the following conditions:

(a) the forum is established for the express purpose of promoting or improving the social, economic and environmental well-being of an area;
(b) its membership is open to individuals who: (i) live in; (ii) work in; or (iii) are elected members of a county, district or London borough of the neighbourhood area;
(c) its membership includes a minimum of 21 individuals that fall within in (b) above;
(d) the forum has a written constitution; and
(e) any other conditions that may be prescribed.

The LPA will also take into account the reasonable steps taken by the prospective designated neighbourhood forum to ensure that at least one individual member of the forum satisfies each of the conditions in TCPA 1990, s.61F(5)(b)(i)–(iii); and that members are drawn from different places in the neighbourhood area and different sections of the community in the area.

New s.61F(6)–(13) of TCPA 1990 provide further rules for the designation of a neighbourhood forum, namely:

- only one forum may be designated in an area (s.61F(7)(b)),
- a designation may cease to have effect after a period of five years (s.61F(8)(a)); and
- reasons must be given where the LPA refuses an application for designation (s.61F(7)(d)).

The LPA may also withdraw a designation if it considers that the neighbourhood forum no longer satisfies the conditions which qualified it for designation (TCPA 1990, s.61F(9)).

7.1.2 Neighbourhood development plan process

New s.38A(3) of PCPA 2004 provides that the process for the making of NDOs under TCPA 1990, Sched.4B is to apply in relation to NDPs (subject to modifications in PCPA 2004, s.38C(5)) including the provision for:

(a) independent examination of NDPs proposed by qualifying bodies; and
(b) the holding of referendums on NDPs proposed by those bodies.

New s.38A(4) of PCPA 2004 provides that an LPA must make an NDP if more than half of those voting in an applicable referendum vote in favour of the proposed NDP. An additional referendum is required where there is a business area, and similarly for a proposed NDP affecting a business area.

The LPA is not subject to the duty to make the NDP if the authority considers that the making of the NDP would infringe any European obligation, or any Convention rights within the meaning of the Human Rights Act 1998. Regulations may be made by the Secretary of State as to the procedures to be followed by the LPA for the making, examination and publication of the approval of an NDP. The regulations may in particular make provision for the holding of an examination, costs, publicity, information provision, consultation and representations (PCPA 2004, new s.38A(7) and (8)). In accordance with new s.38A(9) and (10) of PCPA 2004, the LPA must publish any decision for an NDP and send a copy to the qualifying body. An NDP should specify the period for which it is to have effect and should not include any 'excluded development' defined by TCPA 1990, s.61K (PCPA 2004, new s.38B(6)) and discussed below in relation to NDOs.

If an NDP is in force in relation to a neighbourhood area a qualifying body may make a proposal for the existing NDP to be replaced by a new one (PCPA 2004, s.38A(11)(a)). If so, the process for a replacement plan is the same as the process for the making of the existing plan (PCPA 2004, s.38A(11)(b)).

As with the current provision, in relation to any conflict between policies and any other statement or information in a development plan under PCPA 2004, s.38B(3), the policy in the NDP prevails over any such statement or information.

7.1.3 Supplementary provisions for NDPs

New s.38C of PCPA 2004 specifies the provisions of TCPA 1990, s.61F (authorisation to act in relation to neighbourhood areas), s.61I(2), (3), 61M, 61N, 61O, 61P and Sched.4B that relate to NDOs that are also to apply to the NDP process.

7.1.4 Costs relating to neighbourhood planning

As well as the raft of new provisions for neighbourhood planning within PCPA 2004 and the application of provisions in TCPA 1990, ss.117–120 of the Localism Act 2011 make specific new law in relation to costs including the collection and enforcement of any charges made.

Section 117 of the Act enables LPAs to recover costs which they have incurred in responding to proposals for NDOs or NDPs by means of charges set out in regulations. The section gives the Secretary of State power to make such regulations (with the consent of the Treasury). The charges may be set out in the regulations or the LPA may produce a charging schedule. A charge will be payable when development authorised by an NDO is commenced. Liability for payment of the charge may be imposed on owners or developers and arrangements may be included for other persons to assume liability for payment of the charge.

Any regulations made under s.117 must include provisions for the collection of the charge and different forms of enforcement for payment of the charge. At a minimum, the enforcement of the charge is to be as a civil debt recoverable summarily in the magistrates' court (s.118). Regulations may make provision about procedures to be followed in connection with charges imposed by the regulations. A duty is imposed upon the LPA to have regard to any guidance issued by the Secretary of State.

Finally, on costs and finances, s.120 of the Act empowers the Secretary of State to do anything that is considered appropriate to publicise or promote the making of NDOs and NDPs, or to give advice and assistance in relation to formulating proposals for NDOs and NDPs, including the provision of financial assistance.

7.2 NEIGHBOURHOOD DEVELOPMENT ORDERS

An NDO, once approved, grants planning permission for the development or class of development described in the NDO in relation to the particular specified neighbourhood area (TCPA 1990, s.61E(2)). The concept of planning permission being granted through a development order is not new. The ability to make local development orders already exists in TCPA 1990, ss.61A–61D, while s.59 enables an LPA to make a special development order.

7.2.1 Existing local development orders

To help understand the nature of the new provisions for a neighbourhood development order, the existing provisions under TCPA 1990, ss.61A–61D are summarised below.

A local development order (LDO) allows an LPA to introduce new permitted development rights in planning. A good way to illustrate how an LDO may operate is to consider the provisions in practice. Cornwall Council explains on its website that LDOs:

> are flexible and consistent with local determination, and are part of a move to remove bureaucracy and redefine the issues where planning really makes a contribution to the local area. LDOs are a means for the planning system to incentivise development in a way that meets a whole range of locally specific policy objectives.

The Council adds:

> In Cornwall we now have 2 LDOs – as detailed below:
>
> - **Carnon Downs Local Development Order**
>
>   This was approved by the Secretary of State in April 2011, following considerable consultation, and came into force on 9 June 2011.
>
>   It will provide extended rights which will permit (within certain limitations):
>   - extensions at the front of properties
>   - additions to the roof at the front
>   - porches up to 5 square metres
>
>   Different rights will apply to different character areas within the village and there is a requirement to notify Feock Parish Council using their notification form (an administration fee of £35 applies).
>
>   Further information is available in the Local Development Order, and there is also a simple guidance document which explains what permitted development rights have been extended. These documents and the notification form are available to download below:

- **Newquay Cornwall Airport Local Development Order**

  The proposed Newquay Cornwall Airport Local Development Order (LDO) has been prepared as a facilitative and enabling tool to allow the airport to react to business requirements on a level playing field to other privately owned airports in England.

  Unlike privately owned UK airports and their operators, Newquay Cornwall Airport (NCA) does not benefit from the ability to carry out the operational developments authorised through Classes A, B and I of Part 18 of the GPDO, within its site boundary without the need to obtain planning permission. As a result, over the past three years, as airport development activity focused on the transfer of functions from the former RAF St. Mawgan air base, it was required to make formal planning applications for all development regardless of need and size.

The examples above from Cornwall Council provide a good illustration of the variety and nature of the existing LDO regime: one clarifies permitted development rights in the locality, the other is a project-specific order. The Cornwall Council website (**www.cornwall.gov.uk**) also publishes the relevant orders, guidance and statement of community involvement.

7.2.2 Qualifying and relevant bodies and area necessary for an NDO

In contrast to the existing TCPA 1990 mechanisms for LDOs, the new NDO provisions may be initiated by a 'qualifying body' and, once the NDO has been approved by referendum, the LPA is under a duty to make the NDO as soon as reasonably practicable thereafter (TCPA 1990, new s.61E(4), discussed below).

In order for an LPA to be required to make an NDO there must be a valid application for an NDO relating to a neighbourhood area from a 'relevant body'. In similar fashion to the NDP 'qualifying body' and also the 'qualifying body' that may apply for an NDO (TCPA 1990, new s.61E(6)), 'relevant body' is defined as 'a parish council, or an organisation or body which is, or is capable of being designated as a neighbourhood forum' (TCPA 1990, new s.61G(2)).

In summary, there are up to three phases of designation necessary in order to apply for an NDO:

1. There needs to be a designated 'relevant body' which may be deemed to be designated if it is a parish council (stage 1); but also a designated 'neighbourhood area'.
2. The relevant body applies to the LPA to designate a specific area as a 'neighbourhood area'.
3. The 'qualifying body' may then apply for an NDO in relation to the neighbourhood area.

7.2.3 Designating the neighbourhood area

The legal provisions for an application for an NDO covering all or part of a designated neighbourhood area made by a qualifying body are set out in a new s.61E and Sched.4B inserted into TCPA 1990 (by s.116 of and Scheds.9 and 10 to the Act).

In order to designate the neighbourhood area, the LPA must, under new s.61G of TCPA 1990, be satisfied of the following.

- The area is located in England, and within its own area.
- The body making the request is a parish council, and that the area is located within the area of the parish council. It may be the whole of it or only a part of it.
- If the body making the application is not the parish council, then the area to which the application relates must be outside an area where there is a parish council, i.e. a non-parished area (in practice, this is likely to mean urban or semi-urban areas).
- The LPA must have regard to the desirability of designating the whole of the area of a parish council as a neighbourhood area and the desirability of maintaining the existing boundaries of areas already designated as neighbourhood areas (TCPA 1990, new s.61G(4)(a), (b)).
- Neighbourhood areas must not overlap with each other.
- An LPA can refuse an application to designate an area, and must give reasons for its decision. The LPA may decide that the proposed area is not an area that it is appropriate to designate as a neighbourhood area, but that part of the area would be suitable and modify the designation of the area accordingly (TCPA 1990, s.61G(5)).
- The LPA must also consider whether the area should be designated as a business area (TCPA 1990, s.61H(1)). An area can be designated as a business area if the LPA considers that it is wholly or predominantly business in nature, having regard to certain prescribed matters.
- It is possible for a neighbourhood area to extend into the administrative areas of more than one LPA, as local communities do not necessarily respect administrative boundaries. Regulations will provide for the procedure to be followed in such circumstances (TCPA 1990, s.61I).
- The local planning authority is required to publish a map showing the boundaries of designated neighbourhood areas and business areas.

Power is given to the Secretary of State in new s.61G(11) of TCPA 1990 to make regulations setting out the procedure for making a valid application for designation of a neighbourhood area, and the procedure to be followed by the LPA in designating such an area, including public consultation, the timetable for designation and grounds upon which the authority may decline to consider an application for designation.

7.2.4 Applying for an NDO

The procedure for applying and making an NDO is provided for by a new s.61E(3) and new Sched.4B to TCPA 1990 (Scheds.9 and 10 to the Localism Act 2011). The application for an NDO (referred to as the proposal) must be accompanied by:

> (a) a draft of the order [i.e. the NDO)], and
> (b) a statement which contains a summary of the proposals and sets out the reasons why an order should be made in proposed terms. (TCPA 1990, Sched.4B, para.1(2))

The proposal must be made in the prescribed form, with accompanying documents and other information as prescribed by regulations. The qualifying body making the application is required to send prescribed persons a copy of the application, a copy of the draft order that is being sought, and such other information and documents as may be prescribed (TCPA 1990, Sched.4B, para.1(3), (4)). The draft order should describe the land to which planning permission is to apply. This may be all the land in the neighbourhood area, or only part of it, or a specified site (TCPA 1990, s.61J). The draft order should not seek to give planning permission to any excluded development. Under new s.61K of TCPA 1990 the following development is 'excluded development' for the purpose of new s.61J and Sched.4B:

(a) development that constitutes a county matter within TCPA 1990, Sched.1, para.1(1)(a)–(h), e.g. the winning and working of minerals;
(b) waste development under TCPA 1990, Sched.1, para.1(j)
(c) development that falls within Annex 1 to the EIA Directive 2011/92/EU;
(d) development that consists (wholly or partly) of a nationally significant infrastructure project (within the meaning of PA 2008);
(e) prescribed development or development of a prescribed description (i.e. prescribed by the Secretary of State); or
(f) development in a prescribed area or an area of prescribed description (as prescribed by the Secretary of State).

The LPA must give such advice and assistance to qualifying bodies as, in all the circumstances, it considers appropriate for the purpose of, or in connection with, facilitating the making of proposals for NDOs relating to neighbourhood areas in its area (TCPA 1990, Sched.4B, para.3(1)). The qualifying body may withdraw a proposal at any time before the LPA makes its decision (TCPA 1990, Sched.4B, para.2).

Despite the localism objective, the new provisions contain a power for the Secretary of State to publish a document that sets standards for the preparation of the draft NDO and accompanying documents, the coverage in any accompanying document, the collection, sources, verification, processing and presentation of the information accompanying the application (TCPA 1990, Sched.4B, para.1(5)). The application must comply with these standards or any prescribed steps. These requirements are set out in the Neighbourhood Planning (General) Regulations 2012, SI 2012/637, which came into force on 6 April 2012.

7.2.5 Consideration of proposals for an NDO by the LPA

The initial assessment by an LPA of a proposal for an NDO is whether or not it may decline to consider the proposal in the first place. The LPA can decline to consider an application if it considers that it is a repeat application and it satisfies conditions A and B as to what constitutes a repeat application (TCPA 1990, Sched.4B, para.5(1), (2)):

- Condition A is that, in a period of two years ending with the date that the new application is made, the LPA had refused a similar application, or there had been a referendum where half or less than half of the voters had voted in favour of the application; and

- Condition B is that the LPA considers that there has been no significant change in relevant considerations since the date of the earlier refusal or the holding of the referendum (TCPA 1990, Sched.4B, para.5(3), (4)).

Relevant considerations include:

(a) national policies and advice by the Secretary of State; and
(b) strategic policies contained in the development plan (TCPA 1990, Sched.4B, para.5(5)).

If the LPA declines to consider the proposal it must notify the qualifying body and reasons for declining (TCPA 1990, Sched.4B, para.5(6)).

If the LPA has not exercised its power to decline to consider the application under Sched.4B, para.5 it must then consider the following:

(a) whether the qualifying body is duly authorised to make the proposal having regard to new s.61F of TCPA 1990;
(b) whether the proposal by the body complies with s.61F;
(c) whether the proposal and supporting documentation (including the draft order) comply with the provisions in TCPA 1990, Sched.4B, para.1;
(d) whether the body has complied with the requirements in Sched.4B, para.4; and

further, that the draft NDO complies with TCPA 1990, ss.61E(2), 61J and 61L (all relating to NDOs) and permission pursuant to them (TCPA 1990, Sched.4B, para.6(2), (3)).

Upon consideration of the matters in Sched.4B, para.6(2) and (3), the LPA must notify the qualifying body as to whether or not it is satisfied that the matters in sub-paras.(2) and (3) have been complied with and, where it is not satisfied, refuse the proposal and give reasons to the qualifying body for the refusal (TCPA 1990, Sched.4B, para.6(4)).

7.2.6 Independent examination

If the LPA is satisfied that the proposal meets the requirements for an NDO, it must submit the draft NDO and such other documents that may be prescribed for independent examination (TCPA 1990, Sched.4B, para.7(1), (2)). The LPA may appoint a person to carry out the examination but that appointment must be approved by the qualifying body (Sched.4B, para.7(4)). Further provisions in Sched.4B, para.7 stipulate the requirements to be satisfied in the appointment of the person to undertake the examination.

The examiner is required to consider whether the draft NDO meets the 'basic conditions' defined in Sched.4B, para.8(2) as:

> (a) having regard to national policies and advice contained in guidance issued by the Secretary of State, it is appropriate to make the order,
> (b) having special regard to the desirability of preserving any listed building or its

setting or any features of special architectural or historic interest that it possesses, it is appropriate to make the order,

(c) having special regard to the desirability of preserving or enhancing the character or appearance of any conservation area, it is appropriate to make the order,
(d) the making of the order contributes to the achievement of sustainable development,
(e) the making of the order is in general conformity with the strategic policies contained in the development plan for the area of the authority (or any part of that area),
(f) the making of the order does not breach, and is otherwise compatible with, EU obligations, and
(g) prescribed conditions are met in relation to the order and prescribed matters have been complied with in connection with the proposal for the order.

The general rule is that the examination is to be carried out by means of written representations. The examiner may hold a hearing to hear oral representations on a particular issue. The qualifying body, the LPA, the particular person for whom the hearing is being held in order to give him a fair chance to put a case, and such other prescribed persons are entitled to make oral representations about the need or otherwise for a hearing. The hearing must be in public (TCPA 1990, Sched.4B, para.9).

7.2.7 Referendum on the NDO

Having carried out the examination, the examiner must report on the draft order with a recommendation that:

- the order be submitted to a referendum; or
- the order should be modified and the order as modified submitted to a referendum; or
- the application for the order should be refused (TCPA 1990, Sched.4B, para.10).

The LPA must then consider the recommendations of the examiner and decide whether to make the modifications (if any) recommended by the examiner, or to make other modifications that achieve the same purpose. If the LPA is satisfied that the draft order meets the 'basic conditions', is compatible with the Convention on Human Rights, and other provisions, the authority must hold a referendum (TCPA 1990, Sched.4B, para.12).

The provisions relating to the referendum are contained in TCPA 1990, Sched.4B, para.14. Any person who is entitled to vote in an election of any councillors of the local authority, any of whose constituency is in the referendum area, and who lives in the designated neighbourhood area, has the right to vote in the referendum. However, under Sched.4B, para.12(7) and (8) the referendum area may extend beyond the designated neighbourhood area, but should not be an area that is smaller than the designated neighbourhood area. The LPA may extend the referendum area to the area of another local authority. An additional referendum may be held where the neighbourhood area is a business area. In such circumstances, the persons who have the right to vote in the referendum are non-domestic rate-payers, or meet such other conditions as may be prescribed. The procedure to be followed on a referendum may be set out in regulations. DCLG stated in *Neighbourhood planning regulations: Consultation* (October 2011) (see **www.communities.gov.uk**) that the referendum procedure will be based on that set out in the Local Authorities (Conduct of Referendums) (England) Regulations 2007, SI 2007/2089.

If more than half the persons voting have voted in favour of the order, the LPA must make the NDO as soon as practicably possible after the holding of the referendum (TCPA 1990, s.61E). The planning permission that is granted by the NDO may be unconditional or subject to such conditions and limitations as are mentioned in the order (TCPA 1990, s.61L). Under new s.61M of TCPA 1990, an NDO may be subsequently modified or revoked, in the same way as a planning permission granted under TCPA 1990, s.97 may be modified or revoked. Finally, various actions of the LPA in relation to the NDO and referendum may be challenged by judicial review. However, the time limit for bringing judicial review proceedings is limited to a period of six weeks from the day upon which the decision is published or upon which the referendum is declared (TCPA 1990, s.61N).

7.3 COMMUNITY RIGHT TO BUILD ORDER

The Localism Act 2011, s.116 and Sched.11 insert a new Sched.4C into TCPA 1990. Schedule 4C provides for a particular type of NDO, a 'community right to build order' (CRBO), that provides for community-led site-specific development. Such an order is made in response to a proposal for an order from a community organisation.

7.3.1 Defining a CRBO and a community organisation

The meaning of a CRBO is explained in TCPA 1990, Sched.4C, para.2(1), which provides that:

> A neighbourhood development order is a community right to build order if–
>
> (a) the order is made pursuant to a proposal made by a community organisation,
> (b) the order grants planning permission for specified development in relation to a specified site in the specified neighbourhood area, and
> (c) the specified development does not exceed prescribed limits.

The reference to 'specified' means specified in the CRBO (Sched.4C, para.2(3)), as opposed to any regulations or other provisions. The 'prescribed limits' may be prescribed in regulations (enacted by the Secretary of State) with reference to:

> (a) the area in which the development is to take place,
> (b) the number or type of operations or uses of land constituting the development, or
> (c) any other factor. (TCPA 1990, Sched.4C, para.2(2))

Paragraph 3(1) of Sched.4C states that a 'community organisation' is a body corporate:

(a) which is established for the express purpose of furthering the social, economic and environmental well-being of individuals living, or wanting to live, in a particular area, and
(b) which meets such other conditions in relation to its establishment or constitution as may be prescribed.

Further, para.3(2) of Sched.4C states that regulations under para.1(b) (although not expressly referred to in the sub-paragraph) may make provision in relation to the distribution of profits made by the body to its members, the distribution of assets, and the membership and the control of the body corporate.

7.3.2 Proposals by a community organisation for a CRBO

A community organisation is authorised to make a proposal to the LPA for a CRBO if the area of the community organisation consists of, or includes, the neighbourhood area, and at the time when the proposal is made, more than half of the members of the community organisation live in the area (TCPA 1990, Sched.4C, para.4(1)). It is then a 'qualifying body' for the purposes of s.61E, as explained above (Sched.4C, para.4(2)). The proposal for a CRBO must state that it is for such an order (Sched.4C, para.4(7)).

The LPA can decline to consider a proposal for a CRBO, if there is an outstanding proposal for a CRBO or other NDO relating to the same, or substantially the same, site (TCPA 1990, Sched.4C, para.4(5)). Moreover, under TCPA 1990, Sched.4C, para.6(1), the LPA can decline to consider the proposal for a CRBO if it considers that the specified development:

(a) falls within Annex 2 to the EIA Directive and is likely to have significant effects on the environment by virtue of facts such as its nature, size or location; or
(b) is likely to have significant effects on a qualifying European site within the meaning of a 'European offshore marine site' under the Offshore Marine Conservation (Natural Habitats, etc.) Regulations 2007, SI 2007/1842, or a 'European site' under the Conservation of Habitats and Species Regulations 2010, SI 2010/490.

An application for an NDO is already prohibited for any proposal that falls within Annex 1 to the EIA Directive by virtue of it falling within the meaning of 'excluded development' under TCPA 1990, s.61K.

A proposal for a CRBO is subject to an examination as for an NDO, with similar provisions as to holding a referendum (TCPA 1990, Sched.4C, paras.7–10). Paragraph 11 of Sched.4C sets out powers to disapply or modify certain enfranchisement rights in relation to land the development of which is authorised by the CRBO.

The Neighbourhood Planning (General) Regulations 2012, SI 2012/637 set out the prescribed conditions for CBROs.

7.4 COSTS, COLLECTION AND CONSEQUENTIAL AMENDMENTS

The Secretary of State is given power under s.117 of the Act to make regulations, with the consent of the Treasury, providing for the imposition of charges to meet expenses incurred (or expected to be incurred) by LPAs in connection with the exercise of the neighbourhood planning functions. Any regulations made under s.117 must include provision about the collection and enforcement of charges that are incurred (s.118).

Under s.120(1) of the Act the Secretary of State may do anything he considers appropriate for the purpose of:

(a) publicising or promoting the making of NDPs or NDOs and the benefits expected to arise from them; or
(b) giving advice or assistance to anyone in relation to the making of proposals for such orders or plans or the doing of anything else for the purposes of such proposals, orders or plans.

In particular, the Secretary of State may provide for:

- financial assistance; and
- the making of agreements or other arrangements (s.120(2)).

Advice or assistance includes training or education; financial assistance includes the making of a loan or providing a guarantee or indemnity (s.120(3)). The Explanatory Notes, para.304, suggest that the powers could be used, e.g.

(i) to help fund a neighbourhood forum to develop a draft neighbourhood plan;
(ii) to give assistance to help establish a forum or a community right to build organisation; or
(iii) to support an education campaign about neighbourhood planning.

Consequential amendments to planning legislation to take account of neighbourhood planning are made by s.121 of and Sched.12 to the Localism Act 2011.

7.5 REGULATIONS, GUIDANCE AND ENTRY INTO FORCE

Further detailed provisions relating to NDPs are set out in the Neighbourhood Planning (General) Regulations 2012, SI 2012/637, which came into force on 6 April 2012.

The provisions relating to all aspects of neighbourhood planning, i.e. NDPs, NDOs and CRBOs, are peppered with wide discretion conferred upon the Secretary of State to make regulations and that discretion, notably, TCPA 1990, Sched.4C, para.12 provides that:

> (1) The provision that may be made by regulations under any provision of this Act [i.e. the TCPA 1990] relating to neighbourhood development orders includes different provision in relation to community right to build orders.

(2) Sub-paragraph (1) is not to be read as limiting in any way the generality of section 333(2A) (which provides that regulations may make different provision for different purposes).

Elements of neighbourhood planning provisions, i.e. ss.116 and 121 of and Scheds.9–12 to the Localism Act 2011, so far as they enable the Secretary of State to make regulations, came into force on 15 November 2011 (s.240(5)(j)). The implementation of the substantive changes to TCPA 1990 and PCPA 2004 will enter into force by commencement order. The supplemental provisions relating to costs, collection and enforcement under ss.117–120 came into force on 15 November 2011 (s.240(5)(k)). See **Appendix D** for a list of commencement dates as well as provisions that are not in force as at 20 April 2012.

8 CONSULTATION

Pre-application community consultation on development proposals has become normal practice in recent years. Most LPAs now expect a prospective applicant, certainly those seeking permission for major development proposals, to have carried out some form of consultation with local residents and stakeholders before submitting a planning application. Indeed, this is particularly so where the proposal is one that falls within the scope of the EIA Directive 2011/92/EU. There will also be a need to include a statement of community involvement as part of the supporting documents accompanying the planning application. National guidance on the advisability of pre-application consultation and engagement is found at paras.188–95 of the National Planning Policy Framework. Local planning authorities also have a statutory requirement to carry out consultation for certain development proposals under TCPA 1990, s.71 and art.16 of the Town and Country Planning (Development Management Procedure) (England) Order 2010, SI 2010/2184.

Section 122 of the Act affirms the need for a developer or operator to carry out pre-application community consultation by making consequential amendments to s.62 and inserting new sections into TCPA 1990. The consultation provisions can include an opportunity for consultees to collaborate with the applicant on the design of the proposed development, and there is a duty to take account of the responses to consultation.

It means that there is now an obligation on developers to consult with those people that may be affected by a proposal prior to the planning application being submitted to the planning authority. Previously, pre-application consultation had been a discretionary process.

8.1 SCOPE AND EXTENT OF NEW CONSULTATION REQUIREMENTS

Section 122(1) of the Act inserts a new s.61W into TCPA 1990. This provides under s.61W(1) that where:

(a) a person proposes to make an application for planning permission for the development of any land in England, and

(b) the proposed development is of a description specified in a development order,

the person must carry out consultation on the proposed application in accordance with subsections (2) and (3).

The types of development that are to be subject to mandatory consultation are to be specified in a development order to be made by the Secretary of State, probably by further amendment to the Town and Country Planning (Development Management Procedure) (England) Order 2010.

How the consultation should be carried out is left to the judgment of the applicant, who must publicise the proposed application 'in such manner as the person reasonably considers is likely to bring the proposed application to the attention of a majority of the persons who live at, or otherwise occupy, premises in the vicinity of the land' (TCPA 1990, s.61W(2)).

The current practice of agreeing the extent and method of consultation with the LPA is likely to continue if the applicant wishes to reduce the scope for argument as to whether the manner of consultation that he has chosen was reasonable in the circumstances. Indeed, TCPA 1990, s.61W(7) requires the applicant to have regard to any advice from the LPA about local good practice.

There is an obligation to consult persons specified in a development order (TCPA 1990, s.61W(3), (5)). This is a minimum rather than an exclusive requirement and the applicant may consult other persons if he wishes to do so.

Whatever method of publicity is used, the publicity must make clear how the prospective applicant may be contacted, in order to comment or collaborate on the design of the proposed development, with the timetable for the consultation, which should provide sufficient time to permit persons to respond (TCPA 1990, s.61W(4)).

8.2 OBLIGATION TO TAKE INTO ACCOUNT CONSULTATION RESPONSES

Having carried out the consultation the prospective applicant has an obligation to take account of any responses if he decides to go ahead with the application (TCPA 1990, s.61X). New s.61X(2) then appears to go further and create an obligation upon the applicant to decide whether in fact the application should be made in the same terms as the original proposal (having had regard to the consultation responses). There is no provision for circumstances where an application changes so radically from that originally proposed that the applicant is obliged to re-consult. Prudence suggests that an applicant in these circumstances should re-consult to avoid any argument that the changed proposal is so different that it amounts to a new proposal and that the obligation to consult has not been carried out. Whether the applicant has re-consulted in such circumstances will be something that the LPA can take into account when determining the application.

8.3 SUPPLEMENTARY PROVISIONS BY WAY OF A DEVELOPMENT ORDER

Under new s.61Y of TCPA 1990 a development order may make supplementary provision about, or in connection with, consultation which s.61W(1) requires an applicant to carry out on a proposed application for planning permission. The supplementary provisions may include:

(a) publicising the planning application;
(b) the ways of responding to publicity;
(c) consultation under TCPA 1990, s.61W(3), i.e. with each specified person;
(d) provisions in connection with or collaboration between the applicant and others on the design of the proposal;
(e) matters relating to the timetable and deadlines for the compliance with TCPA 1990, s.61W(1), publicity and consultation;
(f) provision for the applicant to prepare a statement setting out how the person proposes to comply with TCPA 1990, s.61W(1); and
(g) provision for a statement of compliance with the obligations.

8.4 TAKING INTO ACCOUNT THE NEW CONSULTATION PROVISIONS

An account of the consultation undertaken in accordance with the provisions in s.61W must accompany any planning application for development to which the new obligation applies, in order to make it valid. Section 62 of TCPA 1990 is amended by the insertion of new subsections (7) and (8), which state that a development order must require that an application that requires s.61W consultation is accompanied by particulars of how the applicant complied with s.61W, any responses that were received, and what account was taken of these responses.

8.5 REGULATIONS, GUIDANCE AND ENTRY INTO FORCE

The legislation suggests that LPAs may provide advice as to local good practice (TCPA 1990, new s.61W(7)), although there is no requirement to publish this as either practice notes or guidance. There appears to be a considerable degree of flexibility in the new pre-application consultation and the government may find that some general guidance is necessary to ensure that this element of planning is brought into force effectively. The guidance *Community Involvement in Planning* (ODPM, 2004) (archived, but still available at **www.commmunities.gov.uk**) offers some general principles of community consultation that still remain relevant.

The changes brought about by s.122 of the Act appear also to have a limited life. Section 122(3) provides that the amendments brought about by s.122(1) and (2) shall cease to have effect at the end of seven years from the day on which TCPA 1990, s.61W(1) comes fully into force. The time limit in s.122(3) can be extended by secondary legislation. Section 122(4) provides that the Secretary of State may by order provide that the amendments, instead of ceasing to have effect at the time they would otherwise cease to have effect, are extended for a further seven years (s.122(4)). There is no obvious reason why these particular provisions should be time limited.

The new consultation provisions, so far as they relate to development orders, came into force on 15 November 2011 (s.240(5)(l)). The remaining provisions come into force by order (s.240(2)). See **Appendix D** for a list of commencement dates as well as provisions that are not in force as at 20 April 2012.

9 PLANNING ENFORCEMENT

The ability of planning authorities to enforce planning controls has been a fundamental part of land use planning since the Town and Country Planning Act 1947. The amendments introduced by ss.123–127 of the Localism Act 2011 strengthen the planning enforcement regime found in TCPA 1990, Part VII and the body of supporting statutory instruments. The introduction of the new provisions has been subject to considerable debate. The government explained in its regulatory impact assessment: *Localism Bill: enforcement package* (DCLG, Jan 2011) that:

> Local planning authorities have powers to take enforcement action where there have been breaches of planning control. However, certain areas have been identified where the present planning system makes it difficult to take enforcement action or enables those in breach of planning controls to frustrate or evade the enforcement process. In other areas it is considered that the consequences of breaching planning controls could be made tougher to deter potential offenders. These weaknesses in the system can only be remedied by legislative means.

The policy objectives and intended effects of the proposals are also explained in the same publication:

> The package of enforcement measures in the Localism Bill will empower local authorities to take tougher action, and will send a strong message to unscrupulous developers that they will no longer be able to exploit the system to their advantage. This aims to increase confidence in local planning authorities and the planning enforcement system.

In contrast, many organisations opposed the enforcement provisions, concerned that they may have an unintended adverse impact on property dealings. For instance, the Law Society continued to express concern after amendments to the draft provisions were made, noting in the press release 'Government amends planning enforcement regime in response to Law Society warning – but doesn't go far enough' (11 August 2011):

> So, in the Society's view, failing to report a breach would be a concealment and would allow the local authority to enforce. In addition, the Bill would make purchasers liable where the breach had been concealed by their vendor or anyone else. The Society was concerned that this could have a chilling effect on some parts of the property market since, without the certainty that past mistakes could no longer be subject to enforcement action after the limitation period, purchasers would be less willing to buy and lenders less willing to lend.

> Law Society President John Wotton welcomed the amendments which remove inaction from concealment; 'We are very pleased that the Department for Communities and Local Government has listened to our concerns.'
>
> But he said the innocent purchaser is still at risk; 'If there has been concealment in the past, the local authority can still restart the clock and enforce outside the normal time limits.'
>
> The Society's preference was the deletion of the clause. It maintains its view that the provision is unnecessary and will be pressing amendments it has already proposed to protect innocent purchasers.

The new provisions were introduced and relate to two main areas:

- retrospective planning permission; and
- the time limits for taking enforcement proceedings.

9.1 RETROSPECTIVE PLANNING PERMISSIONS

It is considered that persons who may be regarded as 'playing the system' could secure a delay in the operation of an enforcement notice or the hearing of an appeal against an enforcement notice by making a retrospective planning application and then asking the LPA and the Planning Inspectorate to postpone dealing with the enforcement appeal until the retrospective application has been determined. Section 123 of the Localism Act 2011 inserts a new s.70C into TCPA 1990 conferring a power to decline to determine retrospective applications in order to close off this opportunity. It also makes a number of further consequential amendments to the enforcement provisions in TCPA 1990.

9.1.1 Power to decline to determine retrospective applications

A new s.70C of TCPA 1990 provides:

> (1) A local planning authority in England may decline to determine an application for planning permission for the development of any land if granting planning permission for the development would involve granting, whether in relation to the whole or any part of the land to which a pre-existing enforcement notice relates, planning permission in respect of the whole or any part of the matters specified in the enforcement notice as constituting a breach of planning control.
> (2) For the purposes of the operation of this section in relation to any particular application for planning permission, a 'pre-existing enforcement notice' is an enforcement notice issued before the application was received by the local planning authority.

In summary, an LPA can decline to determine a retrospective application if an enforcement notice has been issued for any part of the proposal.

9.1.2 Revision to the appeal provisions relating to enforcement

The associated appeal provisions are also amended by s.123(4) of the Act. The grounds for an appeal against an enforcement notice are set out in TCPA 1990, s.174(2). A new s.174(2A) is inserted in order to remove the ability to lodge an appeal on ground (2)(a) ('ground a') that planning permission ought to be granted, if a retrospective planning application has been made, and an enforcement notice has been issued before the time for determining the planning application has expired.

Section 177 of TCPA 1990 relating to the grant or modification of planning permission on appeals against an enforcement notice is amended by the insertion of a new s.177(1C) which provides that planning permission can only be granted as part of the determination of the appeal where the notice of appeal under s.174(4) specifies 'ground a' (s.123(5) of the Act). A new TCPA 1990, s.177(5) is substituted by s.123(6) of the Act to provide for the slightly different circumstances in Wales where the enforcement legislation is not amended by s.123 of the Act.

9.2 TIME LIMITS FOR ENFORCING CONCEALED BREACHES OF PLANNING CONTROL

9.2.1 Decisions in the *Welwyn-Hatfield* and *Fidler* cases

The provisions in ss.124–126 of the Localism Act 2011 relating to time limits for enforcing concealed breaches of planning control have been introduced by s.124 to address the concerns that arose in the cases of *Secretary of State for Communities and Local Government & anor* v. *Welwyn-Hatfield BC* [2011] UKSC 15 and *R (on the application of Fidler)* v. *Secretary of State for Communities and Local Government* [2011] EWCA Civ 1159 where unauthorised development was effectively concealed from the planning authorities until it was considered to be immune from enforcement through the passage of time.

The facts and appeal grounds in the *Welwyn-Hatfield* case neatly summarise the problems facing enforcing authorities. In 2001, Mr Beesley obtained planning permission to construct a hay barn on open Green Belt land and in 2002 constructed a building which externally appeared to be a hay barn but which internally was a fully fitted dwelling house in which he and his family lived in for four years. In 2006, Mr Beesley applied for a certificate of lawfulness for existing use and development (CLEUD) of the building as a dwelling house contending that the four-year time limit in TCPA 1990, s.171B for taking enforcement action had lapsed. The LPA issued an enforcement notice and this was overturned on appeal to an inspector who granted a CLEUD. The LPA challenged the inspector's decision in the High Court and Court of Appeal. The appeal to the Supreme Court raised two points of public importance:

- whether the building fell within the provisions of TCPA 1990 which impose a time limit for taking planning enforcement action and, in particular, whether there had been a change of use; and
- whether the owner's dishonesty prevented him from benefiting from the time limits within the provisions.

The Supreme Court unanimously allowed the appeal holding that:

(i) there had been no change of use within TCPA 1990, s.171B(2);
(ii) in any event, Mr Beesley's dishonest conduct meant that he could not rely on the enforcement provisions.

In the case of *Fidler*, the landowner built a luxury home in the style of a castle on open Green Belt land while it was concealed within a giant haystack, the top of which was covered with tarpaulin. Mr Fidler had deliberately erected the haystacks in order to conceal the construction of the new dwelling and to attempt to take advantage of the four-year enforcement rule under TCPA 1990, Part VII. The new dwelling was revealed when the straw bales and tarpaulin were eventually removed and after Mr Fidler considered that the four-year period for the substantial completion of the new dwelling had expired. Upon discovering that the home had been built, the LPA issued an enforcement notice. Mr Fidler appealed against the notice on the basis that the time limit for taking enforcement action had expired long before the LPA came to issue the enforcement notice. The inspector dismissed Mr Fidler's appeal on ground (d) (i.e. TCPA 1990, s.174(2)(d) – 'that, at the date when the notice was issued, no enforcement action could be taken in respect of any breach of planning control which may be constituted by those matters'). Mr Fidler's challenge to the appeal decision under TCPA 1990, s.289 was dismissed. In hearing an application to set aside the grant of permission to appeal, the Court of Appeal held:

> 13. It seems to me that upon the facts found by the Inspector, this is a paradigm case of deception which disentitles an appellant from relying upon the four-year rule; it simply does not lie in this appellant's mouth to say that this local planning authority should have spotted the building which he had so carefully concealed at some earlier stage, were he to do so it would indeed frustrate the underlying statutory purpose. It is therefore of no consequence whatsoever whether the bales were or were not part of the building operations; the short point is that this was a deliberate deception which plainly falls within the principles set out in the *Welwyn Hatfield* case, the consequence of which is that this appeal has no prospect whatsoever of succeeding.

9.2.2 New concealment provisions under TCPA 1990

Section 124 of the Act inserts new ss.171BA (relating to time limits), 171BB (relating to procedure) and 171BC (relating to planning enforcement orders) into TCPA 1990 to enable enforcement action to be taken by the LPA when the time limits for doing so have expired and the breach has been concealed. New s.171BA(1) of TCPA 1990 provides:

> Where it appears to the local planning authority that there may have been a breach of planning control in respect of any land in England, the authority may apply to a magistrates' court for an order under this subsection (a 'planning enforcement order') in relation to that apparent breach of planning control.

In order to take enforcement action, the LPA must apply to the magistrates' court for a 'planning enforcement order' in respect of the breach within six months of the date when sufficient evidence is discovered of the breach. A signed certificate by the LPA as to the date when sufficient evidence of the breach was discovered is deemed to be conclusive evidence for the purposes of the application (TCPA 1990, s.171BB(2)). The LPA can also apply for an order before the time limits for taking action have expired, if the expiry date is in dispute.

The LPA must serve a notice of the application for the order upon the persons on whom the enforcement notice would be served, i.e. the owner and occupier of the land as well as any other person having an interest in the land (an interest that, in the opinion of the authority, would be materially affected by the enforcement action) (TCPA 1990, s.171BB(4)). The applicant, the persons served with the application and any other persons having an interest in the land that would be materially affected by the subsequent enforcement action have the right to appear before the magistrates' court (TCPA 1990, s.171BB(5)).

The magistrates' court may make the order only if satisfied, on the balance of probabilities, that a person's actions (including representations or inactions) have resulted in, or contributed to, the full or partial concealment of the breach (TCPA 1990, s.171BC(1)). The LPA then has a year ('the enforcement year') to take enforcement action. The enforcement year commences at the end of 22 days beginning with the date that the proceedings before the magistrates' court are concluded (TCPA 1990, s.171BA(3)).

The planning enforcement order, as with an enforcement notice, should be entered on the register of enforcement and stop notices that is kept by the LPA under TCPA 1990, s.188 (as amended by s.124(2) of the Localism Act 2011).

An amendment is made to TCPA 1990, s.191 relating to CLEUDs to insert references to the time limits that apply to a planning enforcement order (s.124(3) of the Act).

9.2.3 Assurance as regards prosecution for persons served with enforcement notice

A new s.172A is inserted into TCPA 1990 by s.125 of the Localism Act 2011. This amendment allows LPAs to assure anyone receiving an enforcement notice (where the authority does not think they are responsible for the alleged breach of planning control) that they will not be prosecuted if the enforcement notice is not complied with. It provides for the letter to be withdrawn in whole or in part and for the recipient to be given time to comply if the letter is withdrawn. Even if a letter is withdrawn, a recipient could not subsequently be prosecuted in respect of the period during which the assurance was in place. Any assurance would be binding on any prosecutor.

9.3 PLANNING OFFENCES: MISCELLANEOUS AMENDMENTS TO TIME LIMITS AND PENALTIES

Various amendments relating to planning offences in England are made by s.126 of the Localism Act 2011. The maximum penalty for failure to comply with a breach of condition notice under TCPA 1990, s.187A is raised from level 3 on the standard scale (currently £1,000) to level 4 if the land is in England (£2,500) (s.126(2)).

Consistent with the new time limit provisions for enforcement notices, s.126(3) of the Act inserts a new provision in relation to non-compliance with tree preservation regulations where an LPA does not immediately become aware of an offence. Proceedings for the prosecution of offences of lopping or damaging a protected tree under new s.210(4A)–(4E) of TCPA 1990 may be brought within six months of sufficient evidence of the offence coming to the knowledge of the prosecutor (but no more than three years after the offence was committed). The new s.210(4E) makes it clear that the amendment to the time limit does not apply in Wales. The new extended time limit does not extend to the more serious offences under TCPA 1990, s.210(1) of cutting down, uprooting or wilfully destroying a tree in contravention of a tree preservation order. It should be noted that the procedures relating to the making and enforcement of tree preservation orders have been consolidated and updated in the Town and Country Planning (Tree Preservation) (England) Regulations 2012, SI 2012/605 as from 6 April 2012.

Similarly, proceedings for an offence contravening the Control of Advertisement Regulations under TCPA 1990, s.224(3) have been amended by s.126(4) of the Act. Under new s.224(7)–(11) of TCPA 1990, proceedings may be brought within six months of sufficient evidence of the offence coming to the knowledge of the prosecutor (but no more than three years after the offence was committed). New s.244(11) makes it clear that the amendment to the time limit does not apply in Wales.

9.4 UNAUTHORISED ADVERTISEMENTS AND DEFACEMENT OF PREMISES

Further to s.127 of the Act, LPAs are given new powers to deal with fly-posting, graffiti and other unauthorised displays. New ss.225A–225K are inserted into TCPA 1990, Part 8: Special Controls.

9.4.1 Power to remove structures used for unauthorised display

The new power under TCPA 1990, s.225A allows an LPA to remove any display structure in its area which, in its opinion, is used for the display of illegal advertisements. This power cannot be used against a structure within a building to which there is no public right of access (TCPA 1990, s.225A(2)).

The LPA may not remove the structure until a removal notice has been served upon the person who appears to be responsible for the erection or maintenance of the display structure. If the LPA cannot identify such person the removal notice must be fixed to the structure or displayed in the vicinity. If the removal notice is not complied with within the time allowed (not less than 22 days) the LPA may remove the structure and recover its expenses from anyone served with the removal notice. A person who can satisfy the LPA that he was not responsible for either the erection or maintenance of the structure cannot be required to reimburse the expenses incurred. If the LPA damages any land or chattels in removing the structure, it must pay compensation, but not for damage to the structure or for damage reasonably caused in moving the structure. There is a right of appeal to the magistrates' court against a notice under new s.225A on the grounds specified in s.225B(1) including:

- (a) that the display structure concerned is not used for the display of advertisements in contravention of regulations under section 220;
- (b) that there has been some informality, defect or error in, or in connection with, the notice;
- (c) that the period between the date of the notice and the time specified in the notice is not reasonably sufficient for the removal of the display structure;
- (d) that the notice should have been served on another person.

9.4.2 Remedying persistent problems with unauthorised advertisements

If the LPA considers that there is a persistent problem with a display of unauthorised advertisements (fly-posting) on a surface of a building, wall, fence or other structure, or plant or apparatus, it may serve an action notice under new s.225C of TCPA 1990 on the owner or occupier of the land where the surface is situated if known, or if the owner or occupier is unknown, by fixing the notice to the surface. The action notice requires the owner or occupier to take specified measures to prevent or reduce the frequency of the unauthorised advertisements. At least 28 days must be allowed for action to be taken. If action is not taken, the LPA may take the action specified in the notice and recover its expenses from the owner or occupier. Expenses cannot be recovered where the surface is on, or within the curtilage of, or forms part of the boundary curtilage of a dwelling house. New s.225D of TCPA 1990 provides for a right of appeal against a s.255C notice including:

- (a) that there is no problem with the display of unauthorised advertisements on the surface concerned or any such problem is not a persistent one;
- (b) that there has been some informality, defect or error in, or in connection with, the notice;
- (c) that the time within which the measures specified in the notice are to be carried out is not reasonably sufficient for the purpose;
- (d) that the notice should have been served on another person.

Various other provisions are included as insertions into TCPA 1990 dealing with specific circumstances of unlawful advertising, etc., including:

- s.225E, applying s.225C to statutory undertakers' land;
- s.225F, the power to remedy defacement of premises;
- s.225G, considering notices under s.225F in relation to post boxes;
- s.225H, applying the s.225F powers with respect to bus shelters and other street furniture;
- s.225I, providing a right to appeal against notice under s.225F;

- s.225J, provisions to remedy defacement at owner or occupier's request;
- s.225K, relating to action under ss.225A, 225C and 225F in terms of operational land and also replacing certain provisions in the London Local Authorities Acts 1995 and 2007 that only relate to London with those that apply throughout England.

9.5 ENTRY INTO FORCE

The enforcement provisions came into force by order on 6 April 2012 (Localism Act 2011 (Commencement No. 4 and Transitional, Transitory and Saving Provisions) Order 2012, SI 2012/628).

10 NATIONALLY SIGNIFICANT INFRASTRUCTURE PROJECTS

The Planning Act (PA) 2008 introduced an entirely new development consent system for nationally significant infrastructure projects (NSIPs), originally intended to cover the largest forms of development relating to energy, transport, waste and water. The NSIPs planning process operated by an application (or applications) for development consent being made to the Infrastructure Planning Commission (IPC). The decision on the application would be made primarily by the IPC through a single commissioner or panel of commissioners, although the Secretary of State was given a power to intervene. The coalition agreement of May 2010 stated that the government would: 'abolish the unelected Infrastructure Planning Commission and to replace it with an efficient and democratically accountable system that provides a fast-track process for major infrastructure projects'. Put starkly, s.128(1) of the Localism Act 2011 provides that:

> The Infrastructure Planning Commission ceases to exist on the day on which this subsection comes into force.

The subsection came into force on 1 April 2012.

This chapter outlines the purpose and operation of the NSIPs regime as well as discussing the consequential and transitional provisions relating to abolition of the IPC provided for in the Act. It also covers other amendments to PA 2008 relating to NSIPs.

10.1 ABOLITION OF THE IPC

10.1.1 Outline of the infrastructure planning system

A 'nationally significant infrastructure project' is defined under PA 2008, s.14 and is a project which consists of any one of those listed in s.14(1) from (a) to (p) including, for example:

> (a) the construction or extension of a generating station;
>
> ...
>
> (h) highway-related development; [and]
>
> ...
>
> (n) development relating to the transfer of water resources;

The range of projects that may be regarded as an NSIP is not definitive. Indeed, PA 2008, s.14(6) provides that the Secretary of State may amend the project list provided it is a new type of project for the carrying out of works in the fields of:

(a) energy;
(b) transport;
(c) water;
(d) waste water; and
(e) waste.

10.1.2 Transfer of functions from the IPC to the Secretary of State

The IPC came into being on 1 October 2009 with offices in Bristol adjacent to the Planning Inspectorate. Since abolition on 1 April 2012, the operations of the IPC have been integrated into a Major Infrastructure Planning Unit within the Planning Inspectorate (PINS) with its functions being transferred to the Secretary of State (s.128(2) and Sched.13). The government has stated that the 36 Commissioners will be retained to examine major infrastructure applications until September 2014 in order to ensure a smooth transition to the new system.

At the time of writing the IPC has accepted 10 projects, with another 60–70 projects in the pipeline (IPC Chair Michael Pitt at PINS Stakeholders' Group meeting, February 2012). The current programme of projects may be viewed on the IPC website at **http://infrastructure.independent.gov.uk/projects**. These include a range of projects (at varying stages of the planning process):

- The Thames Tunnel project which aims to provide a new storage and transfer tunnel and waste water treatment plants in order to collect London's untreated overflow sewage and transfer it to Beckton Sewage Treatment Works in East London. The tunnel is to follow the line of the River Thames (initial advice given by the IPC, application expected late 2012).
- An underground gas storage facility for up to 900 million cubic metres of natural gas, gas interconnector pipeline, brine outfall pipeline and associated infrastructure at Preesall Sands, Near Fleetwood, Lancashire (project application accepted).
- Hinkley Point C New Nuclear Power Station (project accepted, pre-examination registration closed 23 January 2012).
- An energy from waste facility at Brig y Cwm, Merthyr Tydfil, South Wales (project withdrawn prior to public inquiry).

10.1.3 Retaining the NSIP development control process

The decision-making regime for NSIPs introduced by PA 2008 is retained but with some amendment. Schedule 13 to the Act provides the amendments by revision of PA 2008. For example, para.2 of Sched.13 to the Act deletes PA 2008, ss.1–3 and Sched.1 relating to the establishment and governance of the Commission in their entirety. Schedule 13 also replaces references to the IPC or 'the Commission' with reference to the Secretary of State. By way of illustration, Sched.13, para.3(4), of the Act provides:

> (4) After [s.4(3) of PA 2008] insert –
> '(4) In this section "the Secretary of State's major-infrastructure functions" means –
>
> (a) the Secretary of State's functions under Parts 2 to 8 and under Part 12 so far as applying for the purposes of those Parts,
> (b) the giving of advice to which section 51 applies, and
> (c) the Secretary of State's functions, in relation to proposed applications for orders granting development consent, under statutory provisions implementing –
> (i) Council Directive 85/337/EC on the assessment of the effects of certain public and private projects on the environment, as amended from time to time, or
> (ii) provisions of an EU instrument which from time to time replace provisions of that Directive'.

The determination of NSIPs will continue to be either by a single person, formerly 'the single Commissioner' and to be revised to 'a single appointed person' under PA 2008, ss.78–85, or a panel under PA 2008, ss.64–77. Instead of a panel of Commissioners it will be a panel of members. And therefore, following entry into force of the relevant Localism Act provisions, a revised PA 2008, s.65(1) now reads:

> (1) The Secretary of State must appoint:
>
> (a) three, four or five persons to be members of the Panel, and
> (b) one of those persons to chair the Panel.

10.1.4 Transitional provisions

The Secretary of State is given the power to make a direction about transitional provisions in relation to any applications made before or during the abolition period and the integration into the Planning Inspectorate (s.129). Amendment to the procedure as a result of the abolition of the IPC are found in the Localism Act 2011 (Infrastructure Planning) (Consequential Amendments) Regulations 2012, SI 2012/635 which came into force on 1 April 2012.

10.2 FURTHER REVISION TO NSIPS REGIME

A key aspect of the major infrastructure project regime is the formulation of national policy statements (NPSs) by virtue of PA 2008, ss.5–13. Section 130 of the Localism Act 2011 introduces amendments to the procedure for the approval of an NPS in order to increase the involvement of Parliament (and, in particular, the House of Commons). New ss.6A and 6B are inserted into PA 2008 to take account of the changes to the consideration process by Parliament. The National Planning Policy Framework (NPPF) does not contain specific policies for NSIPs; indeed, para.3 of the introduction to the NPPF states:

> This Framework does not contain specific policies for nationally significant infrastructure projects for which particular considerations apply. These are determined in accordance with the decision-making framework set out in the Planning Act 2008 and relevant national policy statements for major infrastructure, as well as any other matters that are considered both important and relevant (which may include the National Planning Policy Framework). National policy statements form part of the overall framework of national planning policy, and are a material consideration in decisions on planning applications.

Other amendments to PA 2008 are made through ss.131–142 of the Localism Act 2011 in an effort to clarify and regularise the major infrastructure planning regime. These include:

- revisions to PA 2008, s.33 and the power to alter the effect of requirement for development consent on other consent regimes (s.131);
- amending PA 2008, s.35 in relation to the Secretary of State's directions in relation to projects of national significance (s.132);
- clarification of PA 2008, s.43 in relation to the obligation on a proposed developer (an applicant) to undertake pre-application consultation with local authorities (s.133);
- revising the obligation on an applicant to publicise its statement setting out how the applicant proposes to consult the local community (the community consultation statement) under PA 2008, s.47 (s.134);
- revisions to the publicity requirements under PA 2008, s.52 in relation to claiming compensation for the effects of development (s.135);
- revisions to the rights of entry for surveying, etc. land in connection with the proposed project under PA 2008, s.53 (s.136);
- clarification of the requirements in PA 2008, ss.37 and 55 relating to the acceptance of applications for development consent (s.137);
- amendments to PA 2008, s.56 and the insertion of new ss.56A, 88A, 102A and 102B making procedural changes in relation to applications for development consent, e.g. under ss.102A and 102B certain specified persons may make a request to become an interested party (s.138);
- revision to the timetables for reports and decisions on applications for development consent under PA 2008, ss.98 and 107 (s.139);
- amending PA 2008, s.120(2) relating to development consent subject to the need for further approval (s.140);
- amendment to PA 2008, ss.128 and 130 in relation to local authority, statutory undertakers and National Trust land (s.141); and
- changes to the notice requirements for compulsory acquisition under PA 2008, s.134 (s.142).

10.3 ENTRY INTO FORCE

The NSIP provisions came into force by order on 1 April 2012 (Localism Act 2011 (Commencement No. 4 and Transitional, Transitory and Saving Provisions) Order 2012, SI 2012/628).

11 OTHER PLANNING MATTERS

The final chapter of Part 6 of the Localism Act 2011 contains two sections: s.143, relating to applications for planning permission and local finance considerations; and s.144, the application of Part 6 to the Crown.

11.1 APPLICATIONS FOR PLANNING PERMISSION AND LOCAL FINANCE CONSIDERATIONS

Despite being tucked in at the end of Part 6, s.143 of the Act contains a fundamental change to the way in which a planning application should be determined by stating that local financial considerations are material to the determination of a planning application. The general considerations relating to the determination of applications for planning permission in TCPA 1990, s.70 are amended by the insertion of a requirement to take into account any local finance considerations so far as material to the application. Section 70(1) and (2) of TCPA 1990 now reads:

> (1) Where an application is made to a local planning authority for planning permission–
>
> > (a) subject to sections 91 and 92, they may grant planning permission, either unconditionally or subject to such conditions as they think fit; or
> > (b) they may refuse planning permission.
>
> (2) In dealing with such an application the authority shall have regard to–
>
> > (a) the provisions of the development plan, so far as material to the application,
> > *(b) any local finance considerations, so far as material to the application*, and
> > (c) any other material considerations. [Emphasis added to new text.]

Sections 91 and 92 of TCPA 1990 relate to a general condition limiting the duration of permission and outline permission respectively. New s.70(2A) makes it clear that new s.70(2)(b) does not apply in relation to Wales (s.143(3)).

Section 143(4) of the Act inserts a new s.70(4) into TCPA 1990, which states that 'local finance consideration' means:

> (a) a grant or other financial assistance that has been, or will or could be, provided to a relevant authority by a Minister of the Crown, or

(b) sums that a relevant authority has received, or will or could receive, in payment of Community Infrastructure Levy;

It is uncertain how wide the scope of 'other financial assistance' may be as it is not defined in the Act. However, this is likely to extend to financial assistance given in relation to a neighbourhood development order or community right to build order (see **Chapter 7** on neighbourhood planning).

A 'relevant authority' is widely defined and includes not only the usual local authorities such as district councils, county councils, London boroughs, the Mayor of London, the Isles of Scilly Council, and the Broads Authority, but also a National Park authority, Mayoral development corporations, urban development corporations and housing action trusts.

Having made this significant amendment, the Act then emphasises in s.143(5) that the amendments to TCPA 1990, s.70(2) do not alter the requirement to have regard to any particular consideration or the weight to be given to any such consideration. Nevertheless, it will be interesting to see how this amendment inter-relates with the general presumption in favour of sustainable development promoted under the new National Planning Policy Framework (discussed further in **Chapter 14**).

11.2 AMENDMENTS BINDING THE CROWN

Section 144 of the Act provides that the amendments to various Planning Acts as a consequence of Part 6 are also intended to bind the Crown.

11.3 ENTRY INTO FORCE

Section 143 entered into force on 15 January 2012 (s.240(1)(i)). Section 144 entered into force on 15 November 2011 (s.240(5)(m)).

PART C SPECIFIC PLANNING REFORM MEASURES

12 PART 8: LONDON

> Planning is not merely a matter of words and drawings. Nor is it a matter of negative controls. Essentially it is a constructive and creative effort, combining the practical and the aesthetic, within which whole areas of London have been and will be transformed, while elsewhere the results become clearer as the smaller pieces of the mosaic of London's redevelopment come together.
>
> All this concerns everyone. Our planning research and our consultations and discussions bring London's public authorities and many other organisations and people into the planning effort. ... Planning is, above all, the work of a team to which every Londoner can belong. (Sir Isaac Hayward, Leader of the London County Council, in the London Plan (London County Council, 1960))

The Localism Act 2011 gives rise to a number of changes and developments that relate specifically to London. These include revising housing and regeneration functions, the introduction of Mayoral development corporations and revision to the Greater London Authority (GLA) governance. This chapter focuses on elements of this Part of the Act that directly or indirectly relate to land use planning in London. The rights, responsibilities and planning reforms elsewhere in the Act apply to London, consistent with Sir Isaac Hayward's 1960 perspective.

12.1 HOUSING AND REGENERATION FUNCTIONS

12.1.1 New regeneration functions of the GLA

Section 187 of the Act amends Part 7A of the Greater London Authority Act (GLA) 1999 by inserting key regeneration provisions into the GLA's functions relating to land. The Explanatory Notes to the Act helpfully summarise the application of the provisions which include, in relation to land use planning:

- Empowering the GLA to compulsorily acquire land and rights for the purposes of housing or regeneration, subject to authorisation by the Secretary of State.
- Applying the Housing and Regeneration Act (HRA) 2008, Sched.2, Part 1 to compulsory acquisition by the GLA. Part 1 as applied to the GLA, applies the standard procedural model (contained in the Acquisition of Land Act 1981) to the compulsory acquisition of land by the GLA and makes provision for the extinguishment of private rights over land, with compensation to be paid.

- Applying HRA 2008, Sched.3 to land of the GLA held for housing and regeneration. Schedule 3, as applied to the GLA, makes provision that enables the GLA to:
  - override easements;
  - apply to the Secretary of State for a public right of way to be extinguished and prescribes the statutory procedure that must be followed; and
  - use land that is, or forms part of, a burial ground, consecrated land and other land connected to religious worship, and includes power for the Secretary of State to make regulations prescribing requirements about the disposal of such land and about the removal and re-interment of human remains.
- Applying HRA 2008, Sched.4 to land held by the GLA for housing and regeneration purposes. Schedule 4 makes provision for powers in relation to, and for, statutory undertakers including when notices can be served and representations made to the Secretary of State and appropriate minister for an extension of or modification to the functions and obligations of statutory undertakers.
- Making provision to prohibit the GLA from disposing of land held for housing and regeneration purposes for less than the best consideration which can reasonably be obtained unless the Secretary of State consents (with the exception of certain disposals by way of a short tenancy). It provides that the Secretary of State may give consent, where required, generally or specifically.
- Providing that the GLA may authorise a person to enter and survey land in connection with a proposal by the GLA to acquire that land or other land for housing and regeneration purposes, or a claim for compensation in respect of the acquisition of such land.

12.1.2 Abolition of the London Development Agency

Section 191(1) of the Act states that the London Development Agency (LDA) ceases to exist on the day on which the subsection comes into force which, under s.240, will be by order. The date was 15 January 2012, by virtue of the Localism Act 2011 (Commencement No. 2 and Transitional and Saving Provision) Order 2012, SI 2012/57. Schedule 20 to the Act provides for a series of consequential amendments to legislation on abolition of the LDA to e.g. the GLA 1999. Under s.191(2) the Secretary of State may make a scheme for the transfer of property, rights and liabilities of the LDA to various other bodies including the GLA, the Secretary of State, a London borough council or the Common Council of the City of London. However, before making a transfer scheme, the Secretary of State must consult the Mayor of London (s.191(3)). Under s.192 of the Act, the Mayor is required to publish an 'Economic development strategy for London' by inserting a new s.333F into GLA 1999. This replaces similar obligations required of the LDA.

12.2 MAYORAL DEVELOPMENT CORPORATIONS

12.2.1 Establishing a Mayoral development corporation

Chapter 2, Part 8 of the Act provides for the creation and operation of Mayoral development corporations (MDCs) with s.197(1) and (2) enabling the Mayor to designate any area of land or parcels of land in Greater London as a Mayoral development area. The power has procedural requirements including the need for expediency and consultation prior to designation (s.197(3)). The persons who have to be consulted before an area may be designated are those set out in s.197(4) of the Act which include, as relevant to the designated area of the MDC:

(a) the London Assembly;
(b) the Assembly constituents;
(c) the Member(s) of Parliament;
(d) the London borough council(s);
(e) the Common Council of the City of London;
(f) the sub-treasurer of the Inner Temple;
(g) the under treasurer of the Middle Temple; and
(h) any other person whom the Mayor considers appropriate.

If a Mayoral development area is designated, the Mayor must publicise it and notify the Secretary of State of that designation (s.197(6)). Once the Secretary of State receives notification of designation of a Mayoral development area, the Secretary of State must by order, among other things, establish an MDC for the area (s.198(2)(a)).

The object or primary purpose of an MDC is to secure the regeneration of its area (s.201(1)). An MDC has the power to do anything it considers appropriate for the direct or incidental purposes of its object (s.201(2)). An MDC will also have a number of 'specific powers' which are to further the object of the MDC, additional to the primary subsection (2) power (s.201(3)–(5)). The specific powers cannot limit the scope of either the primary object or any other specific power except when the MDC is acting:

(i) in its capacity as a local planning authority; or
(ii) under authorisation pursuant to GLA 1999, s.38 (delegation by Mayor) (s.201(6)–(8)).

Finally, the primary object in s.201(2) must not be used to override a restriction on the exercise of a specific power (s.201(8)(c)).

12.2.2 Planning and infrastructure functions of an MDC

Section 202(2) of the Act provides that:

> The Mayor may decide that the MDC for the area ('the MDC') is to be the local planning authority, for the whole or any portion of the area, for the purposes of any one or more of the following:

(a) Part 3 of the Town and Country Planning Act 1990 [regarding development control],
(b) Part 2 of the Planning and Compulsory Purchase Act 2004 [relating to local development schemes], and
(c) Part 3 of that Act [relating to development plans and sustainable development].

The Mayor may also confer part or all of the following functions on the MDC:

- functions provided under Part 1 of Sched.29 to the Local Government, Planning and Land Act 1980 (relating to urban development corporations) (s.202(3)); and
- functions provided pursuant to s.37 and Sched.8 to the Electricity Act 1989 (consents for overhead lines) (s.202(4)).

Section 202(7) states that the Mayor may only decide to confer the above planning functions on an MDC after:

(a) consulting with the persons specified in s.197(4) (see above);
(b) having had regard to any comments in response; and
(c) publishing reasons for the non-acceptance of any comments received from the Assembly or an affected local authority.

Under s.202(8), the Mayor must:

(i) publicise any transfer of planning functions or other variations under s.202(2)–(6); and
(ii) notify the Secretary of State.

Any decision may be different for different portions of an area affected (s.202(9)) and variation under s.202(6) may include revocation or substitution of an earlier decision (s.202(10)). Once an MDC order has been made, the Mayor can remove or restrict the planning functions by subsequent decision (s.204).

Section 205 of the Act enables the MDC to provide or to facilitate infrastructure. 'Infrastructure' includes the following under s.205(4):

(a) water, electricity, gas, telecommunications, sewerage or other services,
(b) roads or other transport facilities,
(c) retail or other business facilities,
(d) health, educational, employment or training facilities,
(e) social, religious or recreational facilities,
(f) cremation or burial facilities, and
(g) community facilities not falling within paragraphs (a) to (f).

Note that 'provide' is defined in s.205(3) as to 'provide by way of acquisition, construction, conversion, improvement or repair'.

12.2.3 Arrangements for discharge of, or assistance with, planning functions (section 203)

Where an MDC has planning functions in place of a borough council or the City of London, it may make arrangements for the discharge of any of those functions with that council (s.203(1)). Where such arrangements are in force, the council may arrange for the discharge of any functions by committee, sub-committee or officer of the council and s.101 of the Local Government Act 1972 (regarding delegation by committees and sub-committees) applies (s.203(2)). Further, the MDC may seek assistance from the relevant council, and the council may provide assistance in connection with the MDC's discharge of its planning functions under PCPA 2004, Part 2 or 3 (s.203(4), (5)).

12.2.4 Land and other functions of an MDC (sections 206–214)

In addition to its planning functions an MDC may regenerate or develop land or bring about the more effective use of land through a range of activities set out in s.206 of the Act. It may also acquire land in its area or elsewhere subject to certain restrictions in the Act (ss.207–210). An MDC may also adopt private streets (s.211), carry on any business (s.212), give financial assistance to any person (s.213) and provide discretionary relief from non-domestic rates.

12.2.5 Dissolution of an MDC and transfer of property, rights and liabilities (sections 215–218)

Section 215 of the Act requires the Mayor to review, from time to time, the continuation of existing MDCs. The legislation does not make further provision for the review or for any review procedures. Section 217 does, however, provide that the Mayor may request that the Secretary of State revokes the order made under s.198(2) which established an MDC. If such a request is made, the Secretary of State must make an order giving effect to the request (s.217(3)). Where a revocation order under s.217(3) is made, s.217(4) provides that:

(a) the MDC is dissolved on the coming into force of the order; and
(b) the Mayor must revoke the designation of the Mayoral development area for which the MDC was established. Also, the Mayor must publicise and notify the Secretary of State of the revocation (s.217(5)).

A revocation order can only be made if no property, rights or liabilities are vested in an MDC (s.217(1)). Accordingly, ss.216 and 218 of the Act provide for the transfer of property, rights and liabilities.

12.2.6 Guidance, directions and entry into force of provisions relating to MDCs

Under s.219 the Mayor may give guidance to an MDC as to the exercise of any of its functions. Before providing any guidance the Mayor must consult any person(s) he thinks appropriate and must publish any guidance as soon as reasonably practicable after giving it. The Mayor may revoke any guidance given subject to the requirement to consult before revocation. An MDC must have regard to any guidance given to it under this section that is for the time being in force when exercising its functions (s.219(6)). Similarly, an MDC must comply with any directions given by the Mayor either under this Chapter or by any general or specific directions the Mayor may give as to the exercise of an MDCs functions under s.220.

In accordance with s.240(1)(l), the provisions relating to MDCs (i.e. Chapter 2, Part 8 of the Act) entered into force on 15 January 2012, except for s.197(3)(e), (f) and (5) relating to standing orders required to designate a Mayoral development area. All other provisions relating to London come into force by order. Various provisions came into force on 15 January 2012 and 1 April 2012. See **Appendix D** for a list of commencement dates as well as the provisions not yet in force as at 20 April 2012.

12.3 GREATER LONDON AUTHORITY GOVERNANCE

Chapter 3 of Part 8 of the Act amends parts of GLA 1999 relating to GLA governance including, among other things:

- conferring a power to government ministers to delegate certain functions to the Mayor, subject to consultation with London councils and the agreement of the Mayor (s.223);
- revision of the Mayor's Environment Strategy for London (ss.225–226);
- revision of some obligations relating to the Mayoral strategies (ss.227–229); and
- the sharing of administrative functions by London authorities (s.230).

Revision of the Mayor's strategy provisions has some relevance in terms of planning.

12.3.1 The London Environment Strategy

Section 225(1) of the Act inserts a new s.351A into GLA 1999, while Sched.23 of the Act amends GLA 1999, ss.352–370. The net effect is to consolidate six existing London environment strategies into one strategy that the Mayor is required to publish called 'the London Environment Strategy'. New s.351A(2) of GLA 1999 provides that the Strategy must contain a general assessment by the Mayor of the environment in Greater London, so far as relevant to the functions of the GLA or of the Mayor. The London Environment Strategy must contain provisions (reflecting the six distinct strategies) relating to:

(a) biodiversity;
(b) municipal waste management;
(c) climate change mitigation and energy;
(d) adaptation to climate change;
(e) air quality; and
(f) ambient noise.

Under GLA 1999, s.351B, the Secretary of State may give guidance to the Mayor about formulating policies, consultation, evidence of environmental change or its consequences, or the prediction of environmental change. Section 226 of the Act abolishes the Mayor's obligation to publish a four-yearly state of the environment report for London. The new London Environment Strategy is not required to cover matters relating to land use planning, water and transport which each have separate strategic bases, e.g. the London Plan 2011, which is the recently adopted spatial development strategy for Greater London. The present environment strategies inform the London Plan.

12.3.2 Entry into force

The London Environment Strategy provisions come into force by order on a date to be appointed (s.240(2)). See **Appendix D** for a list of commencement dates as well as provisions that are not in force as at 20 April 2012.

13 PART 9: COMPENSATION FOR COMPULSORY ACQUISITION

This is a concise chapter dealing with one discrete topic. Section 232 of the Localism Act 2011 amends the Land Compensation Act (LCA) 1961 in order to reform the assumptions as to planning permission when assessing compensation for compulsory acquisition. The reform is by the substitution of LCA 1961, ss.14–18 with new text; although the substituted text does not provide for a new s.16, the old s.16 is repealed.

Section 14(2) of LCA 1961 provides that, when assessing compensation in respect of a compulsory acquisition of an interest in land, account may be taken:

(a) of planning permission, whether for development on the relevant land or other land, if it is in force at the relevant valuation date, and
(b) of the prospect, on the assumptions set out in subsection (5) but otherwise in the circumstances known to the market at the relevant valuation date, of planning permission being granted on or after that date for development, on the relevant land or other land, other than–

  (i) development for which planning permission is in force at the relevant valuation date, and
  (ii) appropriate alternative development.

The primary assumption within LCA 1961, s.14 is that the scheme of development underlying the acquisition had been cancelled on the launch date. 'Appropriate alternative development' is defined in s.14(4) as development for which planning permission could, at the relevant valuation date, reasonably have been expected to be granted.

New s.18 of LCA 1961 provides that, where the LPA has issued a certificate under s.17 in respect of an interest in land, any appeal against that certificate is made to the Upper Tribunal rather than the Minister as previously provided for. Section 232 comes into force by order on a date to be appointed (s.240(2)). The date was 6 April 2012 by virtue of the Localism Act 2011 (Commencement No. 4 and Transitional, Transitory and Saving Provisions) Order 2012, SI 2012/628.

14 NATIONAL PLANNING POLICY FRAMEWORK

In March 2012, the government published the National Planning Policy Framework (NPPF). It is intended to help simplify the planning process and is central to the localism agenda. Its foreword notes: 'By replacing over a thousand pages of national policy with around fifty, written simply and clearly, we are allowing people and communities back into planning.' The content of the NPPF extends across most, if not all, aspects of planning revised or amended by the introduction of the Localism Act 2011 and it is therefore central to the implementation and understanding of the Act in terms of land use planning. This chapter puts the NPPF in context, and discusses its key parts.

14.1 HOW POLICY FITS INTO THE PLANNING SYSTEM

It is clear from the discussion of the Localism Act 2011 in preceding chapters that modern land use planning, as with most fields of work, is now a mix of European Union rules (e.g. EIA Directive 2011/92/EU), primary legislation (Acts of Parliament), secondary legislation (e.g. statutory instruments, orders, directions and regulations) and policy guidance. Primary and secondary legislation once in force is binding and applicable until it is either revoked or amended, although the detail of any particular legislation may create a power or discretion to act in a particular way. In contrast, any guidance published is non-statutory and is largely persuasive in planning. It can take the form of circulars, e.g. Circular 11/95: *Use of conditions in planning permission*, which provides guidance to planning authorities on the appropriate use of conditions when granting planning permission to regulate and control development, Planning Policy Statements (PPSs), letters from the Chief Planner to LPAs, or even ministerial statements in the House of Commons. Although such policy guidance may be highly material to a particular decision, it is not determinative.

Circulars have been gradually used to provide guidance on process, with politically initiated policies set out in PPSs, e.g. PPS1: *Sustainable Development*. There has also been a range of other policy documents such as Minerals Planning Guidance (MPG), and in Wales, an overarching *Planning Policy Wales*, a series of Technical Advice Notices (TANs) and Mineral Technical Advice Notes (MTANs). Both the overarching aspirational documents and project or sector-specific statements are essentially political comment.

The UK is widely regarded as operating one of the most complex systems of land use planning in the world. It has been a detailed 'command and control' regulatory mechanism, with legislation 'commanding' or directing how the system should apply and planning authorities, primarily LPAs, 'controlling' the system. As part of the localism agenda the government has sought to promote the concept of 'development management', rather than 'development control'. It remains to be seen whether this new emphasis and the Localism Act 2011 have simplified the system in any way at all, arguably not. The government hopes that the NPPF will achieve this objective.

14.2 PURPOSE AND APPROACH OF THE NPPF

14.2.1 Introduction and opening comments

The NPPF covers three main themes:

- achieving sustainable development;
- plan-making; and
- decision-taking.

The ministerial foreword to the NPPF seeks to set out what it regards as the purpose of planning and how it should operate. It states, quite surprisingly for many, that:

> The purpose of planning is to help achieve sustainable development.
>
> ... sustainable development is about positive growth – making economic, environmental and social progress for this and future generations.
>
> The planning system is about helping to make this happen.
>
> Development that is sustainable should go ahead, without delay – a presumption in favour of sustainable development that is the basis for every plan, and every decision. This framework sets out clearly what could make a proposed plan or development unsustainable.

The introduction to the NPPF is not contentious. It explains what the policy framework is intended to do and how the planning policies are expected to be applied. Paragraph 2 of the NPPF refers to TCPA 1990, s.70(2) and PCPA 2004, s.38(6) and states: 'applications for planning permission must be determined in accordance with the development plan, unless material considerations indicate otherwise'. The introduction explains that the NPPF does not contain specific policies for nationally significant infrastructure projects, as expressed through national policy statements (NPSs) (see **Chapter 10**), although it may be relevant in determining such matters (NPPF, para.3). Similarly, it notes that the NPPF does not contain specific waste policies, which will be published as part of the National Waste Management Plan for England (para.5). It also notes that the NPPF should be read in conjunction with the government's planning policy for traveller sites (para.4). This demonstrates that the government has already recognised that what may have been their original aspiration to contain all policy within one document, namely the NPPF, has not been possible.

The introduction is consistent with the planning system that has been in place since the Town and Country Planning Act 1947. It is also consistent with the measures set out in the Localism Act 2011. However, concern has been expressed about the application of the NPPF and the revocation of such a considerable body of formulated and reasonably well-understood detailed policy, which had been interpreted by government and the courts to a reasonable extent.

14.2.2 Structure of the NPPF

The NPPF is set out in full at **Appendix B**. It is concise, with the substantive text on policy covering just 47 pages. It is divided into three sections according to the themes referred to above:

- achieving sustainable development (paras.6–149)
- plan-making (paras.150–85)
- decision-taking (paras.186–207).

As well as providing the focus for the largest policy theme, the concept of sustainable development also informs the sections on plan-making and decision-taking. The first main section, on sustainable development, is divided into 13 discrete policy areas. The main sections on plan-making and decision-taking are also subdivided.

There are also three annexes to the NPPF and a technical guidance note.

- **Annex 1: Implementation.** This states, among other things, that: (i) the NPPF applies from the date of its publication (27 March 2012); (ii) planning law requires applications for planning permission to be determined in accordance with the development plan unless material considerations indicate otherwise; (iii) for 12 months from the date of publication of the NPPF, decision-takers may continue to give full weight to relevant polices adopted since 2004, even if there is a limited degree of conflict with the NPPF; and (iv) after this 12-month period, due weight should only be given to relevant policies in existing plans according to their consistency with the NPPF. These are the transitional provisions, as they effectively impose an obligation upon LPAs to either complete or revise their development plans to accord with the NPPF within this 12-month window, or face the consequences of their decisions being overturned because of non-compliance with the NPPF.
- **Annex 2: Glossary.** The glossary provides eight pages of non-technical clarification of key planning terms from 'affordable housing' to 'windfall sites'.
- **Annex 3: Documents replaced by this framework.** This lists the 44 policy documents which were revoked and replaced by the NPPF on 27 March 2012, as they apply in England. This list includes all Planning Policy Guidance (PPG) and PPSs except for PPS10: *Waste Management*, as well as MPS1, MPS2, MPG2, MPG3, MPG5, MPG7, MPG10, MPG13 and MPG15. It should be noted that

Circular 05/2005: *Planning Obligations* is withdrawn and also Government Office London Circular 1/2008: *Strategic Planning in London*. In addition a series of the letters from the Chief Planner to LPAs has been withdrawn.

- **Technical Guidance to the National Planning Policy Framework.** This 24-page document provides guidance on two specific policy areas, flood risk and mineral extraction, where more detailed technical information was considered necessary. This document is not included at **Appendix B**.

The NPPF and related publications are available at **www.communities.gov.uk**.

14.3 ACHIEVING SUSTAINABLE DEVELOPMENT

The concept of sustainable development runs throughout the NPPF. The foreword states that 'The purpose of planning is to help achieve sustainable development.' Some commentators may disagree with this statement. Whatever the purpose of planning, the principle of sustainable development appears to be central to government thinking on land use planning. Moreover, if the government is serious that sustainable development is critical to how the planning system operates, then inconsistent, vague and inaccurate interpretations of sustainable development will lead to inconsistency, uncertainty and unlawful decision-making. Over two-thirds of the NPPF is devoted to highlighting how sustainable development is to be delivered and seeks to clarify its meaning.

14.3.1 Defining 'sustainable development'

The idea of sustainable development is not new. The report by the World Commission on Environment and Development: *Our Common Future* (OUP, 1987) ('the Brundtland Report', named after the chair of the UN Committee, Gro Harlem Brundtland) defined sustainable development. Page 43 of the report noted that:

> Sustainable development is development that meets the needs of the present without compromising the ability of future generations to meet their own needs. It contains within it two key concepts: the concept of 'needs', in particular the essential needs of the world's poor, to which overriding priority should be given; and the idea of limitations imposed by the state of technology and social organization on the environment's ability to meet present and future needs.

The Brundtland report goes on to explain the concept of sustainable development which includes the satisfaction of human needs and aspirations. It notes that the essential needs of vast numbers of people in developing countries – for food, clothing, shelter, jobs – are not being met, and beyond their basic needs these people have legitimate aspirations for an improved quality of life. The Brundtland report continues at p.44:

> Living standards that go beyond the basic minimum are sustainable only if consumption standards everywhere have regard for long-term sustainability. Yet many of us live beyond the world's ecological means, for instance, in our patterns of energy use.

> Perceived needs are socially and culturally determined, and sustainable development requires the promotion of values that encourage consumption standards that are within the bounds of the ecological possible and to which all can reasonably aspire.

The introductory paragraph to the NPPF section 'Achieving sustainable development' refers to Resolution 42/187 of the United Nations General Assembly and explains that the Resolution 'defined sustainable development as meeting the needs of the present without compromising the ability of future generations to meet their own needs'. Resolution 42/187 agrees with and supports the Brundtland report and its approach to sustainable development. The NPPF also refers to the UK Sustainable Development Strategy *Securing the Future* and notes that this set out five 'guiding principles' of sustainable development:

- living within the planet's environmental limits;
- ensuring a strong, healthy and just society;
- achieving a sustainable economy;
- promoting good governance; and
- using sound science responsibly.

Reference to the five guiding principles appears to follow some of the detailed representations on the draft NPPF; much of the concern was evident in the parliamentary discussion of and debate on the draft NPPF including, for example, the *Communities and Local Government Committee – Eighth Report: The National Planning and Policy Framework* (December 2011).

14.3.2 Communities and Local Government Committee – Eighth Report

The *Communities and Local Government Committee – Eighth Report: The National Planning and Policy Framework* (December 2011) considered the NPPF in detail. The evidence and debate prior to the report outlined many of the key concerns. The government welcomed the Select Committee findings. The Select Committee findings in relation to sustainable development are set out below, as they assist in the understanding of the definition and the government's understanding as to its application:

> 4 THE DEFINITION OF SUSTAINABLE DEVELOPMENT
>
> 48. As we have already noted, the NPPF is a document that both guides the writing of Local Plans, and is intended to be used as a substitute Local Plan where none has been produced by a local authority. Assessing the suitability of the NPPF for this task involves looking both at its sufficiency – addressed in the previous chapter – and at the appropriateness of its content. In the following two chapters we examine two aspects of that content: the definition of sustainable development, and the overall balance of the document.
>
> **The NPPF definition**
>
> 49. The draft NPPF defines sustainable development as:

'Development that meets the needs of the present without compromising the ability of future generations to meet their own needs. It is central to the economic, environmental and social success of the country and is the core principle underpinning planning. Simply stated, the principle recognises the importance of ensuring that all people should be able to satisfy their basic needs and enjoy a better quality of life, both now and in the future.'

50. The definition of sustainable development is at the heart of our discussions on the NPPF. The Framework states that the presumption in favour of sustainable development, 'should be seen as a golden thread running through both plan making and decision taking.' If that is the intention, then the role of sustainable development (considered in Chapter 5) and the way in which the concept is defined become crucial to the document as a whole. We recognise that, if the final NPPF contains an agreed definition of sustainable development which is balanced and comprehensive, then the 'presumption in favour of sustainable development' becomes a very constructive part of the Government's wider environmental, social and economic agendas, rather than solely some sort of stick to compel the completion of Local Plans or, as some of our evidence argues, simply a presumption in favour of development.

51. However, one of the first difficulties encountered is that, on the one hand, the NPPF contains the definition of sustainable development quoted above, but, on the other, the draft Framework also states that:

'When taken as a whole, the policies in this Framework set out the Government's view of what constitutes sustainable development in practice and how the planning system is expected to deliver it.'

As Stuart Hylton, representing the Planning Officers Society, stated, 'What that is saying is you have a definition that runs to 52 pages whose conclusions will inevitably point in all sorts of different directions.' Whilst we can appreciate the thinking behind an approach that encourages users of the NPPF to read it as a whole, we consider that this approach will lead to far more uncertainty and, possibly, legal challenge. The Campaign to Protect Rural England (CPRE) took legal advice on this, among other aspects of the NPPF, and its Chief Executive, Shaun Spiers, stated:

'On the question on sustainability, what the NPPF says is that the sustainable development is the 52 pages. What our lawyer, John Hobson, says is that the problem with this is that the "key sustainable development principles are not easy to identify or extract from the text of the NPPF."'

52. We agree that the Government's statements relating to the need to look at the NPPF as a whole in order to ascertain its view of sustainable development are not helpful in this context. The Government should focus on arriving at an agreed, succinct and useful definition which is clearly identified as such within the NPPF.

53. The evidence we received which addressed the definition of sustainable development can be grouped into five categories: those who deemed it an almost impossible job to define sustainable development; those who felt that the definition in the draft NPPF was sufficient; those who wanted the addition of material from other recent Government documents; and those who felt that the NPPF should present a more positive approach to the environmental aspects of sustainable development. Overlaying these were those who considered that the definition in the NPPF needed to be framed in a way that encouraged local authorities to set out their own definitions in their Local Plans. We deal with each of these approaches in turn. We have also taken into account the conclusions reached by the Environmental Audit Committee which took evidence on this specific issue.

Is the 'Brundtland' definition in the draft NPPF adequate?

54. The evidence to this inquiry has, amongst other things, demonstrated the difficulty of setting down any agreed definition of sustainable development. John Rhodes of Quod told us that:

'Everybody has a different view of sustainability. It is possible I could give you any case study for a development proposal and we could all disagree about whether or not it was sustainable. Trying to identify what sustainability really means is almost the holy grail.'

The difficulty of clarifying the concept in a way that could shed light on practical circumstances was reinforced to us by statements such as 'sustainable development is development that is sustainable, we would argue.'

We do not want to underestimate the difficulties of drafting a definition, but we are of the opinion that a clear definition is a vital component of the NPPF. The definition in the draft NPPF clearly draws on the definition put forward in the 1987 report from the UN World Commission on Environment and Development, the 'Brundtland Report'. This is development that 'meets the needs of the present without compromising the ability of future generations to meet their own needs'. Professor Paul Cheshire queried, 'Who could be against the Brundtland formulation of sustainable development? My worry is: how do you translate that into actual decision making about parcels of land?' The combination of the clarity of the Brundtland definition and the difficulty of adding to it was brought out clearly by Stephen Wright of the John Lewis Partnership:

'I think the NPPF does set out a Brundtland definition; it makes it clear it is about social, economic and environmental considerations. It is very difficult then to come up with a more technical and detailed definition that applies cross-sector and that will pass the test of time.'

55. The 'Brundtland' definition of sustainable development has the advantages of being succinct, of encompassing a number of concepts within one sentence and of being recognisable not only to those most directly involved in seeking to achieve sustainable development but, to an extent, to the wider public. We consider that any definition in the NPPF needs to build on the 'Brundtland' definition rather than starting from scratch.

Should the definition go further?

56. The Environmental Audit Committee, however, found that several groups argued that thinking on sustainable development has moved on somewhat from 1987. A number of witnesses to our inquiry have referred, for example, to the benefits of drawing on the principles in the 2005 Sustainable Development Strategy. The Government set out five guiding principles of sustainable development in that Strategy:

- Living Within Environmental Limits;
- Ensuring a Strong, Healthy and Just Society;
- Achieving a Sustainable Economy;
- Promoting Good Governance; and
- Using Sound Science Responsibly.

Dr Hugh Ellis of the TCPA said that:

'Brundtland is an interesting starting point, but it is now more than 30 years out of date. It is very surprising to see it represented in the NPPF. The 2005 definition is not a partisan one; it represents 25 years' experience of what sustainable development is. I think the five

ideas around sustainable development remain critical, but there is one very important principle that the NPPF deliberately ignores: the concept of environmental limits.'

57. Tony Burton of Civic Voice pointed out that 'there was a lot of consensus about the 2005 Strategy and the key principles around social justice and environmental limits', which he considered needed to be embodied in the Framework. Sustainable development was defined in Planning Policy Statement 1 in terms similar to that of the 2005 Strategy, and the same principles also underpinned the February 2011 Defra document, *Mainstreaming Sustainable Development*. During a debate on the Localism Bill in the House in November 2011, the Minister, Greg Clark, said: 'I could not have been clearer when I said that we have no difficulty with the 2005 strategy or its wording.' We agree, and consider that the five guiding principles from the 2005 Sustainable Development Strategy are useful in identifying key aspirations against which development proposals should be judged. We have heard from a number of witnesses that the concept of 'living within environmental limits' is a particularly useful in this respect.

58. We welcome the constructive approach that the Minister has taken in respect of the definition of sustainable development and, in particular, the fact that he has encouraged us and all those concerned about this issue to go beyond existing definitions. Indeed, the Minister told the Environmental Audit Committee (EAC) that:

'*I think some of the recent thinking in the Natural Environment White Paper [...] goes beyond some of the thinking in 2005 to talk not just about a sort of defensive not breaching limits, but being more ambitious than that, saying we should have net gain, that development and other activities should result in net gain to the environment. We have many habitats in our country that have been despoiled over the years. My view is that we should take the opportunity to restore them. I would not want to set down a definition that was less ambitious than, for example, would have been in the Natural Environment White Paper.*'

59. The Government's 2011 Natural Environment White Paper states that:

'*Through reforms of the planning system, we will take a strategic approach to planning for nature within and across local areas. This approach will guide development to the best locations, encourage greener design and enable development to enhance natural networks. We will retain the protection and improvement of the natural environment as core objectives of the planning system. [...] we will improve the quality and increase the value of the natural environment across England.*'

60. We see great value in an approach to sustainable development that seeks to enhance the value of the natural environment through the development process instead of just protecting it, as valuable as that latter activity is. We share the views of the EAC that:

'*the NPPF should embrace a wider definition of sustainable development than just the Brundtland definition. It should include or refer explicitly to the 2005 Sustainable Development Strategy [...] But it should go further still, and reflect the primacy of environmental limits, couched more firmly in terms of seeking environmental improvement. By doing so, it would encourage local authorities to include in their Local Plans a requirement for some types of development to include environmental gain.*'

The adaptation of a sustainable development definition by local authorities

61. We considered whether there was a tension between a strong national definition of sustainable development in the NPPF and the need for local authorities to set their

own definition according to local circumstances and priorities. Dr Adam Marshall of the British Chambers of Commerce provided an example of contrasting local circumstances:

'I like the fact that local communities will be able to determine for themselves to a certain extent what constitutes "sustainable". I have spent a lot of time in chambers of commerce around the country. When you go to many authorities in the North of England, for example, which have long taken a very positive approach to planning, for them sustainability at the end of the day is about jobs and economic activity. Many years ago one council leader said to me that the best thing in the world that could happen to him was that a B&Q shed should open on a piece of contaminated brownfield land, because it creates jobs and economic activity in the area. Southern local authority representatives have said to me, "The worst thing that could happen to me is the opening of a B&Q shed in this area, because it will create enormous amounts of traffic, pressure on local infrastructure, etc."'

This was echoed by John Slaughter of the Home Builders Federation who agreed that:

'You have to allow for the fact that circumstances do vary from area to area. In terms of balancing sustainability, a point we made in our written evidence is that, in some areas, you would probably in practice give more weight to environmental factors.'

62. We agree that it is both good practice and in the nature of localism that local authorities should be encouraged to apply the definition of sustainable development in a way that meets their local circumstances. The EAC expressed the clear view that a definition of sustainable development in the NPPF that captured the fundamental principles in the 2005 Sustainable Development Strategy would enable 'local authorities to interpret sustainable development for the circumstances of their particular areas.'

Environmental, social and economic aspects

63. There are other issues considered elsewhere in this report that impact directly on the formulation of a definition. These are the need for balance between the 'elements' of sustainable development, and the question of whether the definition should make explicit reference not only to environmental, social and economic aspects, but also to cultural aspects. When giving evidence to the EAC, the Minister stated that 'the economy has always been a part of the definition of sustainability and we do need homes and jobs', but gave the reassurance that any appearance in the NPPF of giving greater weight to the economic pillar was 'not intentional'. This stance reflects that taken by the Prime Minister in a letter to the National Trust in which he stated that:

'I believe that sustainable development has environmental and social dimensions as well as an economic dimension, and we fully recognise the need for a balance between the three. Indeed, the purpose of the planning system as a whole, and of our proposals for it, is to achieve such a balance.'

The Environmental Audit Committee recommended that the Government ensure in the revised NPPF that there is 'no potential for confusion about the equal importance of all three aspects of sustainable development.'

64. As seen in Chapter 3 of this report, we received strong evidence that the NPPF did not pay sufficient attention to the cultural aspects of planning policy and decisions. Witnesses spoke of culture in terms of sport and of the arts but we recognise that the concept of culture can be extended to include all aspects of community life. In the light of these representations we see a compelling case for the definition of sustainable development to include a cultural dimension as part of the social pillar of the definition of sustainable development.

Conclusions on the definition of sustainable development

65. We welcome the Government's willingness to look again at the definition of sustainable development contained in the NPPF. In the course of a debate on the Localism Bill, the Minister for Decentralisation told the House that:

'A cogent case has been made – let me put it that way – for expanding and strengthening the definition in the NPPF. I hope that that demonstrates, on the basis of this House's experience of the scrutiny of the Bill and the commitments the Government have made, that there is no difference in our commitment to the matter. Indeed, I have expressed a personal view that I think we could go a little further than the 2005 strategy. We will reflect on these contributions in the consultation on the NPPF and respond in due course.'

66. Any new definition of sustainable development must contain the following elements:

a) the clear and identifiable use of wording from the Brundtland report as this is well known and understood;
b) the restating of the five guiding principles from the 2005 sustainable development strategy; and
c) an explicit statement of the need to address and to seek to achieve all of the aspects of sustainable development, and not to start by assuming that one aspect can be traded off against another.

67. The definition below is put forward as an example of how these elements may be incorporated into a definition.

Sustainable development is development that meets the needs of the present without compromising the ability of existing communities and future generations to meet their own needs. It is central to the economic, environmental and social success of the country both that these three aspects of development are addressed positively and equally and that planning both serves to protect and to enhance and add value to the environment. This is the core principle underpinning planning.

Policies in plans and decisions on development should be assessed against the principles that the nation and areas within it should live within their environmental limits; should achieve a sustainable economy and should seek to ensure a strong, healthy and just society.

The achievement of sustainable development through planning should be based on the responsible use of a sound evidence base and developed through an open and democratic system.

68. We consider that the definition of sustainable development must give a clear indication of what constitutes sustainable development, while encouraging local authorities to apply this definition to their own local circumstances and allowing them the scope to do so.

What is clear from an appreciation of Resolution 42/187 and the Brundtland report, the discussion surrounding the definition of sustainable development, and the understanding of the legislation and the policy to date is that a presumption in favour of sustainable development will have far reaching implications, far beyond what may presently be anticipated by the government and the commercial sector.

14.3.3 Presumption in favour of sustainable development

The presumption in favour of sustainable development is found at para.14 of the NPPF, which provides that:

> At the heart of the [NPPF] is a **presumption in favour of sustainable development**, which should be seen as a golden thread running through both plan-making and decision-taking.

Paragraph 14 explains that for plan-making the presumption in favour of sustainable development means that LPAs should (subject to exceptions) seek to meet the development needs of their area and that local plans should meet objectively assessed needs. It then explains that for decision-taking the presumption means (subject to exceptions) approving development proposals that accord with the development plan without delay; and that where the development plan is absent, silent or relevant policies are out of date, planning permission should be granted. From the range of responses to the government consultation on the draft NPPF, the presumption in favour of sustainable development was welcomed by many respondents. However, there was also widespread concern about how the presumption would be applied in practice given, among other things, the inconsistency in the draft NPPF.

14.3.4 Core planning principles

Paragraph 17 of the NPPF sets out 12 'core planning principles'. These are that planning should:

- be genuinely plan-led, empowering local people to shape their surroundings ... Plans should be kept up-to-date, and be based on joint working and co-operation ... They should provide a practical framework within which decisions on planning applications can be made with a high degree of predictability and efficiency;
- not simply be about scrutiny ...;
- proactively drive and support sustainable economic development ...;
- always seek to secure high quality design and a good standard of amenity for all existing and future occupants ...;
- take account of the different roles and character of different areas, promoting the vitality of our main urban areas, protecting the Green Belts around them ...;
- support the transition to a low carbon future in a changing climate, taking full account of flood risk and coastal change ...;
- contribute to conserving and enhancing the natural environment and reducing pollution. ...;
- encourage the effective use of land by reusing land that has been previously developed ...;
- promote mixed use developments, and encourage multiple benefits from the use of land ...;
- conserve heritage assets in a manner appropriate to their significance, ...;
- actively manage patterns of growth ...;
- take account of and support local strategies to improve health, social and cultural wellbeing ...

The NPPF is silent on how the core principles are to be applied to the more specific policy statements (discussed below), beyond stating that they should 'underpin both plan-making and decision-taking'.

14.3.5 Delivering sustainable development

Under the sub-heading 'Delivering sustainable development' the NPPF sets out 13 quite specific policy areas which appear to reflect the policy areas of the various

PPSs that have been withdrawn, and which in concise and updated form replace much of the 1,000 pages of prior policy documents. An opportunity has been taken to refocus some of the previous specific policy objectives, so that the text does not merely repeat in edited form the previous PPSs. These policies, summarised below, are set out in full in **Appendix B**.

1. Building a strong, competitive economy

The association between land use planning and the economy was previously found in PPS4: *Planning for Sustainable Economic Growth* (2009). Paragraph 19 of the NPPF highlights this aspect of 'delivering sustainable development' by noting that:

> The Government is committed to ensuring that the planning system does everything it can to support sustainable economic growth. Planning should operate to encourage and not act as an impediment to sustainable growth. Therefore significant weight should be placed on the need to support economic growth through the planning system.

2. Ensuring the vitality of town centres

The policy on promoting and revitalising town centres repeats the application of a sequential test for main town centre uses which prioritises locations in town centres over edge of centre and out of centre sites previously found in PPS4: *Planning for Sustainable Economic Growth*. The introduction to this policy (para.23) provides that:

> Planning policies should be positive, promote competitive town centre environments and set out policies for the management and growth of centres over the plan period.

3. Supporting a prosperous rural economy

This concise policy relating to rural economic growth appears to complement policy 1. It provides that local plans should support sustainable growth and expansion in rural areas, promote development and diversification of agricultural activities, support sustainable rural tourism and promote the retention of local services and facilities. It may be regarded as replacing PPS7: *Sustainable Development in Rural Areas* (2004).

4. Promoting sustainable transport

The policy on sustainable transport is comparatively long and may be regarded as replacing PPG13: *Transport* (as updated in 2011). It notes that transport policies can facilitate sustainable development as well as contribute to 'wider sustainability and health objectives'. The policy recognises that certain transport plans and decisions may be subject to NPSs and the Government Framework for UK Aviation. It also recognises the need to reduce overall greenhouse gas emissions including, for example, an overall need to reduce the use of high-emission vehicles.

5. Supporting high quality communications infrastructure

Paragraph 43 of the NPPF provides that LPAs should support the expansion of electronic communications networks, including telecommunications. This policy may be regarded as replacing PPG8: *Telecommunications* (2001). Its concluding comment is that LPAs must determine applications on planning grounds and not seek to prevent competition between different operators, question the need for the telecommunications system or determine health safeguards if the proposal meets international guidelines for public exposure (para.46).

6. Delivering a wide choice of high quality homes

The NPPF suggests that new housing delivery could more effectively meet housing needs and improve the availability of housing areas whereby LPAs are to identify and update annually a supply of specific deliverable housing sites sufficient to provide a five-year supply with an additional buffer of five per cent to ensure choice and competition in the market for land. Significantly, the updated policy also states: 'Where there has been a record of persistent under delivery of housing, local planning authorities should increase the buffer to 20%'. The purpose of this policy is to 'boost significantly the supply of housing' (para.47). It may be regarded as replacing PPS3: *Housing* (2011), but in doing so it has substantially revisited the policies, e.g. explicit endorsement of the principles of Garden Cities for new settlements or urban extensions.

7. Requiring good design

Policy 7 is a cross-cutting policy. Paragraph 56 notes that:

> Good design is a key aspect of sustainable development, is indivisible from good planning, and should contribute positively to making places better for people.

Paragraphs 57–8 add that it is important to plan positively for the achievement of high quality and inclusive designs for all development and that local plans should develop robust and comprehensive policies that set out the quality of development that will be expected for the area. This policy also covers control over outdoor advertisements (para.67).

8. Promoting healthy communities

Another cross-cutting policy, policy 8 affirms the localism agenda including the principles of neighbourhood planning and CRBOs. It states that LPAs 'should create a shared vision with communities of the residential environment and facilities they wish to see' (para.69). The policy is wide-ranging, covering social, recreational and cultural facilities, public rights of way and access to open spaces, including the designation of land as Local Green Space. It may be regarded as replacing PPG17: *Planning for Open Space, Sport and Recreation* (2002).

9. Protecting Green Belt land

Paragraph 79 of the NPPF states that:

> The fundamental aim of Green Belt policy is to prevent urban sprawl by keeping land permanently open; the essential characteristics of Green Belts are their openness and their permanence.

The NPPF provides no further definition of Green Belt but adds that it serves five purposes (para.80):

- to check the unrestricted sprawl of large built-up areas;
- to prevent neighbouring towns merging into one another;
- to assist in safeguarding the countryside from encroachment;
- to preserve the setting and special character of historic towns; and
- to assist in urban regeneration, by encouraging the recycling of derelict and other urban land.

The NPPF qualifies the use of Green Belt by stating that (para.82):

> The general extent of Green Belts across the country is already established. New Green Belts should only be established in exceptional circumstances ...

Policy 9 may be regarded as replacing PPG2: *Green Belts* (1995).

10. Meeting the challenge of climate change, flooding and coastal change

Policy 10 states that LPAs should adopt proactive strategies to mitigate and adapt to climate change in line with the objectives and provisions of the Climate Change Act 2008, taking full account of flood risk, coastal change and water supply and demand (para.94). Mitigation measures refer to the need to reduce greenhouse gas emissions and support energy efficiency (paras.95–8). Paragraphs 100–4 consider flood risk and should be read in conjunction with the technical guidance on flood risk published alongside the NPPF. Policy 10 may be regarded as replacing PPS: *Planning and Climate Change – Supplement to Planning Policy Statement 1* (2007); PPG20: *Coastal Planning* (1992); PPS25: *Development and Flood Risk* (2010); and PPS25 Supplement: *Development and Coastal Change* (2010).

11. Conserving and enhancing the natural environment

Policy 11 is arguably much wider than its heading suggests and covers pollution and environmental impacts on people and places, including the use and development of the built environment; for example, it provides that planning policies and decisions should aim to avoid noise giving rise to adverse impacts on health and quality of life (para.123) and limit the impact of light pollution from artificial light on local amenity, intrinsically dark landscapes and nature conservation (para.125). The policy notes that the aim in preparing plans should be to minimise pollution and other adverse effects on the local and natural environment (para.110). It adds that planning policies and decisions should encourage the use of brownfield land and recognise the benefits of the best and most versatile agricultural land (paras.111–12). The glossary in Annex 2 to the NPPF further defines 'best and most versatile agricultural land', 'pollution' and 'previously developed land' (brownfield land). This policy may be regarded as replacing PPS9: *Biodiversity and Geological*

Conservation (2005); PPS23: *Planning and Pollution Control* (2004); and PPG24: *Planning and Noise* (1994).

12. Conserving and enhancing the historic environment

A footnote to para.126 provides that policy 12 applies to the heritage-related consent regimes under the Planning (Listed Buildings and Conservation Areas) Act 1990, as well as to plan-making and decision-taking. The policy notes that LPAs should set out in local plans a positive strategy for the conservation and enjoyment of the historic environment. It refers to the designation of conservation areas and the approach to development which relates to or impacts upon heritage assets. 'Heritage asset' is defined in the Annex 2 glossary and includes designated heritage assets and those locally listed by an LPA. This policy may be regarded as replacing PPS5: *Planning for the Historic Environment* (2010).

13. Facilitating the sustainable use of minerals

Policy 13 is supported by further information in the technical guidance to the NPPF. Paragraph 143 states that in preparing local plans LPAs should, among other things:

- identify and include policies for extraction of minerals of local and national importance but should not identify areas for peat extraction;
- consider using recycled and secondary materials and minerals waste before considering the extraction of primary materials;
- define Minerals Safeguarding Areas to ensure specific minerals resources are not sterilised by non-mineral development;
- set out environmental criteria, in line with the policies in the NPPF, against which planning applications will be assessed.

Policy 13 may be regarded as replacing MPS1: *Planning and Minerals* (2006); MPS2: *Controlling and Mitigating the Environmental Effects of Minerals Extraction in England* together with its Annex 1: *Dust* and Annex 2: *Noise* (2005); MPG2: *Applications, Permissions and Conditions* (1998); MPG3: *Coal Mining and Colliery Spoil Disposal* (1999); MPG5: *Stability in Surface Mineral Workings and Tips* (2000); and MPG7: *Reclamation of Minerals Workings* (1996).

14.4 PLAN-MAKING

The second part of the NPPF, plan-making, is divided into the following sections:

- local plans;
- using a proportionate evidence base;
- planning strategically across local boundaries;
- examining local plans; and
- neighbourhood plans.

Paragraphs 150–1 emphasise that local plans are the key to delivering sustainable development that reflects the vision and aspirations of local communities and that they should be prepared with the objective of contributing to the achievement of sustainable development. There is emphasis again that planning decisions must be taken in accordance with the development plan unless material considerations indicate otherwise.

The section on using a proportionate evidence base states that LPAs should have a clear understanding of both housing and business needs (paras.159–61). It adds that LPAs should work alongside others to assess matters related to infrastructure, minerals, health and well-being and defence. It notes that policies and decisions should be based on up-to-date environmental information including evidence about the historic environment. It also refers to the CIL charges and advises that these should be worked up and tested alongside local plans where practical. Paragraphs 178–9 refer to the new duty on LPAs to co-operate on planning issues that cross administrative boundaries, and note that there should be collaborative working with other bodies to ensure that strategic priorities across local boundaries are properly co-ordinated and clearly reflected in local plans.

Paragraph 182 provides that the local plan will be examined by an independent inspector whose role is to assess whether the plan is in accordance with the duty to co-operate and that it is 'sound' – namely that it is positively prepared, justified, effective and consistent with the NPPF. Finally, paras.183–5 discuss and highlight the value of neighbourhood planning.

14.5 DECISION-TAKING

The final part of the NPPF is on decision-taking, otherwise or formerly known as development control or development management. It is the shortest main part of the framework and divided into brief sections on:

- pre-application engagement and front loading;
- determining applications;
- tailoring planning controls to local circumstances;
- planning conditions and obligations; and
- enforcement.

Paragraphs 196–7 again reinforce the points that the planning system is plan-led and that LPAs should apply the presumption in favour of sustainable development. The section on planning conditions appears consistent with Circular 11/95: *Use of conditions in planning permission*, which has not been revoked by the NPPF. The final section on enforcement (para.207) states that 'enforcement action is discretionary'. The operation of this discretion still requires compliance with the UK's obligations under EU law, e.g. EIA Directive 2011/92/EU, and see *Wells* v. *Secretary of State for Transport, Local Government and the Regions* (Case C-201/02) [2004] ECR I-723.

14.6 CONCLUSION

As indicated earlier in this chapter, the draft NPPF prompted widespread concern. Upon Royal Assent of the Localism Act 2011 the Royal Town Planning Institute

(RTPI) reported that, while they supported the objectives of the Localism Bill and very much welcomed the central role of planning at the heart of the localism agenda, they believed that:

> the new Localism Act will fail to deliver a workable planning system unless a number of key issues are resolved including robust transition arrangements, changes to the draft [NPPF] and the Local Planning Regulations and also proper resourcing for the new planning system. ('Localism Bill gets Royal Assent but much still to do to secure a workable planning system', RTPI, 15 November 2011)

The RTPI has welcomed the changes made to the NPPF in response to the consultation, and the transitional arrangements, but still expressed concern in relation to, for example, promoting positive planning:

> There are improvements to the draft here. For example in para 17 the government says that planning is 'not simply about scrutiny'. However the NPPF still seems to regard planning as a largely receptive activity rather than a driving force. For example in para 17 it says that planning should 'take account of and support' Health and Well Being Strategies. Surely it should be saying that planning should 'shape' HWBs. ('NPPF – RTPI responds', RTPI, 27 March 2012)

Similarly, the Law Society consultation response on the NPPF suggested that, notwithstanding the principle of condensing planning policy, there would remain a need for supplementary guidance in the areas of housing, retail/town centres, heritage, enforcement, forward planning, flood risk, noise and unstable land, adding that the scrapping of minerals planning guidance would cause substantial difficulty to minerals authorities in dealing with applications for permission relating to minerals extraction. The need for additional guidance has already been recognised with the simultaneous publication of the technical guidance on flood risk and mineral extraction.

Early commentary on the NPPF and the reforms suggest there is likely to be an increase in appeals, certainly in the short term, where LPA decisions based on existing development plans are subject to challenge on the basis that they are inconsistent with the NPPF (see, e.g. 'Planners warn NPPF will increase number of appeals' by Jamie Carpenter, *Planning*, 5 April 2012; **www.planningresource.co.uk**), especially if the opportunity is not taken to update development plans within the 12-month 'transition' window (NPPF, paras.214–5). It may, for instance, be argued that local plans are incompatible with the NPPF presumption in favour of sustainable development and its policy of promoting economic growth. In the longer term, there may be an increase in appeals as neighbourhood planning begins to inform and influence decision-making and this is regarded as being incompatible with developer's aspirations.

Appendix A
LOCALISM ACT 2011 (EXTRACTS)

PART 1 LOCAL GOVERNMENT

CHAPTER 1 GENERAL POWERS OF AUTHORITIES

1 Local authority's general power of competence

(1) A local authority has power to do anything that individuals generally may do.
(2) Subsection (1) applies to things that an individual may do even though they are in nature, extent or otherwise –

 (a) unlike anything the authority may do apart from subsection (1), or
 (b) unlike anything that other public bodies may do.

(3) In this section 'individual' means an individual with full capacity.
(4) Where subsection (1) confers power on the authority to do something, it confers power (subject to sections 2 to 4) to do it in any way whatever, including –

 (a) power to do it anywhere in the United Kingdom or elsewhere,
 (b) power to do it for a commercial purpose or otherwise for a charge, or without charge, and
 (c) power to do it for, or otherwise than for, the benefit of the authority, its area or persons resident or present in its area.

(5) The generality of the power conferred by subsection (1) ('the general power') is not limited by the existence of any other power of the authority which (to any extent) overlaps the general power.
(6) Any such other power is not limited by the existence of the general power (but see section 5(2)).
(7) Schedule 1 (consequential amendments) has effect.

2 Boundaries of the general power

(1) If exercise of a pre-commencement power of a local authority is subject to restrictions, those restrictions apply also to exercise of the general power so far as it is overlapped by the pre-commencement power.
(2) The general power does not enable a local authority to do –

 (a) anything which the authority is unable to do by virtue of a pre-commencement limitation, or
 (b) anything which the authority is unable to do by virtue of a post-commencement limitation which is expressed to apply –

  (i) to the general power,
  (ii) to all of the authority's powers, or
  (iii) to all of the authority's powers but with exceptions that do not include the general power.

(3) The general power does not confer power to –

 (a) make or alter arrangements of a kind which may be made under Part 6 of the Local Government Act 1972 (arrangements for discharge of authority's functions by committees, joint committees, officers etc);
 (b) make or alter arrangements of a kind which are made, or may be made, by or

under Part 1A of the Local Government Act 2000 (arrangements for local authority governance in England);

(c) make or alter any contracting-out arrangements, or other arrangements within neither of paragraphs (a) and (b), that authorise a person to exercise a function of a local authority.

(4) In this section –

'post-commencement limitation' means a prohibition, restriction or other limitation expressly imposed by a statutory provision that –

(a) is contained in an Act passed after the end of the Session in which this Act is passed, or

(b) is contained in an instrument made under an Act and comes into force on or after the commencement of section 1;

'pre-commencement limitation' means a prohibition, restriction or other limitation expressly imposed by a statutory provision that –

(a) is contained in this Act, or in any other Act passed no later than the end of the Session in which this Act is passed, or

(b) is contained in an instrument made under an Act and comes into force before the commencement of section 1;

'pre-commencement power' means power conferred by a statutory provision that –

(a) is contained in this Act, or in any other Act passed no later than the end of the Session in which this Act is passed, or

(b) is contained in an instrument made under an Act and comes into force before the commencement of section 1.

3 Limits on charging in exercise of general power

(1) Subsection (2) applies where –

(a) a local authority provides a service to a person otherwise than for a commercial purpose, and

(b) its providing the service to the person is done, or could be done, in exercise of the general power.

(2) The general power confers power to charge the person for providing the service to the person only if –

(a) the service is not one that a statutory provision requires the authority to provide to the person,

(b) the person has agreed to its being provided, and

(c) ignoring this section and section 93 of the Local Government Act 2003, the authority does not have power to charge for providing the service.

(3) The general power is subject to a duty to secure that, taking one financial year with another, the income from charges allowed by subsection (2) does not exceed the costs of provision.

(4) The duty under subsection (3) applies separately in relation to each kind of service.

4 Limits on doing things for commercial purpose in exercise of general power

(1) The general power confers power on a local authority to do things for a commercial purpose only if they are things which the authority may, in exercise of the general power, do otherwise than for a commercial purpose.

(2) Where, in exercise of the general power, a local authority does things for a commercial purpose, the authority must do them through a company.

(3) A local authority may not, in exercise of the general power, do things for a commercial

purpose in relation to a person if a statutory provision requires the authority to do those things in relation to the person.

(4) In this section 'company' means –

(a) a company within the meaning given by section 1(1) of the Companies Act 2006, or

(b) a society registered or deemed to be registered under the Co-operative and Community Benefit Societies and Credit Unions Act 1965 or the Industrial and Provident Societies Act (Northern Ireland) 1969.

5 Powers to make supplemental provision

(1) If the Secretary of State thinks that a statutory provision (whenever passed or made) prevents or restricts local authorities from exercising the general power, the Secretary of State may by order amend, repeal, revoke or disapply that provision.

(2) If the Secretary of State thinks that the general power is overlapped (to any extent) by another power then, for the purpose of removing or reducing that overlap, the Secretary of State may by order amend, repeal, revoke or disapply any statutory provision (whenever passed or made).

(3) The Secretary of State may by order make provision preventing local authorities from doing, in exercise of the general power, anything which is specified, or is of a description specified, in the order.

(4) The Secretary of State may by order provide for the exercise of the general power by local authorities to be subject to conditions, whether generally or in relation to doing anything specified, or of a description specified, in the order.

(5) The power under subsection (1), (2), (3) or (4) may be exercised in relation to –

(a) all local authorities,

(b) particular local authorities, or

(c) particular descriptions of local authority.

(6) The power under subsection (1) or (2) to amend or disapply a statutory provision includes power to amend or disapply a statutory provision for a particular period.

(7) Before making an order under subsection (1), (2), (3) or (4) the Secretary of State must consult –

(a) such local authorities,

(b) such representatives of local government, and

(c) such other persons (if any),

as the Secretary of State considers appropriate.

(8) Before making an order under subsection (1) that has effect in relation to Wales, the Secretary of State must consult the Welsh Ministers.

6 Limits on power under section 5(1)

(1) The Secretary of State may not make provision under section 5(1) unless the Secretary of State considers that the conditions in subsection (2), where relevant, are satisfied in relation to that provision.

(2) Those conditions are that –

(a) the effect of the provision is proportionate to the policy objective intended to be secured by the provision;

(b) the provision, taken as a whole, strikes a fair balance between the public interest and the interests of any person adversely affected by it;

(c) the provision does not remove any necessary protection;

(d) the provision does not prevent any person from continuing to exercise any right or freedom which that person might reasonably expect to continue to exercise;

(e) the provision is not of constitutional significance.

(3) An order under section 5(1) may not make provision for the delegation or transfer of any function of legislating.
(4) For the purposes of subsection (3) a 'function of legislating' is a function of legislating by order, rules, regulations or other subordinate instrument.
(5) An order under section 5(1) may not make provision to abolish or vary any tax.

7 Procedure for orders under section 5

(1) If, as a result of any consultation required by section 5(7) and (8) with respect to a proposed order under section 5(1), it appears to the Secretary of State that it is appropriate to change the whole or any part of the Secretary of State's proposals, the Secretary of State must undertake such further consultation with respect to the changes as the Secretary of State considers appropriate.
(2) If, after the conclusion of the consultation required by section 5(7) and (8) and subsection (1), the Secretary of State considers it appropriate to proceed with the making of an order under section 5(1), the Secretary of State must lay before Parliament –

(a) a draft of the order, and
(b) an explanatory document explaining the proposals and giving details of –

(i) the Secretary of State's reasons for considering that the conditions in section 6(2), where relevant, are satisfied in relation to the proposals,
(ii) any consultation undertaken under section 5(7) and (8) and subsection (1),
(iii) any representations received as a result of the consultation, and
(iv) the changes (if any) made as a result of those representations.

(3) Sections 15 to 19 of the Legislative and Regulatory Reform Act 2006 (choosing between negative, affirmative and super-affirmative parliamentary procedure) are to apply in relation to an explanatory document and draft order laid under subsection (2) but as if –

(a) section 18(11) of that Act were omitted,
(b) references to section 14 of that Act were references to subsection (2), and
(c) references to the Minister were references to the Secretary of State.

(4) Provision under section 5(2) may be included in a draft order laid under subsection (2) and, if it is, the explanatory document laid with the draft order must also explain the proposals under section 5(2) and give details of any consultation undertaken under section 5(7) with respect to those proposals.
(5) Section 5(7) does not apply to an order under section 5(3) or (4) which is made only for the purpose of amending an earlier such order –

(a) so as to extend the earlier order, or any provision of the earlier order, to a particular authority or to authorities of a particular description, or
(b) so that the earlier order, or any provision of the earlier order, ceases to apply to a particular authority or to authorities of a particular description.

8 Interpretation of Chapter

(1) In this Chapter –

'the general power' means the power conferred by section 1(1);

'local authority' means –

(a) a county council in England,
(b) a district council,
(c) a London borough council,
(d) the Common Council of the City of London in its capacity as a local authority,
(e) the Council of the Isles of Scilly, or
(f) an eligible parish council;

'statutory provision' means a provision of an Act or of an instrument made under an Act.

(2) A parish council is 'eligible' for the purposes of this Chapter if the council meets the conditions prescribed by the Secretary of State by order for the purposes of this section.

ooo

CHAPTER 4 TRANSFER AND DELEGATION OF FUNCTIONS TO CERTAIN AUTHORITIES

15 Power to transfer local public functions to permitted authorities

(1) The Secretary of State may by order make provision –

(a) transferring a local public function from the public authority whose function it is to a permitted authority;

(b) about the discharge of local public functions that are transferred to permitted authorities under this section (including provision enabling the discharge of those functions to be delegated).

(2) An order under this section may modify any enactment (whenever passed or made) for the purpose of making the provision mentioned in subsection (1).

(3) The power to modify an enactment in subsection (2) is a power –

(a) to apply that enactment with or without modifications,

(b) to extend, disapply or amend that enactment, or

(c) to repeal or revoke that enactment with or without savings.

(4) An order under this section may disapply, or modify the application of, Chapter 4 of Part 1A of the Local Government Act 2000 (changing local authority governance arrangements) in relation to a county council or district council to which the order transfers a local public function.

(5) The Secretary of State may not make an order under this section unless the Secretary of State considers that it is likely that making the order would –

(a) promote economic development or wealth creation, or

(b) increase local accountability in relation to each local public function transferred by the order.

(6) For the purposes of subsection (5)(b), in relation to a local public function, local accountability is increased if the exercise of the function becomes more accountable to persons living or working in the area of the permitted authority to which it is transferred.

(7) The Secretary of State may not make an order under this section unless the Secretary of State considers that the local public function transferred by the order can appropriately be exercised by the permitted authority to which it is transferred.

(8) The Secretary of State may not make an order under this section transferring a local public function to a permitted authority unless the authority has consented to the transfer.

(9) Before making an order under this section, the Secretary of State must consult such persons as the Secretary of State considers appropriate.

16 Delegation of functions by Ministers to permitted authorities

(1) A Minister of the Crown may, to such extent and subject to such conditions as that Minister thinks fit, delegate to a permitted authority any of the Minister's eligible functions.

(2) A function is eligible for the purposes of subsection (1) if –

(a) it does not consist of a power to make regulations or other instruments of a legislative character or a power to fix fees or charges, and
(b) the Minister of the Crown considers that it can appropriately be exercised by the permitted authority.

(3) No delegation under subsection (1), and no variation of a delegation under that subsection, may be made without the agreement of the permitted authority.
(4) Before delegating a function under subsection (1), the Minister of the Crown must consult such persons as the Minister considers appropriate.
(5) A delegation under subsection (1) may be revoked at any time by any Minister of the Crown.

17 Transfer schemes

(1) The Secretary of State may make a scheme for the transfer of property, rights or liabilities from the person who, or body which, would have a local public function but for an order under section 15 to the permitted authority to which the function is transferred.
(2) A Minister of the Crown may make a scheme for the transfer from the Crown to a permitted authority of such property, rights or liabilities as the Minister of the Crown considers appropriate in consequence of a delegation, or the variation of a delegation, under section 16 of a function of any Minister of the Crown to the permitted authority.
(3) A Minister of the Crown may make a scheme for the transfer from a permitted authority to the Crown of such property, rights or liabilities as the Minister of the Crown considers appropriate in consequence of a variation or revocation of a delegation under section 16 of a function of any Minister of the Crown to the permitted authority.
(4) The things that may be transferred under a transfer scheme include –

(a) property, rights or liabilities that could not otherwise be transferred;
(b) property acquired, or rights or liabilities arising, after the making of the order.

(5) A transfer scheme may make consequential, supplementary, incidental and transitional provision and may in particular make provision –

(a) for a certificate issued by a Minister of the Crown to be conclusive evidence that property has been transferred;
(b) creating rights, or imposing liabilities, in relation to property or rights transferred;
(c) about the continuing effect of things done by or in relation to the transferor in respect of anything transferred;
(d) about the continuation of things (including legal proceedings) in the process of being done by, on behalf of or in relation to the transferor in respect of anything transferred;
(e) for references to the transferor in an instrument or other document relating to anything transferred to be treated as references to the transferee;
(f) for the shared ownership or use of property;
(g) that has the same or similar effect as the TUPE regulations (so far as those regulations do not apply in relation to the transfer).

(6) A transfer scheme may provide –

(a) for modification by agreement;
(b) for modifications to have effect from the date when the original scheme came into effect.

(7) For the purposes of this section –

(a) an individual who holds employment in the civil service is to be treated as employed by virtue of a contract of employment, and
(b) the terms of the individual's employment in the civil service are to be regarded as constituting the terms of the contract of employment.

(8) In this section –

'civil service' means the civil service of the State;

'transferee', in relation to a transfer scheme, means the person to whom property, rights or liabilities are transferred by the scheme;

'transferor', in relation to a transfer scheme, means the person from whom property, rights or liabilities are transferred by the scheme;

'transfer scheme' means a scheme for the transfer of property, rights or liabilities under subsection (1), (2) or (3);

'TUPE regulations' means the Transfer of Undertakings (Protection of Employment) Regulations 2006 (S.I. 2006/246);

references to rights and liabilities include rights and liabilities relating to a contract of employment;

references to the transfer of property include the grant of a lease.

18 Duty to consider proposals for exercise of powers under sections 15 and 17

(1) If the Secretary of State receives a relevant proposal from a permitted authority, the Secretary of State must –

(a) consider the proposal, and
(b) notify the permitted authority of what action, if any, the Secretary of State will take in relation to the proposal.

(2) The Secretary of State may by regulations specify criteria to which the Secretary of State must have regard in considering a relevant proposal.

(3) For the purposes of this section, a 'relevant proposal' is a proposal –

(a) for the exercise of the Secretary of State's powers in sections 15 and 17 in relation to the permitted authority, and
(b) that is accompanied by such information and evidence as the Secretary of State may specify by regulations.

(4) Before making regulations under this section, the Secretary of State must consult such persons as the Secretary of State considers appropriate.

19 Orders under section 15: procedure

(1) Before making an order under section 15, the Secretary of State must lay a draft of the instrument containing the order (the 'draft order') before each House of Parliament.

(2) The Secretary of State must have regard to –

(a) any representations,
(b) any resolution of either House of Parliament, and
(c) any recommendations of a committee of either House of Parliament charged with reporting on the draft order,

made during the 60-day period with regard to the draft order.

(3) If, after the expiry of the 60-day period, the Secretary of State wishes to make an order in the terms of the draft order, the Secretary of State must lay before Parliament a statement –

(a) stating whether any representations were made under subsection (2)(a), and
(b) if any representations were so made, giving details of them.

(4) The Secretary of State may after the laying of such a statement make an order in the terms of the draft order if it is approved by a resolution of each House of Parliament.

(5) However, a committee of either House charged with reporting on the draft order may, at any time after the laying of the statement under subsection (3) and before the draft order

is approved by that House under subsection (4), recommend under this subsection that no further proceedings be taken in relation to the draft order.

(6) Where a recommendation is made by a committee of either House under subsection (5) in relation to a draft order, no proceedings may be taken in relation to the draft order in that House under subsection (4) unless the recommendation is, in the same Session, rejected by a resolution of that House.

(7) If, after the expiry of the 60-day period, the Secretary of State wishes to make an order consisting of a version of the draft order with material changes, the Secretary of State must lay before Parliament –

(a) a revised draft order, and
(b) a statement giving details of –

(i) any representations made under subsection (2)(a), and
(ii) the revisions proposed.

(8) The Secretary of State may after laying a revised draft order and statement under subsection (7) make an order in the terms of the revised draft order if it is approved by a resolution of each House of Parliament.

(9) However, a committee of either House charged with reporting on the revised draft order may, at any time after the revised draft order is laid under subsection (7) and before it is approved by that House under subsection (8), recommend under this subsection that no further proceedings be taken in relation to the revised draft order.

(10) Where a recommendation is made by a committee of either House under subsection (9) in relation to a revised draft order, no proceedings may be taken in relation to the revised draft order in that House under subsection (8) unless the recommendation is, in the same Session, rejected by resolution of that House.

(11) For the purposes of subsections (4) and (8) an order is made in the terms of a draft order if it contains no material changes to the provisions of the draft order.

(12) If a draft of an instrument containing an order under section 15 would, apart from this subsection, be treated for the purposes of the standing orders of either House of Parliament as a hybrid instrument, it is to proceed in that House as if it were not such an instrument.

(13) In this section, the '60-day period' means the period of 60 days beginning with the day on which the draft order was laid before Parliament.

(14) In calculating the period mentioned in subsection (13), no account is to be taken of any time during which Parliament is dissolved or prorogued or during which either House is adjourned for more than four days.

20 Interpretation of Chapter

In this Chapter –

'enactment' includes an enactment contained in a local Act or comprised in subordinate legislation (within the meaning of the Interpretation Act 1978);

'Minister of the Crown' has the same meaning as in the Ministers of the Crown Act 1975;

'local public function', in relation to a permitted authority, means a public function in so far as it relates to –

(a) the permitted authority's area, or
(b) persons living, working or carrying on activities in that area;

'permitted authority' means –

(a) a county council in England,
(b) a district council,
(c) an economic prosperity board established under section 88 of the Local Democracy, Economic Development and Construction Act 2009, or
(d) a combined authority established under section 103 of that Act;

'public authority' includes a Minister of the Crown or a government department;

'public function' means a function of a public authority that does not consist of a power to make regulations or other instruments of a legislative character.

CHAPTER 5 GOVERNANCE

21 New arrangements with respect to governance of English local authorities

Schedule 2 (new Part 1A of, including Schedule A1 to, the Local Government Act 2000) has effect.

22 New local authority governance arrangements: amendments

Schedule 3 (minor and consequential amendments relating to local authority governance in England) has effect.

23 Changes to local authority governance in England: transitional provision etc

(1) The Secretary of State may by order make such transitional, transitory or saving provision as the Secretary of State considers appropriate in connection with the coming into force of sections 21 and 22 and Schedules 2 and 3.

(2) An order under subsection (1) may, in particular, include any provision –

- (a) relating to local authorities –
  - (i) ceasing to operate executive arrangements or alternative arrangements under Part 2 of the Local Government Act 2000, and
  - (ii) starting to operate executive arrangements or a committee system under Part 1A of that Act,
- (b) as to whether, and how, anything done, or in the process of being done, under any provision of Part 2 of that Act is to be deemed to have been done, or be in the process of being done, under any provision of Part 1A of that Act (whether generally or for specified purposes), or
- (c) modifying the application of any provision of Chapter 4 of Part 1A of that Act in relation to a change in governance arrangements by a local authority within a specified period.

(3) The reference in subsection (2)(b) to things done includes a reference to things omitted to be done.

(4) In this section –

'change in governance arrangements' has the meaning given by section 9OA of the Local Government Act 2000;

'local authority' means a county council in England, a district council or a London borough council;

'specified' means specified in an order under this section.

24 Timetables for changing English district councils' electoral schemes

(1) The Local Government and Public Involvement in Health Act 2007 is amended as follows.

(2) Omit the following provisions (which provide that councils may pass resolutions to change their electoral schemes only in certain permitted periods) –

- (a) section 33(4), (6) and (7) (district councils changing to whole-council elections),
- (b) section 38(4), (6) and (7) (non-metropolitan district councils reverting to elections by halves), and
- (c) section 40(4), (6) and (7) (district councils reverting to elections by thirds).

(3) In section 33 (resolution for whole-council elections: requirements) after subsection (3) insert –

'(3A) The resolution must specify the year for the first ordinary elections of the council at which all councillors are to be elected.

(3B) In the case of a district council for a district in a county for which there is a county council, the year specified under subsection (3A) may not be a county-council-elections year; and here 'county-council-elections year' means 2013 and every fourth year afterwards.'

(4) In section 34(2) (years in which whole-council elections to a district council are to be held if scheme under section 34 applies) for paragraphs (a) and (b) substitute –

'(a) the year specified under section 33(3A) in the resolution, and
(b) every fourth year afterwards.'

(5) In section 34 (scheme for whole-council elections) after subsection (4) insert –

'(4A) Ordinary elections of councillors of the council under the previous electoral scheme are to be held in accordance with that scheme in any year that –

(a) is earlier than the year specified under section 33(3A) in the resolution for whole-council elections, and
(b) is a year in which, under the previous electoral scheme, ordinary elections of councillors of the council are due to be held.

(4B) In subsection (4A) 'the previous electoral scheme' means the scheme for the ordinary elections of councillors of the council that applied to it immediately before it passed the resolution for whole-council elections.'

(6) After section 31 insert –

'31A Minimum period between resolutions to change electoral schemes

If a council passes a resolution under section 32, 37 or 39 ('the earlier resolution') it may not pass another resolution under any of those sections before the end of five years beginning with the day on which the earlier resolution is passed.'

(7) In section 57 of the Local Democracy, Economic Development and Construction Act 2009 (requests for review of single-member electoral areas by councils subject to a scheme for whole-council elections) after subsection (4) (meaning of 'subject to a scheme for whole-council elections') insert –

'(4A) A district council is also 'subject to a scheme for whole-council elections' for those purposes if –

(a) section 34 of the Local Government and Public Involvement in Health Act 2007 (scheme for whole-council elections) applies to the council, but
(b) by virtue of subsection (4A) of that section (temporary continuation of previous electoral scheme), not all the members of the council are to be elected in a year in which ordinary elections of members of the council are to be held.'

CHAPTER 6 PREDETERMINATION

25 Prior indications of view of a matter not to amount to predetermination etc

(1) Subsection (2) applies if –

(a) as a result of an allegation of bias or predetermination, or otherwise, there is an issue about the validity of a decision of a relevant authority, and

(b) it is relevant to that issue whether the decision-maker, or any of the decision-makers, had or appeared to have had a closed mind (to any extent) when making the decision.

(2) A decision-maker is not to be taken to have had, or to have appeared to have had, a closed mind when making the decision just because –

(a) the decision-maker had previously done anything that directly or indirectly indicated what view the decision-maker took, or would or might take, in relation to a matter, and

(b) the matter was relevant to the decision.

(3) Subsection (2) applies in relation to a decision-maker only if that decision-maker –

(a) is a member (whether elected or not) of the relevant authority, or

(b) is a co-opted member of that authority.

(4) In this section –

'co-opted member', in relation to a relevant authority, means a person who is not a member of the authority but who –

(a) is a member of any committee or sub-committee of the authority, or

(b) is a member of, and represents the authority on, any joint committee or joint sub-committee of the authority,

and who is entitled to vote on any question which falls to be decided at any meeting of the committee or sub-committee;

'decision', in relation to a relevant authority, means a decision made in discharging functions of the authority, functions of the authority's executive, functions of a committee of the authority or functions of an officer of the authority (including decisions made in the discharge of any of those functions otherwise than by the person to whom the function was originally given);

'elected mayor' has the meaning given by section 9H or 39 of the Local Government Act 2000;

'member' –

(a) in relation to the Greater London Authority, means the Mayor of London or a London Assembly member, and

(b) in relation to a county council, district council, county borough council or London borough council, includes an elected mayor of the council;

'relevant authority' means –

(a) a county council,
(b) a district council,
(c) a county borough council,
(d) a London borough council,
(e) the Common Council of the City of London,
(f) the Greater London Authority,
(g) a National Park authority,
(h) the Broads Authority,
(i) the Council of the Isles of Scilly,
(j) a parish council, or
(k) a community council.

(5) This section applies only to decisions made after this section comes into force, but the reference in subsection (2)(a) to anything previously done includes things done before this section comes into force.

CHAPTER 7 STANDARDS

26 Amendments of existing provisions

Schedule 4 (which amends the existing provisions relating to the conduct of local government members and employees in England and makes related provision) has effect.

27 Duty to promote and maintain high standards of conduct

(1) A relevant authority must promote and maintain high standards of conduct by members and co-opted members of the authority.

(2) In discharging its duty under subsection (1), a relevant authority must, in particular, adopt a code dealing with the conduct that is expected of members and co-opted members of the authority when they are acting in that capacity.

(3) A relevant authority that is a parish council –

- (a) may comply with subsection (2) by adopting the code adopted under that subsection by its principal authority, where relevant on the basis that references in that code to its principal authority's register are to its register, and
- (b) may for that purpose assume that its principal authority has complied with section 28(1) and (2).

(4) In this Chapter 'co-opted member', in relation to a relevant authority, means a person who is not a member of the authority but who –

- (a) is a member of any committee or sub-committee of the authority, or
- (b) is a member of, and represents the authority on, any joint committee or joint sub-committee of the authority,

and who is entitled to vote on any question that falls to be decided at any meeting of that committee or sub-committee.

(5) A reference in this Chapter to a joint committee or joint sub-committee of a relevant authority is a reference to a joint committee on which the authority is represented or a sub-committee of such a committee.

(6) In this Chapter 'relevant authority' means –

- (a) a county council in England,
- (b) a district council,
- (c) a London borough council,
- (d) a parish council,
- (e) the Greater London Authority,
- (f) the Metropolitan Police Authority,
- (g) the London Fire and Emergency Planning Authority,
- (h) the Common Council of the City of London in its capacity as a local authority or police authority,
- (i) the Council of the Isles of Scilly,
- (j) a fire and rescue authority in England constituted by a scheme under section 2 of the Fire and Rescue Services Act 2004 or a scheme to which section 4 of that Act applies,
- (k) a police authority (in England or in Wales) established under section 3 of the Police Act 1996,
- (l) a joint authority established by Part 4 of the Local Government Act 1985,
- (m) an economic prosperity board established under section 88 of the Local Democracy, Economic Development and Construction Act 2009,
- (n) a combined authority established under section 103 of that Act,
- (o) the Broads Authority, or
- (p) a National Park authority in England established under section 63 of the Environment Act 1995.

(7) Any reference in this Chapter to a member of a relevant authority –

(a) in the case of a relevant authority to which Part 1A of the Local Government Act 2000 applies, includes a reference to an elected mayor;
(b) in the case of the Greater London Authority, is a reference to the Mayor of London or a London Assembly member.

(8) Functions that are conferred by this Chapter on a relevant authority to which Part 1A of the Local Government Act 2000 applies are not to be the responsibility of an executive of the authority under executive arrangements.
(9) Functions that are conferred by this Chapter on the Greater London Authority are to be exercisable by the Mayor of London and the London Assembly acting jointly on behalf of the Authority.
(10) In this Chapter except section 35 –

(a) a reference to a committee or sub-committee of a relevant authority is, where the relevant authority is the Greater London Authority, a reference to –

(i) a committee or sub-committee of the London Assembly, or
(ii) the standards committee, or a sub-committee of that committee, established under that section,

(b) a reference to a joint committee on which a relevant authority is represented is, where the relevant authority is the Greater London Authority, a reference to a joint committee on which the Authority, the London Assembly or the Mayor of London is represented,
(c) a reference to becoming a member of a relevant authority is, where the relevant authority is the Greater London Authority, a reference to becoming the Mayor of London or a member of the London Assembly, and
(d) a reference to a meeting of a relevant authority is, where the relevant authority is the Greater London Authority, a reference to a meeting of the London Assembly;

and in subsection (4)(b) the reference to representing the relevant authority is, where the relevant authority is the Greater London Authority, a reference to representing the Authority, the London Assembly or the Mayor of London.

28 Codes of conduct

(1) A relevant authority must secure that a code adopted by it under section 27(2) (a 'code of conduct') is, when viewed as a whole, consistent with the following principles –

(a) selflessness;
(b) integrity;
(c) objectivity;
(d) accountability;
(e) openness;
(f) honesty;
(g) leadership.

(2) A relevant authority must secure that its code of conduct includes the provision the authority considers appropriate in respect of the registration in its register, and disclosure, of –

(a) pecuniary interests, and
(b) interests other than pecuniary interests.

(3) Sections 29 to 34 do not limit what may be included in a relevant authority's code of conduct, but nothing in a relevant authority's code of conduct prejudices the operation of those sections.
(4) A failure to comply with a relevant authority's code of conduct is not be dealt with

otherwise than in accordance with arrangements made under subsection (6); in particular, a decision is not invalidated just because something that occurred in the process of making the decision involved a failure to comply with the code.

(5) A relevant authority may –

(a) revise its existing code of conduct, or
(b) adopt a code of conduct to replace its existing code of conduct.

(6) A relevant authority other than a parish council must have in place –

(a) arrangements under which allegations can be investigated, and
(b) arrangements under which decisions on allegations can be made.

(7) Arrangements put in place under subsection (6)(b) by a relevant authority must include provision for the appointment by the authority of at least one independent person –

(a) whose views are to be sought, and taken into account, by the authority before it makes its decision on an allegation that it has decided to investigate, and
(b) whose views may be sought –

(i) by the authority in relation to an allegation in circumstances not within paragraph (a),
(ii) by a member, or co-opted member, of the authority if that person's behaviour is the subject of an allegation, and
(iii) by a member, or co-opted member, of a parish council if that person's behaviour is the subject of an allegation and the authority is the parish council's principal authority.

(8) For the purposes of subsection (7) –

(a) a person is not independent if the person is –

(i) a member, co-opted member or officer of the authority,
(ii) a member, co-opted member or officer of a parish council of which the authority is the principal authority, or
(iii) a relative, or close friend, of a person within sub-paragraph (i) or (ii);

(b) a person may not be appointed under the provision required by subsection (7) if at any time during the 5 years ending with the appointment the person was –

(i) a member, co-opted member or officer of the authority, or
(ii) a member, co-opted member or officer of a parish council of which the authority is the principal authority;

(c) a person may not be appointed under the provision required by subsection (7) unless –

(i) the vacancy for an independent person has been advertised in such manner as the authority considers is likely to bring it to the attention of the public,
(ii) the person has submitted an application to fill the vacancy to the authority, and
(iii) the person's appointment has been approved by a majority of the members of the authority;

(d) a person appointed under the provision required by subsection (7) does not cease to be independent as a result of being paid any amounts by way of allowances or expenses in connection with performing the duties of the appointment.

(9) In subsections (6) and (7) 'allegation', in relation to a relevant authority, means a written allegation –

(a) that a member or co-opted member of the authority has failed to comply with the authority's code of conduct, or

(b) that a member or co-opted member of a parish council for which the authority is the principal authority has failed to comply with the parish council's code of conduct.

(10) For the purposes of subsection (8) a person ('R') is a relative of another person if R is –

(a) the other person's spouse or civil partner,
(b) living with the other person as husband and wife or as if they were civil partners,
(c) a grandparent of the other person,
(d) a lineal descendant of a grandparent of the other person,
(e) a parent, sibling or child of a person within paragraph (a) or (b),
(f) the spouse or civil partner of a person within paragraph (c), (d) or (e), or
(g) living with a person within paragraph (c), (d) or (e) as husband and wife or as if they were civil partners.

(11) If a relevant authority finds that a member or co-opted member of the authority has failed to comply with its code of conduct (whether or not the finding is made following an investigation under arrangements put in place under subsection (6)) it may have regard to the failure in deciding –

(a) whether to take action in relation to the member or co-opted member, and
(b) what action to take.

(12) A relevant authority must publicise its adoption, revision or replacement of a code of conduct in such manner as it considers is likely to bring the adoption, revision or replacement of the code of conduct to the attention of persons who live in its area.

(13) A relevant authority's function of adopting, revising or replacing a code of conduct may be discharged only by the authority.

(14) Accordingly –

(a) in the case of an authority to whom section 101 of the Local Government Act 1972 (arrangements for discharge of functions) applies, the function is not a function to which that section applies;
(b) in the case of the Greater London Authority, the function is not a function to which section 35 (delegation of functions by the Greater London Authority) applies.

29 Register of interests

(1) The monitoring officer of a relevant authority must establish and maintain a register of interests of members and co-opted members of the authority.

(2) Subject to the provisions of this Chapter, it is for a relevant authority to determine what is to be entered in the authority's register.

(3) Nothing in this Chapter requires an entry to be retained in a relevant authority's register once the person concerned –

(a) no longer has the interest, or
(b) is (otherwise than transitorily on re-election or re-appointment) neither a member nor a co-opted member of the authority.

(4) In the case of a relevant authority that is a parish council, references in this Chapter to the authority's monitoring officer are to the monitoring officer of the parish council's principal authority.

(5) The monitoring officer of a relevant authority other than a parish council must secure –

(a) that a copy of the authority's register is available for inspection at a place in the authority's area at all reasonable hours, and
(b) that the register is published on the authority's website.

(6) The monitoring officer of a relevant authority that is a parish council must –

(a) secure that a copy of the parish council's register is available for inspection at a place in the principal authority's area at all reasonable hours,
(b) secure that the register is published on the principal authority's website, and
(c) provide the parish council with any data it needs to comply with subsection (7).

(7) A parish council must, if it has a website, secure that its register is published on its website.
(8) Subsections (5) to (7) are subject to section 32(2).
(9) In this Chapter 'principal authority', in relation to a parish council, means –

(a) in the case of a parish council for an area in a district that has a district council, that district council,
(b) in the case of a parish council for an area in a London borough, the council of that London borough, and
(c) in the case of a parish council for any other area, the county council for the county that includes that area.

(10) In this Chapter 'register', in relation to a relevant authority, means its register under subsection (1).

30 Disclosure of pecuniary interests on taking office

(1) A member or co-opted member of a relevant authority must, before the end of 28 days beginning with the day on which the person becomes a member or co-opted member of the authority, notify the authority's monitoring officer of any disclosable pecuniary interests which the person has at the time when the notification is given.
(2) Where a person becomes a member or co-opted member of a relevant authority as a result of re-election or re-appointment, subsection (1) applies only as regards disclosable pecuniary interests not entered in the authority's register when the notification is given.
(3) For the purposes of this Chapter, a pecuniary interest is a 'disclosable pecuniary interest' in relation to a person ('M') if it is of a description specified in regulations made by the Secretary of State and either –

(a) it is an interest of M's, or
(b) it is an interest of –

(i) M's spouse or civil partner,
(ii) a person with whom M is living as husband and wife, or
(iii) a person with whom M is living as if they were civil partners,

and M is aware that that other person has the interest.
(4) Where a member or co-opted member of a relevant authority gives a notification for the purposes of subsection (1), the authority's monitoring officer is to cause the interests notified to be entered in the authority's register (whether or not they are disclosable pecuniary interests).

31 Pecuniary interests in matters considered at meetings or by a single member

(1) Subsections (2) to (4) apply if a member or co-opted member of a relevant authority –

(a) is present at a meeting of the authority or of any committee, sub-committee, joint committee or joint sub-committee of the authority,
(b) has a disclosable pecuniary interest in any matter to be considered, or being considered, at the meeting, and
(c) is aware that the condition in paragraph (b) is met.

(2) If the interest is not entered in the authority's register, the member or co-opted member must disclose the interest to the meeting, but this is subject to section 32(3).
(3) If the interest is not entered in the authority's register and is not the subject of a pending

notification, the member or co-opted member must notify the authority's monitoring officer of the interest before the end of 28 days beginning with the date of the disclosure.

(4) The member or co-opted member may not –

(a) participate, or participate further, in any discussion of the matter at the meeting, or

(b) participate in any vote, or further vote, taken on the matter at the meeting,

but this is subject to section 33.

(5) In the case of a relevant authority to which Part 1A of the Local Government Act 2000 applies and which is operating executive arrangements, the reference in subsection (1)(a) to a committee of the authority includes a reference to the authority's executive and a reference to a committee of the executive.

(6) Subsections (7) and (8) apply if –

(a) a function of a relevant authority may be discharged by a member of the authority acting alone,

(b) the member has a disclosable pecuniary interest in any matter to be dealt with, or being dealt with, by the member in the course of discharging that function, and

(c) the member is aware that the condition in paragraph (b) is met.

(7) If the interest is not entered in the authority's register and is not the subject of a pending notification, the member must notify the authority's monitoring officer of the interest before the end of 28 days beginning with the date when the member becomes aware that the condition in subsection (6)(b) is met in relation to the matter.

(8) The member must not take any steps, or any further steps, in relation to the matter (except for the purpose of enabling the matter to be dealt with otherwise than by the member).

(9) Where a member or co-opted member of a relevant authority gives a notification for the purposes of subsection (3) or (7), the authority's monitoring officer is to cause the interest notified to be entered in the authority's register (whether or not it is a disclosable pecuniary interest).

(10) Standing orders of a relevant authority may provide for the exclusion of a member or co-opted member of the authority from a meeting while any discussion or vote takes place in which, as a result of the operation of subsection (4), the member or co-opted member may not participate.

(11) For the purpose of this section, an interest is 'subject to a pending notification' if –

(a) under this section or section 30, the interest has been notified to a relevant authority's monitoring officer, but

(b) has not been entered in the authority's register in consequence of that notification.

32 Sensitive interests

(1) Subsections (2) and (3) apply where –

(a) a member or co-opted member of a relevant authority has an interest (whether or not a disclosable pecuniary interest), and

(b) the nature of the interest is such that the member or co-opted member, and the authority's monitoring officer, consider that disclosure of the details of the interest could lead to the member or co-opted member, or a person connected with the member or co-opted member, being subject to violence or intimidation.

(2) If the interest is entered in the authority's register, copies of the register that are made available for inspection, and any published version of the register, must not include details of the interest (but may state that the member or co-opted member has an interest the details of which are withheld under this subsection).

(3) If section 31(2) applies in relation to the interest, that provision is to be read as requiring the member or co-opted member to disclose not the interest but merely the fact that the member or co-opted member has a disclosable pecuniary interest in the matter concerned.

33 Dispensations from section 31(4)

(1) A relevant authority may, on a written request made to the proper officer of the authority by a member or co-opted member of the authority, grant a dispensation relieving the member or co-opted member from either or both of the restrictions in section 31(4) in cases described in the dispensation.

(2) A relevant authority may grant a dispensation under this section only if, after having had regard to all relevant circumstances, the authority –

(a) considers that without the dispensation the number of persons prohibited by section 31(4) from participating in any particular business would be so great a proportion of the body transacting the business as to impede the transaction of the business,

(b) considers that without the dispensation the representation of different political groups on the body transacting any particular business would be so upset as to alter the likely outcome of any vote relating to the business,

(c) considers that granting the dispensation is in the interests of persons living in the authority's area,

(d) if it is an authority to which Part 1A of the Local Government Act 2000 applies and is operating executive arrangements, considers that without the dispensation each member of the authority's executive would be prohibited by section 31(4) from participating in any particular business to be transacted by the authority's executive, or

(e) considers that it is otherwise appropriate to grant a dispensation.

(3) A dispensation under this section must specify the period for which it has effect, and the period specified may not exceed four years.

(4) Section 31(4) does not apply in relation to anything done for the purpose of deciding whether to grant a dispensation under this section.

34 Offences

(1) A person commits an offence if, without reasonable excuse, the person –

(a) fails to comply with an obligation imposed on the person by section 30(1) or 31(2), (3) or (7),

(b) participates in any discussion or vote in contravention of section 31(4), or

(c) takes any steps in contravention of section 31(8).

(2) A person commits an offence if under section 30(1) or 31(2), (3) or (7) the person provides information that is false or misleading and the person –

(a) knows that the information is false or misleading, or

(b) is reckless as to whether the information is true and not misleading.

(3) A person who is guilty of an offence under this section is liable on summary conviction to a fine not exceeding level 5 on the standard scale.

(4) A court dealing with a person for an offence under this section may (in addition to any other power exercisable in the person's case) by order disqualify the person, for a period not exceeding five years, for being or becoming (by election or otherwise) a member or co-opted member of the relevant authority in question or any other relevant authority.

(5) A prosecution for an offence under this section is not to be instituted except by or on behalf of the Director of Public Prosecutions.

(6) Proceedings for an offence under this section may be brought within a period of 12

months beginning with the date on which evidence sufficient in the opinion of the prosecutor to warrant the proceedings came to the prosecutor's knowledge.

(7) But no such proceedings may be brought more than three years –

(a) after the commission of the offence, or
(b) in the case of a continuous contravention, after the last date on which the offence was committed.

(8) A certificate signed by the prosecutor and stating the date on which such evidence came to the prosecutor's knowledge is conclusive evidence of that fact; and a certificate to that effect and purporting to be so signed is to be treated as being so signed unless the contrary is proved.

(9) The Local Government Act 1972 is amended as follows.

(10) In section 86(1)(b) (authority to declare vacancy where member becomes disqualified otherwise than in certain cases) after '2000' insert 'or section 34 of the Localism Act 2011'.

(11) In section 87(1)(ee) (date of casual vacancies) –

(a) after '2000' insert 'or section 34 of the Localism Act 2011 or', and
(b) after 'decision' insert 'or order'.

(12) The Greater London Authority Act 1999 is amended as follows.

(13) In each of sections 7(b) and 14(b) (Authority to declare vacancy where Assembly member or Mayor becomes disqualified otherwise than in certain cases) after sub-paragraph (i) insert –

'(ia) under section 34 of the Localism Act 2011,'.

(14) In section 9(1)(f) (date of casual vacancies) –

(a) before 'or by virtue of' insert 'or section 34 of the Localism Act 2011', and
(b) after 'that Act' insert 'of 1998 or that section'.

35 Delegation of functions by Greater London Authority

(1) The Mayor of London and the London Assembly, acting jointly, may arrange for any of the functions conferred on them by or under this Chapter to be exercised on their behalf by –

(a) a member of staff of the Greater London Authority, or
(b) a committee appointed in accordance with provision made by virtue of this section.

(2) Standing orders of the Greater London Authority may make provision regulating the exercise of functions by any member of staff of the Authority pursuant to arrangements under subsection (1).

(3) Standing orders of the Greater London Authority may make provision for the appointment of a committee ('the standards committee') to exercise functions conferred on the Mayor of London and the London Assembly by or under this Chapter in accordance with arrangements under subsection (1).

(4) Standing orders of the Greater London Authority may make provision about the membership and procedure of the standards committee.

(5) The provision that may be made under subsection (4) includes –

(a) provision for the standards committee to arrange for the discharge of its functions by a sub-committee of that committee;
(b) provision about the membership and procedure of such a sub-committee.

(6) Subject to subsection (7), the standards committee and any sub-committee of that committee –

(a) is not to be treated as a committee or (as the case may be) sub-committee of the London Assembly for the purposes of the Greater London Authority Act 1999, but

(b) is a committee or (as the case may be) sub-committee of the Greater London Authority for the purposes of Part 3 of the Local Government Act 1974 (investigations by Commission for Local Administration in England).

(7) Sections 6(3)(a) (failure to attend meetings) and 73(6) (functions of monitoring officer) of the Greater London Authority Act 1999 apply to the standards committee or any sub-committee of that committee as they apply to a committee of the London Assembly or any sub-committee of such a committee.

(8) Part 5A of the Local Government Act 1972 (access to meetings and documents) applies to the standards committee or any sub-committee of that committee as if –

(a) it were a committee or (as the case may be) a sub-committee of a principal council within the meaning of that Part, and

(b) the Greater London Authority were a principal council in relation to that committee or sub-committee.

(9) Arrangements under this section for the exercise of any function by –

(a) a member of staff of the Greater London Authority, or

(b) the standards committee,

do not prevent the Mayor of London and the London Assembly from exercising those functions.

(10) References in this section to the functions of the Mayor of London and the London Assembly conferred by or under this Chapter do not include their functions under this section.

(11) In this section 'member of staff of the Greater London Authority' has the same meaning as in the Greater London Authority Act 1999 (see section 424(1) of that Act).

36 Amendment of section 27 following abolition of police authorities

In section 27(6) (which defines 'relevant authority' for the purposes of this Chapter) omit –

(a) paragraph (f) (the Metropolitan Police Authority), and

(b) paragraph (k) (police authorities).

37 Transitional provision

(1) An order under section 240(2) may, in particular, provide for any provision made by or under Part 3 of the Local Government Act 2000 to have effect with modifications in consequence of any partial commencement of any of the amendments to, or repeals of, provisions of that Part made by Schedule 4.

(2) An order under section 240(2) may, in particular, make provision for an allegation or a case that is being investigated under Part 3 of the Local Government Act 2000 by the Standards Board for England or an ethical standards officer –

(a) to be referred to an authority of a kind specified in or determined in accordance with the order;

(b) to be dealt with in accordance with provision made by the order.

(3) The provision that may be made by virtue of subsection (2)(b) includes –

(a) provision corresponding to any provision made by or under Part 3 of the Local Government Act 2000;

(b) provision applying any provision made by or under that Part with or without modifications.

ooo

PART 2 EU FINANCIAL SANCTIONS

48 Power to require public authorities to make payments in respect of certain EU financial sanctions

(1) A Minister of the Crown may, in accordance with the provisions of this Part, require public authorities to make payments of amounts determined by a Minister of the Crown in respect of an EU financial sanction to which this Part applies.

(2) A requirement to make a payment under this Part –

- (a) may only be imposed on a public authority if –
  - (i) the authority has been designated under section 52; and
  - (ii) the EU financial sanction concerned is one to which the designation applies; and
- (b) must be imposed by a notice given to the authority under section 56 (referred to in this Part as a final notice).

(3) If a final notice is registered in accordance with rules of court or any practice direction, it is enforceable in the same manner as an order of the High Court.

(4) Any sums paid by a public authority under this Part are to be paid into the Consolidated Fund.

(5) In this Part –

- (a) 'EU financial sanction' means a sanction consisting of a lump sum or penalty payment (or both) imposed by the Court of Justice in Article 260(2) proceedings for an infraction of EU law;
- (b) 'infraction of EU law', in relation to an EU financial sanction, means the failure to comply with a judgment of the Court of Justice given in proceedings under Article 258 or 259 of the Treaty on the Functioning of the European Union; and
- (c) 'Article 260(2) proceedings' means proceedings under Article 260(2) of that Treaty.

49 Duty of the Secretary of State to issue a policy statement

(1) The Secretary of State must publish a statement of policy with respect to –

- (a) the designation of public authorities under section 52;
- (b) the imposition and variation of requirements to make payments under this Part; and
- (c) such other matters relating to the operation of the provisions of this Part as the Secretary of State may think it appropriate to include in the statement.

(2) The Secretary of State may from time to time revise and republish the statement of policy required by this section.

(3) A revised statement of policy may include saving or transitional provisions relating to the continued application for any purpose of any provisions of an earlier published version of the statement.

(4) The Secretary of State must consult such persons as the Secretary of State considers appropriate before publishing, or revising and republishing, the statement of policy required by this section.

(5) In exercising functions under this Part in relation to an EU financial sanction which has been or may be imposed on the United Kingdom –

- (a) a Minister of the Crown, and
- (b) a panel established under section 53,

must have regard to the statement of policy most recently published under this section.

50 The EU financial sanctions to which Part 2 applies

(1) This Part applies to any EU financial sanction imposed on the United Kingdom after the commencement of this Part, subject to subsection (2).

(2) If a Minister of the Crown gives a certificate –

(a) specifying a part or parts of an EU financial sanction, and
(b) stating that this Part is not to apply to that part, or those parts, of the sanction,

this Part applies to that EU financial sanction as if it did not include that part or those parts.

(3) A certificate under subsection (2) –

(a) may make different provision about any of the following –

(i) the lump sum (if any) paid by the United Kingdom;
(ii) any periodic payment due from the United Kingdom under the terms of the EU financial sanction before the certificate is given; and
(iii) any subsequent periodic payment that may fall due from the United Kingdom under those terms; and

(b) must be given in such form and published in such manner as the Minister of the Crown giving it thinks fit.

(4) Any provision of a certificate under subsection (2) which has the effect of excluding the whole or part of any periodic payment mentioned in subsection (3)(a)(iii) (including any such payment which has fallen due from the United Kingdom since the earlier certificate was given) may be varied by a further certificate under subsection (2).

51 Meaning of 'public authority' and related terms

(1) This section defines various terms used in this Part.

(2) 'Public authority' means –

(a) a local authority to which subsection (3) applies; or
(b) any other person or body which has any non-devolved functions.

(3) This subsection applies to –

(a) any of the following in England –

(i) a county council, district council or London borough council;
(ii) the Common Council of the City of London (in its capacity as a local authority);
(iii) the Greater London Authority; and
(iv) the Council of the Isles of Scilly;

(b) a council constituted under section 2 of the Local Government etc. (Scotland) Act 1994;
(c) a district council within the meaning of the Local Government Act (Northern Ireland) 1972;
(d) a council of a county or county borough in Wales.

(4) References to functions are to functions of a public nature.

(5) References to non-devolved functions are to functions which are not devolved functions.

(6) References to devolved functions are to –

(a) Scottish devolved functions, that is to say functions the exercise of which would be within devolved competence (within the meaning of section 54 of the Scotland Act 1998);
(b) Northern Ireland devolved functions, that is to say functions which could be conferred by provision included in an Act of the Northern Ireland Assembly

made without the consent of the Secretary of State (see sections 6 to 8 of the Northern Ireland Act 1998); or

(c) Welsh devolved functions, that is to say functions which are exercisable in relation to Wales and could be conferred by provision falling within the legislative competence of the National Assembly for Wales as defined in section 108 of the Government of Wales Act 2006.

(7) References to a public authority with mixed functions are to a public authority which has both non-devolved and devolved functions.

(8) The 'appropriate national authority', in relation to a public authority with mixed functions, means the following national authority or authorities (according to whichever one or more of the following paragraphs apply to that public authority) –

(a) the Scottish Ministers, if the public authority has any Scottish devolved functions;

(b) the relevant Northern Ireland department, if the public authority has any Northern Ireland devolved functions; and

(c) the Welsh Ministers, if the public authority has any Welsh devolved functions.

52 Designation of public authorities

(1) A Minister of the Crown may by order designate a public authority for the purposes of this Part.

(2) The order must –

(a) specify the public authority by name;

(b) identify any EU financial sanction to which the designation applies; and

(c) describe the activities of the authority which are covered by the designation.

(3) The order may identify an EU financial sanction for the purposes of subsection (2)(b) by –

(a) specifying an EU financial sanction that has been imposed on the United Kingdom;

(b) specifying any Article 260(2) proceedings that have been commenced and providing that the designation is to apply to any EU financial sanction that may be imposed on the United Kingdom in those proceedings;

(c) specifying a judgment of the Court of Justice finding that the United Kingdom has failed to comply with an EU obligation and providing that the designation is to apply to any EU financial sanction that may be imposed on the United Kingdom for failing to comply with that judgment; or

(d) specifying or describing any proceedings under Article 258 or 259 of the Treaty on the Functioning of the European Union that have been or may be commenced and providing that the designation is to apply to any EU financial sanction that may be imposed on the United Kingdom for failing to comply with a judgment of the Court of Justice given in those proceedings.

(4) The order may, for the purposes of subsection (3)(d), describe any proceedings under Article 258 or 259 that may be commenced by reference to the subject-matter of –

(a) a Reasoned Opinion addressed to the United Kingdom under Article 258 or 259 (as the case may be); or

(b) any other document sent to the Government of the United Kingdom by the Commission of the European Union or by another member State which gives notice to the Government of the possibility of proceedings being commenced against the United Kingdom.

(5) The activities described for the purposes of subsection (2)(c) must be activities of the public authority which –

(a) are carried out in the exercise of non-devolved functions of the public authority; and
(b) take place after the provisions of the order describing the activities come into force.

(6) The following may not be designated under this section –

(a) the House of Commons, the House of Lords, the Scottish Parliament, the Northern Ireland Assembly or the National Assembly for Wales;
(b) a Minister of the Crown or a United Kingdom government department;
(c) a member of the Scottish Executive;
(d) the First Minister or the deputy First Minister for Northern Ireland, a Northern Ireland Minister or a Northern Ireland Department;
(e) a member of the Welsh Assembly Government;
(f) a court or tribunal.

(7) Before making an order designating a public authority a Minister of the Crown must consult –

(a) the public authority concerned; and
(b) if it is a public authority with mixed functions, the appropriate national authority.

(8) In sections 54 to 56 references to 'acts', in relation to a public authority which has been designated under this section, are to acts within a description of activities covered by the designation.

53 Establishment of independent panel

(1) This section applies where –

(a) an EU financial sanction to which this Part applies has been imposed by the Court of Justice; and
(b) at least one public authority is the subject of a designation order under section 52 which applies to that EU financial sanction.

(2) A Minister of the Crown must establish a panel for the purpose of carrying out any functions it may be given by or under any provision of this Part in relation to that EU financial sanction.
(3) The panel must be established before any warning notice is given to a public authority in relation to that EU financial sanction.
(4) The panel is to consist of one or more individuals appointed by a Minister of the Crown who appear to a Minister of the Crown to have suitable qualifications, expertise or experience to carry out their duties.
(5) A Minister of the Crown may invite nominations for appointment to the panel from such organisations as a Minister of the Crown considers appropriate.
(6) The validity of any acts of the panel is not affected by a vacancy among its members.
(7) A Minister of the Crown may pay to a member of the panel such fees, allowances or expenses as a Minister of the Crown may determine.
(8) A Minister of the Crown may provide such staff, accommodation or other facilities as a Minister of the Crown may consider necessary to enable the panel to carry out its functions.

54 Warning notices

(1) Before a public authority which has been designated under section 52 can be required to make any payment under this Part in respect of an EU financial sanction to which the designation applies –

(a) a Minister of the Crown must give a warning notice under this section to the public authority;

(b) the procedures set out in the warning notice (with any changes made under subsection (9)) must be followed; and

(c) a Minister of the Crown must determine the matters mentioned in section 55(4).

(2) A warning notice is a notice stating that a Minister of the Crown, having regard to the judgment of the Court of Justice imposing the EU financial sanction, believes –

(a) that acts of the authority may have caused or contributed to the infraction of EU law for which the EU financial sanction was imposed, and

(b) that, if acts of the authority did cause or contribute to that infraction of EU law, it would be appropriate to consider requiring the authority to make payments under this Part (which may be or include ongoing payments) in respect of the EU financial sanction.

(3) The warning notice must also –

(a) identify the EU financial sanction to which the notice relates;

(b) specify the total amount of that sanction (see subsection (7));

(c) if that sanction is or includes a penalty payment, specify the amount and frequency of any periodic payments that fall due from the United Kingdom under the terms of the penalty payment (see subsection (8));

(d) set out the reasons for making the statement required by subsection (2);

(e) set out the proposed procedures and arrangements for determining the matters mentioned in section 55(4) (which may include arrangements for securing that matters arising under the notice are dealt together with matters arising under other warning notices given to other public authorities in respect of the same EU financial sanction);

(f) propose a timetable for those procedures and for any steps to be taken by the panel or a Minister of the Crown before any requirement to make a payment can be imposed on the authority;

(g) invite the authority to make representations to a Minister of the Crown about the matters mentioned in paragraphs (e) and (f);

(h) invite the authority to make representations to the panel (with any supporting evidence) about anything the authority considers relevant to the matters mentioned in section 55(4), including its response to any representations made (and any supporting evidence submitted) to the panel –

(i) by a Minister of the Crown or a government department (whether in relation to matters arising from the notice or matters arising from any other warning notice given to another public authority in relation to the same EU financial sanction);

(ii) by another public authority which has been given a warning notice in relation to the same EU financial sanction; or

(iii) by the appropriate national authority in response to an invitation under paragraph (j) included in the notice; and

(j) if the authority has mixed functions, invite the appropriate national authority to make representations about anything contained in or arising from the notice.

(4) The warning notice may contain other such information as the Minister of the Crown giving it considers appropriate.

(5) Before a Minister of the Crown gives a warning notice to the authority, the Minister of the Crown must consult the panel as to the contents of the notice (including in particular the proposed procedures and timetable mentioned in subsection (3)(e) and (f)).

(6) If the authority has mixed functions, a Minister of the Crown must –

(a) consult the appropriate national authority before deciding to give a warning notice to the authority; and

(b) give the appropriate national authority a copy of any warning notice the Minister of the Crown decides to give.

(7) In subsection (3)(b) the 'total amount of the sanction' means the sum of the following –

(a) the amount of the lump sum (if any) due from the United Kingdom under the terms of the EU financial sanction (disregarding any amount that falls to be excluded from the lump sum by virtue of section 50(2)); and
(b) the total amount of the periodic payments (if any) which have fallen due from the United Kingdom on or before a day specified in the notice (disregarding any amount that falls to be excluded from any of those payments by virtue of section 50(2));

and the day specified for the purposes of paragraph (b) must be no later than the day on which the warning notice is given to the authority.

(8) The periodic payments to be taken into account for the purposes of subsection (3)(c) do not include –

(a) any periodic payment taken into account in calculating the total amount of the sanction for the purposes of subsection (3)(b); or
(b) any periodic payment, or any part of a periodic payment, that falls to be excluded from the EU financial sanction by virtue of section 50(2).

(9) A Minister of the Crown may, after considering any representations made by the authority under subsection (3)(g) but before the matters mentioned in section 55(4) are determined, give the authority –

(a) a notice stating any changes that the Minister has decided to make to the procedures or timetable as originally set out in the warning notice under subsection (3)(e) and (f); and
(b) a copy of the warning notice incorporating those changes.

(10) A Minister of the Crown must consult the panel before making any changes under subsection (9).

(11) A warning notice given to a public authority may be withdrawn at any time before the matters mentioned in section 55(4) are determined, but this does not prevent another warning notice being given to the authority in relation to the same EU financial sanction.

(12) In this section and section 55 'the panel' means the panel established under section 53 to deal with the EU financial sanction to which the notice relates.

55 Matters to be determined before a final notice is given

(1) This section applies where –

(a) a warning notice has been given to a public authority; and
(b) the panel has considered all representations made to it under the procedures set out in that notice.

(2) The panel must make, to a Minister of the Crown, a report on the matters to which the representations made to the panel relate.

(3) The report –

(a) may be published by the panel in such manner as the panel thinks fit and, if not published by the panel, must be published by the Minister of the Crown to whom it is made in such manner as the Minister of the Crown thinks fit;
(b) must include recommendations as to the determination of the matters mentioned in subsection (4)(a) and (b);
(c) if the authority has made representations to the panel about anything the authority considers relevant to any of the matters mentioned in paragraphs (c)

to (e) of subsection (4), must include recommendations as to the determination of the matters mentioned in those paragraphs; and

(d) must include the panel's reasons for any recommendations included in the report.

(4) After having had regard to the report, a Minister of the Crown must determine the following matters –

(a) whether any acts of the authority did cause or contribute to the infraction of EU law concerned and, in relation to any periodic payments, whether any acts of the authority have continued, and will continue, to cause or contribute to the continuation of that infraction;

(b) the proportion of –

(i) the total amount of the sanction (being the amount to be specified under section 56(2)(b) if a final notice is given), and

(ii) any periodic payments not included in that total amount (including both payments that have fallen due since the date specified under section 54(7)(b) and future periodic payments),

that, in the light of the acts of the authority which are determined to be relevant for the purposes of paragraph (a), is to be regarded as reflecting the authority's share of the responsibility for the infraction of EU law concerned or, in relation to a periodic payment mentioned in sub-paragraph (ii), the continuing infraction of EU law concerned;

(c) whether the authority should be required to make any payment or payments in respect of the EU financial sanction;

(d) if so, what payment or payments the authority should make towards –

(i) the total amount of the sanction referred to in paragraph (b)(i); and

(ii) any periodic payments referred to in paragraph (b)(ii); and

(e) when any such payment or payments should be made.

(5) In determining the matters mentioned in subsection (4)(c), (d) and (e) the Minister of the Crown must have regard to –

(a) the effect on the authority's finances of any amount it may be required to pay and in particular, if the authority has mixed functions, the need to avoid any prejudicial effect on the performance by the authority of its devolved functions;

(b) the determination under subsection (4)(b); and

(c) any other relevant considerations.

(6) Before making a final decision on the matters mentioned in subsection (4)(c), (d) and (e), the Minister of the Crown must invite –

(a) representations from the authority about the potential effect on its finances and, if it has mixed functions, the effect on its devolved functions of any amount it may be required to pay; and

(b) if the authority has mixed functions, representations from the appropriate national authority.

56 Final notices

(1) A Minister of the Crown may give a final notice to a public authority only if a Minister of the Crown has decided in accordance with section 55 to impose a requirement under this Part on the authority.

(2) The final notice must –

(a) identify the EU financial sanction to which the notice relates;

(b) specify the total amount of the sanction (see subsection (3)) and, where relevant, the amount and frequency of any future periodic payments (see subsection (4));

(c) describe the acts of the authority that a Minister of the Crown has under section 55(4) determined –

 (i) have caused or contributed to the infraction of EU law concerned; or

 (ii) have caused or contributed, or will continue to cause or contribute, to the continuation of that infraction;

and set out the reasons for that determination;

(d) summarise the other determinations made by a Minister of the Crown under section 55(4) and set out the reasons for making them;

(e) specify the amount required to be paid by the authority towards the total amount of the sanction and when it is to be paid (and if it is to be paid in instalments, the instalments and the date on which they become payable);

(f) specify the amount or proportion required to be paid towards any future periodic payment (as defined for the purposes of paragraph (b)) and the time when that amount is to be paid (or, if the notice so provides, the time when two or more such amounts are to be paid); and

(g) specify how and to whom payments are to be made.

(3) In subsection (2)(b) and (e) the 'total amount of the sanction' means the sum of the following –

(a) the amount of the lump sum (if any) due from the United Kingdom under the terms of the EU financial sanction (disregarding any amount that falls to be excluded from the lump sum by virtue of section 50(2)); and

(b) the total amount of the periodic payments (if any) which have fallen due from the United Kingdom on or before a day specified in the final notice (disregarding any amount that falls to be excluded from any of those payments by virtue of section 50(2));

and the day specified for the purposes of paragraph (b) must be no later than the day on which the final notice is given to the authority.

(4) In subsection (2)(b) 'future periodic payments' means periodic payments due from the United Kingdom other than –

(a) any periodic payment taken into account in calculating the total amount of the sanction; or

(b) any periodic payment, or any part of a periodic payment, that falls to be excluded from the EU financial sanction by virtue of section 50(2).

(5) The requirement to make payments towards periodic payments falling due from the United Kingdom after the notice is given continues so long as those periodic payments continue to fall due, unless a Minister of the Crown gives the authority a notice under this subsection terminating the requirement or varying it so as to make it less onerous for the authority.

(6) A notice under subsection (5) may be given, either on the application of the authority or without such an application, where a Minister of the Crown considers it appropriate in the light of a change in the circumstances which applied when the final notice was given or when it was last varied (as the case may be).

(7) A Minister of the Crown may –

(a) consult the panel, or refer any matter relating to the possible termination or variation of the requirement for its advice or recommendations;

(b) invite the authority to make representations; and

(c) if the authority has mixed functions, invite the appropriate national authority to make representations, before deciding whether to terminate or vary the requirement mentioned in subsection (5).

(8) If the authority makes an application under subsection (6) a Minister of the Crown may by notice to the authority suspend the requirement until further notice (but this does not affect the liability to make any payment once the suspension is ended, unless the final notice is varied to have that effect).

57 Interpretation of Part: general

In this Part –

'act' includes omission;

'the appropriate national authority', in relation to a public authority with mixed functions, has the meaning given by section 51(8);

'Article 260(2) proceedings' has the meaning given by section 48(5)(c);

'Court of Justice' means the Court of Justice of the European Union;

'EU financial sanction' has the meaning given by section 48(5)(a);

'final notice' means a notice under section 56;

'functions', 'non-devolved functions' and 'devolved functions' are to be construed in accordance with section 51;

'infraction of EU law', in relation to an EU financial sanction, has the meaning given by section 48(5)(b);

'Minister of the Crown' has the same meaning as in the Ministers of the Crown Act 1975;

'periodic payment', in relation to an EU financial sanction that is or includes a penalty payment, means a payment due under the terms of the penalty payment;

'public authority' has the meaning given in section 51(2);

'public authority with mixed functions' has the meaning given by section 51(7);

'warning notice' means a notice under section 54.

ooo

PART 5 COMMUNITY EMPOWERMENT

ooo

CHAPTER 2 COMMUNITY RIGHT TO CHALLENGE

81 Duty to consider expression of interest

(1) A relevant authority must consider an expression of interest in accordance with this Chapter if –

(a) it is submitted to the authority by a relevant body, and
(b) it is made in writing and complies with such other requirements for expressions of interest as the Secretary of State may specify by regulations.

This is subject to section 82 (timing of expressions of interest).

(2) In this Chapter 'relevant authority' means –

(a) a county council in England,
(b) a district council,
(c) a London borough council, or

(d) such other person or body carrying on functions of a public nature as the Secretary of State may specify by regulations.

(3) The persons or bodies who may be specified by regulations under subsection (2)(d) include a Minister of the Crown or a government department.

(4) In this Chapter 'expression of interest', in relation to a relevant authority, means an expression of interest in providing or assisting in providing a relevant service on behalf of the authority.

(5) In this Chapter 'relevant service', in relation to a relevant authority, means a service provided by or on behalf of that authority in the exercise of any of its functions in relation to England, other than a service of a kind specified in regulations made by the Secretary of State.

(6) In this Chapter 'relevant body' means –

(a) a voluntary or community body,
(b) a body of persons or a trust which is established for charitable purposes only,
(c) a parish council,
(d) in relation to a relevant authority, two or more employees of that authority, or
(e) such other person or body as may be specified by the Secretary of State by regulations.

(7) For the purposes of subsection (6) 'voluntary body' means a body, other than a public or local authority, the activities of which are not carried on for profit.

(8) The fact that a body's activities generate a surplus does not prevent it from being a voluntary body for the purposes of subsection (6) so long as that surplus is used for the purposes of those activities or invested in the community.

(9) For the purposes of subsection (6) 'community body' means a body, other than a public or local authority, that carries on activities primarily for the benefit of the community.

(10) The Secretary of State may by regulations –

(a) amend or repeal any of paragraphs (a) to (d) of subsection (6);
(b) amend or repeal any of subsections (7) to (9);
(c) make other amendments to this Chapter (including amendments to any power to make regulations) in consequence of provision made under subsection (2)(d) or (6)(e) or paragraph (a) or (b) of this subsection.

82 Timing of expressions of interest

(1) Subject as follows, a relevant body may submit an expression of interest to a relevant authority at any time.

(2) A relevant authority may specify periods during which expressions of interest, or expressions of interest in respect of a particular relevant service, may be submitted to the authority.

(3) The relevant authority must publish details of each specification under subsection (2) in such manner as it thinks fit (which must include publication on the authority's website).

(4) The relevant authority may refuse to consider an expression of interest submitted outside a period specified under subsection (2).

83 Consideration of expression of interest

(1) The relevant authority must –

(a) accept the expression of interest, or
(b) reject the expression of interest.

This is subject to section 84(1) (modification of expression of interest).

(2) If the relevant authority accepts the expression of interest it must carry out a procurement exercise relating to the provision on behalf of the authority of the relevant service to which the expression of interest relates.

(3) The exercise required by subsection (2) must be such as is appropriate having regard to the value and nature of the contract that may be awarded as a result of the exercise.

(4) A relevant authority must specify –

(a) the minimum period that will elapse between –

(i) the date of the relevant authority's decision to accept an expression of interest, and

(ii) the date on which it will begin the procurement exercise required by subsection (2) as a result of that acceptance, and

(b) the maximum period that will elapse between those dates.

(5) The relevant authority may specify different periods for different cases.

(6) The relevant authority must publish details of a specification under subsection (4) in such manner as it thinks fit (which must include publication on the authority's website).

(7) The relevant authority must comply with a specification under subsection (4).

(8) A relevant authority must, in considering an expression of interest, consider whether acceptance of the expression of interest would promote or improve the social, economic or environmental well-being of the authority's area.

(9) A relevant authority must, in carrying out the exercise referred to in subsection (2), consider how it might promote or improve the social, economic or environmental well-being of the authority's area by means of that exercise.

(10) Subsection (9) applies only so far as is consistent with the law applying to the awarding of contracts for the provision on behalf of the authority of the relevant service in question.

(11) The relevant authority may reject the expression of interest only on one or more grounds specified by the Secretary of State by regulations.

84 Consideration of expression of interest: further provisions

(1) A relevant authority that is considering an expression of interest from a relevant body may modify the expression of interest.

(2) A relevant authority may exercise the power in subsection (1) only if –

(a) the authority thinks that the expression of interest would not otherwise be capable of acceptance, and

(b) the relevant body agrees to the modification.

(3) A relevant authority must specify the maximum period that will elapse between –

(a) the date on which it receives an expression of interest submitted by a relevant body, and

(b) the date on which it notifies the relevant body of its decision in respect of the expression of interest.

(4) The relevant authority may specify different periods for different cases.

(5) The relevant authority must publish details of a specification under subsection (3) in such manner as it thinks fit (which must include publication on the authority's website).

(6) A relevant authority that receives an expression of interest from a relevant body in accordance with this Chapter must notify the relevant body in writing of the period within which it expects to notify the relevant body of its decision in respect of the expression of interest.

(7) The relevant authority must give the notification under subsection (6) –

(a) where the expression of interest is one to which a specification under section 82(2) relates and is made within a period so specified, within the period of 30 days beginning immediately after the end of the period so specified, or

(b) otherwise, within the period of 30 days beginning with the day on which the relevant authority receives the expression of interest.

(8) The relevant authority must –

(a) notify the relevant body in writing of its decision in respect of the expression of interest within the period specified by it under subsection (3), and

(b) if the authority's decision is to modify or reject the expression of interest, give reasons for that decision in the notification.

(9) The relevant authority must publish the notification in such manner as it thinks fit (which must include publication on the authority's website).

(10) A relevant body may withdraw an expression of interest after submitting it to a relevant authority (whether before or after a decision has been made by the authority in respect of the expression of interest).

(11) The withdrawal of an expression of interest, or the refusal of a relevant body to agree to modification of an expression of interest, does not prevent the relevant authority from proceeding as described in section 83(2) if the relevant authority thinks that it is appropriate to do so.

85 Supplementary

(1) The Secretary of State may by regulations make further provision about the consideration by a relevant authority of an expression of interest submitted by a relevant body.

(2) A relevant authority must, in exercising its functions under or by virtue of this Chapter, have regard to guidance issued by the Secretary of State.

86 Provision of advice and assistance

(1) The Secretary of State may do anything that the Secretary of State considers appropriate for the purpose of giving advice or assistance to a relevant body in relation to –

(a) the preparation of an expression of interest for submission to a relevant authority and its submission to a relevant authority,

(b) participation in a procurement exercise carried out by a relevant authority in response to an expression of interest, or

(c) the provision of a relevant service on behalf of a relevant authority following such a procurement exercise.

(2) The Secretary of State may do anything that the Secretary of State considers appropriate for the purpose of giving advice or assistance about the operation of this Chapter to a body or person other than a relevant body.

(3) The things that the Secretary of State may do under this section include, in particular –

(a) the provision of financial assistance to a relevant body;

(b) the making of arrangements with a body or person (whether or not a relevant body), including arrangements for things that may be done by the Secretary of State under this section to be done by that body or person;

(c) the provision of financial assistance to a body or person other than a relevant body in connection with arrangements under paragraph (b).

(4) In this section references to a relevant body include a body that the Secretary of State considers was formed wholly or partly by employees or former employees of the relevant authority for the purposes of, or for purposes including –

(a) participating in a procurement exercise carried out by the authority, or

(b) providing a relevant service on the authority's behalf.

(5) In this section –

(a) the reference to giving advice or assistance includes providing training or education, and

(b) any reference to the provision of financial assistance is to the provision of financial assistance by any means (including the making of a loan and the giving of a guarantee or indemnity).

CHAPTER 3 ASSETS OF COMMUNITY VALUE

List of assets of community value

87 List of assets of community value

(1) A local authority must maintain a list of land in its area that is land of community value.
(2) The list maintained under subsection (1) by a local authority is to be known as its list of assets of community value.
(3) Where land is included in a local authority's list of assets of community value, the entry for that land is to be removed from the list with effect from the end of the period of 5 years beginning with the date of that entry (unless the entry has been removed with effect from some earlier time in accordance with provision in regulations under subsection (5)).
(4) The appropriate authority may by order amend subsection (3) for the purpose of substituting, for the period specified in that subsection for the time being, some other period.
(5) The appropriate authority may by regulations make further provision in relation to a local authority's list of assets of community value, including (in particular) provision about –

(a) the form in which the list is to be kept;
(b) contents of an entry in the list (including matters not to be included in an entry);
(c) modification of an entry in the list;
(d) removal of an entry from the list;
(e) cases where land is to be included in the list and –

(i) different parts of the land are in different ownership or occupation, or
(ii) there are multiple estates or interests in the land or any part or parts of it;

(f) combination of the list with the local authority's list of land nominated by unsuccessful community nominations.

(6) Subject to any provision made by or under this Chapter, it is for a local authority to decide the form and contents of its list of assets of community value.

88 Land of community value

(1) For the purposes of this Chapter but subject to regulations under subsection (3), a building or other land in a local authority's area is land of community value if in the opinion of the authority –

(a) an actual current use of the building or other land that is not an ancillary use furthers the social wellbeing or social interests of the local community, and
(b) it is realistic to think that there can continue to be non-ancillary use of the building or other land which will further (whether or not in the same way) the social wellbeing or social interests of the local community.

(2) For the purposes of this Chapter but subject to regulations under subsection (3), a building or other land in a local authority's area that is not land of community value as a result of subsection (1) is land of community value if in the opinion of the local authority –

(a) there is a time in the recent past when an actual use of the building or other land that was not an ancillary use furthered the social wellbeing or interests of the local community, and

(b) it is realistic to think that there is a time in the next five years when there could be non-ancillary use of the building or other land that would further (whether or not in the same way as before) the social wellbeing or social interests of the local community.

(3) The appropriate authority may by regulations –

(a) provide that a building or other land is not land of community value if the building or other land is specified in the regulations or is of a description specified in the regulations;

(b) provide that a building or other land in a local authority's area is not land of community value if the local authority or some other person specified in the regulations considers that the building or other land is of a description specified in the regulations.

(4) A description specified under subsection (3) may be framed by reference to such matters as the appropriate authority considers appropriate.

(5) In relation to any land, those matters include (in particular) –

(a) the owner of any estate or interest in any of the land or in other land;
(b) any occupier of any of the land or of other land;
(c) the nature of any estate or interest in any of the land or in other land;
(d) any use to which any of the land or other land has been, is being or could be put;
(e) statutory provisions, or things done under statutory provisions, that have effect (or do not have effect) in relation to –

(i) any of the land or other land, or
(ii) any of the matters within paragraphs (a) to (d);

(f) any price, or value for any purpose, of any of the land or other land.

(6) In this section –

'legislation' means –

(a) an Act, or
(b) a Measure or Act of the National Assembly for Wales;

'social interests' includes (in particular) each of the following –

(a) cultural interests;
(b) recreational interests;
(c) sporting interests;

'statutory provision' means a provision of –

(a) legislation, or
(b) an instrument made under legislation.

89 Procedure for including land in list

(1) Land in a local authority's area which is of community value may be included by a local authority in its list of assets of community value only –

(a) in response to a community nomination, or
(b) where permitted by regulations made by the appropriate authority.

(2) For the purposes of this Chapter 'community nomination', in relation to a local authority, means a nomination which –

(a) nominates land in the local authority's area for inclusion in the local authority's list of assets of community value, and
(b) is made –

(i) by a parish council in respect of land in England in the parish council's area,
(ii) by a community council in respect of land in Wales in the community council's area, or
(iii) by a person that is a voluntary or community body with a local connection.

(3) Regulations under subsection (1)(b) may (in particular) permit land to be included in a local authority's list of assets of community value in response to a nomination other than a community nomination.
(4) The appropriate authority may by regulations make provision as to –

(a) the meaning in subsection (2)(b)(iii) of 'voluntary or community body';
(b) the conditions that have to be met for a person to have a local connection for the purposes of subsection (2)(b)(iii);
(c) the contents of community nominations;
(d) the contents of any other nominations which, as a result of regulations under subsection (1)(b), may give rise to land being included in a local authority's list of assets of community value.

(5) The appropriate authority may by regulations make provision for, or in connection with, the procedure to be followed where a local authority is considering whether land should be included in its list of assets of community value.

90 Procedure on community nominations

(1) This section applies if a local authority receives a community nomination.
(2) The authority must consider the nomination.
(3) The authority must accept the nomination if the land nominated –

(a) is in the authority's area, and
(b) is of community value.

(4) If the authority is required by subsection (3) to accept the nomination, the authority must cause the land to be included in the authority's list of assets of community value.
(5) The nomination is unsuccessful if subsection (3) does not require the authority to accept the nomination.
(6) If the nomination is unsuccessful, the authority must give, to the person who made the nomination, the authority's written reasons for its decision that the land could not be included in its list of assets of community value.

91 Notice of inclusion or removal

(1) Subsection (2) applies where land –

(a) is included in, or
(b) removed from,

a local authority's list of assets of community value.
(2) The authority must give written notice of the inclusion or removal to the following persons –

(a) the owner of the land,
(b) the occupier of the land if the occupier is not also the owner,
(c) if the land was included in the list in response to a community nomination, the person who made the nomination, and
(d) any person specified, or of a description specified, in regulations made by the appropriate authority,

but where it appears to the authority that it is not reasonably practicable to give a notice under this subsection to a person to whom it is required to be given, the authority must instead take reasonable alternative steps for the purpose of bringing the notice to the person's attention.

(3) A notice under subsection (2) of inclusion of land in the list must describe the provision made by and under this Chapter, drawing particular attention to –

(a) the consequences for the land and its owner of the land's inclusion in the list, and
(b) the right to ask for review under section 92.

(4) A notice under subsection (2) of removal of land from the list must state the reasons for the removal.

92 Review of decision to include land in list

(1) The owner of land included in a local authority's list of assets of community value may ask the authority to review the authority's decision to include the land in the list.
(2) If a request is made –

(a) under subsection (1), and
(b) in accordance with the time limits (if any) provided for in regulations under subsection (5),

the authority concerned must review its decision.
(3) Where under subsection (2) an authority reviews a decision, the authority must notify the person who asked for the review –

(a) of the decision on the review, and
(b) of the reasons for the decision.

(4) If the decision on a review under subsection (2) is that the land concerned should not have been included in the authority's list of assets of community value –

(a) the authority must remove the entry for the land from the list, and
(b) where the land was included in the list in response to a community nomination –

(i) the nomination becomes unsuccessful, and
(ii) the authority must give a written copy of the reasons mentioned in subsection (3)(b) to the person who made the nomination.

(5) The appropriate authority may by regulations make provision as to the procedure to be followed in connection with a review under this section.
(6) Regulations under subsection (5) may (in particular) include –

(a) provision as to time limits;
(b) provision requiring the decision on the review to be made by a person of appropriate seniority who was not involved in the original decision;
(c) provision as to the circumstances in which the person asking for the review is entitled to an oral hearing, and whether and by whom that person may be represented at the hearing;
(d) provision for appeals against the decision on the review.

List of land nominated by unsuccessful community nominations

93 List of land nominated by unsuccessful community nominations

(1) A local authority must maintain a list of land in its area that has been nominated by an unsuccessful community nomination (see sections 90(5) and 92(4)(b)(i)).
(2) The list maintained under subsection (1) by a local authority is to be known as its list of land nominated by unsuccessful community nominations.
(3) Where land is included in a local authority's list of land nominated by unsuccessful community nominations, the entry in the list for the land –

(a) may (but need not) be removed from the list by the authority after it has been in the list for 5 years, and

(b) while it is in the list, is to include the reasons given under section 90(6) or 92(3)(b) for not including the land in the authority's list of assets of community value.

(4) Subject to any provision made by or under this Chapter, it is for a local authority to decide the form and contents of its list of land nominated by unsuccessful community nominations.

Provisions common to both lists

94 Publication and inspection of lists

(1) A local authority must publish –

(a) its list of assets of community value, and
(b) its list of land nominated by unsuccessful community nominations.

(2) A local authority must at a place in its area make available, for free inspection by any person, both –

(a) a copy of its list of assets of community value, and
(b) a copy of its list of land nominated by unsuccessful community nominations.

(3) A local authority must provide a free copy of its list of assets of community value to any person who asks it for a copy, but is not required to provide to any particular person more than one free copy of the same version of the list.
(4) A local authority must provide a free copy of its list of land nominated by unsuccessful community nominations to any person who asks it for a copy, but is not required to provide to any particular person more than one free copy of the same version of the list.
(5) In this section 'free' means free of charge.

Moratorium on disposing of listed land

95 Moratorium

(1) A person who is an owner of land included in a local authority's list of assets of community value must not enter into a relevant disposal of the land unless each of conditions A to C is met.
(2) Condition A is that that particular person has notified the local authority in writing of that person's wish to enter into a relevant disposal of the land.
(3) Condition B is that either –

(a) the interim moratorium period has ended without the local authority having received during that period, from any community interest group, a written request (however expressed) for the group to be treated as a potential bidder in relation to the land, or
(b) the full moratorium period has ended.

(4) Condition C is that the protected period has not ended.
(5) Subsection (1) does not apply in relation to a relevant disposal of land –

(a) if the disposal is by way of gift (including a gift to trustees of any trusts by way of settlement upon the trusts),
(b) if the disposal is by personal representatives of a deceased person in satisfaction of an entitlement under the will, or on the intestacy, of the deceased person,
(c) if the disposal is by personal representatives of a deceased person in order to raise money to –

(i) pay debts of the deceased person,
(ii) pay taxes,
(iii) pay costs of administering the deceased person's estate, or

(iv) pay pecuniary legacies or satisfy some other entitlement under the will, or on the intestacy, of the deceased person,

(d) if the person, or one of the persons, making the disposal is a member of the family of the person, or one of the persons, to whom the disposal is made,

(e) if the disposal is a part-listed disposal of a description specified in regulations made by the appropriate authority, and for this purpose 'part-listed disposal' means a disposal of an estate in land –

(i) part of which is land included in a local authority's list of assets of community value, and

(ii) part of which is land not included in any local authority's list of assets of community value,

(f) if the disposal is of an estate in land on which a business is carried on and is at the same time, and to the same person, as a disposal of that business as a going concern,

(g) if the disposal is occasioned by a person ceasing to be, or becoming, a trustee,

(h) if the disposal is by trustees of any trusts –

(i) in satisfaction of an entitlement under the trusts, or

(ii) in exercise of a power conferred by the trusts to re-settle trust property on other trusts,

(i) if the disposal is occasioned by a person ceasing to be, or becoming, a partner in a partnership, or

(j) in cases of a description specified in regulations made by the appropriate authority.

(6) In subsections (3) and (4) –

'community interest group' means a person specified, or of a description specified, in regulations made by the appropriate authority,

'the full moratorium period', in relation to a relevant disposal, means the six months beginning with the date on which the local authority receives notification under subsection (2) in relation to the disposal,

'the interim moratorium period', in relation to a relevant disposal, means the six weeks beginning with the date on which the local authority receives notification under subsection (2) in relation to the disposal, and

'the protected period', in relation to a relevant disposal, means the eighteen months beginning with the date on which the local authority receives notification under subsection (2) in relation to the disposal.

(7) For the purposes of subsection (5)(d), a person ('M') is a member of the family of another person if M is –

(a) that other person's spouse or civil partner, or

(b) a lineal descendant of a grandparent of that other person.

(8) For the purposes of subsection (7)(b) a relationship by marriage or civil partnership is to be treated as a relationship by blood.

(9) For the meaning of 'relevant disposal', and for when a relevant disposal is entered into, see section 96.

96 Meaning of 'relevant disposal' etc in section 95

(1) This section applies for the purposes of section 95.

(2) A disposal of the freehold estate in land is a relevant disposal of the land if it is a disposal with vacant possession.

(3) A grant or assignment of a qualifying leasehold estate in land is a relevant disposal of the land if it is a grant or assignment with vacant possession.

(4) If a relevant disposal within subsection (2) or (3) is made in pursuance of a binding agreement to make it, the disposal is entered into when the agreement becomes binding.
(5) Subject to subsection (4), a relevant disposal within subsection (2) or (3) is entered into when it takes place.
(6) In this section 'qualifying leasehold estate', in relation to any land, means an estate by virtue of a lease of the land for a term which, when granted, had at least 25 years to run.
(7) The appropriate authority may by order amend this section.

97 Publicising receipt of notice under section 95(2)

(1) This section applies if a local authority receives notice under section 95(2) in respect of land included in the authority's list of assets of community value.
(2) The authority must cause the entry in the list for the land to reveal –

(a) that notice under section 95(2) has been received in respect of the land,
(b) the date when the authority received the notice, and
(c) the ends of the initial moratorium period, the full moratorium period and the protected period that apply under section 95 as a result of the notice.

(3) If the land is included in the list in response to a community nomination, the authority must give written notice, to the person who made the nomination, of the matters mentioned in subsection (2)(a), (b) and (c).
(4) The authority must make arrangements for those matters to be publicised in the area where the land is situated.

98 Informing owner of request to be treated as bidder

(1) Subsection (2) applies if –

(a) after a local authority has received notice under section 95(2) in respect of land included in the authority's list of assets of community value, and
(b) before the end of the interim moratorium period that applies under section 95 as a result of the notice,

the authority receives from a community interest group a written request (however expressed) for the group to be treated as a potential bidder in relation to the land.
(2) The authority must, as soon after receiving the request as is practicable, either pass on the request to the owner of the land or inform the owner of the details of the request.
(3) In this section 'community interest group' means a person who is a community interest group for the purposes of section 95(3) as a result of regulations made under section 95(6) by the appropriate authority.

99 Compensation

(1) The appropriate authority may by regulations make provision for the payment of compensation in connection with the operation of this Chapter.
(2) Regulations under subsection (1) may (in particular) –

(a) provide for any entitlement conferred by the regulations to apply only in cases specified in the regulations;
(b) provide for any entitlement conferred by the regulations to be subject to conditions, including conditions as to time limits;
(c) make provision about –

(i) who is to pay compensation payable under the regulations;
(ii) who is to be entitled to compensation under the regulations;
(iii) what compensation under the regulations is to be paid in respect of;
(iv) the amount, or calculation, of compensation under the regulations;
(v) the procedure to be followed in connection with claiming compensation under the regulations;

(vi) the review of decisions made under the regulations;
(vii) appeals against decisions made under the regulations.

Miscellaneous

100 Local land charge

If land is included in a local authority's list of assets of community value –

(a) inclusion in the list is a local land charge, and
(b) that authority is the originating authority for the purposes of the Local Land Charges Act 1975.

101 Enforcement

(1) The appropriate authority may by regulations make provision –

(a) with a view to preventing, or reducing the likelihood of, contraventions of section 95(1);
(b) as to the consequences applicable in the event of contraventions of section 95(1).

(2) The provision that may be made under subsection (1) includes (in particular) –

(a) provision for transactions entered into in breach of section 95(1) to be set aside or to be ineffective;
(b) provision about entries on registers relating to land.

(3) The provision that may be made under subsection (1) includes provision amending –

(a) legislation, or
(b) an instrument made under legislation.

(4) In subsection (3) 'legislation' means –

(a) an Act, or
(b) a Measure or Act of the National Assembly for Wales.

102 Co-operation

If different parts of any land are in different local authority areas, the local authorities concerned must co-operate with each other in carrying out functions under this Chapter in relation to the land or any part of it.

103 Advice and assistance in relation to land of community value in England

(1) The Secretary of State may do anything that the Secretary of State considers appropriate for the purpose of giving advice or assistance –

(a) to anyone in relation to doing any of the following –

(i) taking steps under or for purposes of provision contained in, or made under, this Chapter so far as applying in relation to England, or
(ii) preparing to, or considering or deciding whether to, take steps within sub-paragraph (i), or

(b) to a community interest group in relation to doing any of the following –

(i) bidding for, or acquiring, land in England that is included in a local authority's list of assets of community value,
(ii) preparing to, or considering or deciding whether or how to, bid for or acquire land within sub-paragraph (i), or
(iii) preparing to, or considering or deciding whether or how to, bring land within sub-paragraph (i) into effective use.

(2) The things that the Secretary of State may do under this section include, in particular –

(a) the provision of financial assistance to any body or other person;
(b) the making of arrangements with a body or other person, including arrangements for things that may be done by the Secretary of State under this section to be done by that body or other person.

(3) In this section –

(a) the reference to giving advice or assistance includes providing training or education,
(b) 'community interest group' means a person who is a community interest group for the purposes of section 95(3) as a result of regulations made under section 95(6) by the Secretary of State, and
(c) the reference to the provision of financial assistance is to the provision of financial assistance by any means (including the making of a loan and the giving of a guarantee or indemnity).

104 Advice and assistance in relation to land of community value in Wales

(1) The Welsh Ministers may do anything that they consider appropriate for the purpose of giving advice or assistance –

(a) to anyone in relation to doing any of the following –

(i) taking steps under or for purposes of provision contained in, or made under, this Chapter so far as applying in relation to Wales, or
(ii) preparing to, or considering or deciding whether to, take steps within sub-paragraph (i), or

(b) to a community interest group in relation to doing any of the following –

(i) bidding for, or acquiring, land in Wales that is included in a local authority's list of assets of community value,
(ii) preparing to, or considering or deciding whether or how to, bid for or acquire land within sub-paragraph (i), or
(iii) preparing to, or considering or deciding whether or how to, bring land within sub-paragraph (i) into effective use.

(2) The things that the Welsh Ministers may do under this section include, in particular –

(a) the provision of financial assistance to any body or other person;
(b) the making of arrangements with a body or other person, including arrangements for things that may be done by the Welsh Ministers under this section to be done by that body or other person.

(3) In this section –

(a) the reference to giving advice or assistance includes providing training or education,
(b) 'community interest group' means a person who is a community interest group for the purposes of section 95(3) as a result of regulations made under section 95(6) by the Welsh Ministers, and
(c) the reference to the provision of financial assistance is to the provision of financial assistance by any means (including the making of a loan and the giving of a guarantee or indemnity).

105 Crown application

This Chapter binds the Crown.

Interpretation of Chapter

106 Meaning of 'local authority'

(1) In this Chapter 'local authority' in relation to England means –

(a) a district council,
(b) a county council for an area in England for which there are no district councils,
(c) a London borough council,
(d) the Common Council of the City of London, or
(e) the Council of the Isles of Scilly.

(2) The Secretary of State may by order amend this section for the purpose of changing the meaning in this Chapter of 'local authority' in relation to England.
(3) In this Chapter 'local authority' in relation to Wales means –

(a) a county council in Wales, or
(b) a county borough council.

(4) The Welsh Ministers may by order amend this section for the purpose of changing the meaning in this Chapter of 'local authority' in relation to Wales.

107 Meaning of 'owner'

(1) In this Chapter 'owner', in relation to land, is to be read as follows.
(2) The owner of any land is the person in whom the freehold estate in the land is vested, but not if there is a qualifying leasehold estate in the land.
(3) If there is just one qualifying leasehold estate in any land, the owner of the land is the person in whom that estate is vested.
(4) If there are two or more qualifying leasehold estates in the same land, the owner of the land is the person in whom is vested the qualifying leasehold estate that is more or most distant (in terms of the number of intervening leasehold estates) from the freehold estate.
(5) In this section 'qualifying leasehold estate', in relation to any land, means an estate by virtue of a lease of the land for a term which, when granted, had at least 25 years to run.
(6) The appropriate authority may by order amend this section –

(a) for the purpose of changing the definition of 'owner' for the time being given by this section;
(b) for the purpose of defining 'owner' for the purposes of this Chapter in a case where, for the time being, this section does not define that expression.

108 Interpretation of Chapter: general

(1) In this Chapter –

'appropriate authority' –

(a) in relation to England means the Secretary of State, and
(b) in relation to Wales means the Welsh Ministers;

'building' includes part of a building;

'community nomination' has the meaning given by section 89(2);

'land' includes –

(a) part of a building,
(b) part of any other structure, and
(c) mines and minerals, whether or not held with the surface;

'land of community value' is to be read in accordance with section 88;

'local authority' is to be read in accordance with section 106;

'owner', in relation to any land, is to read in accordance with section 107;

'unsuccessful', in relation to a community nomination, has the meaning given by sections 90(5) and 92(4)(b)(i).

(2) For the meaning of 'list of assets of community value' see section 87(2).

(3) For the meaning of 'list of land nominated by unsuccessful community nominations' see section 93(2).

PART 6 PLANNING

CHAPTER 1 PLANS AND STRATEGIES

109 Abolition of regional strategies

(1) The following provisions are repealed –

(a) sections 70(5), 82(1) and (2) and 83 of the Local Democracy, Economic Development and Construction Act 2009 (interpretation and effect of regional strategies), and
(b) the remaining provisions of Part 5 of that Act (regional strategy).

(2) Subsection (1)(b) does not apply to –

(a) section 85(1) (consequential provision) of that Act,
(b) Schedule 5 to that Act (regional strategy: amendments) (but see Part 16 of Schedule 25 to this Act), or
(c) Part 4 of Schedule 7 to that Act (regional strategy: repeals).

(3) The Secretary of State may by order revoke the whole or any part of a regional strategy under Part 5 of that Act.
(4) An order under subsection (3) may, in particular, revoke all of the regional strategies (or all of the remaining regional strategies) under Part 5 of that Act.
(5) The Secretary of State may by order revoke the whole or any part of a direction under paragraph 1(3) of Schedule 8 to the Planning and Compulsory Purchase Act 2004 (directions preserving development plan policies) if and so far as it relates to a policy contained in a structure plan.
(6) An order under subsection (5) may, in particular, revoke all directions (or all remaining directions) under paragraph 1(3) of that Schedule so far as they relate to policies contained in structure plans.
(7) Schedule 8 (which contains amendments that are consequential on this section) has effect.

110 Duty to co-operate in relation to planning of sustainable development

(1) In Part 2 of the Planning and Compulsory Purchase Act 2004 (local development) after section 33 insert –

'33A Duty to co-operate in relation to planning of sustainable development

(1) Each person who is –

(a) a local planning authority,
(b) a county council in England that is not a local planning authority, or
(c) a body, or other person, that is prescribed or of a prescribed description,

must co-operate with every other person who is within paragraph (a), (b) or (c) or subsection (9) in maximising the effectiveness with which activities within subsection (3) are undertaken.

(2) In particular, the duty imposed on a person by subsection (1) requires the person –

(a) to engage constructively, actively and on an ongoing basis in any process by means of which activities within subsection (3) are undertaken, and

(b) to have regard to activities of a person within subsection (9) so far as they are relevant to activities within subsection (3).

(3) The activities within this subsection are –

(a) the preparation of development plan documents,
(b) the preparation of other local development documents,
(c) the preparation of marine plans under the Marine and Coastal Access Act 2009 for the English inshore region, the English offshore region or any part of either of those regions,
(d) activities that can reasonably be considered to prepare the way for activities within any of paragraphs (a) to (c) that are, or could be, contemplated, and
(e) activities that support activities within any of paragraphs (a) to (c),

so far as relating to a strategic matter.

(4) For the purposes of subsection (3), each of the following is a 'strategic matter' –

(a) sustainable development or use of land that has or would have a significant impact on at least two planning areas, including (in particular) sustainable development or use of land for or in connection with infrastructure that is strategic and has or would have a significant impact on at least two planning areas, and
(b) sustainable development or use of land in a two-tier area if the development or use –

(i) is a county matter, or
(ii) has or would have a significant impact on a county matter.

(5) In subsection (4) –

'county matter' has the meaning given by paragraph 1 of Schedule 1 to the principal Act (ignoring sub-paragraph 1(1)(i)),

'planning area' means –

(a) the area of –

(i) a district council (including a metropolitan district council),
(ii) a London borough council, or
(iii) a county council in England for an area for which there is no district council,

but only so far as that area is neither in a National Park nor in the Broads,

(b) a National Park,
(c) the Broads,
(d) the English inshore region, or
(e) the English offshore region, and

'two-tier area' means an area –

(a) for which there is a county council and a district council, but
(b) which is not in a National Park.

(6) The engagement required of a person by subsection (2)(a) includes, in particular –

(a) considering whether to consult on and prepare, and enter into and publish, agreements on joint approaches to the undertaking of activities within subsection (3), and

(b) if the person is a local planning authority, considering whether to agree under section 28 to prepare joint local development documents.

(7) A person subject to the duty under subsection (1) must have regard to any guidance given by the Secretary of State about how the duty is to be complied with.

(8) A person, or description of persons, may be prescribed for the purposes of subsection (1)(c) only if the person, or persons of that description, exercise functions for the purposes of an enactment.

(9) A person is within this subsection if the person is a body, or other person, that is prescribed or of a prescribed description.

(10) In this section –

'the English inshore region' and 'the English offshore region' have the same meaning as in the Marine and Coastal Access Act 2009, and

'land' includes the waters within those regions and the bed and subsoil of those waters.'

(2) In section 16 of the Planning and Compulsory Purchase Act 2004 (applying Part 2 for purposes of a county council's minerals and waste development scheme) after subsection (4) insert –

'(5) Also, subsection (3)(b) does not apply to section 33A(1)(a) and (b).'

(3) In section 20(5) of the Planning and Compulsory Purchase Act 2004 (development plan documents: purpose of independent examination) after paragraph (b) insert '; and

(c) whether the local planning authority complied with any duty imposed on the authority by section 33A in relation to its preparation.'

111 Local development schemes

(1) Section 15 of the Planning and Compulsory Purchase Act 2004 (preparation, revision and promulgation of local development schemes) is amended as follows.

(2) Omit subsection (3) (requirements as to preparation of schemes).

(3) In subsection (4) (Secretary of State or Mayor of London may direct that scheme be amended) after 'thinks appropriate' insert 'for the purpose of ensuring effective coverage of the authority's area by the development plan documents (taken as a whole) for that area'.

(4) In subsection (6A)(b) (provision about directions given by Mayor of London under subsection (4)) for 'the scheme is not to be brought into effect' substitute 'effect is not to be given to the direction'.

(5) For subsection (7) (regulations about publicity, inspection and bringing schemes into effect) substitute –

'(7) To bring the scheme into effect, the local planning authority must resolve that the scheme is to have effect and in the resolution specify the date from which the scheme is to have effect.'

(6) After subsection (8A) insert –

'(8AA) A direction may be given under subsection (8)(b) only if the person giving the direction thinks that revision of the scheme is necessary for the purpose of ensuring effective coverage of the authority's area by the development plan documents (taken as a whole) for that area.'

(7) After subsection (9) insert –

'(9A) The local planning authority must make the following available to the public –

(a) the up-to-date text of the scheme,
(b) a copy of any amendments made to the scheme, and
(c) up-to-date information showing the state of the authority's compliance (or non-compliance) with the timetable mentioned in subsection (2)(f).'

112 Adoption and withdrawal of development plan documents

(1) The Planning and Compulsory Purchase Act 2004 is amended as follows.
(2) For section 20(7) (independent examiner must make recommendations with reasons) substitute –

'(7) Where the person appointed to carry out the examination –

(a) has carried it out, and
(b) considers that, in all the circumstances, it would be reasonable to conclude –

(i) that the document satisfies the requirements mentioned in subsection (5)(a) and is sound, and
(ii) that the local planning authority complied with any duty imposed on the authority by section 33A in relation to the document's preparation,

the person must recommend that the document is adopted and give reasons for the recommendation.

(7A) Where the person appointed to carry out the examination –

(a) has carried it out, and
(b) is not required by subsection (7) to recommend that the document is adopted,

the person must recommend non-adoption of the document and give reasons for the recommendation.

(7B) Subsection (7C) applies where the person appointed to carry out the examination –

(a) does not consider that, in all the circumstances, it would be reasonable to conclude that the document satisfies the requirements mentioned in subsection (5)(a) and is sound, but
(b) does consider that, in all the circumstances, it would be reasonable to conclude that the local planning authority complied with any duty imposed on the authority by section 33A in relation to the document's preparation.

(7C) If asked to do so by the local planning authority, the person appointed to carry out the examination must recommend modifications of the document that would make it one that –

(a) satisfies the requirements mentioned in subsection (5)(a), and
(b) is sound.'

(3) For section 23(2) and (3) (adoption of development plan documents, whether as prepared or with modifications, must be in accordance with independent examiner's recommendations) substitute –

'(2) If the person appointed to carry out the independent examination of a development plan document recommends that it is adopted, the authority may adopt the document –

(a) as it is, or

(b) with modifications that (taken together) do not materially affect the policies set out in it.

(2A) Subsection (3) applies if the person appointed to carry out the independent examination of a development plan document –

(a) recommends non-adoption, and
(b) under section 20(7C) recommends modifications ('the main modifications').

(3) The authority may adopt the document –

(a) with the main modifications, or
(b) with the main modifications and additional modifications if the additional modifications (taken together) do not materially affect the policies that would be set out in the document if it was adopted with the main modifications but no other modifications.'

(4) Omit section 22(2) (development plan document not to be withdrawn once submitted for independent examination unless examiner or Secretary of State directs that it be withdrawn).
(5) In section 21 (intervention by Secretary of State) after subsection (9) insert –

'(9A) The Secretary of State may at any time –

(a) after a development plan document has been submitted for independent examination under section 20, but
(b) before it is adopted under section 23,

direct the local planning authority to withdraw the document.'

(6) The amendments made by subsections (2) and (3) apply in relation to all adoptions of development plan documents that take place after the coming into force of those subsections, including an adoption where steps in relation to the document have taken place before then.

113 Local development: monitoring reports

(1) Section 35 of the Planning and Compulsory Purchase Act 2004 (local planning authority must make annual report to Secretary of State) is amended as follows.
(2) Omit subsection (1) (duty to make annual report).
(3) In subsection (2) (contents of annual report) for 'The annual report must contain' substitute 'Every local planning authority must prepare reports containing'.
(4) In subsection (3) (rules about annual reports) for the words from the beginning to the end of paragraph (b) substitute –

'A report under subsection (2) must –

(a) be in respect of a period –

(i) which the authority considers appropriate in the interests of transparency,
(ii) which begins with the end of the period covered by the authority's most recent report under subsection (2), and
(iii) which is not longer than 12 months or such shorter period as is prescribed;'.

(5) After subsection (3) insert –

'(4) The authority must make the authority's reports under this section available to the public.'

(6) In the heading for 'Annual' substitute 'Authorities' and for 'report' substitute 'reports'.

CHAPTER 2 COMMUNITY INFRASTRUCTURE LEVY

114 Community Infrastructure Levy: approval of charging schedules

(1) The Planning Act 2008 is amended as follows.
(2) In section 211 (amount of levy) after subsection (7) insert –

'(7A) A charging authority must use appropriate available evidence to inform the charging authority's preparation of a charging schedule.
(7B) CIL regulations may make provision about the application of subsection (7A) including, in particular –

(a) provision as to evidence that is to be taken to be appropriate,
(b) provision as to evidence that is to be taken to be not appropriate,
(c) provision as to evidence that is to be taken to be available,
(d) provision as to evidence that is to be taken to be not available,
(e) provision as to how evidence is, and as to how evidence is not, to be used,
(f) provision as to evidence that is, and as to evidence that is not, to be used,
(g) provision as to evidence that may, and as to evidence that need not, be used, and
(h) provision as to how the use of evidence is to inform the preparation of a charging schedule.'

(3) For section 212(4) to (7) (draft must be accompanied by declaration of compliance with requirements, and examiner must consider the requirements and make recommendations with reasons) substitute –

'(4) In this section and sections 212A and 213 'the drafting requirements' means the requirements of this Part and CIL regulations (including the requirements to have regard to the matters listed in section 211(2) and (4)), so far as relevant to the drafting of the schedule.
(7) The examiner must consider whether the drafting requirements have been complied with and –

(a) make recommendations in accordance with section 212A, and
(b) give reasons for the recommendations.'

(4) After section 212 insert –

'212A Charging schedule: examiner's recommendations

(1) This section applies in relation to the examination, under section 212, of a draft charging schedule.
(2) If the examiner considers –

(a) that there is any respect in which the drafting requirements have not been complied with, and
(b) that the non-compliance with the drafting requirements cannot be remedied by the making of modifications to the draft,

the examiner must recommend that the draft be rejected.
(3) Subsection (4) applies if the examiner considers –

(a) that there is any respect in which the drafting requirements have not been complied with, and
(b) that the non-compliance with the drafting requirements could be remedied by the making of modifications to the draft.

(4) The examiner must –

(a) specify the respects in which the drafting requirements have not been complied with,
(b) recommend modifications that the examiner considers sufficient and necessary to remedy that non-compliance, and
(c) recommend that the draft be approved with –

(i) those modifications, or
(ii) other modifications sufficient and necessary to remedy that non-compliance.

(5) Subject to subsections (2) to (4), the examiner must recommend that the draft be approved.
(6) If the examiner makes recommendations under subsection (4), the examiner may recommend other modifications with which the draft should be approved in the event that it is approved.
(7) If the examiner makes recommendations under subsection (5), the examiner may recommend modifications with which the draft should be approved in the event that it is approved.'

(5) For section 213(1) (charging authority has to follow examiner's recommendations when approving charging schedule) substitute –

'(1) A charging authority may approve a charging schedule only if –

(a) the examiner makes recommendations under section 212A(4) or (5), and
(b) the charging authority has had regard to those recommendations and the examiner's reasons for them.

(1A) Accordingly, a charging authority may not approve a charging schedule if, under section 212A(2), the examiner recommends rejection.
(1B) If the examiner makes recommendations under section 212A(4), the charging authority may approve the charging schedule only if it does so with modifications that are sufficient and necessary to remedy the non-compliance specified under section 212A(4)(a) (although those modifications need not be the ones recommended under section 212A(4)(b)).
(1C) If a charging authority approves a charging schedule, it may do so with all or none, or some one or more, of the modifications (if any) recommended under section 212A(6) or (7).
(1D) The modifications with which a charging schedule may be approved include only –

(a) modifications required by subsection (1B), and
(b) modifications allowed by subsection (1C).'

(6) In section 213 (approval of charging schedules) after subsection (3) insert –

'(3A) Subsection (3B) applies if –

(a) the examiner makes recommendations under section 212A(4), and
(b) the charging schedule is approved by the charging authority.

(3B) The charging authority must publish a report setting out how the charging schedule as approved remedies the non-compliance specified under section 212A(4)(a).
(3C) CIL regulations may make provision about the form or contents of a report under subsection (3B).'

(7) In section 213 after subsection (4) insert –

'(5) In this section 'examiner' means examiner under section 212.'

(8) The amendments made by this section do not apply in relation to cases where an examiner submits recommendations to a charging authority before the coming into force of this section, but subject to that the cases in relation to which the amendments apply include a case in which steps in relation to the charging schedule have been taken before then.

115 Use of Community Infrastructure Levy

(1) The Planning Act 2008 is amended as follows.
(2) In section 205(2) (requirement to aim to ensure that overall purpose of the levy is to ensure that costs of providing infrastructure to support development of an area can be funded by owners or developers of land) –

(a) for 'providing infrastructure to support' substitute 'supporting', and
(b) after 'land' insert 'in a way that does not make development of the area economically unviable'.

(3) In the Table in section 205(3) (which describes the provisions of the Part) for 'Section 216' substitute 'Sections 216 to 216B'.
(4) In section 211(4) (particular provision that may be included in regulations about setting rates, or other criteria, by reference to which the amount of levy chargeable is to be determined) after paragraph (a) insert –

'(aa) to have regard, to the extent and in the manner specified by the regulations, to actual and expected costs of anything other than infrastructure that is concerned with addressing demands that development places on an area (whether by reference to lists prepared by virtue of section 216(5)(a) or otherwise);
(ab) to have regard, to the extent and in the manner specified by the regulations, to other actual and expected sources of funding for anything other than infrastructure that is concerned with addressing demands that development places on an area;'.

(5) In section 216 (application of levy) –

(a) in subsection (1) (levy to be used to fund infrastructure, or pay compensation under section 219) –

(i) for 'section' substitute 'sections 216A(1), 216B(2) and', and
(ii) for 'funding infrastructure' substitute 'supporting development by funding the provision, improvement, replacement, operation or maintenance of infrastructure',

(b) in subsection (2) (meaning of 'infrastructure' in subsection (1)) for 'subsection (1)' substitute 'this section (except subsection (3)) and sections 216A(2) and 216B(2)',
(c) in subsection (4)(a) (power to specify facilities that are to be, or not to be, funded) for 'that are to be, or not to' substitute 'whose provision, improvement or replacement may or is to be, or may not',
(d) in subsection (4) (matters that may be specified by regulations) after paragraph (a) insert –

'(aa) maintenance activities and operational activities (including operational activities of a promotional kind) in connection with infrastructure that may or are to be, or may not be, funded by CIL,
(ab) things within section 216A(2)(b) that may or are to be, or may not be, funded by CIL passed to a person in discharge of a duty under section 216A(1),
(ac) things within section 216B(2)(b) that may or are to be, or may not be, funded by CIL to which provision under section 216B(2) relates,',

(e) in subsection (4)(b) (power to specify criteria for determining areas in relation to which infrastructure may be funded) for 'in relation to which infrastructure may be funded' substitute 'that may benefit from funding',
(f) in subsection (5)(a) (power to require authorities to list projects that are to be, or may be, funded) for 'projects that are' substitute 'what is',
(g) in subsection (5)(c) (power to make provision about funding projects not on list) for 'projects' substitute 'anything',
(h) in subsection (6)(b) (regulations about funding may permit levy to be reserved for expenditure on future projects) for 'on future projects' substitute 'in the future',
(i) in subsection (6)(c) (regulations may permit funding of administrative expenses in connection with infrastructure) after 'infrastructure' insert 'or anything within section 216A(2)(b) or 216B(2)(b)', and
(j) in subsection (6)(e) (regulations may make provision for the use of funding where the projects to be funded no longer require funding) –
   (i) for 'the projects' substitute 'anything', and
   (ii) for 'require' substitute 'requires'.

(6) After section 216 insert –

'216A Duty to pass receipts to other persons

(1) CIL regulations may require that CIL received in respect of development of land in an area is to be passed by the charging authority that charged the CIL to a person other than that authority.
(2) CIL regulations must contain provision to secure that money passed to a person in discharge of a duty under subsection (1) is used to support the development of the area to which the duty relates, or of any part of that area, by funding –
   (a) the provision, improvement, replacement, operation or maintenance of infrastructure, or
   (b) anything else that is concerned with addressing demands that development places on an area.
(3) A duty under subsection (1) may relate to –
   (a) the whole of a charging authority's area or the whole of the combined area of two or more charging authorities, or
   (b) part only of such an area or combined area.
(4) CIL regulations may make provision about the persons to whom CIL may or must, or may not, be passed in discharge of a duty under subsection (1).
(5) A duty under subsection (1) may relate –
   (a) to all CIL (if any) received in respect of the area to which the duty relates, or
   (b) such part of that CIL as is specified in, or determined under or in accordance with, CIL regulations.
(6) CIL regulations may make provision in connection with the timing of payments in discharge of a duty under subsection (1).
(7) CIL regulations may, in relation to CIL passed to a person in discharge of a duty under subsection (1), make provision about –
   (a) accounting for the CIL,
   (b) monitoring its use,
   (c) reporting on its use,
   (d) responsibilities of charging authorities for things done by the person in connection with the CIL,

(e) recovery of the CIL, and any income or profits accruing in respect of it or from its application, in cases where –

(i) anything to be funded by it has not been provided, or
(ii) it has been misapplied,

including recovery of sums or other assets representing it or any such income or profits, and

(f) use of anything recovered in cases where –

(i) anything to be funded by the CIL has not been provided, or
(ii) the CIL has been misapplied.

(8) This section does not limit section 216(7)(f).

216B Use of CIL in an area to which section 216A(1) duty does not relate

(1) Subsection (2) applies where –

(a) there is an area to which a particular duty under section 216A(1) relates, and
(b) there is also an area to which that duty does not relate ('the uncovered area').

(2) CIL regulations may provide that the charging authority that charges CIL received in respect of development of land in the uncovered area may apply the CIL, or cause it to be applied, to –

(a) support development by funding the provision, improvement, replacement, operation or maintenance of infrastructure, or
(b) support development of the uncovered area, or of any part of that area, by funding anything else that is concerned with addressing demands that development places on an area.

(3) Provision under subsection (2) may relate to the whole, or part only, of the uncovered area.

(4) Provision under subsection (2) may relate –

(a) to all CIL (if any) received in respect of the area to which the provision relates, or
(b) such part of that CIL as is specified in, or determined under or in accordance with, CIL regulations.'

CHAPTER 3 NEIGHBOURHOOD PLANNING

116 Neighbourhood planning

(1) Schedule 9 (which makes provision about neighbourhood development orders and neighbourhood development plans) has effect.
(2) After Schedule 4A to the Town and Country Planning Act 1990 insert the Schedule 4B set out in Schedule 10 to this Act.
(3) After the inserted Schedule 4B to that Act insert the Schedule 4C set out in Schedule 11 to this Act.

117 Charges for meeting costs relating to neighbourhood planning

(1) The Secretary of State may with the consent of the Treasury make regulations providing for the imposition of charges for the purpose of meeting expenses incurred (or expected to be incurred) by local planning authorities in, or in connection with, the exercise of their neighbourhood planning functions.

(2) A local planning authority's 'neighbourhood planning functions' are any of their functions exercisable under any provision made by or under –

(a) any of sections 61E to 61Q of, or Schedule 4B or 4C to, the Town and Country Planning Act 1990 (neighbourhood development orders),
(b) any of sections 38A to 38C of the Planning and Compulsory Purchase Act 2004 (neighbourhood development plans), or
(c) this section.

(3) The regulations must secure –

(a) that the charges are payable in relation to development for which planning permission is granted by a neighbourhood development order made under section 61E of the Town and Country Planning Act 1990,
(b) that the charges become payable when the development is commenced (determined in accordance with the regulations), and
(c) that the charges are payable to local planning authorities.

(4) The regulations may authorise local planning authorities to set the amount of charges imposed by the regulations; and, if so, the regulations may –

(a) provide for the charges not to be payable at any time unless at that time a document (a 'charging document') has been published by the authority setting out the amounts chargeable under the regulations in relation to development in their area,
(b) make provision about the approval and publication of a charging document,
(c) prescribe matters to which the authorities must have regard in setting the charges,
(d) require the authorities, in setting the charges, to disregard such expenditure expected to be incurred as mentioned in subsection (1) as falls within a description prescribed by the regulations,
(e) authorise the authorities to set different charges for different cases, circumstances or areas (either generally or only to the extent specified in the regulations), and
(f) authorise the authorities to make exceptions (either generally or only to the extent specified in the regulations).

(5) The regulations must make provision about liability to pay a charge imposed by the regulations.
(6) The regulations may make provision –

(a) enabling any person to assume (in accordance with any procedural provision made by the regulations) the liability to pay a charge imposed by the regulations before it becomes payable,
(b) about assumption of partial liability,
(c) about the withdrawal of assumption of liability,
(d) about the cancellation by a local planning authority of assumption of liability,
(e) for the owner or developer of land to be liable to pay the charge in cases prescribed by the regulations,
(f) about joint liability (with or without several liability),
(g) about liability of partnerships,
(h) about apportionment of liability, including provision for referral to a specified body or other person for determination and provision for appeals, and
(i) about transfer of liability (whether before or after the charge becomes due and whether or not liability has been assumed).

(7) In subsection (6)(e) –

(a) 'owner' of land means a person who owns an interest in land, and

(b) 'developer' means a person who is wholly or partly responsible for carrying out a development.

(8) The provision for appeals that may be made as a result of subsection (6)(h) includes provision about –

(a) the period within which the right of appeal may be exercised,
(b) the procedure on appeals, and
(c) the payment of fees, and award of costs, in relation to appeals (including provision requiring local planning authorities to bear expenses incurred in connection with appeals).

118 Regulations under section 117: collection and enforcement

(1) Regulations under section 117 must include provision about the collection of charges imposed by the regulations.
(2) The regulations may make provision –

(a) for payment on account or by instalments,
(b) about repayment (with or without interest) in cases of overpayment, and
(c) about the source of payments in respect of a Crown interest or Duchy interest (within the meaning of section 227(3) or (4) of the Planning Act 2008).

(3) Regulations under section 117 must include provision about enforcement of charges imposed by the regulations; and that provision must include provision –

(a) for a charge (or other amount payable under the regulations) to be treated as a civil debt due to a local planning authority, and
(b) for the debt to be recoverable summarily.

(4) The regulations may make provision –

(a) about the consequences of failure to assume liability, to give a notice or to comply with another procedure under the regulations,
(b) for the payment of interest (at a rate specified in, or determined in accordance with, the regulations),
(c) for the imposition of a penalty or surcharge (of an amount specified in, or determined in accordance with, the regulations),
(d) replicating or applying (with or without modifications) any provision made by any of sections 324 to 325A of the Town and Country Planning Act 1990 (rights of entry), and
(e) for enforcement in the case of death or insolvency of a person liable for the charge.

119 Regulations under section 117: supplementary

(1) Regulations under section 117 may make provision about procedures to be followed in connection with charges imposed by the regulations.
(2) The regulations may make provision about –

(a) procedures to be followed by a local planning authority proposing to start or stop imposing a charge,
(b) procedures to be followed by a local planning authority in relation to the imposition of a charge,
(c) the arrangements of a local planning authority for the making of any decision prescribed by the regulations,
(d) consultation,
(e) the publication or other treatment of reports,
(f) timing and methods of publication,
(g) making documents available for inspection,
(h) providing copies of documents (with or without charge),

(i) the form and content of documents,
(j) giving notice,
(k) serving notices or other documents, and
(l) procedures to be followed in connection with actual or potential liability for a charge.

(3) Provision made by the regulations as a result of subsection (2)(c) is to have effect despite provision made by any enactment as to the arrangements of a local planning authority for the exercise of their functions (such as section 101 of the Local Government Act 1972 or section 13 of the Local Government Act 2000).
(4) Regulations under section 117 may make provision binding the Crown.
(5) Regulations under section 117 may make –

(a) provision applying any enactment (with or without modifications), and
(b) provision for exceptions.

(6) A local planning authority must have regard to any guidance issued by the Secretary of State in the exercise of any of their functions under regulations under section 117.
(7) For the purposes of sections 117 and 118 and this section 'local planning authority' means an authority that have made or have power to make –

(a) a neighbourhood development order under section 61E of the Town and Country Planning Act 1990, or
(b) a neighbourhood development plan under section 38A of the Planning and Compulsory Purchase Act 2004.

(8) Nothing in section 117, 118 or this section that authorises the inclusion of any particular kind of provision in regulations under section 117 is to be read as restricting the generality of the provision that may be included in the regulations.

120 Financial assistance in relation to neighbourhood planning

(1) The Secretary of State may do anything that the Secretary of State considers appropriate –

(a) for the purpose of publicising or promoting the making of neighbourhood development orders or neighbourhood development plans and the benefits expected to arise from their making, or
(b) for the purpose of giving advice or assistance to anyone in relation to the making of proposals for such orders or plans or the doing of anything else for the purposes of, or in connection with, such proposals or such orders or plans.

(2) The things that the Secretary of State may do under this section include, in particular –

(a) the provision of financial assistance (or the making of arrangements for its provision) to any body or other person, and
(b) the making of agreements or other arrangements with any body or other person (under which payments may be made to the person).

(3) In this section –

(a) the reference to giving advice or assistance includes providing training or education,
(b) any reference to the provision of financial assistance is to the provision of financial assistance by any means (including the making of a loan and the giving of a guarantee or indemnity),
(c) any reference to a neighbourhood development order is to a neighbourhood development order under section 61E of the Town and Country Planning Act 1990, and
(d) any reference to a neighbourhood development plan is to a neighbourhood development plan under section 38A of the Planning and Compulsory Purchase Act 2004.

121 Consequential amendments

Schedule 12 (neighbourhood planning: consequential amendments) has effect.

CHAPTER 4 CONSULTATION

122 Consultation before applying for planning permission

(1) In the Town and Country Planning Act 1990, before section 62 (and before the italic heading which precedes that section) insert –

'*Consultation before applying for planning permission*

61W Requirement to carry out pre-application consultation

(1) Where –

(a) a person proposes to make an application for planning permission for the development of any land in England, and
(b) the proposed development is of a description specified in a development order,

the person must carry out consultation on the proposed application in accordance with subsections (2) and (3).
(2) The person must publicise the proposed application in such manner as the person reasonably considers is likely to bring the proposed application to the attention of a majority of the persons who live at, or otherwise occupy, premises in the vicinity of the land.
(3) The person must consult each specified person about the proposed application.
(4) Publicity under subsection (2) must –

(a) set out how the person ('P') may be contacted by persons wishing to comment on, or collaborate with P on the design of, the proposed development, and
(b) give such information about the proposed timetable for the consultation as is sufficient to ensure that persons wishing to comment on the proposed development may do so in good time.

(5) In subsection (3) 'specified person' means a person specified in, or of a description specified in, a development order.
(6) Subsection (1) does not apply –

(a) if the proposed application is an application under section 293A, or
(b) in cases specified in a development order.

(7) A person subject to the duty imposed by subsection (1) must, in complying with that subsection, have regard to the advice (if any) given by the local planning authority about local good practice.

61X Duty to take account of responses to consultation

(1) Subsection (2) applies where a person –

(a) has been required by section 61W(1) to carry out consultation on a proposed application for planning permission, and
(b) proposes to go ahead with making an application for planning permission (whether or not in the same terms as the proposed application).

(2) The person must, when deciding whether the application that the person is

actually to make should be in the same terms as the proposed application, have regard to any responses to the consultation that the person has received.

61Y Power to make supplementary provision

(1) A development order may make provision about, or in connection with, consultation which section 61W(1) requires a person to carry out on a proposed application for planning permission.

(2) The provision that may be made under subsection (1) includes (in particular) –

(a) provision about, or in connection with, publicising the proposed application;
(b) provision about, or in connection with, the ways of responding to the publicity;
(c) provision about, or in connection with, consultation under section 61W(3);
(d) provision about, or in connection with, collaboration between the person and others on the design of the proposed development;
(e) provision as to the timetable (including deadlines) for –

(i) compliance with section 61W(1),
(ii) responding to publicity under section 61W(2), or
(iii) responding to consultation under section 61W(3);

(f) provision for the person to prepare a statement setting out how the person proposes to comply with section 61W(1);
(g) provision for the person to comply with section 61W(1) in accordance with a statement required by provision under paragraph (f).

(3) Provision under subsection (1) may be different for different cases.'

(2) In section 62 of the Town and Country Planning Act 1990 (applications for planning permission) after subsection (6) insert –

'(7) In subsection (8) 'a relevant application' means the application for planning permission in a case where a person –

(a) has been required by section 61W(1) to carry out consultation on a proposed application for planning permission, and
(b) is going ahead with making an application for planning permission (whether or not in the same terms as the proposed application).

(8) A development order must require that a relevant application be accompanied by particulars of –

(a) how the person complied with section 61W(1),
(b) any responses to the consultation that were received by the person, and
(c) the account taken of those responses.'

(3) The amendments made by subsections (1) and (2) cease to have effect at the end of 7 years beginning with the day on which the inserted section 61W(1) comes fully into force, but this is subject to subsection (4).

(4) The Secretary of State may by order provide that the amendments are, instead of ceasing to have effect at the time they would otherwise cease to have effect, to cease to have effect at the end of a period of not more than 7 years from that time.

CHAPTER 5 ENFORCEMENT

123 Retrospective planning permission

(1) The Town and Country Planning Act 1990 is amended as follows.

(2) After section 70B insert –

'70C **Power to decline to determine retrospective application**

(1) A local planning authority in England may decline to determine an application for planning permission for the development of any land if granting planning permission for the development would involve granting, whether in relation to the whole or any part of the land to which a pre-existing enforcement notice relates, planning permission in respect of the whole or any part of the matters specified in the enforcement notice as constituting a breach of planning control.

(2) For the purposes of the operation of this section in relation to any particular application for planning permission, a 'pre-existing enforcement notice' is an enforcement notice issued before the application was received by the local planning authority.'

(3) In section 78(2)(aa) (which refers to an authority not having given notice that it has exercised its power under section 70A or 70B to decline to determine an application) after 'or 70B' insert 'or 70C'.

(4) In section 174 (appeal against enforcement notice) after subsection (2) insert –

'(2A) An appeal may not be brought on the ground specified in subsection (2)(a) if –

(a) the land to which the enforcement notice relates is in England, and
(b) the enforcement notice was issued at a time –

(i) after the making of a related application for planning permission, but
(ii) before the end of the period applicable under section 78(2) in the case of that application.

(2B) An application for planning permission for the development of any land is, for the purposes of subsection (2A), related to an enforcement notice if granting planning permission for the development would involve granting planning permission in respect of the matters specified in the enforcement notice as constituting a breach of planning control.'

(5) In section 177 (grant or modification of planning permission on appeals against enforcement notice) after subsection (1B) insert –

'(1C) If the land to which the enforcement notice relates is in England, subsection (1)(a) applies only if the statement under section 174(4) specifies the ground mentioned in section 174(2)(a).'

(6) In section 177(5) (deemed application for planning permission where appeal brought against enforcement notice) for the words from the beginning to 'the appellant' substitute –

'Where an appeal against an enforcement notice is brought under section 174 and –

(a) the land to which the enforcement notice relates is in Wales, or
(b) that land is in England and the statement under section 174(4) specifies the ground mentioned in section 174(2)(a),

the appellant'.

124 Time limits for enforcing concealed breaches of planning control

(1) In the Town and Country Planning Act 1990 after section 171B insert –

'171BA Time limits in cases involving concealment

(1) Where it appears to the local planning authority that there may have been a breach of planning control in respect of any land in England, the authority may apply to a magistrates' court for an order under this subsection (a 'planning enforcement order') in relation to that apparent breach of planning control.

(2) If a magistrates' court makes a planning enforcement order in relation to an apparent breach of planning control, the local planning authority may take enforcement action in respect of –

(a) the apparent breach, or
(b) any of the matters constituting the apparent breach,

at any time in the enforcement year.

(3) 'The enforcement year' for a planning enforcement order is the year that begins at the end of 22 days beginning with the day on which the court's decision to make the order is given, but this is subject to subsection (4).

(4) If an application under section 111(1) of the Magistrates' Courts Act 1980 (statement of case for opinion of High Court) is made in respect of a planning enforcement order, the enforcement year for the order is the year beginning with the day on which the proceedings arising from that application are finally determined or withdrawn.

(5) Subsection (2) –

(a) applies whether or not the time limits under section 171B have expired, and
(b) does not prevent the taking of enforcement action after the end of the enforcement year but within those time limits.

171BB Planning enforcement orders: procedure

(1) An application for a planning enforcement order in relation to an apparent breach of planning control may be made within the 6 months beginning with the date on which evidence of the apparent breach of planning control sufficient in the opinion of the local planning authority to justify the application came to the authority's knowledge.

(2) For the purposes of subsection (1), a certificate –

(a) signed on behalf of the local planning authority, and
(b) stating the date on which evidence sufficient in the authority's opinion to justify the application came to the authority's knowledge,

is conclusive evidence of that fact.

(3) A certificate stating that matter and purporting to be so signed is to be deemed to be so signed unless the contrary is proved.

(4) Where the local planning authority apply to a magistrates' court for a planning enforcement order in relation to an apparent breach of planning control in respect of any land, the authority must serve a copy of the application –

(a) on the owner and on the occupier of the land, and
(b) on any other person having an interest in the land that is an interest which, in the opinion of the authority, would be materially affected by the taking of enforcement action in respect of the apparent breach.

(5) The persons entitled to appear before, and be heard by, the court hearing an application for a planning enforcement order in relation to an apparent breach of planning control in respect of any land include –

(a) the applicant,
(b) any person on whom a copy of the application was served under subsection (4), and
(c) any other person having an interest in the land that is an interest which, in the opinion of the court, would be materially affected by the taking of enforcement action in respect of the apparent breach.

(6) In this section 'planning enforcement order' means an order under section 171BA(1).

171BC Making a planning enforcement order

(1) A magistrates' court may make a planning enforcement order in relation to an apparent breach of planning control only if –

(a) the court is satisfied, on the balance of probabilities, that the apparent breach, or any of the matters constituting the apparent breach, has (to any extent) been deliberately concealed by any person or persons, and
(b) the court considers it just to make the order having regard to all the circumstances.

(2) A planning enforcement order must –

(a) identify the apparent breach of planning control to which it relates, and
(b) state the date on which the court's decision to make the order was given.

(3) In this section 'planning enforcement order' means an order under section 171BA(1).'

(2) In section 188 of the Town and Country Planning Act 1990 (register of enforcement and stop notices) –

(a) in subsection (1) (matters to which registers apply) before paragraph (a) insert –

'(za) to planning enforcement orders,',

(b) in subsection (2)(a) (development order may make provision about removal of entries from register) –

(i) before 'enforcement notice' insert 'planning enforcement order,',
(ii) before 'any such notice' insert 'any planning enforcement order or', and
(iii) after 'specified in the' insert 'development',

(c) in subsection (2)(b) (development order may make provision about supply of information by county planning authority) after 'served by' insert ', and planning enforcement orders made on applications made by,',
(d) after subsection (3) insert –

'(4) In this section 'planning enforcement order' means an order under section 171BA(1).', and

(e) in the heading after 'and stop notices' insert 'and other enforcement action'.

(3) In section 191 of the Town and Country Planning Act 1990 (certificate of lawfulness of existing use or development) after subsection (3) insert –

'(3A) In determining for the purposes of this section whether the time for taking enforcement action in respect of a matter has expired, that time is to be taken not to have expired if –

(a) the time for applying for an order under section 171BA(1) (a 'planning enforcement order') in relation to the matter has not expired,
(b) an application has been made for a planning enforcement order in relation to the matter and the application has neither been decided nor been withdrawn, or
(c) a planning enforcement order has been made in relation to the matter, the order has not been rescinded and the enforcement year for the order (whether or not it has begun) has not expired.'

125 Assurance as regards prosecution for person served with enforcement notice

In the Town and Country Planning Act 1990 after section 172 (issue and service of enforcement notice) insert –

'172A Assurance as regards prosecution for person served with notice

(1) When, or at any time after, an enforcement notice is served on a person, the local planning authority may give the person a letter –

(a) explaining that, once the enforcement notice had been issued, the authority was required to serve the notice on the person,
(b) giving the person one of the following assurances –

(i) that, in the circumstances as they appear to the authority, the person is not at risk of being prosecuted under section 179 in connection with the enforcement notice, or
(ii) that, in the circumstances as they appear to the authority, the person is not at risk of being prosecuted under section 179 in connection with the matters relating to the enforcement notice that are specified in the letter,

(c) explaining, where the person is given the assurance under paragraph (b)(ii), the respects in which the person is at risk of being prosecuted under section 179 in connection with the enforcement notice, and
(d) stating that, if the authority subsequently wishes to withdraw the assurance in full or part, the authority will first give the person a letter specifying a future time for the withdrawal that will allow the person a reasonable opportunity to take any steps necessary to avoid any risk of prosecution that is to cease to be covered by the assurance.

(2) At any time after a person has under subsection (1) been given a letter containing an assurance, the local planning authority may give the person a letter withdrawing the assurance (so far as not previously withdrawn) in full or part from a time specified in the letter.
(3) The time specified in a letter given under subsection (2) to a person must be such as will give the person a reasonable opportunity to take any steps necessary to avoid any risk of prosecution that is to cease to be covered by the assurance.
(4) Withdrawal under subsection (2) of an assurance given under subsection (1) does not withdraw the assurance so far as relating to prosecution on account of there being a time before the withdrawal when steps had not been taken or an activity had not ceased.
(5) An assurance given under subsection (1) (so far as not withdrawn under subsection (2)) is binding on any person with power to prosecute an offence under section 179.'

126 Planning offences: time limits and penalties

(1) The Town and Country Planning Act 1990 is amended as follows.

(2) In section 187A(12) (maximum penalty of level 3 on standard scale for offence of being in breach of a breach of condition notice) for 'fine not exceeding level 3 on the standard scale' substitute 'fine –

(a) not exceeding level 4 on the standard scale if the land is in England;
(b) not exceeding level 3 on the standard scale if the land is in Wales'.

(3) In section 210 (penalties for non-compliance with tree preservation regulations) after subsection (4) insert –

'(4A) Proceedings for an offence under subsection (4) may be brought within the period of 6 months beginning with the date on which evidence sufficient in the opinion of the prosecutor to justify the proceedings came to the prosecutor's knowledge.
(4B) Subsection (4A) does not authorise the commencement of proceedings for an offence more than 3 years after the date on which the offence was committed.
(4C) For the purposes of subsection (4A), a certificate –

(a) signed by or on behalf of the prosecutor, and
(b) stating the date on which evidence sufficient in the prosecutor's opinion to justify the proceedings came to the prosecutor's knowledge,

is conclusive evidence of that fact.
(4D) A certificate stating that matter and purporting to be so signed is to be deemed to be so signed unless the contrary is proved.
(4E) Subsection (4A) does not apply in relation to an offence in respect of a tree in Wales.'

(4) In section 224 (enforcement of control as to advertisements) after subsection (6) insert –

'(7) Proceedings for an offence under subsection (3) may be brought within the period of 6 months beginning with the date on which evidence sufficient in the opinion of the prosecutor to justify the proceedings came to the prosecutor's knowledge.
(8) Subsection (7) does not authorise the commencement of proceedings for an offence more than 3 years after the date on which the offence was committed.
(9) For the purposes of subsection (7), a certificate –

(a) signed by or on behalf of the prosecutor, and
(b) stating the date on which evidence sufficient in the prosecutor's opinion to justify the proceedings came to the prosecutor's knowledge,

is conclusive evidence of that fact.
(10) A certificate stating that matter and purporting to be so signed is to be deemed to be so signed unless the contrary is proved.
(11) Subsection (7) does not apply in relation to an offence in respect of an advertisement in Wales.'

(5) An amendment made by this section applies only in relation to offences committed after the amendment has come into force.

127 Powers in relation to: unauthorised advertisements; defacement of premises

(1) In Part 8 of the Town and Country Planning Act 1990 (special controls) in Chapter 3 (advertisements) after section 225 insert –

'225A Power to remove structures used for unauthorised display

(1) Subject to subsections (2), (3) and (5) and the right of appeal under section 225B, the local planning authority for an area in England may remove, and then dispose of, any display structure –

(a) which is in their area; and
(b) which, in the local planning authority's opinion, is used for the display of advertisements in contravention of regulations under section 220.

(2) Subsection (1) does not authorise the removal of a display structure in a building to which there is no public right of access.
(3) The local planning authority may not under subsection (1) remove a display structure unless the local planning authority have first served a removal notice on a person who appears to the local planning authority to be responsible for the erection or maintenance of the display structure.
(4) Subsection (3) applies only if there is a person –

(a) who appears to the local planning authority to be responsible for the erection or maintenance of the display structure; and
(b) whose name and address are either known by the local planning authority or could be ascertained by the local planning authority after reasonable enquiry.

(5) If subsection (3) does not apply, the local planning authority may not under subsection (1) remove a display structure unless the local planning authority have first –

(a) fixed a removal notice to the display structure or exhibited a removal notice in the vicinity of the display structure; and
(b) served a copy of that notice on the occupier of the land on which the display structure is situated.

(6) Subsection (5)(b) applies only if the local planning authority know who the occupier is or could identify the occupier after reasonable enquiry.
(7) Where –

(a) the local planning authority has served a removal notice in accordance with subsection (3) or (5)(b), and
(b) the display structure is not removed by the time specified in the removal notice,

the local planning authority may recover, from any person on whom the removal notice has been served under subsection (3) or (5)(b), expenses reasonably incurred by the local planning authority in exercising the local planning authority's power under subsection (1).
(8) Expenses are not recoverable under subsection (7) from a person if the person satisfies the local planning authority that the person was not responsible for the erection of the display structure and is not responsible for its maintenance.
(9) Where in the exercise of power under subsection (1) any damage is caused to land or chattels, compensation may be recovered by any person suffering the damage from the local planning authority exercising the power, but compensation is not recoverable under this subsection or section 325(6) –

(a) for damage caused to the display structure; or
(b) for damage reasonably caused in removing the display structure.

(10) The provisions of section 118 apply in relation to compensation under subsection (9) as they apply in relation to compensation under Part 4.

(11) In this section 'removal notice', in relation to a display structure, means notice –

(a) stating that in the local planning authority's opinion the display structure is used for the display of advertisements in contravention of regulations under section 220;
(b) stating that the local planning authority intend after a time specified in the notice to remove the display structure; and
(c) stating the effect of subsections (7) and (8).

(12) A time specified under subsection (11)(b) may not be earlier than the end of 22 days beginning with the date of the notice.

(13) In this section 'display structure' means (subject to subsection (14)) –

(a) a hoarding or similar structure used, or designed or adapted for use, for the display of advertisements;
(b) anything (other than a hoarding or similar structure) principally used, or designed or adapted principally for use, for the display of advertisements;
(c) a structure that is itself an advertisement; or
(d) fitments used to support anything within any of paragraphs (a) to (c).

(14) Something is a 'display structure' for the purpose of this section only if –

(a) its use for the display of advertisement requires consent under this Chapter, and
(b) that consent has not been granted and is not deemed to have been granted.

(15) In subsection (13) 'structure' includes movable structure.

225B Appeal against notice under section 225A

(1) A person on whom a removal notice has been served in accordance with section 225A(3) or (5)(b) may appeal to a magistrates' court on any of the following grounds –

(a) that the display structure concerned is not used for the display of advertisements in contravention of regulations under section 220;
(b) that there has been some informality, defect or error in, or in connection with, the notice;
(c) that the period between the date of the notice and the time specified in the notice is not reasonably sufficient for the removal of the display structure;
(d) that the notice should have been served on another person.

(2) For the purposes of subsection (3), a person is a 'permitted appellant' in relation to a removal notice if –

(a) the removal notice has been fixed or exhibited in accordance with section 225A(5)(a);
(b) the person is an owner or occupier of the land on which the display structure concerned is situated; and
(c) no copy of the removal notice has been served on the person in accordance with section 225A(5)(b).

(3) A person who is a permitted appellant in relation to a removal notice may appeal to a magistrates' court on any of the following grounds –

(a) that the display structure concerned is not used for the display of advertisements in contravention of regulations under section 220;

(b) that there has been some informality, defect or error in, or in connection with, the notice;

(c) that the period between the date of the notice and the time specified in the notice is not reasonably sufficient for the removal of the display structure.

(4) So far as an appeal under this section is based on the ground mentioned in subsection (1)(b) or (3)(b), the court must dismiss the appeal if it is satisfied that the informality, defect or error was not a material one.

(5) If an appeal under subsection (1) is based on the ground mentioned in subsection (1)(d), the appellant must serve a copy of the notice of appeal on each person who the appellant considers is a person on whom the removal notice should have been served in accordance with section 225A(3) or (5)(b).

(6) If –

(a) a removal notice is served on a person in accordance with section 225A(3) or (5)(b), and

(b) the local planning authority bring proceedings against the person for the recovery under section 225A(7) of any expenses,

it is not open to the person to raise in the proceedings any question which the person could have raised in an appeal under subsection (1).

(7) In this section 'removal notice' and 'display structure' have the same meaning as in section 225A.

225C Remedying persistent problems with unauthorised advertisements

(1) Subsections (2) and (3) apply if the local planning authority for an area in England have reason to believe that there is a persistent problem with the display of unauthorised advertisements on a surface of –

(a) any building, wall, fence or other structure or erection; or

(b) any apparatus or plant.

(2) The local planning authority may serve an action notice on the owner or occupier of the land in or on which the surface is situated.

(3) If after reasonable enquiry the local planning authority –

(a) are unable to ascertain the name and address of the owner, and

(b) are unable to ascertain the name and address of the occupier,

the local planning authority may fix an action notice to the surface.

(4) For the purposes of this section 'an action notice', in relation to a surface, is a notice requiring the owner or occupier of the land in or on which the surface is situated to carry out the measures specified in the notice by a time specified in the notice.

(5) A time may be specified in an action notice if it is a reasonable time not earlier than the end of 28 days beginning with the date of the notice.

(6) Measures may be specified in an action notice if they are reasonable measures to prevent or reduce the frequency of the display of unauthorised advertisements on the surface concerned.

(7) The time by which an owner or occupier must comply with an action notice may be postponed by the local planning authority.

(8) This section has effect subject to –

(a) the other provisions of the enactments relating to town and country planning;
(b) the provisions of the enactments relating to historic buildings and ancient monuments; and
(c) Part 2 of the Food and Environmental Protection Act 1985 (which relates to deposits in the sea).

(9) Subsection (10) applies if –

(a) an action notice is served under subsection (2) or fixed under subsection (3); and
(b) the measures specified in the notice are not carried out by the time specified in the notice.

(10) The local planning authority may –

(a) carry out the measures; and
(b) recover expenses reasonably incurred by the local planning authority in doing that from the person required by the action notice to do it.

(11) Power under subsection (10)(a) is subject to the right of appeal under section 225D.

(12) Where in the exercise of power under subsection (10)(a) any damage is caused to land or chattels, compensation may be recovered by any person suffering the damage from the local planning authority exercising the power, but compensation is not recoverable under this subsection for damage reasonably caused in carrying out the measures.

(13) The provisions of section 118 apply in relation to compensation under subsection (12) as they apply in relation to compensation under Part 4.

(14) The local planning authority may not recover expenses under subsection (10)(b) in respect of a surface that –

(a) forms part of a flat or a dwellinghouse;
(b) is within the curtilage of a dwellinghouse; or
(c) forms part of the boundary of the curtilage of a dwellinghouse.

(15) Each of sections 275 and 291 of the Public Health Act 1936 (provision for authority to agree to take the required measures at expense of owner or occupier, and provision for expenses to be recoverable also from owner's successor or from occupier and to be charged on premises concerned) applies as if the reference in that section to that Act included a reference to this section.

(16) In this section –

'dwellinghouse' does not include a building containing one or more flats, or a flat contained within such a building;

'flat' means a separate and self-contained set of premises constructed or adapted for use as a dwelling and forming part of a building from some other part of which it is divided horizontally;

'unauthorised advertisement' means an advertisement in respect of which an offence –

(a) under section 224(3), or
(b) under section 132 of the Highways Act 1980 (unauthorised marks on highway),

is committed after the coming into force of this section.

225D Right to appeal against notice under section 225C

(1) A person on whom notice has been served under section 225C(2) may appeal to a magistrates' court on any of the following grounds –

(a) that there is no problem with the display of unauthorised advertisements on the surface concerned or any such problem is not a persistent one;
(b) that there has been some informality, defect or error in, or in connection with, the notice;
(c) that the time within which the measures specified in the notice are to be carried out is not reasonably sufficient for the purpose;
(d) that the notice should have been served on another person.

(2) The occupier or owner of premises which include a surface to which a notice has been fixed under section 225C(3) may appeal to a magistrates' court on any of the following grounds –

(a) that there is no problem with the display of unauthorised advertisements on the surface concerned or any such problem is not a persistent one;
(b) that there has been some informality, defect or error in, or in connection with, the notice;
(c) that the time within which the measures specified in the notice are to be carried out is not reasonably sufficient for the purpose.

(3) So far as an appeal under this section is based on the ground mentioned in subsection (1)(b) or (2)(b), the court must dismiss the appeal if it is satisfied that the informality, defect or error was not a material one.

(4) If an appeal under subsection (1) is based on the ground mentioned in subsection (1)(d), the appellant must serve a copy of the notice of appeal on each person who the appellant considers is a person on whom the notice under section 225C(2) should have been served.

(5) If –

(a) notice under section 225C(2) is served on a person, and
(b) the local planning authority bring proceedings against the person for the recovery under section 225C(10)(b) of any expenses,

it is not open to the person to raise in the proceedings any question which the person could have raised in an appeal under subsection (1).

225E Applying section 225C to statutory undertakers' operational land

(1) Subsection (2) and (3) apply where the local planning authority serves a notice under section 225C(2) requiring a statutory undertaker to carry out measures in respect of the display of unauthorised advertisements on a surface on its operational land.

(2) The statutory undertaker may, within 28 days beginning with the date of service of the notice, serve a counter-notice on the local planning authority specifying alternative measures which will in the statutory undertaker's reasonable opinion have the effect of preventing or reducing the frequency of the display of unauthorised advertisements on the surface to at least the same extent as the measures specified in the notice.

(3) Where a counter-notice is served under subsection (2), the notice under section 225C(2) is to be treated –

(a) as requiring the alternative measures specified in the counter-notice to be carried out (instead of the measures actually required by the notice under section 225C(2)); and

(b) as having been served on the date on which the counter-notice is served.

(4) The time by which a statutory undertaker must carry out the measures specified in a counter-notice served under subsection (2) may be postponed by the local planning authority.'

(2) In Part 8 of the Town and Country Planning Act 1990 (special controls) after Chapter 3 insert –

'CHAPTER 4 Remedying defacement of premises

225F Power to remedy defacement of premises

(1) Subsections (2) and (3) apply if –

(a) premises in England include a surface that is readily visible from a place to which the public have access;
(b) either –

(i) the surface does not form part of the operational land of a statutory undertaker, or
(ii) the surface forms part of the operational land of a statutory undertaker and subsection (11) applies to the surface;

(c) there is a sign on the surface; and
(d) the local planning authority consider the sign to be detrimental to the amenity of the area or offensive.

(2) The local planning authority may serve on the occupier of the premises a notice requiring the occupier to remove or obliterate the sign by a time specified in the notice.
(3) If it appears to the local planning authority that there is no occupier of the premises, the local planning authority may fix to the surface a notice requiring the owner or occupier of the premises to remove or obliterate the sign by a time specified in the notice.
(4) A time specified under subsection (2) or (3) may not be earlier than the end of 15 days beginning the date of service or fixing of the notice.
(5) Subsection (6) applies if –

(a) a notice is served under subsection (2) or fixed under subsection (3); and
(b) the sign is neither removed nor obliterated by the time specified in the notice.

(6) The local planning authority may –

(a) remove or obliterate the sign; and
(b) recover expenses reasonably incurred by the local planning authority in doing that from the person required by the notice to do it.

(7) Power under subsection (6)(a) is subject to the right of appeal under section 225I.
(8) Expenses may not be recovered under subsection (6)(b) if the surface –

(a) forms part of a flat or a dwellinghouse;
(b) is within the curtilage of a dwellinghouse; or
(c) forms part of the boundary of the curtilage of a dwellinghouse.

(9) Section 291 of the Public Health Act 1936 (provision for expenses to be recoverable also from owner's successor or from occupier and to be charged

on premises concerned) applies as if the reference in that section to that Act included a reference to this section.

(10) For the purposes of this section, a universal postal service provider is treated as being the occupier of any plant or apparatus that consists of a universal postal service letter box or a universal postal service pouch-box belonging to it.

(11) This subsection applies to a surface if the surface abuts on, or is one to which access is given directly from, either –

(a) a street; or
(b) any place, other than a street, to which the public have access as of right.

(12) In this section –

'dwellinghouse' does not include a building containing one or more flats, or a flat contained within such a building;

'flat' means a separate and self-contained set of premises constructed or adapted for use as a dwelling and forming part of a building from some other part of which it is divided horizontally;

'premises' means building, wall, fence or other structure or erection, or apparatus or plant;

'sign' –

(a) includes any writing, letter, picture, device or representation, but
(b) does not include an advertisement;

'statutory undertaker' does not include a relevant airport operator (within the meaning of Part 5 of the Airports Act 1986);

'street' includes any highway, any bridge carrying a highway and any road, lane, mews, footway, square, court, alley or passage, whether a thoroughfare or not;

'universal postal service letter box' has the meaning given in section 86(4) of the Postal Services Act 2000;

'universal postal service pouch-box' has the meaning given in paragraph 1(10) of Schedule 6 to that Act.

225G Notices under section 225F in respect of post boxes

(1) The local planning authority may serve a notice under section 225F(2) on a universal postal service provider in respect of a universal postal service letter box, or universal postal service pouch-box, belonging to the provider only if –

(a) the authority has served on the provider written notice of the authority's intention to do so; and
(b) the period of 28 days beginning with the date of service of that notice has ended.

(2) In this section –

'universal postal service letter box' has the meaning given in section 86(4) of the Postal Services Act 2000;

'universal postal service pouch-box' has the meaning given in paragraph 1(10) of Schedule 6 to that Act.

225H Section 225F powers as respects bus shelters and other street furniture

(1) The local planning authority may exercise the power conferred by section 225F(6)(a) to remove or obliterate a sign from any surface on a bus shelter, or other street furniture, of a statutory undertaker that is not situated on operational land of the statutory undertaker only if –

(a) the authority has served on the statutory undertaker notice of the authority's intention to do so;
(b) the notice specified the bus shelter, or other street furniture, concerned; and
(c) the period of 28 days beginning with the date of service of the notice has ended.

(2) In this section 'statutory undertaker' does not include an airport operator (within the meaning of Part 5 of the Airports Act 1986).

225I Right to appeal against notice under section 225F

(1) A person on whom notice has been served under section 225F(2) may appeal to a magistrates' court on any of the following grounds –

(a) that the sign concerned is neither detrimental to the amenity of the area nor offensive;
(b) that there has been some informality, defect or error in, or in connection with, the notice;
(c) that the time within which the sign concerned is to be removed or obliterated is not reasonably sufficient for the purpose;
(d) that the notice should have been served on another person.

(2) The occupier or owner of premises which include a surface to which a notice has been fixed under section 225F(3) may appeal to a magistrates' court on any of the following grounds –

(a) that the sign concerned is neither detrimental to the amenity of the area nor offensive;
(b) that there has been some informality, defect or error in, or in connection with, the notice;
(c) that the time within which the sign concerned is to be removed or obliterated is not reasonably sufficient for the purpose.

(3) So far as an appeal under this section is based on the ground mentioned in subsection (1)(b) or (2)(b), the court must dismiss the appeal if it is satisfied that the informality, defect or error was not a material one.
(4) If an appeal under subsection (1) is based on the ground mentioned in subsection (1)(d), the appellant must serve a copy of the notice of appeal on each person who the appellant considers is a person on whom the notice under section 225F(2) should have been served.
(5) If –

(a) notice under section 225F(2) is served on a person, and
(b) the local planning authority bring proceedings against the person for the recovery under section 225F(6)(b) of any expenses,

it is not open to the person to raise in the proceedings any question which the person could have raised in an appeal under subsection (1).

225J Remedying defacement at owner or occupier's request

(1) Subsection (2) applies if –

(a) premises in England include a surface that is readily visible from a place to which the public have access;
(b) there is a sign on the surface; and
(c) the owner or occupier of the premises asks the local planning authority to remove or obliterate the sign.

(2) The local planning authority may –

(a) remove or obliterate the sign; and
(b) recover expenses reasonably incurred by the local planning authority in doing that from the person who asked the local planning authority to do it.

(3) In this section 'premises' means building, wall, fence or other structure or erection, or apparatus or plant.
(4) In this section 'sign' –

(a) includes –

(i) any writing, letter, picture, device or representation, and
(ii) any advertisement, but

(b) does not include an advertisement for the display of which deemed or express consent has been granted under Chapter 3.

Chapter 5 Application of provisions of Chapters 3 and 4 to statutory undertakers

225K Action under sections 225A, 225C and 225F: operational land

(1) This section applies in relation to the exercise by the local planning authority of –

(a) power conferred by section 225A(1), or section 324(3) so far as applying for the purposes of section 225A(1), to –

(i) enter on any operational land of a statutory undertaker, or
(ii) remove a display structure situated on operational land of a statutory undertaker;

(b) power conferred by section 225C(10)(a), or section 324(3) so far as applying for the purposes of section 225C(10)(a), to –

(i) enter on any operational land of a statutory undertaker, or
(ii) carry out any measures to prevent or reduce the frequency of the display of unauthorised advertisements on a surface on operational land of a statutory undertaker; or

(c) power conferred by section 225F(6)(a), or section 324(3) so far as applying for the purposes of section 225F(6)(a), to –

(i) enter on any operational land of a statutory undertaker, or
(ii) remove or obliterate a sign on a surface of premises that are, or are on, operational land of a statutory undertaker.

(2) The authority may exercise the power only if –

(a) the authority has served on the statutory undertaker notice of the authority's intention to do so;
(b) the notice specified the display structure, surface or sign concerned and its location; and
(c) the period of 28 days beginning with the date of service of the notice has ended.

(3) If –

(a) a notice under subsection (2) is served on a statutory undertaker, and
(b) within 28 days beginning with the date the notice is served, the statutory undertaker serves a counter-notice on the local planning authority specifying conditions subject to which the power is to be exercised,

the power may only be exercised subject to, and in accordance with, the conditions specified in the counter-notice.

(4) The conditions which may be specified in a counter-notice under subsection (3) are conditions which are –

(a) necessary or expedient in the interests of safety or the efficient and economic operation of the undertaking concerned; or
(b) for the protection of any works, apparatus or other property not vested in the statutory undertaker which are lawfully present on, in, under or over the land upon which entry is proposed to be made.

(5) If –

(a) a notice under subsection (2) is served on a statutory undertaker, and
(b) within 28 days beginning with the date the notice is served, the statutory undertaker serves a counter-notice on the local planning authority requiring the local planning authority to refrain from exercising the power,

the power may not be exercised.

(6) A counter-notice under subsection (5) may be served only if the statutory undertaker has reasonable grounds to believe, for reasons connected with the operation of its undertaking, that the power cannot be exercised under the circumstances in question –

(a) without risk to the safety of any person; or
(b) without unreasonable risk to the efficient and economic operation of the statutory undertaker's undertaking.

(7) In this section 'statutory undertaker' does not include an airport operator (within the meaning of Part 5 of the Airports Act 1986).'

(3) In section 324(3) of the Town and Country Planning Act 1990 (power of entry where necessary for purposes of section 225) after '225' insert ', 225A(1), 225C(10)(a) or 225F(6)(a)'.

(4) In the London Local Authorities Act 1995 (c. x) omit sections 11 to 13 (provision as respects London which is generally superseded as a result of the provision as respects England made by the preceding provisions of this section).

(5) In section 11 of the London Local Authorities Act 2007 (c. ii) after subsection (10) insert –

'(11) The definition of 'an advertising offence' given by section 4 of this Act applies for the purposes of subsection (10) above with –

(a) the omission of paragraphs (a) and (b), and
(b) in paragraph (d), the substitution of 'paragraph' for 'paragraphs (a) to'.'

CHAPTER 6 NATIONALLY SIGNIFICANT INFRASTRUCTURE PROJECTS

128 Abolition of Infrastructure Planning Commission

(1) The Infrastructure Planning Commission ceases to exist on the day on which this subsection comes into force.

(2) Schedule 13 (amendments in consequence of Commission's abolition, including amendments transferring its functions to Secretary of State) has effect.

(3) On the coming into force of this subsection, the property, rights and liabilities of the Infrastructure Planning Commission vest by virtue of this subsection in the Secretary of State.

(4) Subsection (3) operates in relation to property, rights and liabilities –

- (a) whether or not they would otherwise be capable of being transferred,
- (b) without any instrument or other formality being required, and
- (c) irrespective of any requirement for consent that would otherwise apply.

(5) The transfer by virtue of subsections (2) to (4) is to be treated as a relevant transfer for the purposes of the Transfer of Undertakings (Protection of Employment) Regulations 2006 (S.I. 2006/246) if it would not otherwise be a relevant transfer for those purposes.

(6) Subsections (3) and (4) do not affect the operation of those Regulations in relation to that transfer.

129 Transitional provision in connection with abolition

(1) The Secretary of State may, in connection with the operation of the abolition provisions, give a direction about the handling on and after the abolition date of –

- (a) an application received by the Infrastructure Planning Commission before the abolition date that purports to be an application for an order granting development consent under the Planning Act 2008,
- (b) a proposed application notified to the Commission under section 46 of that Act before the abolition date, or
- (c) an application received by the Secretary of State on or after the abolition date where –
  - (i) the application purports to be an application for an order granting development consent under that Act, and
  - (ii) a proposed application that has become that application was notified to the Commission under section 46 of that Act before the abolition date.

(2) A direction under subsection (1) may (in particular) –

- (a) make provision about the effect on and after the abolition date of things done before that date;
- (b) provide for provisions of or made under the Planning Act 2008 to apply on and after that date as they applied before that date, with or without modifications specified in the direction;
- (c) provide for provisions of or made under that Act to apply on and after the abolition date with modifications specified in the direction;
- (d) make provision for a person who immediately before the abolition date –
  - (i) is a member of the Commission, and
  - (ii) is a member of the Panel, or is the single Commissioner, handling an application for an order granting development consent under that Act,

  to be, or to be treated as being, a member of the Panel that under Chapter 2 of Part 6 of that Act, or the appointed person who under Chapter 3 of that Part, is to handle the application on and after the abolition date;
- (e) make other transitional provision and savings;
- (f) make provision binding the Crown.

(3) In this section –

'the abolition date' means the date on which section 128(1) comes into force;

'the abolition provisions' means section 128, Schedule 13 and Part 20 of Schedule 25.

130 National policy statements

(1) The Planning Act 2008 is amended as follows.

(2) In section 5(4) (statement may be designated as national policy statement only if consultation, publicity and parliamentary requirements have been complied with) after 'have been complied with in relation to it' insert 'and –

(a) the consideration period for the statement has expired without the House of Commons resolving during that period that the statement should not be proceeded with, or

(b) the statement has been approved by resolution of the House of Commons –

(i) after being laid before Parliament under section 9(8), and

(ii) before the end of the consideration period.'

(3) In section 5 (national policy statements) after subsection (4) insert –

'(4A) In subsection (4) 'the consideration period', in relation to a statement, means the period of 21 sitting days beginning with the first sitting day after the day on which the statement is laid before Parliament under section 9(8), and here 'sitting day' means a day on which the House of Commons sits.'

(4) In section 5(9) omit paragraph (b) (designated statement must be laid before Parliament).

(5) In section 6(7) (national policy statement may be amended only if consultation, publicity and parliamentary requirements have been complied with) after 'have been complied with in relation to the proposed amendment' insert 'and –

(a) the consideration period for the amendment has expired without the House of Commons resolving during that period that the amendment should not be proceeded with, or

(b) the amendment has been approved by resolution of the House of Commons –

(i) after being laid before Parliament under section 9(8), and

(ii) before the end of the consideration period.'

(6) In section 6 (review and amendment of national policy statements) after subsection (7) insert –

'(7A) In subsection (7) 'the consideration period', in relation to an amendment, means the period of 21 sitting days beginning with the first sitting day after the day on which the amendment is laid before Parliament under section 9(8), and here 'sitting day' means a day on which the House of Commons sits.'

(7) In section 6(8) (subsections (6) and (7) do not apply if amendment does not materially affect national policy) for 'and (7)' substitute 'to (7A)'.

(8) After section 6 insert –

'6A Interpretation of sections 5(4) and 6(7)

(1) This section applies for the purposes of section 5(4) and 6(7).

(2) The consultation and publicity requirements set out in section 7 are to be treated as having been complied with in relation to a statement or proposed amendment ('the final proposal') if –

(a) they have been complied with in relation to a different statement or proposed amendment ('the earlier proposal'),

(b) the final proposal is a modified version of the earlier proposal, and

(c) the Secretary of State thinks that the modifications do not materially affect the policy as set out in the earlier proposal.

(3) The consultation and publicity requirements set out in section 7 are also to

be treated as having been complied with in relation to a statement or proposed amendment ('the final proposal') if –

(a) they have been complied with –

(i) in relation to a different statement or proposed amendment ('the earlier proposal'), and
(ii) in relation to modifications of the earlier proposal ('the main modifications'),

(b) the final proposal is a modified version of the earlier proposal, and
(c) there are no modifications other than the main modifications or, where the modifications include modifications other than the main modifications, the Secretary of State thinks that those other modifications do not materially affect the policy as set out in the earlier proposal modified by the main modifications.

(4) If section 9(8) has been complied with in relation to a statement or proposed amendment ('the final proposal'), the parliamentary requirements set out in section 9(2) to (7) are to be treated as having been complied with in relation to the final proposal where –

(a) the final proposal is not the same as what was laid under section 9(2), but
(b) those requirements have been complied with in relation to what was laid under section 9(2).

(5) Ignore any corrections of clerical or typographical errors in what was laid under section 9(8).

6B Extension of consideration period under section 5(4A) or 6(7A)

(1) The Secretary of State may –

(a) in relation to a proposed national policy statement, extend the period mentioned in section 5(4A), or
(b) in relation to a proposed amendment of a national policy statement, extend the period mentioned in section 6(7A),

by 21 sitting days or less.

(2) The Secretary of State does that by laying before the House of Commons a statement –

(a) indicating that the period is to be extended, and
(b) setting out the length of the extension.

(3) The statement under subsection (2) must be laid before the period would have expired without the extension.
(4) The Secretary of State must publish the statement under subsection (2) in a way the Secretary of State thinks appropriate.
(5) The period may be extended more than once.'

(9) In section 8(1)(a) (local authorities within subsection (2) or (3) to be consulted about publicity required for proposed statement identifying a location) for 'or (3)' substitute ', (3) or (3A)'.

(10) In section 8(3) (consultation with local authorities that share a boundary with the local authority ('B') whose area contains a location) before the 'and' at the end of paragraph (a) insert –

'(aa) B is a unitary council or a lower-tier district council,'.

(11) In section 8 (consultation on publicity requirements) after subsection (3) insert –

'(3A) If any of the locations concerned is in the area of an upper-tier county council ('C'), a local authority ('D') is within this subsection if –

(a) D is not a lower-tier district council, and
(b) any part of the boundary of D's area is also part of the boundary of C's area.'

(12) In section 8, after subsection (4) (meaning of 'local authority') insert –

'(5) In this section –

'lower-tier district council' means a district council in England for an area for which there is a county council;

'unitary council' means a local authority that is not an upper-tier county council, a lower-tier district council, a National Park authority or the Broads Authority;

'upper-tier county council' means a county council in England for each part of whose area there is a district council.'

(13) In section 9 (parliamentary requirements for national policy statements and their amendments) after subsection (7) insert –

'(8) After the end of the relevant period, but not before the Secretary of State complies with subsection (5) if it applies, the Secretary of State must lay the proposal before Parliament.
(9) If after subsection (8) has been complied with –

(a) something other than what was laid under subsection (8) becomes the proposal, or
(b) what was laid under subsection (8) remains the proposal, or again becomes the proposal, despite the condition in section 5(4)(a) not having been met in relation to it,

subsection (8) must be complied with anew.
(10) For the purposes of subsection (9)(a) and (b) ignore any proposal to correct clerical or typographical errors in what was laid under subsection (8).'

(14) Section 12 (power to designate pre-commencement statements of policy and to take account of pre-commencement consultation etc) is repealed.

131 Power to alter effect of requirement for development consent on other consent regimes

(1) The Planning Act 2008 is amended as follows.
(2) In section 33 (effect of requirement for development consent on other consent regimes) after subsection (4) insert –

'(5) The Secretary of State may by order –

(a) amend subsection (1) or (2) –

(i) to add or remove a type of consent, or
(ii) to vary the cases in relation to which a type of consent is within that subsection;

(b) make further provision, or amend or repeal provision, about –

(i) the types of consent that are, and are not, within subsection (1) or (2), or
(ii) the cases in relation to which a type of consent is, or is not, within either of those subsections.

(6) In this section 'consent' means –

(a) a consent or authorisation that is required, under legislation, to be obtained for development,
(b) a consent, or authorisation, that –

(i) may authorise development, and
(ii) is given under legislation, or

(c) a notice that is required by legislation to be given in relation to development.

(7) In subsection (6) 'legislation' means an Act or an instrument made under an Act.
(8) An order under subsection (5) may not affect –

(a) a requirement for a devolved consent to be obtained for, or given in relation to, development, or
(b) whether development may be authorised by a devolved consent.

(9) A consent is 'devolved' for the purposes of subsection (8) if –

(a) provision for the consent would be within the legislative competence of the National Assembly for Wales if the provision were contained in an Act of the Assembly,
(b) provision for the consent is, or could be, made by the Welsh Ministers in an instrument made under an Act,
(c) the consent is not within subsection (6)(c) and the Welsh Ministers have a power or duty –

(i) to decide, or give directions as to how to decide, whether the consent is given,
(ii) to decide, or give directions as to how to decide, some or all of the terms on which the consent is given, or
(iii) to revoke or vary the consent, or

(d) the consent is within subsection (6)(c) and the notice has to be given to the Welsh Ministers or otherwise brought to their attention.

(10) An order under subsection (5)(b) may amend this Act.'

(3) In section 232 (orders and regulations) –

(a) in subsection (5)(d) (orders not subject to annulment by either House of Parliament) after '14(3),' insert '33(5),', and
(b) in subsection (6) (orders that must be approved in draft by both Houses of Parliament before being made) after '14(3),' insert '33(5),'.

(4) In paragraph 4 of Schedule 12 (application of section 33 to Scotland: modifications) –

(a) in sub-paragraph (a) for paragraph (i) substitute –

'(i) for 'none of the following is' there were substituted 'the following are not', and',

(b) omit the 'and' at the end of sub-paragraph (a),
(c) in sub-paragraph (b) for 'subsections (2) to (4)' substitute 'paragraphs (a) to (c) of subsection (2), and subsections (3) and (4),', and
(d) after sub-paragraph (b) insert ', and

(c) in subsection (7) 'Act' includes an Act of the Scottish Parliament.'

132 Secretary of State's directions in relation to projects of national significance

(1) Section 35 of the Planning Act 2008 (directions in relation to projects of national significance) is amended in accordance with subsections (2) to (9).

(2) In subsection (1) (circumstances in which the Secretary of State may give directions) –

(a) omit paragraph (a) (requirement that an application for a consent or authorisation mentioned in section 33(1) or (2) has been made), and
(b) in paragraph (b) –

(i) omit 'the', and
(ii) after 'project' insert ', or proposed project,'.

(3) For subsection (4) (directions the Secretary of State may give) substitute –

'(4) The Secretary of State may direct the development to be treated as development for which development consent is required.
(4A) If no relevant application has been made, the power under subsection (4) is exercisable only in response to a qualifying request.
(4B) If the Secretary of State gives a direction under subsection (4), the Secretary of State may –

(a) if a relevant application has been made, direct the application to be treated as an application for an order granting development consent;
(b) if a person proposes to make a relevant application, direct the proposed application to be treated as a proposed application for development consent.

(4C) A direction under subsection (4) or (4B) may be given so as to apply for specified purposes or generally.'

(4) In subsection (5) (power to modify application of statutory provisions in relation to an application etc) –

(a) for 'subsection (4)' substitute 'subsection (4B)',
(b) in paragraph (a) after 'application' insert ', or proposed application,', and
(c) in paragraph (b) after 'application' insert 'or proposed application'.

(5) In subsection (6) (authority to which an application for a consent or authorisation mentioned in section 33(1) or (2) has been made to refer the application to the Commission) –

(a) for 'subsection (4)' substitute 'subsection (4B)', and
(b) after 'application' insert ', or proposed application,'.

(6) In subsection (7) (power to direct authority considering application for consent or authorisation mentioned in section 33(1) or (2) to take no further action) –

(a) for 'subsection (4)' substitute 'subsection (4B)', and
(b) after 'application' insert ', or proposed application,'.

(7) In subsection (8) (power to require authority considering application for consent or authorisation mentioned in section 33(1) or (2) to provide information) for 'the relevant authority' substitute 'an authority within subsection (8A)'.
(8) After subsection (8) insert –

'(8A) An authority is within this subsection if a relevant application has been, or may be, made to it.'

(9) After subsection (9) insert –

'(10) In this section –

'qualifying request' means a written request, for a direction under subsection (4) or (4B), that –

(a) specifies the development to which it relates, and
(b) explains why the conditions in subsection (1)(b) and (c) are met in relation to the development;

'relevant application' means an application, relating to the development, for a consent or authorisation mentioned in section 33(1) or (2);

'relevant authority' –

(a) in relation to a relevant application that has been made, means the authority to which the application was made, and
(b) in relation to a relevant application that a person proposes to make, means the authority to which the person proposes to make the application.'

(10) In the Planning Act 2008 after section 35 insert –

'35A Timetable for deciding request for direction under section 35

(1) This section applies if the Secretary of State receives a qualifying request from a person ('R').
(2) The Secretary of State must make a decision on the qualifying request before the primary deadline, subject to subsection (3).
(3) Subsection (2) does not apply if, before the primary deadline, the Secretary of State asks R to provide the Secretary of State with information for the purpose of enabling the Secretary of State to decide –

(a) whether to give the direction requested, and
(b) the terms in which it should be given.

(4) If R –

(a) is asked under subsection (3) to provide information, and
(b) provides the information sought within the period of 14 days beginning with the day on which R is asked to do so,

the Secretary of State must make a decision on the qualifying request before the end of the period of 28 days beginning with the day the Secretary of State receives the information.
(5) In this section –

'the primary deadline' means the end of the period of 28 days beginning with the day on which the Secretary of State receives the qualifying request;

'qualifying request' has the meaning given by section 35(10).'

133 Pre-application consultation with local authorities

(1) Section 43 of the Planning Act 2008 (local authorities for the purposes of the consultation requirements in section 42) is amended as follows.
(2) In subsection (2) (provision requiring consultation with local authorities that share a boundary with the local authority ('B') in whose area the development is to take place) before the 'and' at the end of paragraph (a) insert –

'(aa) B is a unitary council or a lower-tier district council,'.

(3) After subsection (2) insert –

'(2A) If the land is in the area of an upper-tier county council ('C'), a local authority ('D') is within this section if –

(a) D is not a lower-tier district council, and
(b) any part of the boundary of D's area is also part of the boundary of C's area.'

(4) For subsection (3) (definition of local authority) substitute –

'(3) In this section –

'local authority' means –

(a) a county council, or district council, in England;
(b) a London borough council;
(c) the Common Council of the City of London;
(d) the Council of the Isles of Scilly;
(e) a county council, or county borough council, in Wales;
(f) a council constituted under section 2 of the Local Government etc (Scotland) Act 1994;
(g) a National Park authority;
(h) the Broads Authority;

'lower-tier district council' means a district council in England for an area for which there is a county council;

'unitary council' means a local authority that is not an upper-tier county council, a lower-tier district council, a National Park authority or the Broads Authority;

'upper-tier county council' means a county council in England for each part of whose area there is a district council.'

134 Reform of duties to publicise community consultation statement

In section 47(6) of the Planning Act 2008 (duties of applicant for development consent to publicise the statement setting out how the applicant proposes to consult the local community) –

(a) for 'must publish it –' substitute 'must –

(za) make the statement available for inspection by the public in a way that is reasonably convenient for people living in the vicinity of the land,',

(b) in paragraph (a) (duty to publish statement in local newspaper) –

(i) at the beginning insert 'publish,', and
(ii) after 'land' insert ', a notice stating where and when the statement can be inspected', and

(c) in paragraph (b) (duty to publish statement in any other prescribed manner) for 'in such other manner' substitute 'publish the statement in such manner'.

135 Claimants of compensation for effects of development

(1) The Planning Act 2008 is amended as follows.
(2) In section 52(1) (obtaining information about interests in land) for 'subsection (2) applies' substitute 'subsections (2) and (2A) apply'.
(3) In section 52 after subsection (2) insert –

'(2A) The Secretary of State may authorise the applicant to serve a notice on a person mentioned in subsection (3) requiring the person ('the recipient') to give to the applicant in writing the name and address of any person the recipient believes is a person who, if the order sought by the application or proposed application were to be made and fully implemented, would or might be entitled –

(a) as a result of the implementing of the order,
(b) as a result of the order having been implemented, or
(c) as a result of the use of the land once the order has been implemented,

to make a relevant claim.'

(4) In section 52(4), (6) and (7) after 'subsection (2)' insert 'or (2A)'.

(5) In section 52 after subsection (5) insert –

'(5A) A notice under subsection (2A) must explain the circumstances in which a person would or might be entitled as mentioned in that subsection.'

(6) In section 52(10) for '(2) and (3)' substitute '(2) to (3)'.
(7) In section 52 after subsection (11) insert –

'(12) In subsection (3) as it applies for the purposes of subsection (2A) 'the land' also includes any relevant affected land (see subsection (13)).
(13) Where the applicant believes that, if the order sought by the application or proposed application were to be made and fully implemented, there would or might be persons entitled –

(a) as a result of the implementing of the order,
(b) as a result of the order having been implemented, or
(c) as a result of the use of the land once the order has been implemented,

to make a relevant claim in respect of any land or in respect of an interest in any land, that land is 'relevant affected land' for the purposes of subsection (12).
(14) In this section 'relevant claim' means –

(a) a claim under section 10 of the Compulsory Purchase Act 1965 (compensation where satisfaction not made for compulsory purchase of land or not made for injurious affection resulting from compulsory purchase);
(b) a claim under Part 1 of the Land Compensation Act 1973 (compensation for depreciation of land value by physical factors caused by use of public works);
(c) a claim under section 152(3).'

(8) In section 44(6) (meaning of 'relevant claim' in section 44(4)) after paragraph (b) insert ';

(c) a claim under section 152(3).'

(9) In section 57(6) (meaning of 'relevant claim' in section 57(4)) after paragraph (b) insert ';

(c) a claim under section 152(3).'

(10) In Schedule 12 (application of Act to Scotland: modifications) in paragraph 6 (application of section 52) after sub-paragraph (c) insert –

'(d) in subsection (14) for paragraph (a) there were substituted –

'(a) a claim arising by virtue of paragraph 1 of the Second Schedule to the Acquisition of Land (Authorisation Procedure) (Scotland) Act 1947 (c. 42);', and

(e) in subsection (14)(b) the reference to Part 1 of the Land Compensation Act 1973 were a reference to Part 1 of the Land Compensation (Scotland) Act 1973.'

136 Rights of entry for surveying etc in connection with applications

(1) The Planning Act 2008 is amended as follows.
(2) In section 53(1) (person may be authorised to enter land for the purpose of surveying and taking levels of it) after 'taking levels of it' insert ', or in order to facilitate compliance with the provisions mentioned in subsection (1A),'.
(3) In section 53 after subsection (1) insert –

'(1A) Those provisions are any provision of or made under an Act for the purpose of implementing –

(a) Council Directive 85/337/EEC of 27 June 1985 on the assessment of the effects of certain public and private projects on the environment, as amended from time to time,
(b) Council Directive 92/43/EC of 21 May 1992 on the conservation of natural habitats and of wild fauna and flora, as amended from time to time, or
(c) any EU instrument from time to time replacing all or any part of either of those Directives.'

(4) Omit section 53(2)(b) and (c) (until proposed application is made, entry for surveying may be authorised only if compulsory acquisition may be involved and section 42 has been complied with).
(5) In section 53 after subsection (3) insert –

'(3A) Power conferred by subsection (1) for the purpose of complying with the provisions mentioned in subsection (1A) includes power to take, and process, samples of or from any of the following found on, in or over the land –

(a) water,
(b) air,
(c) soil or rock,
(d) its flora,
(e) bodily excretions, or dead bodies, of non-human creatures, or
(f) any non-living thing present as a result of human action.'

(6) In section 54(1) (application of section 53(1) to (3) to Crown land) for 'to (3)' substitute 'to (3A)'.
(7) In paragraph 7 of Schedule 12 (modifications of section 53 for the purposes of its application to Scotland) before sub-paragraph (a) insert –

'(za) in subsection (1A), the reference to an Act included an Act of the Scottish Parliament,'.

137 Acceptance of applications for development consent

(1) The Planning Act 2008 is amended as follows.
(2) In section 55(3) (conditions for acceptance of application) omit paragraphs (b) and (d) (application may be accepted only if it complies with requirements as to form and contents and with any standards set, and gives reasons for any failure to follow applicable guidance).
(3) In section 55(3) after paragraph (e) insert ', and

(f) that the application (including accompaniments) is of a standard that the Secretary of State considers satisfactory.'

(4) In section 55 after subsection (5) insert –

'(5A) The Secretary of State, when deciding whether the Secretary of State may reach the conclusion in subsection (3)(f), must have regard to the extent to which –

(a) the application complies with the requirements in section 37(3) (form and contents of application) and any standards set under section 37(5), and
(b) any applicable guidance given under section 37(4) has been followed in relation to the application.'

(5) In section 37(3) (requirements as to form and contents of application) after 'must' insert ', so far as necessary to secure that the application (including accompaniments) is of a standard that the Secretary of State considers satisfactory'.

138 Procedural changes relating to applications for development consent

(1) The Planning Act 2008 is amended as follows.

(2) In section 56(2) (persons to be notified of the acceptance of an application for an order granting development consent) for paragraph (b) (relevant local authorities under section 102(5)) substitute –

'(b) each local authority that is within section 56A,'.

(3) After section 56 insert –

'56A Local authorities for the purposes of sections 56(2)(b) and 60(2)(a)

(1) A local authority is within this section if the land is in the authority's area.

(2) A local authority ('A') is within this section if –

(a) the land is in the area of another local authority ('B'),
(b) B is a unitary council or a lower-tier district council, and
(c) any part of the boundary of A's area is also a part of the boundary of B's area.

(3) If the land is in the area of an upper-tier county council ('C'), a local authority ('D') is within this section if –

(a) D is not a lower-tier district council, and
(b) any part of the boundary of D's area is also part of the boundary of C's area.

(4) In this section –

'the land' means the land to which the application concerned relates or any part of that land;

'local authority' has the meaning given in section 102(8);

'lower-tier district council' means a district council in England for an area for which there is a county council;

'unitary council' means a local authority that is not an upper-tier county council, a lower-tier district council, a National Park authority or the Broads Authority;

'upper-tier county council' means a county council in England for each part of whose area there is a district council.'

(4) In section 60(2) (persons who the Commission must invite to submit local impact reports) for paragraph (a) (relevant local authorities under section 102(5)) substitute –

'(a) each local authority that is within section 56A, and'.

(5) In section 88 (initial assessment of issues, and preliminary meeting) –

(a) in subsection (3) (persons who must be invited to preliminary meeting) omit the 'and' at the end of paragraph (a),
(b) in that subsection after paragraph (b) insert –

'(c) each statutory party, and
(d) each local authority that is within section 88A,', and

(c) after that subsection insert –

'(3A) In subsection (3)(c) 'statutory party' means a person specified in, or of a description specified in, regulations made by the Secretary of State.'

(6) After section 88 insert –

'88A Local authorities for the purposes of section 88(3)(d)

(1) A local authority ('A') is within this section if –

(a) the land is in the area of another local authority ('B'),
(b) B is a unitary council or a lower-tier district council, and
(c) any part of the boundary of A's area is also a part of the boundary of B's area.

(2) If the land is in the area of an upper-tier county council ('C'), a local authority ('D') is within this section if –

(a) D is not a lower-tier district council, and
(b) any part of the boundary of D's area is also part of the boundary of C's area.

(3) In this section –

'the land' means the land to which the application relates or any part of that land;

'local authority' has the meaning given in section 102(8);

'lower-tier district council' means a district council in England for an area for which there is a county council;

'unitary council' means a local authority that is not an upper-tier county council, a lower-tier district council, a National Park authority or the Broads Authority;

'upper-tier county council' means a county council in England for each part of whose area there is a district council.'

(7) In section 89 (Examining authority's decisions about how application is to be examined and the notification of those decisions to parties) after subsection (2) insert –

'(2A) Upon making the decisions required by subsection (1), the Examining authority must inform each person mentioned in section 88(3)(c) and (d) –

(a) of those decisions, and
(b) that the person may notify the Examining authority in writing that the person is to become an interested party.'

(8) In section 102 (interpretation of Chapter 4: 'interested party' and other expressions) –

(a) in subsection (1) for paragraph (b) (statutory party is interested party) substitute –

'(aa) the person has been notified of the acceptance of the application in accordance with section 56(2)(d),
(ab) the Examining authority has under section 102A decided that it considers that the person is within one or more of the categories set out in section 102B,',

(b) in subsection (1) for paragraph (c) (relevant local authority is interested party) insert –

'(c) the person is a local authority in whose area the land is located,
(ca) the person –

(i) is mentioned in section 88(3)(c) or (d), and
(ii) has notified the Examining authority as mentioned in section 89(2A)(b),',

(c) after subsection (1) (definition of interested party) insert –

'(1ZA)But a person ceases to be an 'interested party' for the purposes of this Chapter upon notifying the Examining authority in writing that the person no longer wishes to be an interested party.',

(d) omit subsection (3) (definition of statutory party),
(e) omit subsections (5) to (7) (which further define the local authorities that are relevant local authorities), and
(f) in subsection (8) (definition of local authority) for 'subsections (5) to (7)' substitute 'subsection (1)(c)'.

(9) After section 102 insert –

'102A Persons in certain categories may ask to become interested parties etc

(1) Subsection (2) applies if –

(a) a person makes a request to the Examining authority to become an interested party,
(b) the request states that the person claims to be within one or more of the categories set out in section 102B,
(c) the person has not been notified of the acceptance of the application in accordance with section 56(2)(d), and
(d) the applicant has issued a certificate under section 58 in relation to the application.

(2) The Examining authority must decide whether it considers that the person is within one or more of the categories set out in section 102B.
(3) If the Examining authority decides that it considers that the person is within one or more of the categories set out in section 102B, the Examining authority must notify the person, and the applicant, that the person has become an interested party under section 102(1)(ab).
(4) If the Examining authority thinks that a person might successfully make a request mentioned in subsection (1)(a), the Examining authority may inform the person about becoming an interested party under section 102(1)(ab).

But the Examining authority is under no obligation to make enquiries in order to discover persons who might make such a request.

102B Categories for the purposes of section 102A

(1) A person is within Category 1 if the person is an owner, lessee, tenant (whatever the tenancy period) or occupier of the land.
(2) A person is within Category 2 if the person –

(a) is interested in the land, or
(b) has power –

(i) to sell and convey the land, or
(ii) to release the land.

(3) An expression, other than 'the land', that appears in subsection (2) of this section and also in section 5(1) of the Compulsory Purchase Act 1965 has in subsection (2) the meaning that it has in section 5(1) of that Act.
(4) A person is within Category 3 if, should the order sought by the application be made and fully implemented, the person would or might be entitled –

(a) as a result of the implementing of the order,
(b) as a result of the order having been implemented, or
(c) as a result of use of the land once the order has been implemented,

to make a relevant claim.

(5) In subsection (4) 'relevant claim' means –

(a) a claim under section 10 of the Compulsory Purchase Act 1965 (compensation where satisfaction not made for the taking, or injurious affection, of land subject to compulsory purchase);
(b) a claim under Part 1 of the Land Compensation Act 1973 (compensation for depreciation of land value by physical factors caused by use of public works);
(c) a claim under section 152(3).

(6) In this section 'the land' means the land to which the application relates or any part of that land.'

(10) In Schedule 12 (application of Act to Scotland: modifications) after paragraph 9 insert –

'9A Section 102B applies as if –

(a) in subsection (2)(b), the words from 'or' to the end were omitted,
(b) in subsection (3), references to section 5(1) of the Compulsory Purchase Act 1965 were references to section 17 of the Lands Clauses Consolidation (Scotland) Act 1845, and
(c) in subsection (5) –

(i) for paragraph (a) there were substituted –

'(a) a claim arising by virtue of paragraph 1 of the Second Schedule to the Acquisition of Land (Authorisation Procedure) (Scotland) Act 1947'; and

(ii) in paragraph (b), the reference to Part 1 of the Land Compensation Act 1973 were a reference to Part 1 of the Land Compensation (Scotland) Act 1973.'

139 Timetables for reports and decisions on applications for development consent

(1) The Planning Act 2008 is amended as follows.
(2) In section 98(3) (Examining authority must report on application within 3 months beginning with deadline for completing its examination) for the words from 'beginning' onwards substitute 'beginning with –

(a) the deadline for completion of its examination of the application, or
(b) (if earlier) the end of the day on which it completes the examination.'

(3) In section 107(1) (which provides for the application to be decided within 3 months of the start day but is amended by this Act to provide for decision within 3 months of the deadline under section 98(3)) –

(a) for 'with the' substitute 'with –

(a) the', and

(b) at the end insert ', or

(b) (if earlier) the end of the day on which the Secretary of State receives a report on the application under section 74(2)(b) or 83(1)(b).'

140 Development consent subject to requirement for further approval

In section 120(2) of the Planning Act 2008 (provision relating to requirements that may be included in order granting development consent) –

(a) after 'in particular include' insert '–

(a)', and

(b) after 'development' insert ';

(b) requirements to obtain the approval of the Secretary of State or any other person, so far as not within paragraph (a)'.

141 Local authority, statutory undertakers' and National Trust land

(1) The Planning Act 2008 is amended as follows.

(2) In section 128(3) (order authorising compulsory acquisition of local authority or statutory undertakers' land subject to special parliamentary procedure if representation made by the authority or statutory undertakers and not withdrawn) –

(a) after paragraph (a) (but before the 'and' at the end of that paragraph) insert –

'(aa) the representation contains an objection to the compulsory acquisition of the land,', and

(b) in paragraph (b) (condition that representation has not been withdrawn) for 'representation' substitute 'objection'.

(3) In section 130(3) (order authorising compulsory acquisition of certain National Trust land subject to special parliamentary procedure if representation made by National Trust and not withdrawn) –

(a) after paragraph (a) (but before the 'and' at the end of that paragraph) insert –

'(aa) the representation contains an objection to the compulsory acquisition of the land,', and

(b) in paragraph (b) (condition that representation has not been withdrawn) for 'representation' substitute 'objection'.

142 Changes to notice requirements for compulsory acquisition

(1) Section 134 of the Planning Act 2008 (notice of authorisation of compulsory acquisition) is amended as follows.

(2) In subsection (3) (steps the prospective purchaser must take after order granting development consent is made that includes provision authorising compulsory acquisition) –

(a) before paragraph (a) insert –

'(za) make a copy of the order available, at a place in the vicinity of the land, for inspection by the public at all reasonable hours,', and

(b) in paragraph (a) omit 'and a copy of the order'.

(3) In subsection (7) (contents of a compulsory acquisition notice) before the 'and' at the end of paragraph (c) insert –

'(ca) stating where and when a copy of the order is available for inspection in accordance with subsection (3)(za),'.

(4) Omit subsection (8) (compulsory acquisition notice affixed to object on or near the order land to say where order granting development consent can be inspected).

CHAPTER 7 OTHER PLANNING MATTERS

143 Applications for planning permission: local finance considerations

(1) Section 70 of the Town and Country Planning Act 1990 (determination of applications for planning permission: general considerations) is amended as follows.

(2) In subsection (2) (local planning authority to have regard to material considerations in dealing with applications) for the words from 'to the provisions' to the end substitute

'to –

(a) the provisions of the development plan, so far as material to the application,
(b) any local finance considerations, so far as material to the application, and
(c) any other material considerations.'

(3) After subsection (2) insert –

'(2A) Subsection (2)(b) does not apply in relation to Wales.'

(4) After subsection (3) insert –

'(4) In this section –

'local finance consideration' means –

(a) a grant or other financial assistance that has been, or will or could be, provided to a relevant authority by a Minister of the Crown, or
(b) sums that a relevant authority has received, or will or could receive, in payment of Community Infrastructure Levy;

'Minister of the Crown' has the same meaning as in the Ministers of the Crown Act 1975;

'relevant authority' means –

(a) a district council;
(b) a county council in England;
(c) the Mayor of London;
(d) the council of a London borough;
(e) a Mayoral development corporation;
(f) an urban development corporation;
(g) a housing action trust;
(h) the Council of the Isles of Scilly;
(i) the Broads Authority;
(j) a National Park authority in England;
(k) the Homes and Communities Agency; or
(l) a joint committee established under section 29 of the Planning and Compulsory Purchase Act 2004.'

(5) The amendments made by this section do not alter –

(a) whether under subsection (2) of section 70 of the Town and Country Planning Act 1990 regard is to be had to any particular consideration, or
(b) the weight to be given to any consideration to which regard is had under that subsection.

144 Application of this Part to the Crown

An amendment made by this Part in –

(a) the Town and Country Planning Act 1990,
(b) the Planning (Listed Buildings and Conservation Areas) Act 1990,
(c) the Planning and Compulsory Purchase Act 2004, or
(d) the Planning Act 2008,

binds the Crown.

ooo

PART 8 LONDON

CHAPTER 1 HOUSING AND REGENERATION FUNCTIONS

ooo

187 New housing and regeneration functions of the Authority

(1) Part 7A of the Greater London Authority Act 1999 is amended as follows.
(2) In the heading to that Part, after 'Housing' insert 'and regeneration'.
(3) Before section 333A insert –

'Functions in relation to land

333ZA Compulsory acquisition of land

(1) The Authority may acquire land in Greater London compulsorily for the purposes of housing or regeneration.
(2) The Authority may exercise the power in subsection (1) only if the Secretary of State authorises it to do so.
(3) The power in subsection (1) includes power to acquire new rights over land.
(4) Subsection (5) applies where –

(a) land forming part of a common, open space or allotment is being acquired under subsection (1), or
(b) new rights are being acquired under subsection (1) over land forming part of a common, open space or allotment.

(5) The power under subsection (1) includes power to acquire land compulsorily for giving in exchange for that land or those new rights.
(6) Part 1 of Schedule 2 to the Housing and Regeneration Act 2008 (compulsory acquisition of land by the Homes and Communities Agency) applies in relation to the acquisition of land under subsection (1) as it applies in relation to the acquisition of land under section 9 of that Act.
(7) In that Part of that Schedule as applied by subsection (6) –

(a) references to section 9 of that Act are to be read as references to subsection (1),
(b) references to the Homes and Communities Agency are to be read as references to the Authority, and
(c) references to Part 1 of that Act are to be read as references to this Part.

(8) The provisions of Part 1 of the Compulsory Purchase Act 1965 (other than section 31) apply, so far as applicable, to the acquisition by the Authority of land by agreement for the purposes of housing or regeneration.
(9) In this section –

'allotment' means any allotment set out as a fuel allotment, or a field garden allotment, under an Inclosure Act;

'common' has the meaning given by section 19(4) of the Acquisition of Land Act 1981;

'open space' means any land which is –

(a) laid out as a public garden,

(b) used for the purposes of public recreation, or
(c) a disused burial ground.

333ZB Powers in relation to land held for housing or regeneration purposes

(1) Schedule 3 to the Housing and Regeneration Act 2008 (powers in relation to land of the Homes and Communities Agency) applies in relation to the Authority and land held by it for the purposes of housing or regeneration as it applies in relation to the Homes and Communities Agency and its land.
(2) In that Schedule as applied by subsection (1) –

(a) references to the Homes and Communities Agency are to be read as references to the Authority, and
(b) references to the Homes and Communities Agency's land are to the Authority's land held by it for the purposes of housing or regeneration.

(3) Schedule 4 to that Act (powers in relation to, and for, statutory undertakers) applies in relation to the Authority and land held by it for the purposes of housing or regeneration as it applies in relation to the Homes and Communities Agency and its land.
(4) In that Schedule as applied by subsection (3) –

(a) references to the Homes and Communities Agency are to be read as references to the Authority,
(b) references to the Homes and Communities Agency's land are to the Authority's land held by it for the purposes of housing or regeneration,
(c) references to Part 1 of that Act are to be read as references to this Part, and
(d) references to the functions of the Homes and Communities Agency under Part 1 of that Act are to be read as references to the functions of the Authority relating to housing or regeneration.

333ZC Disposal etc of land held for housing and regeneration purposes

(1) The Authority may not dispose of land held by it for the purposes of housing or regeneration for less than the best consideration which can reasonably be obtained unless the Secretary of State consents.
(2) Consent under subsection (1) –

(a) may be general or specific;
(b) may be given unconditionally or subject to conditions.

(3) Subsection (1) does not apply to a disposal by way of a short tenancy if the disposal consists of –

(a) the grant of a term of not more than 7 years, or
(b) the assignment of a term which, at the date of assignment, has not more than 7 years to run.

(4) A disposal of land by the Authority is not invalid merely because any consent required by subsection (1) has not been given.
(5) A person dealing with –

(a) the Authority, or
(b) a person claiming under the Authority,

in relation to any land need not be concerned as to whether any consent required by subsection (1) has been given.

333ZD Power to enter and survey land

(1) Sections 17 and 18 of the Housing and Regeneration Act 2008 (power to enter and survey land) apply in relation to the Authority and land in Greater London as they apply in relation to the Homes and Communities Agency and land outside Greater London.

(2) In those sections as applied by subsection (1) –

(a) references to the Homes and Communities Agency are to be read as references to the Authority,

(b) references to land are to land in Greater London, and

(c) the reference to a proposal for the Homes and Communities Agency to acquire land is a reference to a proposal for the Authority to acquire land for the purposes of housing or regeneration.

Social housing

333ZE Social housing

(1) Subject to subsection (2), sections 31 to 36 of the Housing and Regeneration Act 2008 (social housing functions) apply in relation to the Authority as they apply in relation to the Homes and Communities Agency.

(2) In those sections as applied by subsection (1) –

(a) references to the Homes and Communities Agency are to be read as references to the Authority,

(b) the definition of 'social housing assistance' in section 32(13) is to be read as if the reference to financial assistance given under section 19 of that Act were to financial assistance given by the Authority,

(c) section 34 is to be read as if subsection (1) were omitted, and

(d) section 35(1) is to be read as if the reference to section 19 of the Housing and Regeneration Act 2008 were omitted and as if the reference in paragraph (b) to a dwelling in England outside Greater London were to a dwelling in Greater London.

(3) Sums received by the Authority in respect of repayments of grants made by it for the purposes of social housing are to be used by it for those purposes.

333ZF Relationship with the Regulator of Social Housing: general

(1) The Authority must, in the exercise of its housing and regeneration functions, co-operate with the Regulator of Social Housing (referred to in this Part as 'the Regulator').

(2) In particular, the Authority must consult the Regulator on matters likely to interest the Regulator in the exercise of its social housing functions.

(3) The Regulator must, in the exercise of its social housing functions, co-operate with the Authority.

(4) In particular, the Regulator must consult the Authority on matters likely to interest the Authority in the exercise of its housing and regeneration functions.

333ZG Relationship with the Regulator of Social Housing: directions

(1) The Regulator may direct the Authority not to give financial assistance in connection with social housing to a specified registered provider of social housing.

(2) A direction may be given if –

(a) the Regulator has decided to hold an inquiry into affairs of the registered provider of social housing under section 206 of the Housing and Regeneration Act 2008 (and the inquiry is not concluded),

(b) the Regulator has received notice in respect of the registered provider of social housing under section 145 of that Act, or

(c) the Regulator has appointed an officer of the registered provider of social housing under section 269 of that Act (and the person appointed has not vacated office).

(3) A direction may prohibit the Authority from giving assistance of a specified kind (whether or not in pursuance of a decision already taken and communicated to the registered provider of social housing).

(4) A direction may not prohibit grants to a registered provider of social housing in respect of discounts given by the provider on disposals of dwellings to tenants.

(5) A direction has effect until withdrawn.

(6) In this section the following terms have the same meaning as in Part 2 of the Housing and Regeneration Act 2008 –

'disposal' (see section 273 of that Act);

'dwelling' (see section 275 of that Act);

'tenant' (see section 275 of that Act).

333ZH Relationship with the Regulator of Social Housing: further provisions

(1) Subsection (2) applies if the Authority is proposing to give financial assistance on condition that the recipient provides low cost home ownership accommodation.

(2) The Authority must consult the Regulator about the proposals.

(3) The Authority must notify the Regulator at least 14 days before exercising, in relation to a registered provider of social housing, any of the powers conferred by section 32(2) to (4) of the Housing and Regeneration Act 2008 (recovery etc of social housing assistance).

(4) The Authority must consult the Regulator before making a general determination under section 32 or 33 of the Housing and Regeneration Act 2008.

(5) For the purposes of this section a person provides low cost home ownership accommodation if (and only if) the person acquires, constructs or converts any housing or other land for use as low cost home ownership accommodation or ensures such acquisition, construction or conversion by another.

(6) In this section 'low cost home ownership accommodation' has the meaning given by section 70 of the Housing and Regeneration Act 2008.

Exercise of functions in relation to certain property etc

333ZI Exercise of functions by the Authority in relation to certain property etc

(1) The Authority may do in relation to any property, rights or liabilities, or any undertaking, to which this section applies anything that the Commission for the New Towns or (as the case may be) an urban development corporation could do in relation to the property, rights or liabilities or the undertaking.

(2) This section applies to –

(a) any property, rights or liabilities that –

(i) have been or are to be transferred to the Authority from the Homes and Communities Agency by virtue of section 190 of the Localism Act 2011, and

(ii) were transferred to the Homes and Communities Agency from the Commission for the New Towns by virtue of section 51 of and Schedule 6 to the Housing and Regeneration Act 2008,

(b) an undertaking, or part of an undertaking, of an urban development corporation that has been or is to be transferred to the Authority by virtue of an agreement under section 165 of the Local Government, Planning and Land Act 1980,

(c) any property, rights or liabilities of an urban development corporation that have been or are to be transferred to the Authority by virtue of an order under section 165B of the Local Government, Planning and Land Act 1980, and

(d) any property, rights or liabilities that –

(i) have been or are to be transferred to the Authority from the Homes and Communities Agency by virtue of section 190 of the Localism Act 2011, and

(ii) were transferred to the Homes and Communities Agency from an urban development corporation by virtue of an order under section 165B of the Local Government, Planning and Land Act 1980.

(3) In any enactment (whenever passed or made) references to the Authority's new towns and urban development functions are to its functions in relation to any property, rights or liabilities, or any undertaking, to which this section applies (whether exercisable by virtue of this section or otherwise).

(4) In subsection (3) 'enactment' includes an enactment comprised in subordinate legislation (within the meaning of the Interpretation Act 1978).

Grants for housing and regeneration purposes

333ZJ Grants to the Authority for housing and regeneration purposes

(1) The Secretary of State may pay to the Authority grants of such amounts as the Secretary of State may, with the Treasury's consent, determine in respect of the exercise of the Authority's functions relating to housing and regeneration.

(2) A grant under this section may be paid at such times, or in such instalments at such times, as the Secretary of State may, with the Treasury's consent, determine.

(3) A grant under this section may be made subject to such conditions as the Secretary of State may determine.

(4) Conditions under subsection (3) may, in particular, include –

(a) provision as to the use of the grant;

(b) provision as to the use of any funds generated by activities funded by the grant;

(c) provision as to the circumstances in which the whole or part of the grant must be repaid.'

(4) After section 333D insert –

'Interpretation

333E Interpretation of Part 7A

In this Part –

'building' means a building or other structure (including a house-boat or caravan);

'caravan' has the meaning given by section 29(1) of the Caravan Sites and Control of Development Act 1960;

'housing' means a building, or part of a building, occupied or intended to be occupied as a dwelling or as more than one dwelling; and includes a hostel which provides temporary residential accommodation;

'land' includes housing or other buildings (and see also the definition in Schedule 1 to the Interpretation Act 1978);

'the Regulator' has the meaning given by section 333ZF(1);

'social housing' (except as part of the expression 'social housing functions') has the same meaning as in Part 2 of the Housing and Regeneration Act 2008 (see section 68 of that Act).'

ooo

191 Abolition of London Development Agency and transfer of its property etc

(1) The London Development Agency ceases to exist on the day on which this subsection comes into force.

(2) The Secretary of State may at any time make a scheme (a 'transfer scheme') transferring the property, rights and liabilities of the London Development Agency that are specified in the scheme to –

(a) the Greater London Authority,
(b) a functional body,
(c) a company that is a subsidiary of the Greater London Authority,
(d) the Secretary of State,
(e) a London borough council, or
(f) the Common Council of the City of London.

(3) Before making a transfer scheme, the Secretary of State must consult the Mayor of London.

(4) The Secretary of State may by order specify another person, or a description of other persons, to whom property, rights or liabilities of the London Development Agency may be transferred by a transfer scheme.

(5) In this section –

'company' means –

(a) a company within the meaning given by section 1(1) of the Companies Act 2006, or
(b) a society registered or deemed to be registered under the Co-operative and Community Benefit Societies and Credit Unions Act 1965 or the Industrial and Provident Societies Act (Northern Ireland) 1969;

'functional body' has the meaning given by section 424(1) of the Greater London Authority Act 1999;

'rights' and 'liabilities' include rights, or (as the case may be) liabilities, in relation to a contract of employment;

'subsidiary' has the meaning given by section 1159 of the Companies Act 2006.

ooo

CHAPTER 2 MAYORAL DEVELOPMENT CORPORATIONS

Introductory

196 Interpretation of Chapter

In this Chapter –

'the Mayor' means the Mayor of London;

'MDC' means a Mayoral development corporation (see section 198).

Establishment and areas

197 Designation of Mayoral development areas

(1) The Mayor may designate any area of land in Greater London as a Mayoral development area.
(2) Separate parcels of land may be designated as one Mayoral development area.
(3) The Mayor may designate a Mayoral development area only if –

(a) the Mayor considers that designation of the area is expedient for furthering any one or more of the Greater London Authority's principal purposes,
(b) the Mayor has consulted the persons specified by subsection (4),
(c) the Mayor has had regard to any comments made in response by the consultees,
(d) in the event that those comments include comments made by the London Assembly or a consultee under subsection (4)(d), (e), (f) or (g) that are comments that the Mayor does not accept, the Mayor has published a statement giving the reasons for the non-acceptance,
(e) the Mayor has laid before the London Assembly, in accordance with standing orders of the Greater London Authority, a document stating that the Mayor is proposing to designate the area, and
(f) the consideration period for the document has expired without the London Assembly having rejected the proposal.

(4) The persons who have to be consulted before an area may be designated are –

(a) the London Assembly,
(b) each constituency member of the London Assembly whose Assembly constituency contains any part of the area,
(c) each Member of Parliament whose parliamentary constituency contains any part of the area,
(d) each London borough council whose borough contains any part of the area,
(e) the Common Council of the City of London if any part of the area is within the City,
(f) the sub-treasurer of the Inner Temple if any part of the area is within the Inner Temple,
(g) the under treasurer of the Middle Temple if any part of the area is within the Middle Temple, and
(h) any other person whom the Mayor considers it appropriate to consult.

(5) For the purposes of subsection (3)(f) –

(a) the 'consideration period' for a document is the 21 days beginning with the day the document is laid before the London Assembly in accordance with standing orders of the Greater London Authority, and
(b) the London Assembly rejects a proposal if it resolves to do so on a motion –

(i) considered at a meeting of the Assembly throughout which members of the public are entitled to be present, and
(ii) agreed to by at least two thirds of the Assembly members voting.

(6) If the Mayor designates a Mayoral development area, the Mayor must –

(a) publicise the designation,
(b) notify the Secretary of State of the designation, and
(c) notify the Secretary of State of the name to be given to the Mayoral development corporation for the area.

(7) Section 30(2) of the Greater London Authority Act 1999 (interpretation of references to the Authority's principal purposes) applies for the purposes of subsection (3)(a).

198 Mayoral development corporations: establishment

(1) Subsection (2) applies if the Secretary of State receives notification under section 197(6) of the designation of a Mayoral development area.
(2) The Secretary of State must by order –

(a) establish a corporation for the area,
(b) give the corporation the name notified to the Secretary of State by the Mayor, and
(c) give effect to any decisions notified under section 202(8) (decisions about planning functions, but see also sections 199(4) and 214(6) as regards other decisions to which effect has to be given).

(3) A corporation established under subsection (2) is a Mayoral development corporation.
(4) A Mayoral development corporation is a body corporate having the name given to it by the order establishing it.
(5) In exercising power under subsection (2) to make provision of the kind mentioned in section 235(2)(b), the Secretary of State is to have regard to any relevant representations received from the Mayor.
(6) Schedule 21 (further provision about MDCs) has effect.

199 Exclusion of land from Mayoral development areas

(1) The Mayor may alter the boundaries of a Mayoral development area so as to exclude any area of land.
(2) Before making an alteration, the Mayor must consult –

(a) the London Assembly, and
(b) any other person whom the Mayor considers it appropriate to consult.

(3) If the Mayor makes an alteration, the Mayor must –

(a) publicise the alteration,
(b) notify the Secretary of State of the alteration, and
(c) notify the MDC for the area (if an MDC has been established for that area).

(4) If the Secretary of State receives notification under subsection (3) of an alteration, the Secretary of State must give effect to the alteration –

(a) when making the order under section 198(2) that establishes an MDC for the Mayoral development area concerned, or
(b) by exercising the power to amend that order (see section 14 of the Interpretation Act 1978).

200 Transfers of property etc to a Mayoral development corporation

(1) The Secretary of State may at any time make a scheme transferring to an MDC property, rights and liabilities of a person within subsection (3).
(2) Before making a scheme under subsection (1), the Secretary of State must consult –

(a) the person whose property, rights or liabilities would be transferred, and
(b) the Mayor.

(3) A person is within this subsection if the person is –

(a) a London borough council,
(b) the Common Council of the City of London in its capacity as a local authority,
(c) the Homes and Communities Agency,
(d) a development corporation established under the New Towns Act 1981 for a new town all or part of whose area is in Greater London,
(e) an urban development corporation for an urban development area all or part of which is in Greater London,
(f) the Olympic Delivery Authority,
(g) any company, or other body corporate, which is a wholly-owned subsidiary of the Olympic Delivery Authority,
(h) any company, or other body corporate, which –

(i) is a subsidiary of the Olympic Delivery Authority, and
(ii) is a subsidiary of at least one other public authority, and
(iii) is not a subsidiary of any person who is not a public authority,

(i) a Minister of the Crown or a government department,
(j) any company all the shares in which are held by a Minister of the Crown, or
(k) any company whose members –

(i) include the Mayor and a Minister of the Crown, and
(ii) do not include anyone who is neither the Mayor nor a Minister of the Crown.

(4) The Mayor may at any time make a scheme transferring to an MDC property, rights and liabilities of –

(a) the Greater London Authority,
(b) a functional body other than that MDC, or
(c) a company that is a subsidiary of the Greater London Authority.

(5) The Mayor must publish a scheme under subsection (4) as soon after it is made as is reasonably practicable.
(6) The Secretary of State may by order specify another person, or a description of other persons, from whom property, rights or liabilities may be transferred under subsection (1) or (4).
(7) In subsection (3)(g) 'wholly-owned subsidiary' has the meaning given by section 1159 of the Companies Act 2006.
(8) For the purposes of subsection (3)(h) and paragraph (b) of this subsection, a body corporate ('C') is a 'subsidiary' of another person ('P') if –

(a) P, or P's nominee, is a member of C, or
(b) C is a subsidiary of a body corporate that is itself a subsidiary of P.

(9) In subsection (4)(c) –

'company' means –

(a) a company within the meaning given by section 1(1) of the Companies Act 2006, or
(b) a society registered or deemed to be registered under the Co-operative and Community Benefit Societies and Credit Unions Act 1965 or the Industrial and Provident Societies Act (Northern Ireland) 1969, and

'subsidiary' has the meaning given by section 1159 of the Companies Act 2006.

(10) In this section –

'functional body' has the meaning given by section 424(1) of the Greater London Authority Act 1999;

'Minister of the Crown' has the same meaning as in the Ministers of the Crown Act 1975;

'public authority' means a public body or a Minister of the Crown or other holder of a public office;

'urban development corporation' means a corporation established by an order under section 135 of the Local Government, Planning and Land Act 1980.

Object and main power

201 Object and powers

(1) The object of an MDC is to secure the regeneration of its area.
(2) An MDC may do anything it considers appropriate for the purposes of its object or for purposes incidental to those purposes.
(3) In this section 'specific power', in relation to an MDC, means any of the MDC's powers other than its powers under subsection (2).
(4) An MDC's specific powers are to be exercised for the purposes of its object or for purposes incidental to those purposes.
(5) Each of an MDC's specific powers may be exercised separately or together with, or as part of, another of its specific powers.
(6) None of an MDC's specific powers limits the scope of its other specific powers.
(7) None of an MDC's specific powers limits the scope of its powers under subsection (2).
(8) But –

(a) subsections (4) and (5) do not apply to an MDC in its capacity as a local planning authority as a result of decisions under section 202 or in its exercise of other functions as a result of decisions under that section,
(b) subsection (4) does not apply to the exercise of a function by an MDC in consequence of an authorisation under section 38 of the Greater London Authority Act 1999 (delegation by Mayor), and
(c) the powers conferred by subsection (2) must not be used to override a restriction imposed on the exercise of a specific power.

Planning and infrastructure functions

202 Functions in relation to Town and Country Planning

(1) Subsections (2) to (4) apply if the Mayor designates a Mayoral development area.
(2) The Mayor may decide that the MDC for the area ('the MDC') is to be the local planning authority, for the whole or any portion of the area, for the purposes of any one or more of the following –

(a) Part 3 of the Town and Country Planning Act 1990,
(b) Part 2 of the Planning and Compulsory Purchase Act 2004, and
(c) Part 3 of that Act.

(3) The Mayor may decide that the MDC is to have, in the whole or any portion of the area, the functions conferred on the local planning authority by the provisions mentioned in Part 1 of Schedule 29 to the Local Government, Planning and Land Act 1980.
(4) The Mayor may decide that the MDC is to have, in the whole or any portion of the area, the functions conferred on the relevant planning authority by Schedule 8 to the Electricity Act 1989 so far as applying to applications for consent under section 37 of that Act.
(5) If the Mayor makes a decision under subsection (3), the Mayor may decide that the provisions specified in Part 2 of Schedule 29 to the Local Government, Planning and

Land Act 1980 are to have effect, in relation to land in the whole or any portion of the area and to the MDC, subject to the modifications specified in that Part of that Schedule.

(6) The Mayor may, at any time before the order establishing the MDC is made, decide that a decision under any of subsections (2) to (5) (whether as originally made or as varied under this subsection) should be subject to variations specified in the decision under this subsection.

(7) The Mayor may make a decision under any of subsections (2) to (6) only if –

(a) the Mayor has consulted the persons specified by section 197(4) in relation to the area,

(b) the Mayor has had regard to any comments made in response by the consultees, and

(c) in the event that those comments include comments made by the London Assembly or an affected local authority that are comments that the Mayor does not accept, the Mayor has published a statement giving the reasons for the non-acceptance.

In paragraph (c) 'affected local authority' means a person specified by section 197(4)(d), (e), (f) or (g) in relation to the area.

(8) If the Mayor makes a decision under any of subsections (2) to (6), the Mayor must –

(a) publicise the decision, and

(b) notify the Secretary of State of the decision.

(9) A decision under subsection (2), or a decision under subsection (6) varying a decision under subsection (2), may make different provision for different portions of the area.

(10) For the purposes of subsection (6) 'variation', in relation to a decision, includes a variation that involves –

(a) revocation of all or part of the decision, or

(b) substitution of something new for all or part of the decision, including substitution of something wholly unlike what it replaces.

203 Arrangements for discharge of, or assistance with, planning functions

(1) Where an MDC, as a result of being the local planning authority for purposes of Part 3 of the Town and Country Planning Act 1990 in relation to any area, has functions in place of a London borough council or the Common Council of the City of London, the MDC may make arrangements for the discharge of any of those functions by that council.

(2) Where arrangements are in force under subsection (1) for the discharge of any functions of an MDC by a council –

(a) that council may arrange for the discharge of those functions by a committee, sub-committee or officer of the council, and

(b) section 101(2) of the Local Government Act 1972 (delegation by committees and sub-committees) applies in relation to those functions as it applies in relation to the functions of that council.

(3) Arrangements under subsection (1) for the discharge of any functions do not prevent the MDC from exercising those functions.

(4) Subsection (5) applies where an MDC, as a result of being the local planning authority for purposes of Part 2 or 3 of the Planning and Compulsory Purchase Act 2004 in relation to any area, has functions in place of a London borough council or the Common Council of the City of London.

(5) The MDC may seek from that council, and that council may give, assistance in connection with the MDC's discharge of any of those functions.

204 Removal or restriction of planning functions

(1) This section applies if an order establishing an MDC ('the MDC') has been made.

(2) The Mayor may decide in relation to a function conferred on the MDC as a result of a decision under section 202(2), (3) or (4) –

(a) that the MDC is to cease to have the function, whether in all respects or in respects specified in the decision, or
(b) that the exercise of the function by the MDC is to be subject to restrictions specified in the decision.

(3) If the Mayor makes a decision under subsection (2) ('the new decision'), the Mayor may decide that any provision made under section 198(2) in consequence of a decision under section 202(5) should, in consequence of the new decision, be amended or revoked as specified in the decision under this subsection.
(4) A reference in subsection (2) or (3) to a decision under a provision of section 202 is, where that decision has been varied (whether once or more than once) under section 202(6), a reference to that decision as varied.
(5) If the Mayor makes a decision under subsection (2) or (3), the Mayor must –

(a) publicise the decision, and
(b) notify the Secretary of State of the decision.

(6) The Secretary of State must give effect to a decision notified under subsection (5) by exercising the power to amend the order under 198(2) that establishes the MDC (see section 14 of the Interpretation Act 1978).

205 Powers in relation to infrastructure

(1) An MDC may provide infrastructure.
(2) An MDC may facilitate the provision of infrastructure.
(3) In this section 'provide' includes provide by way of acquisition, construction, conversion, improvement or repair (and 'provision' is to be read in the same way).
(4) In this section 'infrastructure' means –

(a) water, electricity, gas, telecommunications, sewerage or other services,
(b) roads or other transport facilities,
(c) retail or other business facilities,
(d) health, educational, employment or training facilities,
(e) social, religious or recreational facilities,
(f) cremation or burial facilities, and
(g) community facilities not falling within paragraphs (a) to (f).

Land functions

206 Powers in relation to land

(1) An MDC may regenerate or develop land.
(2) An MDC may bring about the more effective use of land.
(3) An MDC may provide buildings or other land.
(4) An MDC may carry out any of the following activities in relation to land –

(a) acquiring, holding, improving, managing, reclaiming, repairing or disposing of buildings, other land, plant, machinery, equipment or other property,
(b) carrying out building and other operations (including converting or demolishing buildings), and
(c) creating an attractive environment.

(5) An MDC may facilitate –

(a) the regeneration or development of land,
(b) the more effective use of land,
(c) the provision of buildings or other land, or
(d) the carrying out of activities mentioned in subsection (4).

(6) In this section –

(a) a reference to a 'building' is a reference to –

(i) a building or other structure (including a house-boat or caravan), or
(ii) any part of something within sub-paragraph (i);

(b) 'develop' includes redevelop (and 'development' includes redevelopment);
(c) 'improve', in relation to buildings, includes refurbish, equip and fit out;
(d) 'provide' includes provide by way of acquisition, construction, conversion, improvement or repair (and 'provision' is to be read in the same way).

207 Acquisition of land

(1) An MDC may by agreement acquire land in its area or elsewhere.
(2) An MDC may acquire land in its area, or elsewhere in Greater London, compulsorily if the Secretary of State authorises it to do so.
(3) An MDC must obtain the consent of the Mayor of London before submitting a compulsory purchase order authorising an acquisition under subsection (2) to the Secretary of State for confirmation.
(4) The power under subsection (2) includes power to acquire new rights over land.
(5) Subsection (6) applies where –

(a) land forming part of a common, open space or allotment is being acquired under subsection (2), or
(b) new rights are being acquired under subsection (2) over land forming part of a common, open space or allotment.

(6) The power under subsection (2) includes power to acquire land compulsorily for giving in exchange for that land or those new rights.
(7) Part 1 of Schedule 2 to the Housing and Regeneration Act 2008 (compulsory acquisition of land by the Homes and Communities Agency) applies in relation to the acquisition of land under subsection (2) as it applies in relation to the acquisition of land under section 9 of that Act.
(8) In that Part of that Schedule as applied by subsection (7) –

(a) references to section 9 of that Act are to be read as references to subsection (2),
(b) references to the Homes and Communities Agency are to be read as references to the MDC concerned, and
(c) references to Part 1 of that Act are to be read as references to this Chapter.

(9) The provisions of Part 1 of the Compulsory Purchase Act 1965 (other than section 31) apply, so far as applicable, to the acquisition by an MDC of land by agreement.
(10) In subsection (5) –

'allotment' means any allotment set out as a fuel allotment, or a field garden allotment, under an Inclosure Act;

'common' has the meaning given by section 19(4) of the Acquisition of Land Act 1981;

'open space' means any land which is –

(a) laid out as a public garden,
(b) used for the purposes of public recreation, or
(c) a disused burial ground.

208 Powers in relation to acquired land

(1) Schedule 3 to the Housing and Regeneration Act 2008 (powers, in relation to land of the Homes and Communities Agency, to override easements etc, to extinguish public rights of way, and in relation to burial grounds and consecrated land) applies in relation to an MDC and its land as it applies in relation to the Homes and Communities Agency and its land.

(2) In that Schedule as applied by subsection (1), references to the Homes and Communities Agency are to be read as references to the MDC concerned.
(3) The power of the Secretary of State under Part 2 of that Schedule (extinguishment of public rights of way) as applied by subsection (1) is exercisable only with the consent of the Mayor.
(4) Schedule 4 to that Act (powers in relation to, and for, statutory undertakers) applies in relation to an MDC and its land as it applies in relation to the Homes and Communities Agency and its land.
(5) In that Schedule as applied by subsection (4) –

(a) references to the Homes and Communities Agency are to be read as references to the MDC concerned, and
(b) references to Part 1 of that Act are to be read as references to this Chapter.

209 Restrictions on disposal of land

(1) An MDC may not dispose of land for less than the best consideration which can reasonably be obtained unless the Mayor consents.
(2) Subsection (1) does not apply to a disposal by way of a short tenancy if the disposal consists of –

(a) the grant of a term of not more than 7 years, or
(b) the assignment of a term which, at the date of assignment, has not more than 7 years to run.

(3) An MDC may not dispose of land which has been compulsorily acquired by it under this Chapter unless the Mayor consents.
(4) Subject to subsections (1) to (3), an MDC may dispose of land held by it in any way it considers appropriate.

210 Power to enter and survey land

(1) Sections 17 and 18 of the Housing and Regeneration Act 2008 (power to enter and survey land) apply in relation to an MDC as they apply in relation to the Homes and Communities Agency.
(2) In those sections as applied by subsection (1), references to that Agency are to be read as references to the MDC concerned.

Other functions

211 Adoption of private streets

(1) Where any street works have been executed on any land in a Mayoral development area which was then or has since become a private street (or part of a private street), the MDC for the area may serve a notice (an 'adoption notice') on the street works authority requiring the authority to declare the private street (or part) to be a highway which for the purposes of the Highways Act 1980 is a highway maintainable at the public expense.
(2) Subsections (2) to (5) of section 157 of the Local Government, Planning and Land Act 1980 (appeal against corresponding notice served by an urban development corporation, and deemed adoption where no appeal or compliance) apply in relation to an adoption notice under subsection (1) of this section as they apply in relation to an adoption notice under subsection (1) of that section.
(3) Section 157(6) of that Act (interpretation) applies for the purposes of this section.

212 Businesses, subsidiaries and other companies

(1) An MDC may carry on any business.
(2) An MDC may with the consent of the Mayor –

(a) form, or

(b) acquire interests in,

bodies corporate.

(3) An MDC must ensure that no subsidiary of the MDC engages in an activity which the MDC would not be required or permitted to carry on.

(4) An MDC must ensure that no subsidiary of the MDC –

(a) borrows from a person other than the MDC, or
(b) raises money by the issue of shares or stock to a person other than the MDC,

without the consent of the Mayor.

(5) In subsection (1) 'business' includes undertaking.

(6) In this section 'subsidiary' has the meaning given by section 1159 of the Companies Act 2006.

213 Financial assistance

(1) An MDC may, with the consent of the Mayor, give financial assistance to any person.

(2) Financial assistance under this section may be given in any form.

(3) Financial assistance under this section may, in particular, be given by way of –

(a) grants,
(b) loans,
(c) guarantee or indemnity,
(d) investment, or
(e) incurring expenditure for the benefit of the person assisted.

(4) Financial assistance under this section may be given on such terms and conditions as the MDC giving it considers appropriate (including provision for repayment, with or without interest).

214 Powers in relation to discretionary relief from non-domestic rates

(1) Subsection (2) applies if the Mayor designates a Mayoral development area.

(2) The Mayor may decide that the MDC for the area is to have –

(a) in relation to qualifying hereditaments in the area, the function of making decisions (under section 47(3) and (6) of the 1988 Act) to the effect that section 47 of the 1988 Act applies as regards a hereditament, and
(b) in relation to a hereditament as regards which that section applies as a result of a decision made by the MDC, the function of making the determinations mentioned in section 47(1)(a) of the Local Government Finance Act 1988 (determination of amount of discretionary relief).

(3) The Mayor may at any time decide that a decision under subsection (2) should be revoked.

(4) The Mayor may make a decision under subsection (2) or (3) only if –

(a) the Mayor has consulted the persons specified by section 197(4) in relation to the area,
(b) the Mayor has had regard to any comments made in response by the consultees, and
(c) in the event that those comments include comments made by the London Assembly or an affected local authority that are comments that the Mayor does not accept, the Mayor has published a statement giving the reasons for the non-acceptance.

In paragraph (c) 'affected local authority' means a person specified by section 197(4)(d), (e), (f) or (g) in relation to the area.

(5) If the Mayor makes a decision under subsection (2) or (3), the Mayor must –

(a) publicise the decision, and

(b) notify the Secretary of State of the decision.

(6) If the Secretary of State receives notification under subsection (5) of a decision, the Secretary of State must give effect to the decision –

(a) when making the order under section 198(2) that establishes an MDC for the area, or

(b) by exercising the power to amend that order (see section 14 of the Interpretation Act 1978).

(7) Exercise by an MDC of functions mentioned in subsection (2) requires the Mayor's consent.

(8) If an MDC has the functions mentioned in subsection (2) it has them in place of the authority that would otherwise have them.

(9) For the purposes of subsection (2), a hereditament is a 'qualifying hereditament' on a day if neither –

(a) section 43(6) of the 1988 Act (charities and community amateur sports clubs), nor

(b) section 47(5B) of the 1988 Act (certain organisations not established or conducted for profit),

applies on that day.

Dissolution

215 Reviews

It is the duty of the Mayor to review, from time to time, the continuing in existence of any existing MDCs.

216 Transfers of property, rights and liabilities

(1) The Mayor may at any time make a scheme (a 'transfer scheme') transferring to a permitted recipient, upon such terms as the Mayor considers appropriate, any property, rights or liabilities which are for the time being vested in an MDC.

(2) A transfer scheme may provide for a transfer to a person within paragraph (d), (e) or (f) of the definition of 'permitted recipient' in subsection (4) only if the person consents.

(3) The Mayor must publish a transfer scheme as soon after it is made as is reasonably practicable.

(4) In this section –

'company' means –

(a) a company within the meaning given by section 1(1) of the Companies Act 2006, or

(b) a society registered or deemed to be registered under the Co-operative and Community Benefit Societies and Credit Unions Act 1965 or the Industrial and Provident Societies Act (Northern Ireland) 1969;

'functional body' has the meaning given by section 424(1) of the Greater London Authority Act 1999;

'permitted recipient' means –

(a) the Greater London Authority,
(b) a functional body other than the MDC concerned,
(c) a company that is a subsidiary of the Greater London Authority,
(d) a London borough council,
(e) the Common Council of the City of London, or
(f) any other person;

'subsidiary' has the meaning given by section 1159 of the Companies Act 2006.

217 Dissolution: final steps

(1) Subsection (2) applies if no property, no rights and no liabilities are vested in an MDC ('the MDC').
(2) The Mayor may request the Secretary of State to revoke the order under section 198(2) which established the MDC.
(3) If the Secretary of State receives a request under subsection (2), the Secretary of State must make an order giving effect to the request.
(4) Where the Secretary of State makes an order under subsection (3) –

(a) the MDC is dissolved on the coming into force of the order, and
(b) the Mayor must revoke the designation of the Mayoral development area for which the MDC was established.

(5) Where the Mayor makes a revocation under subsection (4)(b), the Mayor must –

(a) publicise the revocation, and
(b) notify the Secretary of State of the revocation.

General

218 Transfer schemes: general provisions

(1) In this section –

'transfer scheme' means a scheme under section 200(1) or (4) or 216(1);

'transferee', in relation to a transfer scheme, means the person to whom property, rights or liabilities are transferred by the scheme;

'transferor', in relation to a transfer scheme, means the person from whom property, rights or liabilities are transferred by the scheme.

(2) The things that may be transferred under a transfer scheme include –

(a) property, rights or liabilities that could not otherwise be transferred;
(b) property acquired, and rights and liabilities arising, after the making of the scheme.

(3) A transfer scheme may make consequential, supplementary, incidental or transitional provision and may in particular –

(a) make provision for certificates issued by the Secretary of State to be conclusive evidence that property has been transferred;
(b) create rights, or impose liabilities, in relation to property or rights transferred;
(c) make provision about the continuing effect of things done (or having effect as if done) by or in relation to the transferor in respect of anything transferred;
(d) make provision about the continuation of things (including legal proceedings) in the process of being done by, on behalf of or in relation to the transferor in respect of anything transferred;
(e) make provision for references to the transferor in an instrument or other document in respect of anything transferred to be treated as references to the transferee;
(f) make provision for the shared ownership or use of property.

(4) The Transfer of Undertakings (Protection of Employment) Regulations 2006 (S.I. 2006/246) apply to a transfer under a transfer scheme where the transfer relates to rights or liabilities under a contract of employment (whether or not it is a relevant transfer for the purposes of those regulations).
(5) A transfer scheme may provide –

(a) for modification by agreement;
(b) for modifications to have effect from the date when the original scheme came into effect.

(6) In this section 'rights' and 'liabilities' include rights, or (as the case may be) liabilities, in relation to a contract of employment.

219 Guidance by the Mayor

(1) The Mayor may give guidance to an MDC as to the exercise of any of the MDC's functions.
(2) Before giving guidance under this section, the Mayor must consult such persons as the Mayor considers appropriate.
(3) The Mayor must publish any guidance given under this section as soon as reasonably practicable after giving it.
(4) The Mayor may revoke guidance given under this section.
(5) The Mayor must –

  (a) consult, before revoking guidance given under this section, such persons as the Mayor considers appropriate, and
  (b) publish the fact that guidance given under this section has been revoked as soon as reasonably practicable after the revocation of the guidance.

(6) An MDC must, in exercising its functions, have regard to any guidance given to it under this section that is for the time being in force.
(7) References in this section to giving guidance include references to giving guidance by varying existing guidance.

220 Directions by the Mayor

(1) The Mayor may give an MDC general or specific directions as to the exercise of any of the MDC's functions.
(2) The Mayor must publish any directions given under this Chapter by the Mayor as soon as reasonably practicable after giving them.
(3) The Mayor –

  (a) may revoke any directions given under this Chapter by the Mayor, and
  (b) must publish the fact that directions given under this Chapter have been revoked as soon as reasonably practicable after the revocation.

(4) An MDC must comply with any directions given by the Mayor under this Chapter that are in force in relation to the MDC.
(5) Subsections (2) and (3)(b) do not apply to directions given under paragraph 8(1) of Schedule 21.
(6) References in this Chapter to the Mayor giving directions include references to the Mayor giving directions by varying existing directions.

221 Consents

(1) A relevant consent may be given –

  (a) unconditionally or subject to conditions, and
  (b) generally or specifically.

(2) The Mayor may vary or revoke a relevant consent except in the case of anything already done, or agreed to be done, on the authority of it.
(3) A variation or revocation under subsection (2) does not have effect until the Mayor has served notice of it on the person to whom the relevant consent was given.
(4) In this section 'relevant consent' means a consent of the Mayor required under this Chapter.

222 Consequential and other amendments

Schedule 22 (Mayoral development corporations: consequential and other amendments) has effect.

CHAPTER 3 GREATER LONDON AUTHORITY GOVERNANCE

223 Delegation of functions by Ministers to the Mayor

(1) The Greater London Authority Act 1999 is amended as follows.
(2) After section 39 insert –

'Delegation to Mayor of Ministers' functions

39A Delegation by Ministers

(1) A Minister of the Crown may, to such extent and subject to such conditions as that Minister thinks fit, delegate to the Mayor any of that Minister's eligible functions.
(2) A function is eligible for the purposes of subsection (1) above if –

(a) it does not consist of a power to make regulations or other instruments of a legislative character or a power to fix fees or charges, and
(b) the Secretary of State considers that it can appropriately be exercised by the Mayor.

(3) No delegation under subsection (1) above, and no variation of a delegation under subsection (1) above, may be made without the agreement of the Mayor.
(4) Before making or varying a delegation under subsection (1) above, a Minister of the Crown must consult –

(a) each London borough council,
(b) the Common Council, and
(c) the Assembly.

(5) A delegation under subsection (1) above may be revoked at any time by any Minister of the Crown.
(6) Section 38 above does not apply in relation to functions delegated under subsection (1) above.'

(3) In section 409 (schemes for the transfer of property, rights and liabilities) –

(a) after subsection (1) (Ministers may make schemes transferring property etc of the Crown) insert –

'(1A) A Minister of the Crown may make a scheme for the transfer from the Authority to the Crown of such property, rights or liabilities as the Minister of the Crown may consider appropriate in consequence of the revocation of a delegation under section 39A(1) above of a function of any Minister of the Crown.', and

(b) in subsections (6) and (7) (provision that may be included in scheme under subsection (1) or (2)) after 'subsection (1)' insert ', (1A)'.

224 Authority may be required to carry on commercial activities through a taxable body

(1) The Greater London Authority Act 1999 is amended as follows.
(2) After section 34 insert –

'34A Restriction on exercise of certain powers except through a taxable body

(1) The Authority may carry on specified activities for a commercial purpose only if it does so –

(a) through a company that is a subsidiary of the Authority, or

(b) in pursuance of an authorisation under section 38(1), through –

(i) a body that is specified in section 38(2) and is within the charge to corporation tax, or
(ii) a company that is a subsidiary of a body specified in section 38(2).

(2) Subsection (3) applies if –

(a) the Authority carries on a specified activity for a commercial purpose otherwise than as permitted by subsection (1), and
(b) the activity is actually carried on by a body (whether the Authority or another) that, disregarding this section, is in respect of the carrying-on of the activity exempt from corporation tax and income tax.

(3) The body mentioned in subsection (2)(b) is to be treated in respect of the carrying-on of the activity as not being a local authority for the purposes of –

(a) section 984 of the Corporation Tax Act 2010 (exemption of local authorities from corporation tax),
(b) section 838 of the Income Tax Act 2007 (exemption of local authorities from income tax), and
(c) section 271 of the Taxation of Chargeable Gains Act 1992 (exemption of local authorities from capital gains tax).

(4) In this section –

'company' means –

(a) a company within the meaning given by section 1(1) of the Companies Act 2006, or
(b) a society registered or deemed to be registered under the Co-operative and Community Benefit Societies and Credit Unions Act 1965 or the Industrial and Provident Societies Act (Northern Ireland) 1969, and

'specified activity' means an activity specified in an order made by the Secretary of State with the consent of the Treasury.'

(3) In section 420(8) (orders subject to annulment) after the entry for section 25 insert – 'section 34A;'.

225 The London Environment Strategy

(1) Before section 352 of the Greater London Authority Act 1999 insert –

'The Mayor's Environment Strategy for London

351A The London Environment Strategy

(1) The Mayor shall prepare and publish a document to be known as the 'London Environment Strategy' ('the Strategy').
(2) The Strategy must contain a general assessment by the Mayor of the environment in Greater London, so far as relevant to the functions of the Authority or of the Mayor.
(3) The Strategy must contain provisions dealing with the Mayor's policies and proposals in relation to each of the following matters in relation to Greater London –

(a) biodiversity;
(b) municipal waste management;
(c) climate change mitigation and energy;

(d) adaptation to climate change;
(e) air quality; and
(f) ambient noise.

(4) The provisions of the Strategy dealing with a matter specified in a paragraph of subsection (2) must also contain anything required to be included in them by any other provision of this Act.
(5) The Strategy may also include provisions dealing with the Mayor's policies and proposals in relation to any other matter relating to the environment in Greater London.
(6) In preparing or revising the provisions of the Strategy dealing with a matter mentioned in subsection (3), the Mayor's duty under section 42(1)(e) applies as if it were a duty to consult any person or body whom the Mayor considers it appropriate to consult in relation to those provisions (and section 42(2) applies accordingly).
(7) Where the Strategy is revised, the Mayor must publish it as revised.
(8) In this Act references to the London Environment Strategy include, unless the context otherwise requires, a reference to the Strategy as revised.

351B Guidance

(1) The Secretary of State may give to the Mayor guidance –

(a) about the content of the London Environment Strategy;
(b) in relation to the preparation or revision of that Strategy.

(2) The guidance that may be given under subsection (1)(a) includes guidance as to matters which the Secretary of State considers the Mayor should, or should not, consider dealing with by formulating policies and proposals under section 351A(5).
(3) The guidance that may be given under subsection (1)(b) includes –

(a) guidance specifying or describing the bodies or persons whom the Secretary of State considers the Mayor should consult in preparing or revising the London Environment Strategy or, as the case may be, the provisions dealing with a matter specified in the guidance;
(b) guidance as to the evidence of environmental change or its consequences, or the predictions of environmental change or its consequences, to which the Secretary of State considers the Mayor should have regard in preparing or revising that Strategy or, as the case may be, the provisions dealing with a matter specified in the guidance.

(4) In preparing or revising the London Environment Strategy the Mayor must have regard to any relevant guidance given under this section.

351C Directions as to the content of the London Environment Strategy

(1) Where the Secretary of State considers that any of the conditions specified in subsection (2) is satisfied in relation to any provisions of the London Environment Strategy, the Secretary of State may give the Mayor a direction as to the content of those provisions.
(2) The conditions are –

(a) that the provisions are inconsistent with any policies announced by Her Majesty's government with respect to the matters to which they relate and the inconsistency would have a detrimental effect on achieving any of the objectives of those policies;
(b) that the provisions or their implementation are likely to be detrimental to any area outside Greater London;

(c) that the provisions are inconsistent with any EU obligation of the United Kingdom.

(3) A direction under this section may require the Mayor to make specified revisions of the London Environmental Strategy.
(4) The power of the Secretary of State to give a direction under this section may only be exercised after consultation with the Mayor.
(5) Where the Secretary of State gives a direction under this section, the Mayor must comply with the direction.'

(2) Schedule 23 (which contains minor and consequential amendments to the Greater London Authority Act 1999 relating to the London Environment Strategy) has effect.

226 Abolition of Mayor's duty to prepare state of the environment reports

Section 351 of the Greater London Authority Act 1999 (which provides for four-yearly reports by the Mayor on the environment in Greater London) ceases to have effect.

227 Mayoral strategies: general duties

(1) Section 41 of the Greater London Authority Act 1999 (general duties of the Mayor in relation to his strategies) is amended as follows.
(2) In subsection (5)(a), for 'and with such international obligations' substitute ', with the EU obligations of the United Kingdom and with such other international obligations of the United Kingdom'.
(3) After subsection (9) insert –

'(9A) In exercising any function the Mayor must have regard to any strategy mentioned in subsection (1) which is relevant to the exercise of that function.'

(4) Subsection (10) ceases to have effect.

228 Simplification of the consultation process for the Mayor's strategies

(1) Section 42A of the Greater London Authority Act 1999 (which requires the Mayor to follow a two stage process in preparing or revising a strategy to which section 42 applies) ceases to have effect.
(2) In section 335 of that Act (public participation in preparation of the spatial development strategy) –

(a) subsections (1) to (1B) cease to have effect,
(b) in subsection (2), for the words from the beginning to 'finally' substitute 'Before', and
(c) in subsection (3), after paragraph (a) insert –

'(aa) the Assembly and the functional bodies;'.

229 London Assembly's power to reject draft strategies

Before section 43 of the Greater London Authority Act 1999 (publicity and availability of strategies) insert –

'42B Assembly's power to reject draft strategies

(1) This section applies where the Mayor has prepared, and is ready to publish, a draft of any of the strategies to which section 41 applies (including a revised version of the strategy).
(2) But this section does not apply to a revised version of a strategy containing only revisions which –

(a) are specified in a direction as to the contents of the strategy which is

given to the Mayor under this Act (or which the Mayor considers are necessary in consequence of any revisions so specified); or
(b) are not so specified but the Mayor considers to be necessary to comply with such a direction.

(3) Before publishing the strategy (or, in the case of the housing strategy, before submitting the draft to the Secretary of State) the Mayor must lay a copy of the draft before the Assembly in accordance with the standing orders of the Authority.
(4) The Mayor must not publish the strategy (or, in the case of the housing strategy, submit the draft to the Secretary of State) if, within the period of 21 days beginning with the day on which the copy is laid before the Assembly, the Assembly resolves to reject the draft.
(5) A motion for the Assembly to reject a draft strategy –

(a) must be considered at a meeting of the Assembly throughout which members of the public are entitled to be present; and
(b) is not carried unless it is agreed to by at least two thirds of the Assembly members voting.'

230 Sharing of administrative etc services by London authorities

(1) Section 401A of the Greater London Authority Act 1999 (sharing of administrative etc services by the Greater London Authority and functional bodies) is amended as follows.
(2) In subsection (1) (definition of 'constituent body') –

(a) for 'constituent body' substitute 'relevant London authority', and
(b) at the end of paragraph (b) insert ',

(c) the London Pensions Fund Authority,
(d) the London Transport Users' Committee,
(e) the Commissioner of Police of the Metropolis, and
(f) such person or body falling within subsection (1A) as the Secretary of State may specify by order.'

(3) After that subsection insert –

'(1A) A person or body falls within this subsection if the person or body exercises functions of a public nature in relation only to –

(a) Greater London,
(b) a part of Greater London, or
(c) a part of England including Greater London or a part of Greater London.'

(4) In subsection (2) (power of constituent bodies to enter into arrangements for provision of administrative etc services) for 'constituent bodies' substitute 'relevant London authorities'.
(5) In subsection (3) (arrangements may include discharge of functions by one constituent body on behalf of another) –

(a) for 'constituent bodies' substitute 'relevant London authorities', and
(b) for 'constituent body' substitute 'relevant London authority'.

(6) In subsection (4) (power of constituent bodies to form joint committees) for 'constituent bodies' substitute 'relevant London authorities'.
(7) In subsection (5) (joint committee to be treated as separate from constituent bodies for purposes of section) –

(a) for 'constituent body' substitute 'relevant London authority', and
(b) for 'constituent bodies' substitute 'relevant London authorities'.

(8) After subsection (6) insert –

'(6A) The Secretary of State must consult a person or body before making an order under subsection (1)(f) specifying that person or body.'

(9) In section 420(8) of that Act (orders subject to annulment) after the entry for section 395 insert 'section 401A(1)(f);'.

ooo

PART 9 COMPENSATION FOR COMPULSORY ACQUISITION

232 Taking account of planning permission when assessing compensation

(1) The Land Compensation Act 1961 is amended as follows.
(2) For sections 14 to 16 (assumptions as to planning permission) substitute –

'14 Taking account of actual or prospective planning permission

(1) This section is about assessing the value of land in accordance with rule (2) in section 5 for the purpose of assessing compensation in respect of a compulsory acquisition of an interest in land.
(2) In consequence of that rule, account may be taken –

(a) of planning permission, whether for development on the relevant land or other land, if it is in force at the relevant valuation date, and
(b) of the prospect, on the assumptions set out in subsection (5) but otherwise in the circumstances known to the market at the relevant valuation date, of planning permission being granted on or after that date for development, on the relevant land or other land, other than –

(i) development for which planning permission is in force at the relevant valuation date, and
(ii) appropriate alternative development.

(3) In addition, it may be assumed –

(a) that planning permission is in force at the relevant valuation date for any development that is appropriate alternative development to which subsection (4)(b)(i) applies, and
(b) that, in the case of any development that is appropriate alternative development to which subsection (4)(b)(ii) applies and subsection (4)(b)(i) does not apply, it is certain at the relevant valuation date that planning permission for that development will be granted at the later time at which at that date it could reasonably have been expected to be granted.

(4) For the purposes of this section, development is 'appropriate alternative development' if –

(a) it is development, on the relevant land alone or on the relevant land together with other land, other than development for which planning permission is in force at the relevant valuation date, and
(b) on the assumptions set out in subsection (5) but otherwise in the circumstances known to the market at the relevant valuation date, planning permission for the development could at that date reasonably have been expected to be granted on an application decided –

(i) on that date, or
(ii) at a time after that date.

(5) The assumptions referred to in subsections (2)(b) and (4)(b) are –

(a) that the scheme of development underlying the acquisition had been cancelled on the launch date,
(b) that no action has been taken (including acquisition of any land, and any development or works) by the acquiring authority wholly or mainly for the purposes of the scheme,
(c) that there is no prospect of the same scheme, or any other project to meet the same or substantially the same need, being carried out in the exercise of a statutory function or by the exercise of compulsory purchase powers, and
(d) if the scheme was for use of the relevant land for or in connection with the construction of a highway ('the scheme highway'), that no highway will be constructed to meet the same or substantially the same need as the scheme highway would have been constructed to meet.

(6) In subsection (5)(a) 'the launch date' means whichever of the following dates applies –

(a) if the acquisition is authorised by a compulsory purchase order, the date of first publication of the notice required under section 11 of the Acquisition of Land Act 1981 or (as the case may be) paragraph 2 of Schedule 1 to that Act,
(b) if the acquisition is authorised by any other order –

(i) the date of first publication, or
(ii) the date of service,

of the first notice that, in connection with the acquisition, is published or served in accordance with any provision of or made under any Act, or
(c) if the acquisition is authorised by a special enactment other than an order, the date of first publication of the first notice that, in connection with the acquisition, is published in accordance with any Standing Order of either House of Parliament relating to private bills;

and in paragraph (a) 'compulsory purchase order' has the same meaning as in the Acquisition of Land Act 1981.
(7) In subsection (5)(d) references to the construction of a highway include its alteration or improvement.
(8) If there is a dispute as to what is to be taken to be the scheme mentioned in subsection (5) ('the underlying scheme') then, for the purposes of this section, the underlying scheme is to be identified by the Upper Tribunal as a question of fact, subject as follows –

(a) the underlying scheme is to be taken to be the scheme provided for by the Act, or other instrument, which authorises the compulsory acquisition unless it is shown (by either party) that the underlying scheme is a scheme larger than, but incorporating, the scheme provided for by that instrument, and
(b) except by agreement or in special circumstances, the Upper Tribunal may permit the acquiring authority to advance evidence of such a larger scheme only if that larger scheme is one identified in the following read together –

(i) the instrument which authorises the compulsory acquisition, and
(ii) any documents published with it.

(9) For the purposes of the references to planning permission in subsections (2)(a) and (b)(i) and (4)(a) and section 15(1)(b), it is immaterial whether any planning permission was granted –

(a) unconditionally or subject to conditions, or
(b) on an ordinary application, on an outline application or by virtue of a development order,

or is planning permission that, in accordance with any direction or provision given or made by or under any enactment, is deemed to have been granted.

15 Planning permission to be assumed for acquiring authority's proposals

(1) In a case where –

(a) the relevant interest is to be acquired for purposes which involve the carrying out of proposals of the acquiring authority for development of the relevant land or part of it, and
(b) planning permission for that development is not in force at the relevant valuation date,

it is to be assumed for the purposes of section 14(2)(a) and (b)(i) and (4)(a) that planning permission is in force at the relevant valuation date for the development of the relevant land or that part of it, as the case may be, in accordance with the proposals of the acquiring authority.

(2) For the purposes of subsection (1)(b), no account is to be taken of any planning permission so granted as not to enure (while the permission remains in force) for the benefit of the land and of all persons for the time being interested in the land.'

(3) For sections 17 and 18 (certification of appropriate alternative development and appeals against certificates) substitute –

'17 Certificates of appropriate alternative development

(1) Where an interest in land is proposed to be acquired by an authority possessing compulsory purchase powers, either of the parties directly concerned may (subject to subsection (2)) apply to the local planning authority for a certificate containing whichever of the following statements is the applicable statement –

(a) that in the local planning authority's opinion there is development that, for the purposes of section 14, is appropriate alternative development in relation to the acquisition;
(b) that in the local planning authority's opinion there is no development that, for the purposes of section 14, is appropriate alternative development in relation to the acquisition.

(2) If –

(a) the acquiring authority have served a notice to treat in respect of the interest or an agreement has been made for the sale of the interest to that authority, and
(b) a reference has been made to the Upper Tribunal to determine the amount of the compensation payable in respect of the interest,

no application for a certificate under this section may be made after the making of that reference by either of the parties directly concerned except with the consent in writing of the other party directly concerned or the permission of the Upper Tribunal.

(3) An application for a certificate under this section –

(a) must contain whichever of the following statements is the applicable statement –

(i) that in the applicant's opinion there is development that, for the purposes of section 14, is appropriate alternative development in relation to the acquisition concerned;
(ii) that in the applicant's opinion there is no development that, for the purposes of section 14, is appropriate alternative development in relation to the acquisition concerned;

(b) must, if it contains a statement under paragraph (a)(i), specify –

(i) each description of development that in the applicant's opinion is, for the purposes of section 14, appropriate alternative development in relation to the acquisition, and
(ii) the applicant's reasons for holding that opinion; and

(c) must be accompanied by a statement specifying the date on which a copy of the application has been or will be served on the other party directly concerned.

(4) Where an application is made to the local planning authority for a certificate under this section in respect of an interest in land, the local planning authority must not, without the agreement of the other party directly concerned, issue a certificate to the applicant before the end of 22 days beginning with the date specified in the statement under subsection (3)(c).

(5) If a certificate under this section contains a statement under subsection (1)(a) it must also –

(a) identify every description of development (whether specified in the application or not) that in the local planning authority's opinion is, for the purposes of section 14, appropriate alternative development in relation to the acquisition concerned, and
(b) give a general indication –

(i) of any conditions to which planning permission for the development could reasonably have been expected to be subject,
(ii) of when the permission could reasonably have been expected to be granted if it is one that could reasonably have been expected to be granted only at a time after the relevant valuation date, and
(iii) of any pre-condition for granting the permission (for example, entry into an obligation) that could reasonably have been expected to have to be met.

(6) If a certificate under this section contains a statement under subsection (1)(a) –

(a) then, for the purposes of section 14, development is appropriate alternative development in relation to the acquisition concerned if, and only if, it is of a description identified in accordance with subsection (5)(a) in the certificate, and
(b) the matters indicated in accordance with subsection (5)(b) in the certificate are to be taken to apply in relation to the planning permission that under section 14(3) may be assumed to be in force for that development.

(7) If a certificate under this section contains a statement under subsection

(1)(b) then, for the purposes of section 14, there is no development that is appropriate alternative development in relation to the acquisition concerned.

(8) References in subsections (5) to (7) to a certificate under this section include references to the certificate as varied and to any certificate issued in place of the certificate.

(9) On issuing to one of the parties directly concerned a certificate under this section in respect of an interest in land, the local planning authority must serve a copy of the certificate on the other of those parties.

(10) In assessing any compensation payable to any person in respect of any compulsory acquisition, there must be taken into account any expenses reasonably incurred by the person in connection with the issue of a certificate under this section (including expenses incurred in connection with an appeal under section 18 where any of the issues are determined in the person's favour).

(11) For the purposes of this section and sections 18 to 20, the Broads Authority is the sole district planning authority for the Broads; and here 'the Broads' has the same meaning as in the Norfolk and Suffolk Broads Act 1988.

18 Appeal to Upper Tribunal against certificate under section 17

(1) Where the local planning authority have issued a certificate under section 17 in respect of an interest in land –

(a) the person for the time being entitled to that interest, or
(b) any authority possessing compulsory purchase powers by whom that interest is proposed to be, or is, acquired,

may appeal to the Upper Tribunal against that certificate.

(2) On any appeal under this section against a certificate, the Upper Tribunal –

(a) must consider the matters to which the certificate relates as if the application for a certificate under section 17 had been made to the Upper Tribunal in the first place, and
(b) must –

(i) confirm the certificate, or
(ii) vary it, or
(iii) cancel it and issue a different certificate in its place,

as the Upper Tribunal may consider appropriate.

(3) Where an application is made for a certificate under section 17, and at the expiry of the time prescribed by a development order for the issue of the certificate (or, if an extended period is at any time agreed upon in writing by the parties and the local planning authority, at the end of that period) no certificate has been issued by the local planning authority in accordance with that section, the preceding provisions of this section apply as if the local planning authority has issued such a certificate containing a statement under section 17(1)(b).'

(4) In section 20 (power to prescribe matters relevant to Part 3) omit –

(a) in the opening words –

(i) the words 'and appeals under section eighteen of this Act', and
(ii) the word 'respectively',

(b) paragraph (b) (manner of and time for giving notice of appeal), and
(c) paragraph (d) (which refers to provisions of section 17 not re-enacted in the section 17 substituted by this Act).

(5) Omit section 21 (proceedings for challenging validity of decision on appeal under section 18).

(6) In section 22 (interpretation of Part 3) –

(a) in subsection (1) (meaning of 'the parties directly concerned') for 'authority by whom it is proposed to be acquired' substitute 'acquiring authority', and

(b) in subsection (2) (interpretation of sections 17 and 18) for 'and eighteen' substitute 'to nineteen'.

(7) In each of paragraph 11 of Schedule 27 to the Local Government, Planning and Land Act 1980 and paragraph 8 of Schedule 9 to the Housing Act 1988 (modifications of section 17(2) of the 1961 Act) –

(a) for 'authority proposing to acquire it' substitute 'acquiring authority',

(b) for 'in respect thereof,' substitute 'in respect of the interest', and

(c) for 'sale thereof' substitute 'sale of the interest'.

(8) The amendments made in the Land Compensation Act 1961 by this section apply to the Crown to the extent set out in section 33 of that Act (Act applies in relation to acquisition by government department, including any Minister of the Crown, that is an authority possessing compulsory purchase powers as it applies to other authorities possessing those powers).

PART 10 GENERAL

ooo

235 Orders and regulations

(1) Any power of a Minister of the Crown or the Welsh Ministers to make an order or regulations under this Act is exercisable by statutory instrument.

(2) Any power of a Minister of the Crown or the Welsh Ministers to make an order or regulations under this Act (other than a power under section 240) includes –

(a) power to make different provision for different cases, circumstances or areas, and

(b) power to make incidental, supplementary, consequential, transitional or transitory provision or savings.

(3) The power under subsection (2)(a) includes, in particular, power to make different provision for different authorities or descriptions of authority (including descriptions framed by reference to authorities in particular areas).

(4) Provision or savings made under subsection (2)(b) may take the form of amendments, or revocations, of provisions of an instrument made under legislation.

(5) The generality of the power under subsection (2)(a) is not to be taken to be prejudiced by any specific provision of this Act authorising differential provision.

(6) A Minister of the Crown may not make an order or regulations to which subsection (7) applies unless a draft of the statutory instrument containing the order or regulations (whether alone or with other provisions) has been laid before, and approved by a resolution of, each House of Parliament.

(7) This subsection applies to –

(a) an order under section 5(2) that –

(i) amends any Act or provision of an Act, and

(ii) is not made (in reliance on section 7(4)) in accordance with sections 15 to 19 of the Legislative and Regulatory Reform Act 2006 as applied by section 7(3);

(b) an order under section 5(3), other than one that is made only for the purpose mentioned in section 7(5)(b);
(c) an order under section 5(4), other than one that is made only for that purpose or for imposing conditions on the doing of things for a commercial purpose;
(d) an order under section 8(2);
(e) an order under section 52;
(f) regulations under section 81(2)(d), (6)(e) or (10) or 83(11);
(g) an order under section 87(4) or 96(7);
(h) regulations under section 101;
(i) an order under section 106(2) or 107(6);
(j) regulations under section 117;
(k) an order or regulations under section 236 which amend or repeal a provision of an Act otherwise than in consequence of provision made by or under section 232;
(l) an order or regulations under section 236 which, in consequence of provision made by section 232, amend or repeal a provision of an Act other than a local or private Act.

(8) A statutory instrument that –

(a) contains an order or regulations made by a Minister of the Crown under this Act,
(b) is not subject to any requirement that a draft of the instrument be laid before, and approved by a resolution of, each House of Parliament, and
(c) is not subject to any requirement that a draft of the instrument be laid before, and approved by a resolution of, the House of Commons,

is subject to annulment in pursuance of a resolution of either House of Parliament.

(9) Subsection (8) does not apply to –

(a) an order under section 5(1) (but see section 7),
(b) an order under section 5(2) which (in reliance on section 7(4)) is made in accordance with sections 15 to 19 of the Legislative and Regulatory Reform Act 2006 as applied by section 7(3),
(c) an order under section 15 (but see section 19),
(d) an order or regulations under Schedule 24, or
(e) an order under section 240.

(10) A statutory instrument that contains an order or regulations made by the Treasury under Schedule 24 is subject to annulment in pursuance of a resolution of the House of Commons.

(11) The Welsh Ministers may not make –

(a) an order or regulations under section 236 which amend or repeal a provision of legislation,
(b) an order under section 62,
(c) an order under section 87(4) or 96(7),
(d) regulations under section 101, or
(e) an order under section 106(4) or 107(6),

unless a draft of the statutory instrument containing the order or regulations (whether alone or with other provisions) has been laid before, and approved by a resolution of, the National Assembly for Wales.

(12) A statutory instrument that –

(a) contains an order or regulations made by the Welsh Ministers under this Act, and
(b) is not subject to any requirement that a draft of the instrument be laid before, and approved by a resolution of, the National Assembly for Wales,

is subject to annulment in pursuance of a resolution of the National Assembly for Wales.

(13) Subsection (12) does not apply to an order under section 240.

(14) If a draft of a statutory instrument containing an order under section 52 would, apart from this subsection, be treated for the purposes of the standing orders of either House of Parliament as a hybrid instrument, it is to proceed in that House as if it were not such an instrument.

(15) In this section –

'legislation' means –

(a) an Act, or
(b) a Measure or Act of the National Assembly for Wales;

'Minister of the Crown' has the same meaning as in the Ministers of the Crown Act 1975.

ooo

237 Repeals and revocations

Schedule 25 (repeals and revocations) has effect.

ooo

240 Commencement

(1) The following provisions come into force at the end of 2 months beginning with the day on which this Act is passed –

(a) section 25,
(b) Chapter 8 of Part 1 so far as relating to England,
(c) section 44,
(d) section 45,
(e) section 47,
(f) section 71,
(g) section 80,
(h) sections 111 to 113,
(i) section 143,
(j) section 177,
(k) section 183 and Schedule 18,
(l) Chapter 2 of Part 8, except section 197(3)(e) and (f) and (5), and
(m) Parts 6, 8, 14, 17 and 29 of Schedule 25, and section 237 so far as relating to those Parts.

(2) Subject to subsections (1) and (3) to (6), provisions of this Act come into force on such day as the Secretary of State may by order appoint.

(3) The following provisions so far as relating to Wales come into force on such day as the Welsh Ministers may by order appoint –

(a) Chapter 8 of Part 1,
(b) section 46,
(c) section 68,
(d) section 69,
(e) Chapter 3 of Part 5 except so far as it is brought into force by subsection (5)(f) and (g),
(f) sections 148, 149 and 162(3)(b) and (c), and
(g) Parts 7, 9, 10 and 22 of Schedule 25, and section 237 so far as relating to those Parts.

(4) The following provisions come into force on such day as the Welsh Ministers may by order appoint –

(a) section 9(1) so far as it inserts –

(i) new sections 5A and 5B so far as relating to fire and rescue authorities in Wales,

(ii) new sections 5C and 5D so far as relating to power of the Welsh Ministers to make orders, and

(iii) new sections 5F to 5L,

(b) section 9(2) so far as relating to fire and rescue authorities in Wales,

(c) section 9(3), (6) and (7)(a) and (c),

(d) section 9(7)(b) so far as it inserts new section 62(1A)(a) and (d),

(e) section 9(7)(b) so far as it inserts new section 62(1A)(b) so far as relating to power of the Welsh Ministers to make orders,

(f) section 10(1) to (3) and (5) so far as relating to fire and rescue authorities in Wales,

(g) section 10(4),

(h) Part 3,

(j) the following so far as relating to fire and rescue authorities in Wales –

(i) in Part 2 of Schedule 25, the entries for sections 5 and 19 of the Fire and Rescue Services Act 2004, and

(ii) section 237 so far as relating to those entries, and

(k) in Part 2 of Schedule 25, the entry for section 62(3) of the Fire and Rescue Services Act 2004, and section 237 so far as relating to that entry.

(5) The following provisions come into force on the day on which this Act is passed –

(a) section 23,

(b) paragraphs 57 and 58 of Schedule 4, and section 26 so far as relating to those paragraphs,

(c) section 37,

(d) Chapter 2 of Part 5 so far as it confers power on the Secretary of State to make regulations,

(e) section 86,

(f) Chapter 3 of Part 5 so far as it confers power on the Secretary of State, or the Welsh Ministers, to make regulations or orders,

(g) sections 103 and 104,

(h) section 109(1)(b) and (2) to (6), paragraphs 1, 13(1), 18 and 19 of Schedule 8 and section 109(7) so far as relating to those provisions of that Schedule,

(i) section 110,

(j) sections 116 and 121 and Schedules 9 to 12 so far as those sections or Schedules confer power on the Secretary of State to make regulations or publish documents setting standards,

(k) sections 117 to 120,

(l) the provisions inserted by section 122 so far as they require or authorise the making of provision in a development order,

(m) section 144,

(n) sections 168 to 175,

(o) section 233 and Schedule 24 so far as they confer power on the Treasury to make regulations or orders,

(p) sections 234, 235, 236, 238, 239, this section and section 241, and

(q) Part 15 of Schedule 25, and section 237 so far as relating to that Part.

(6) Section 114 comes into force on the day after the day on which this Act is passed.

(7) An order under subsection (2), (3) or (4) may –

(a) appoint different days for different purposes;

(b) make such transitory or transitional provision, or savings, as the person making the order considers appropriate.

(8) The appropriate authority may by order make such transitory or transitional provision, or savings, as the appropriate authority considers appropriate in connection with the coming into force of any provision of this Act mentioned in subsection (1), (5) or (6).

(9) In subsection (8) 'appropriate authority' –

(a) in relation to sections 25 and 45, and Part 6 of Schedule 25 and section 237 so far as relating to that Part, means –

(i) the Secretary of State in relation to England, and
(ii) the Welsh Ministers in relation to Wales,

(b) in relation to sections 80 and 104, and Chapter 3 of Part 5 so far as it confers power on the Welsh Ministers to make regulations or orders, means the Welsh Ministers, and

(c) in relation to any other provision mentioned in subsection (1), (5) or (6) means the Secretary of State.

SCHEDULE 2 NEW ARRANGEMENTS WITH RESPECT TO GOVERNANCE OF ENGLISH LOCAL AUTHORITIES

Section 21

PART 1 NEW PART 1A OF THE LOCAL GOVERNMENT ACT 2000

1 After Part 1 of the Local Government Act 2000 insert –

'PART 1A ARRANGEMENTS WITH RESPECT TO LOCAL AUTHORITY GOVERNANCE IN ENGLAND

CHAPTER 1 Permitted forms of governance

9B Permitted forms of governance for local authorities in England

(1) A local authority must operate –

(a) executive arrangements,
(b) a committee system, or
(c) prescribed arrangements.

(2) Executive arrangements must conform with any provisions made by or under this Part which relate to such arrangements (see, in particular, Chapter 2).

(3) A committee system must conform with any provisions made by or under this Part which relate to such a system (see, in particular, Chapter 3).

(4) In this Part –

'a committee system' means the arrangements made by a local authority, which does not operate executive arrangements or prescribed arrangements, for or in connection with the discharge of its functions in accordance with –

(a) Part 6 of the Local Government Act 1972, and
(b) this Part;

'executive arrangements' means arrangements by a local authority –

(a) for and in connection with the creation and operation of an executive of the authority, and
(b) under which certain functions of the authority are the responsibility of the executive;

'prescribed arrangements' means such arrangements as may be prescribed in regulations made by the Secretary of State under section 9BA.

9BA Power of Secretary of State to prescribe additional permitted governance arrangements

(1) The Secretary of State may by regulations make provision prescribing arrangements that local authorities may operate for and in connection with the discharge of their functions.

(2) In particular, the regulations –

(a) must include provision about how, and by whom, the functions of a local authority are to be discharged, and

(b) may include provision enabling functions to be delegated.

(3) Regulations under this section may, in particular, include provision which applies or reproduces (with or without modifications) any provisions of, or any provision made under, Chapters 2 to 4 of this Part.

(4) In considering whether or how to exercise the power in this section, the Secretary of State must have regard to any proposals made under subsection (5).

(5) A local authority may propose to the Secretary of State that the Secretary of State make regulations prescribing arrangements specified in the proposal if the authority considers that the conditions in subsection (6) are met.

(6) The conditions are –

(a) that the operation by the authority of the proposed arrangements would be an improvement on the arrangements which the authority has in place for the discharge of its functions at the time that the proposal is made to the Secretary of State,

(b) that the operation by the authority of the proposed arrangements would be likely to ensure that the decisions of the authority are taken in an efficient, transparent and accountable way, and

(c) that the arrangements, if prescribed under this section, would be appropriate for all local authorities, or for any particular description of local authority, to consider.

(7) A proposal under subsection (5) –

(a) must describe the provision which the authority considers should be made under subsection (2) in relation to the proposed arrangements, and

(b) explain why the conditions in subsection (6) are met in relation to the proposed arrangements.

CHAPTER 2 Executive arrangements

Local authority executives

9C Local authority executives

(1) The executive of a local authority must take a form specified in subsection (2) or (3).

(2) The executive may consist of –

(a) an elected mayor of the authority, and

(b) two or more councillors of the authority appointed to the executive by the elected mayor.

Such an executive is referred to in this Part as a mayor and cabinet executive.

(3) The executive may consist of –

(a) a councillor of the authority (referred to in this Part as the executive leader) elected as leader of the executive by the authority, and
(b) two or more councillors of the authority appointed to the executive by the executive leader.

Such an executive is referred to in this Part as a leader and cabinet executive (England).
(4) A local authority executive may not include the chairman or vice-chairman of the authority.
(5) The number of members of a local authority executive may not exceed 10 or such other number as may be specified in regulations made by the Secretary of State.
(6) Section 101 of the Local Government Act 1972 (arrangements for discharge of functions by local authorities) does not apply to the function of electing a leader under subsection (3)(a).

Executive functions

9D Functions which are the responsibility of an executive

(1) This section has effect for the purposes of determining which of the functions of a local authority that operates executive arrangements are the responsibility of an executive of the authority under those arrangements.
(2) Subject to any provision made by this Act or by any enactment which is passed or made after the day on which this Act is passed, any function of the local authority which is not specified in regulations under subsection (3) is to be the responsibility of an executive of the authority under executive arrangements.
(3) The Secretary of State may by regulations make provision for any function of a local authority specified in the regulations –

(a) to be a function which is not to be the responsibility of an executive of the authority under executive arrangements,
(b) to be a function which may be the responsibility of such an executive under such arrangements, or
(c) to be a function which –

(i) to the extent provided by the regulations, is to be the responsibility of such an executive under such arrangements, and
(ii) to the extent provided by the regulations, is not to be the responsibility of such an executive under such arrangements.

(4) Executive arrangements must make provision for any function of a local authority falling within subsection (3)(b) –

(a) to be a function which is to be the responsibility of an executive of the authority,
(b) to be a function which is not to be the responsibility of such an executive, or
(c) to be a function which –

(i) to the extent provided by the arrangements, is to be the responsibility of such an executive, and
(ii) to the extent provided by the arrangements, is not to be the responsibility of such executive.

(5) The power under subsection (3)(c) or (4)(c) includes power in relation to any function of a local authority that operates executive arrangements –

(a) to designate any action in connection with the discharge of that function which is to be the responsibility of an executive of the local authority, and
(b) to designate any action in connection with the discharge of that function which is not to be the responsibility of such an executive.

(6) The Secretary of State may by regulations specify cases or circumstances in which any function of a local authority which, by virtue of the preceding provisions of this section, would otherwise be the responsibility of an executive of the authority to any extent is not to be the responsibility of such an executive to that or any particular extent.
(7) A function of a local authority may, by virtue of this section, be the responsibility of an executive of the authority to any extent notwithstanding that section 101 of the Local Government Act 1972, or any provision of that section, does not apply to that function.
(8) Any reference in this section to a function specified in regulations includes a reference to a function of a description specified in regulations.
(9) In this section –

'action' in relation to any function includes any action (of whatever nature and whether or not separately identified by any enactment) involving –

(a) the taking of any step in the course of, or otherwise for the purposes of or in connection with, the discharge of the function,
(b) the doing of anything incidental or conducive to the discharge of the function, or
(c) the doing of anything expedient in connection with the discharge of the function or any action falling within paragraph (a) or (b);

'function' means a function of any nature, whether conferred or otherwise arising before, on or after the passing of this Act.

9DA Functions of an executive: further provision

(1) Any reference in the following provisions of this Chapter to any functions which are, or are not, the responsibility of an executive of a local authority under executive arrangements is a reference to the functions of the authority to the extent to which they are or (as the case may be) are not, by virtue of section 9D, the responsibility of the executive under such arrangements.
(2) Any function which is the responsibility of an executive of a local authority under executive arrangements –

(a) is to be regarded as exercisable by the executive on behalf of the authority, and
(b) may be discharged only in accordance with any provisions made by or under this Part or section 236 of the Local Government and Public Involvement in Health Act 2007 (exercise of functions by local councillors in England) which apply to the discharge of any such function by that form of executive.

(3) Accordingly, any function which is the responsibility of an executive of a local authority under executive arrangements –

(a) may not be discharged by the authority,
(b) is not to be a function to which section 101(1) of the Local Government Act 1972 applies, and
(c) may be the subject of arrangements made under section 101(5) of that Act only if permitted by any provision made under section 9EB.

(4) Subject to any provision made under subsection (5), any function of a local

authority that operates executive arrangements which, under those arrangements, is not the responsibility of the executive of the local authority is to be discharged in any way which would be permitted or required apart from the provisions made by or under this Chapter.

(5) The Secretary of State may by regulations make provision with respect to the discharge of any function of a local authority that operates executive arrangements which, under those arrangements, is not the responsibility of the executive of the local authority (including provision disapplying section 101 of the Local Government Act 1972 or any provision of that section).

(6) In this section 'function' has the same meaning as in section 9D.

Discharge of functions

9E Discharge of functions: general

(1) Subject to any provision made under section 9EA or 9EB, any functions which, under executive arrangements, are the responsibility of –

(a) a mayor and cabinet executive, or
(b) a leader and cabinet executive (England),

are to be discharged in accordance with this section.

(2) The senior executive member –

(a) may discharge any of those functions, or
(b) may arrange for the discharge of any of those functions –

(i) by the executive,
(ii) by another member of the executive,
(iii) by a committee of the executive,
(iv) by an area committee, or
(v) by an officer of the authority.

(3) Where by virtue of this section any functions may be discharged by a local authority executive, then, unless the senior executive member otherwise directs, the executive may arrange for the discharge of any of those functions –

(a) by a committee of the executive,
(b) by an area committee, or
(c) by an officer of the authority.

(4) Where by virtue of this section any functions may be discharged by a member of a local authority executive, then, unless the senior executive member otherwise directs, the member who may discharge the functions may arrange for the discharge of any of those functions –

(a) by an area committee, or
(b) by an officer of the authority.

(5) Where by virtue of this section any functions may be discharged by a committee of a local authority executive, then, unless the senior executive member otherwise directs, the committee may arrange for the discharge of any of those functions –

(a) by an area committee, or
(b) by an officer of the authority.

(6) Where by virtue of this section any functions may be discharged by an area committee, then, unless the senior executive member otherwise directs, the

committee may arrange for the discharge of any of those functions by an officer of the authority.

(7) Any arrangements made by virtue of this section by a senior executive member, executive, member or committee for the discharge of any functions by an executive, member, committee or officer are not to prevent the senior executive member, executive, member or committee by whom the arrangements are made from exercising those functions.

(8) In this section –

'area committee', in relation to a local authority, means a committee or sub-committee of the authority which satisfies the conditions in subsection (9);

'senior executive member' means –

(a) in the case of a mayor and cabinet executive, the elected mayor;
(b) in the case of a leader and cabinet executive (England), the executive leader.

(9) A committee or sub-committee of a local authority satisfies the conditions in this subsection if –

(a) the committee or sub-committee is established to discharge functions in respect of part of the area of the authority, and
(b) the members of the committee or sub-committee who are members of the authority are elected for electoral divisions or wards which fall wholly or partly within that part.

9EA Discharge of functions of and by another local authority

(1) The Secretary of State may by regulations make provision for or in connection with enabling an executive of a local authority, or a committee or specified member of such an executive, to arrange for the discharge of any functions which, under executive arrangements, are the responsibility of the executive –

(a) by a relevant authority (other than the local authority), or
(b) by a relevant executive (other than an executive of the local authority) or a committee or specified member of such an executive.

(2) The Secretary of State may by regulations make provision for or in connection with enabling a relevant authority in England to arrange for the discharge of any of its functions by a relevant executive (other than an executive of the relevant authority) or a committee or specified member of such an executive.

(3) The reference in subsection (2) to the functions of a relevant authority in England, in a case where the authority is operating executive arrangements, is a reference to the functions which, under those arrangements, are not the responsibility of the authority's executive.

(4) Regulations under subsection (1) or (2) may, in particular, include provision –

(a) requiring, in the case of arrangements for the discharge of any functions by a relevant executive or a committee or member of such an executive, the approval of the authority of which the executive is part to such arrangements;
(b) which, in the case of arrangements for the discharge of any functions by a relevant authority, enables any of those functions to be delegated;
(c) which, in the case of arrangements for the discharge of any functions

by a relevant executive or a committee or member of such an executive, enables any of those functions to be delegated.

(5) The provision made under subsection (4)(b) may, in particular, apply or reproduce (with or without modifications) any provisions of section 101(2) to (4) of the Local Government Act 1972.

(6) The provision made under subsection (4)(c) may, in particular, apply or reproduce (with or without modifications) any provisions of section 9E.

(7) In this section –

'relevant authority' means a local authority within the meaning of section 101 of the Local Government Act 1972;

'relevant executive' means an executive of a local authority under either this Part or Part 2;

'specified' means specified in regulations under this section.

9EB Joint exercise of functions

(1) The Secretary of State may by regulations make provision for or in connection with permitting arrangements under section 101(5) of the Local Government Act 1972 where any of the functions which are the subject of the arrangements are the responsibility of an executive of a local authority under executive arrangements.

(2) The provision which may be made under subsection (1) includes, in particular, provision –

(a) as to the circumstances in which the executive, or a committee or specified member of the executive, is to be a party to the arrangements in place of the authority,

(b) as to the circumstances in which –

(i) the authority, and

(ii) the executive or a committee or specified member of the executive,

are both to be parties to the arrangements,

(c) as to the circumstances in which any functions of the local authority under section 101(2) or 102(1)(b), (2) or (3) of the Local Government Act 1972, so far as they relate to any joint committee falling within section 101(5)(a) of that Act, are instead to be exercised by the executive or a committee or specified member of the executive,

(d) as to the circumstances in which any functions of the local authority under section 101(2) or 102(1)(b), (2) or (3) of that Act, so far as they relate to any such joint committee, are to be exercised by the authority,

(e) as to the circumstances in which appointments to any such joint committee by the executive, or a committee or specified member of the executive, need not be made in accordance with the political balance requirements,

(f) as to the persons (including officers of the authority) who may be appointed to any such joint committee by the executive or a committee or specified member of the executive.

(3) In this section 'specified' means specified in regulations under this section.

Overview and scrutiny committees

9F Overview and scrutiny committees: functions

(1) Executive arrangements by a local authority must include provision for the

appointment by the authority of one or more committees of the authority (referred to in this Chapter as overview and scrutiny committees).

(2) Executive arrangements by a local authority must ensure that its overview and scrutiny committee has power (or its overview and scrutiny committees, and any joint overview and scrutiny committees, have power between them) –

(a) to review or scrutinise decisions made, or other action taken, in connection with the discharge of any functions which are the responsibility of the executive,

(b) to make reports or recommendations to the authority or the executive with respect to the discharge of any functions which are the responsibility of the executive,

(c) to review or scrutinise decisions made, or other action taken, in connection with the discharge of any functions which are not the responsibility of the executive,

(d) to make reports or recommendations to the authority or the executive with respect to the discharge of any functions which are not the responsibility of the executive,

(e) to make reports or recommendations to the authority or the executive on matters which affect the authority's area or the inhabitants of that area,

(f) in the case of the overview and scrutiny committee, or committees, of an authority to which section 244 of the National Health Service Act 2006 applies –

(i) to review and scrutinise, in accordance with regulations under that section, matters relating to the health service (within the meaning given by that Act as extended by that section) in the authority's area, and

(ii) to make reports and recommendations on such matters in accordance with the regulations.

(3) In subsection (2) 'joint overview and scrutiny committee', in relation to a local authority ('the authority concerned'), means –

(a) a joint overview and scrutiny committee within the meaning given by subsection (2)(a) of section 245 of the National Health Service Act 2006 appointed by the authority concerned and one or more other local authorities,

(b) an overview and scrutiny committee of another local authority exercising relevant functions (within the meaning given by subsection (1) of that section) of the authority concerned by virtue of arrangements made under regulations under subsection (2)(b) of that section, or

(c) a joint overview and scrutiny committee within the meaning of section 123 of the Local Government and Public Involvement in Health Act 2007 (joint overview and scrutiny committees) appointed by two or more local authorities including the authority concerned.

(4) The power of an overview and scrutiny committee under subsection (2)(a) to review or scrutinise a decision made but not implemented includes power –

(a) to recommend that the decision be reconsidered by the person who made it, or

(b) to arrange for its function under subsection (2)(a), so far as it relates to the decision, to be exercised by the authority.

(5) An overview and scrutiny committee of a local authority may not discharge any functions other than –

(a) its functions under this section and sections 9FA to 9FI, or
(b) its functions under section 19 of the Police and Justice Act 2006 (local authority scrutiny of crime and disorder matters).

9FA Overview and scrutiny committees: supplementary provision

(1) An overview and scrutiny committee of a local authority –

(a) may appoint one or more sub-committees, and
(b) may arrange for the discharge of any of its functions by any such sub-committee.

(2) A sub-committee of an overview and scrutiny committee may not discharge any functions other than those conferred on it under subsection (1)(b).
(3) An overview and scrutiny committee of a local authority, or a sub-committee of such a committee, may not include any member of the authority's executive.
(4) An overview and scrutiny committee of a local authority, or any sub-committee of such a committee, may include persons who are not members of the authority.
(5) Subject to any provision made by or under paragraphs 6 to 8 of Schedule A1 and to section 20(6) of the Police and Justice Act 2006, any persons who are not members of the local authority are not entitled to vote at any meeting of its overview and scrutiny committee, or any sub-committee of such a committee, on any question which falls to be decided at that meeting, unless permitted to do so under paragraphs 11 and 12 of that Schedule.
(6) An overview and scrutiny committee of a local authority, or a sub-committee of such a committee, is to be treated –

(a) as a committee or sub-committee of a principal council for the purposes of Part 5A of the Local Government Act 1972 (access to meetings and documents of certain authorities, committees and sub-committees), and
(b) as a body to which section 15 of the Local Government and Housing Act 1989 (duty to allocate seats to political groups) applies.

(7) Subsections (2) and (5) of section 102 of the Local Government Act 1972 apply to an overview and scrutiny committee of a local authority, or a sub-committee of such a committee, as they apply to a committee appointed under that section.
(8) An overview and scrutiny committee of a local authority or a sub-committee of such a committee –

(a) may require members of the executive, and officers of the authority, to attend before it to answer questions,
(b) may require any other member of the authority to attend before it to answer questions relating to any function which is exercisable by the member by virtue of section 236 of the Local Government and Public Involvement in Health Act 2007 (exercise of functions by local councillors in England), and
(c) may invite other persons to attend meetings of the committee.

(9) It is the duty of any member or officer mentioned in paragraph (a) or (b) of subsection (8) to comply with any requirement mentioned in that paragraph.
(10) A person is not obliged by subsection (9) to answer any question which the

person would be entitled to refuse to answer in or for the purposes of proceedings in a court in England and Wales.

(11) In exercising, or deciding whether to exercise, any of its functions an overview and scrutiny committee of a local authority, or a sub-committee of such a committee, must have regard to any guidance for the time being issued by the Secretary of State.

(12) Guidance under subsection (11) may make different provision for different cases or for different descriptions of committee or sub-committee.

9FB Scrutiny officers

(1) Subject as follows, a local authority must designate one of its officers to discharge the functions in subsection (2).

(2) Those functions are –

- (a) to promote the role of the authority's overview and scrutiny committee or committees,
- (b) to provide support to the authority's overview and scrutiny committee or committees and the members of that committee or those committees,
- (c) to provide support and guidance to –
    - (i) members of the authority,
    - (ii) members of the executive of the authority, and
    - (iii) officers of the authority,

  in relation to the functions of the authority's overview and scrutiny committee or committees.

(3) An officer designated by a local authority under this section is to be known as the authority's 'scrutiny officer'.

(4) A local authority may not designate any of the following under this section –

- (a) the head of the authority's paid service designated under section 4 of the Local Government and Housing Act 1989;
- (b) the authority's monitoring officer designated under section 5 of that Act;
- (c) the authority's chief finance officer, within the meaning of that section.

(5) The duty in subsection (1) does not apply to a district council for an area for which there is a county council.

(6) In this section, references to an overview and scrutiny committee include any sub-committee of that committee.

9FC Reference of matters to overview and scrutiny committee etc

(1) Executive arrangements by a local authority must include provision which –

- (a) enables any member of an overview and scrutiny committee of the authority to refer to the committee any matter which is relevant to the functions of the committee,
- (b) enables any member of a sub-committee of such a committee to refer to the sub-committee any matter which is relevant to the functions of the sub-committee, and
- (c) enables any member of the authority to refer to an overview and scrutiny committee of the authority of which the member of the authority is not a member any matter which is relevant to the functions of the committee and is not an excluded matter.

(2) For the purposes of subsection (1), provision enables a person to refer a

matter to a committee or sub-committee if it enables the person to ensure that the matter is included in the agenda for, and discussed at, a meeting of the committee or sub-committee.

(3) In considering whether to exercise the power which a member of an authority has by virtue of subsection (1)(c) in any case, the member must have regard to any guidance for the time being issued by the Secretary of State.

(4) Guidance under subsection (3) may make different provision for different cases.

(5) In subsection (1)(c) 'excluded matter' means any matter which is –

(a) a local crime and disorder matter within the meaning of section 19 of the Police and Justice Act 2006 (local authority scrutiny of crime and disorder matters), or

(b) a matter of any description specified in an order made by the Secretary of State for the purposes of this section.

9FD Dealing with references under section 9FC(1)(c)

(1) This section applies where a matter is referred to an overview and scrutiny committee by a member of a local authority in accordance with provision made pursuant to section 9FC(1)(c).

(2) In considering whether or not to exercise any of its powers under section 9F(2) in relation to the matter, the committee may have regard to –

(a) any powers which the member may exercise in relation to the matter by virtue of section 236 of the Local Government and Public Involvement in Health Act 2007 (exercise of functions by local councillors in England), and

(b) any representations made by the member as to why it would be appropriate for the committee to exercise any of its powers under section 9F(2) in relation to the matter.

(3) If the committee decides not to exercise any of those powers in relation to the matter, it must notify the member of –

(a) its decision, and

(b) the reasons for it.

(4) The committee must provide the member with a copy of any report or recommendations which it makes to the authority or the executive under section 9F(2) in relation to the matter.

(5) Subsection (4) is subject to section 9FG (confidential and exempt information).

9FE Duty of authority or executive to respond to overview and scrutiny committee

(1) This section applies where an overview and scrutiny committee of a local authority makes a report or recommendations to the authority or the executive, otherwise than –

(a) by virtue of subsection (1)(b) of section 19 of the Police and Justice Act 2006 (local authority scrutiny of crime and disorder matters), or

(b) by virtue of subsection (3)(a) of that section.

(2) The overview and scrutiny committee may publish the report or recommendations.

(3) The overview and scrutiny committee must by notice in writing require the authority or executive –

(a) to consider the report or recommendations,
(b) to respond to the overview and scrutiny committee indicating what (if any) action the authority, or the executive, proposes to take,
(c) if the overview and scrutiny committee has published the report or recommendations under subsection (2), to publish the response, and
(d) if the overview and scrutiny committee provided a copy of the report or recommendations to a member of the authority under section 9FD(4), to provide the member with a copy of the response.

(4) The notice served under subsection (3) must require the authority or executive to comply with it within two months beginning with the date on which the authority or executive received the report or recommendations or (if later) the notice.
(5) It is the duty of an authority or executive to which a notice is given under subsection (3) to comply with the requirements specified in the notice.
(6) Subsections (2) and (5) are subject to section 9FG and to any provision made under section 9GA(8) (confidential and exempt information).
(7) In this section –

(a) references to an overview and scrutiny committee include references to a sub-committee of such a committee;
(b) references to 'the authority' or 'the executive', in relation to an overview and scrutiny committee, or a sub-committee of such a committee, are to the authority by which the overview and scrutiny committee is established or to the executive of that authority.

9FF Reports and recommendations of overview and scrutiny committees: duties of certain partner authorities

(1) This section applies where –

(a) a relevant committee makes a report or recommendations to the authority or the executive, otherwise than –

(i) by virtue of subsection (1)(b) of section 19 of the Police and Justice Act 2006 (local authority scrutiny of crime and disorder matters), or
(ii) by virtue of subsection (3)(a) of that section, and

(b) the report or any of the recommendations relates to functions of a relevant partner authority so far as exercisable in relation to –

(i) the authority's area, or
(ii) the inhabitants of that area.

(2) The relevant committee may by notice in writing to the relevant partner authority require the relevant partner authority to have regard to the report or recommendation in question in exercising its functions.
(3) A notice under subsection (2) must be accompanied by a copy of the report or recommendations.
(4) It is the duty of a relevant partner authority to which a notice is given under subsection (2) to comply with the requirement specified in the notice.
(5) Subsection (2) does not apply if –

(a) the relevant partner authority is a health service body, and
(b) either –

(i) the relevant committee is a non-unitary district council committee, or
(ii) by virtue of section 244 of the National Health Service Act

2006, the report was, or the recommendations were, made to the health service body (as well as to the authority or the executive).

(6) In subsection (5) 'health service body' means –

(a) a National Health Service trust,
(b) an NHS foundation trust, or
(c) a Primary Care Trust.

(7) Subsections (2) and (3) are subject to section 9FG (confidential and exempt information).

(8) In this section –

'the authority', in relation to a relevant committee, means –

(a) in the case of an overview and scrutiny committee, the local authority by which it is established, and
(b) in the case of a sub-committee of an overview and scrutiny committee, the local authority by which the overview and scrutiny committee is established,

'the executive', in relation to a relevant committee, means the executive of the authority,

'non-unitary district council committee' means –

(a) an overview and scrutiny committee of a district council for a district in a county for which there is a county council, or
(b) a sub-committee of such a committee,

'relevant committee' means an overview and scrutiny committee or a sub-committee of such a committee,

'relevant partner authority', in relation to a relevant committee other than a non-unitary district council committee, means any person who is a partner authority in relation to the authority for the purposes of Chapter 1 of Part 5 of the Local Government and Public Involvement in Health Act 2007, other than a chief officer of police, and

'relevant partner authority', in relation to a relevant committee that is a non-unitary district council committee, means –

(a) the county council for the county concerned, or
(b) any person (other than the district council concerned) who is a partner authority in relation to that county council for the purposes of Chapter 1 of Part 5 of the Local Government and Public Involvement in Health Act 2007, other than a chief officer of police.

9FG Publication etc of reports, recommendations and responses: confidential and exempt information

(1) This section applies to –

(a) the publication under section 9FE of any document comprising –
  (i) a report or recommendations of an overview and scrutiny committee, or
  (ii) a response of a local authority to any such report or recommendations, and
(b) the provision of a copy of such a document –

(i) to a member of a local authority under section 9FD(4) or section 9FE, or
(ii) to a relevant partner authority under section 9FF,

by an overview and scrutiny committee or a local authority.

(2) The overview and scrutiny committee or the local authority, in publishing the document or providing a copy of the document to a relevant partner authority –

(a) must exclude any confidential information, and
(b) may exclude any relevant exempt information.

(3) The overview and scrutiny committee or the local authority, in providing a copy of the document to a member of the local authority, may exclude any confidential information or relevant exempt information.

(4) Where information is excluded under subsection (2) or (3), the overview and scrutiny committee or the local authority, in publishing, or providing a copy of, the document –

(a) may replace so much of the document as discloses the information with a summary which does not disclose that information, and
(b) must do so if, in consequence of excluding the information, the document published, or copy provided, would be misleading or not reasonably comprehensible.

(5) Subsection (6) applies if, by virtue of subsection (2), (3) or (4), an overview and scrutiny committee, in publishing or providing a copy of a report or recommendations –

(a) excludes information, or
(b) replaces part of the report or recommendations with a summary.

(6) The overview and scrutiny committee is nevertheless to be taken for the purposes of section 9FE(3)(c) or (d) to have published or provided a copy of the report or recommendations.

(7) In this section, references to relevant exempt information are references to –

(a) in relation to a report or recommendations of an overview and scrutiny committee, exempt information of a description specified in a resolution of the overview and scrutiny committee under section 100A(4) of the Local Government Act 1972 which applied to the proceedings, or part of the proceedings, at any meeting of the overview and scrutiny committee at which the report was, or recommendations were, considered, and
(b) in relation to a response of the authority, exempt information of a description specified in such a resolution of the authority which applied to the proceedings, or part of the proceedings, at any meeting of the authority at which the report or response was, or recommendations were, considered.

(8) In this section –

'confidential information' has the meaning given by section 100A(3) of the Local Government Act 1972 (admission to meetings of principal councils),

'exempt information' has the meaning given by section 100I of that Act and, in relation to –

(a) any report or recommendations of an overview and scrutiny committee which has functions under section 9F(2)(f) (national health service functions), or
(b) any response to such a report or recommendations,

also includes information which is exempt information under section 246 of the National Health Service Act 2006, and

'relevant partner authority', in relation to an overview and scrutiny committee which is a relevant committee within the meaning of section 9FF, has the same meaning as in that section.

(9) In this section, references to an overview and scrutiny committee include references to a sub-committee of such a committee.

9FH Overview and scrutiny committees: flood risk management

(1) This section applies to a local authority that operates executive arrangements and that is a lead local flood authority.
(2) The arrangements required under section 9F(2) include arrangements to review and scrutinise the exercise by risk management authorities of flood risk management functions or coastal erosion risk management functions which may affect the local authority's area.
(3) A risk management authority must comply with a request made by an overview and scrutiny committee, in the course of arrangements under subsection (2), for –

(a) information;
(b) a response to a report.

(4) The Secretary of State may make regulations about the duty under subsection (3) which may, in particular, include provision –

(a) about the procedure to be followed in relation to requests and compliance with them,
(b) about notices to be served in relation to requests,
(c) for exemptions from the duty,
(d) requiring persons to attend to give information orally,
(e) about the nature of the information and responses that may be requested, and
(f) about the publication of requests, information and responses.

(5) A risk management authority must have regard to reports and recommendations of an overview and scrutiny committee made in the course of arrangements under subsection (2).
(6) Regulations under section 123 of the Local Government and Public Involvement in Health Act 2007 may make provision about the application of this section in relation to joint overview and scrutiny committees.
(7) Expressions used in this section have the same meaning as in Part 1 of the Flood and Water Management Act 2010.

9FI Overview and scrutiny committees: provision of information etc by certain partner authorities

(1) The Secretary of State may by regulations make provision, in relation to a relevant committee –

(a) as to information which relevant partner authorities must provide to the relevant committee, and
(b) as to information which may not be disclosed by a relevant partner authority to the relevant committee.

(2) In subsection (1), references to information do not include information in respect of which provision may be made in exercise of the power conferred by –

(a) section 20(5)(c) or (d) of the Police and Justice Act 2006 (guidance and regulations regarding crime and disorder matters), or
(b) section 244(2)(d) or (e) of the National Health Service Act 2006 (functions of overview and scrutiny committees).

(3) For the purposes of subsection (1), 'relevant committee' and 'relevant partner authority' have the meanings given by section 9FF.
(4) Regulations under this section may make different provision in relation to different persons or committees or descriptions of person or committee.
(5) The power conferred by subsection (4) does not affect the power conferred by section 105(2)(b).

Further provision in relation to executives

9G Meetings and access to information etc

(1) Meetings of a local authority executive, or a committee of such an executive, are to be open to the public or held in private.
(2) Subject to regulations under section 9GA(4), it is for a local authority executive to decide which of its meetings, and which of the meetings of any committee of the executive, are to be open to the public and which of those meetings are to be held in private.
(3) A written record must be kept of prescribed decisions made at meetings of local authority executives, or committees of such executives, which are held in private.
(4) A written record must be kept of prescribed decisions made by individual members of local authority executives.
(5) Written records under subsection (3) or (4) must include reasons for the decisions to which they relate.
(6) In this section 'prescribed' means prescribed by regulations made by the Secretary of State.

9GA Meetings and access to information etc: further provision and regulations

(1) Written records under section 9G(3) and (4), together with such reports, background papers or other documents as may be prescribed, must be made available to members of the public in accordance with regulations made by the Secretary of State.
(2) Regulations under subsection (1) may make provision for or in connection with preventing the whole or part of any record or document containing prescribed information from being made available to members of the public.
(3) The Secretary of State may by regulations make provision –

(a) with respect to the access of the public to meetings of joint committees, or sub-committees of such committees, at which decisions are made in connection with the discharge of functions which are the responsibility of executives (including provision enabling such meetings to be held in private),
(b) for or in connection with requiring written records to be kept of decisions made at meetings which by virtue of paragraph (a) are held in private,
(c) for or in connection with requiring written records falling within paragraph (b) to include reasons,
(d) for or in connection with requiring any such written records to be made available to members of the public,

(e) for or in connection with requiring documents connected with decisions to which any such written records relate to be made available to members of the public.

(4) The Secretary of State may by regulations make provision –

(a) as to the circumstances in which meetings mentioned in section 9G(2), or particular proceedings at such meetings, must be open to the public,
(b) as to the circumstances in which meetings mentioned in section 9G(2), or particular proceedings at such meetings, must be held in private,
(c) with respect to the information which is to be included in written records kept by virtue of this section or section 9G,
(d) with respect to the reasons which are to be included in any such written records,
(e) with respect to the persons who are to produce, keep or make available any such written records,
(f) for or in connection with requiring any such written records to be made available to members of local authorities or to overview and scrutiny committees or sub-committees,
(g) for or in connection with requiring documents connected with decisions to which any such written records relate to be made available to members of local authorities or to overview and scrutiny committees or sub-committees,
(h) for or in connection with requiring information to be made available by electronic means,
(i) for or in connection with conferring rights on members of the public or members of local authorities, overview and scrutiny committees or sub-committees in relation to records or documents,
(j) for or in connection with the creation of offences in respect of any rights or requirements conferred or imposed by virtue of this section or section 9G.

(5) The Secretary of State may by regulations make provision for or in connection with requiring prescribed information about prescribed decisions made in connection with the discharge of functions which are the responsibility of a local authority executive to be made available to members of the public or members of the authority.
(6) The provision which may be made under subsection (5) includes provision –

(a) requiring prescribed information to be made available in advance of the prescribed decisions mentioned in that subsection,
(b) as to the way or form in which prescribed information is to be made available.

(7) The Secretary of State may by regulations make provision which, in relation to meetings of –

(a) local authority executives or committees of such executives, or
(b) joint committees, or sub-committees of such committees, falling within subsection (3)(a),

applies or reproduces (with or without modifications) any provisions of Part 5A of the Local Government Act 1972.
(8) The Secretary of State may by regulations make provision, in relation to –

(a) the publication by executives of local authorities under section 9FE of responses to reports or recommendations of overview and scrutiny committees and sub-committees of such committees, or

(b) the provision by such executives under that section of copies of such responses,

which applies or reproduces (with or without modifications) any provisions of section 9FG (confidential and exempt information).

(9) In this section –

'joint committee' means a joint committee falling within section 101(5)(a) of the Local Government Act 1972,

'prescribed' means prescribed by regulations made by the Secretary of State.

9GB Further provision

Schedule A1 (which makes further provision in relation to executive arrangements under this Part) has effect.

9GC Absence of requirement for political balance

Neither –

(a) a local authority executive, nor

(b) a committee of a local authority executive,

is to be regarded as a body to which section 15 of the Local Government and Housing Act 1989 (duty to allocate seats to political groups) applies.

Elected mayors etc

9H Elected mayors etc

(1) In this Part 'elected mayor', in relation to a local authority, means an individual elected as mayor of the authority by the local government electors for the authority's area in accordance with the provisions made by or under this Part.

(2) An elected mayor is to be entitled to the style of 'mayor'.

(3) A reference in any enactment (whenever passed or made) to –

(a) a member of a local authority, or

(b) a councillor of a local authority,

does not include a reference to an elected mayor of the authority.

(4) But subsection (3) is subject to –

(a) regulations made by the Secretary of State under this paragraph which provide that an elected mayor is to be treated as a member or councillor of a local authority for the purposes of an enactment (whenever passed or made), and

(b) any other contrary intention that appears in any enactment (whenever passed or made).

(5) Section 2(2A) of, and paragraph 5C(1) of Schedule 2 to, the Local Government Act 1972 are not to be taken to indicate any contrary intention for the purposes of subsection (4)(b).

(6) Elections for the return of an elected mayor are to take place on the ordinary day of election in each of the relevant election years.

(7) The term of office of an elected mayor of a local authority is to be four years.

(8) This section is subject to regulations under section 9HB or 9HE.

9HA Election as elected mayor and councillor

(1) If the person who is returned at an election as the elected mayor of a local authority is also returned at an election held at the same time as a councillor of the authority, a vacancy arises in the office of councillor.

(2) If the person who is returned at an election ('the mayoral election') as the elected mayor of a local authority –

(a) is a councillor of the authority, and
(b) was returned as such a councillor at an election held at an earlier time than the mayoral election,

a vacancy shall arise in the office of councillor.

(3) Subject to subsection (4), a person who is the elected mayor of a local authority may not be a candidate in an election for the return of a councillor or councillors of the authority.

(4) A person who is the elected mayor of a local authority may be a candidate in an election for the return of a councillor or councillors of the authority if the election is held at the same time as an election for the return of the elected mayor of the authority, but subsection (1) applies if the person is a candidate in both such elections and is returned both as the elected mayor and as a councillor.

9HB Time of elections etc

The Secretary of State may by regulations make provision –

(a) as to the dates on which and years in which elections for the return of elected mayors may or must take place,
(b) as to the intervals between elections for the return of elected mayors,
(c) as to the term of office of elected mayors, and
(d) as to the filling of vacancies in the office of elected mayor.

9HC Voting at elections of elected mayors

(1) Each person entitled to vote as an elector at an election for the return of an elected mayor is to have the following vote or votes –

(a) one vote (referred to in this Part as a first preference vote) which may be given for the voter's first preference from among the candidates to be the elected mayor, and
(b) if there are three or more candidates to be the elected mayor, one vote (referred to in this Part as a second preference vote) which may be given for the voter's second preference from among those candidates

(2) The elected mayor is to be returned under the simple majority system, unless there are three or more candidates.

(3) If there are three or more candidates to be the elected mayor, the elected mayor is to be returned under the supplementary vote system in accordance with Schedule 2.

9HD Entitlement to vote

(1) The persons entitled to vote as electors at an election for the return of an elected mayor are those who on the day of the poll –

(a) would be entitled to vote as electors at an election of councillors for an electoral area which is situated within the area of the local authority concerned, and

(b) are registered in the register of local government electors at an address within the authority's area.

(2) A person is not entitled as an elector to cast more than one first preference vote, or more than one second preference vote, at an election for the return of an elected mayor.

9HE Power to make provision about elections

(1) The Secretary of State may by regulations make provision as to –

(a) the conduct of elections for the return of elected mayors, and
(b) the questioning of elections for the return of elected mayors and the consequences of irregularities.

(2) Regulations made under subsection (1)(a) may, in particular, include provision –

(a) about the registration of electors,
(b) for disregarding alterations in a register of electors,
(c) about the limitation of election expenses (and the creation of criminal offences in connection with the limitation of such expenses), and
(d) for the combination of polls at elections for the return of elected mayors and other elections.

(3) Regulations under this section may –

(a) apply or incorporate, with or without modifications or exceptions, any provision of, or made under, the Representation of the People Acts or any provision of any other enactment (whenever passed or made) relating to parliamentary elections or local government elections,
(b) modify any form contained in, or in regulations or rules made under, the Representation of the People Acts so far as may be necessary to enable it to be used both for the original purpose and in relation to elections for the return of elected mayors, and
(c) so far as may be necessary in consequence of any provision made by or under this Part or any regulations under this section, amend any provision of any enactment (whenever passed or made) relating to the registration of parliamentary electors or local government electors.

(4) Before making any regulations under this section, the Secretary of State must consult the Electoral Commission.
(5) In addition, the power of the Secretary of State to make regulations under this section so far as relating to matters mentioned in subsection (2)(c) is exercisable only on, and in accordance with, a recommendation of the Electoral Commission, except where the Secretary of State considers that it is expedient to exercise that power in consequence of changes in the value of money.
(6) No return of an elected mayor at an election is to be questioned except by an election petition under the provisions of Part 3 of the Representation of the People Act 1983 as applied by or incorporated in regulations under this section.

Leader and cabinet executives (England)

9I Election and term of office of leader

Executive arrangements by a local authority which provide for a leader and cabinet executive (England) –

(a) must include provision with respect to the election of the executive leader, including provision for an election where there is a vacancy in the office of executive leader, and
(b) may include provision with respect to the term of office of the executive leader.

9IA Removal of leader

(1) Executive arrangements by a local authority which provide for a leader and cabinet executive (England) must include provision for the council to remove the executive leader by resolution.
(2) If a council passes a resolution to remove the executive leader, a new executive leader is to be elected –

(a) at the meeting at which the leader is removed from office, or
(b) at a subsequent meeting.

9IB Leader to continue to hold office as councillor

(1) A person who is the executive leader of a leader and cabinet executive (England) remains a member of the council during the period that the person is the executive leader.
(2) Accordingly, any enactment which provides for the person's earlier retirement as a councillor does not apply.
(3) This section does not affect anything by which the executive leader may cease to be a councillor otherwise than by retirement (including disqualification or resignation).

9IC No other means of removing leader

(1) This section applies to a local authority which operates a leader and cabinet executive (England).
(2) An executive leader may not be removed from office except in accordance with section 9IA or regulations under section 9ID.

9ID Regulations

(1) The Secretary of State may by regulations make provision –

(a) as to the election and removal from office of executive leaders of leader and cabinet executives (England),
(b) as to the term of office of an executive leader of a leader and cabinet executive (England), and
(c) as to the filling of vacancies in the office of executive leader of a leader and cabinet executive (England).

(2) Sections 9I to 9IC are subject to regulations under this section.

CHAPTER 3 The committee system

9J Secretary of State's power to prohibit delegation of functions etc

(1) The Secretary of State may by regulations –

(a) specify or describe any function of a committee system local authority that is to be a non-delegable function;
(b) specify or describe cases or circumstances in which any specified or described function of a committee system local authority is to be a non-delegable function;
(c) specify or describe any action in connection with the discharge of a function of a committee system local authority that is to be a non-delegable action;

(d) specify or describe cases or circumstances in which any specified or described action in connection with the discharge of a function of a committee system local authority is to be a non-delegable action.

(2) If a function or action is non-delegable –

(a) it must be carried out by the local authority, and
(b) such provisions of section 101 of the Local Government Act 1972 as may be specified in regulations under this section do not apply to it.

(3) In this Part 'committee system local authority' means a local authority that operates a committee system.
(4) For the purposes of this section, something is specified or described if it is specified or described in regulations made by the Secretary of State under this section.
(5) In this section –

'action' in relation to any function includes any action (of whatever nature and whether or not separately identified by any enactment) involving –

(a) the taking of any step in the course of, or otherwise for the purposes of or in connection with, the discharge of the function,
(b) the doing of anything incidental or conducive to the discharge of the function, or
(c) the doing of anything expedient in connection with the discharge of the function or any action within paragraph (a) or (b);

'function' means a function of any nature, whether conferred or otherwise arising before, on or after this section comes into force.

9JA Overview and scrutiny committee

(1) A committee system local authority may by resolution appoint one or more committees as the authority's overview and scrutiny committee or, as the case may be, committees.
(2) The Secretary of State may by regulations make provision about –

(a) the functions, composition and procedure of a committee that has been appointed as an overview and scrutiny committee under this section, and
(b) the appointment by committee system local authorities of joint committees and sub-committees as overview and scrutiny committees.

(3) Provision under subsection (2) may, in particular, include provision which applies or reproduces (with or without modifications) any provision of, or made under, sections 9F to 9FI or paragraphs 6 to 13 of Schedule A1.

9JB Overview and scrutiny: flood risk management

(1) A committee system local authority that is a lead local flood authority must review and scrutinise the exercise by risk management authorities of –

(a) flood risk management functions, or
(b) coastal erosion risk management functions,

which may affect the local authority's area.
(2) A local authority may issue such reports and recommendations as it considers appropriate in the course of exercising the function in subsection (1).
(3) A risk management authority must comply with a request made by a local authority in the course of exercising the function in subsection (1) for –

(a) information;
(b) a response to a report.

(4) The Secretary of State may make regulations about the duty under subsection (3) which may, in particular, include provision –

(a) about the procedure to be followed in relation to requests and compliance with them,
(b) about notices to be served in relation to requests,
(c) for exemptions from the duty,
(d) requiring persons to attend to give information orally,
(e) about the nature of the information and responses that may be requested, and
(f) about the publication of requests, information and responses.

(5) A risk management authority must have regard to any reports or recommendations mentioned in subsection (2) that relate to it.
(6) Expressions used in this section have the same meaning as in Part 1 of the Flood and Water Management Act 2010.

CHAPTER 4 Changing governance arrangements

Changes to governance arrangements by local authorities: general provision

9K Changing from one form of governance to another

(1) A local authority may –

(a) cease to operate its existing form of governance, and
(b) start to operate a different form of governance.

(2) This section is subject to section 9NA (effect of order requiring, and giving effect to, referendum on change to mayor and cabinet executive).

9KA Executive arrangements: different form of executive

(1) A local authority which operates executive arrangements may –

(a) vary the arrangements so that they provide for a different form of executive, and
(b) if it makes such a variation, vary the arrangements in such other respects (if any) as it considers appropriate.

(2) This section is subject to section 9NA (effect of order requiring, and giving effect to, referendum on change to mayor and cabinet executive).

9KB Executive arrangements: other variation of arrangements

A local authority which operates executive arrangements may vary those arrangements so that they –

(a) differ from the existing arrangements in any respect, but
(b) still provide for the same form of executive.

9KC Resolution of local authority

(1) A resolution of a local authority is required in order for the authority to make a change in governance arrangements.
(2) As soon as practicable after passing such a resolution a local authority must –

(a) secure that copies of a document setting out the provisions of the arrangements that are to have effect following the resolution are available at its principal office for inspection by members of the public, and

(b) publish in one or more newspapers circulating in its area a notice which –

(i) states that the authority has resolved to make a change in its governance arrangements,

(ii) states the date on which the change is to have effect,

(iii) describes the main features of the change,

(iv) states that copies of a document setting out the provisions of the arrangements that are to have effect following the resolution are available at the authority's principal office for inspection by members of the public, and

(v) specifies the address of the authority's principal office.

(3) Subsection (4) applies if a local authority passes a resolution in accordance with this section ('Resolution A') which makes a change in governance arrangements of the kind set out in –

(a) section 9K (change from one form of governance to another), or

(b) section 9KA (change to a different form of executive).

(4) The local authority may not pass another resolution that makes a change in governance arrangements of a kind mentioned in subsection (3) ('Resolution B') before the end of the period of 5 years beginning with the date Resolution A is passed, unless Resolution B is approved in a referendum held in accordance with this Chapter.

(5) This section does not apply to a change in governance arrangements effected by an order under section 9N (power by order to require, and give effect to, referendum on change to mayor and cabinet executive).

Implementation of certain changes to governance arrangements

9L Implementation: change in form of governance or change in form of executive

(1) This section applies if a local authority passes a resolution which makes a change in governance arrangements of the kind set out in –

(a) section 9K (change from one form of governance to another), or

(b) section 9KA (change to a different form of executive).

(2) At a relevant change time, the local authority must –

(a) cease operating the old form of governance or (as the case may be) old form of executive, and

(b) start operating the form of governance or (as the case may be) form of executive which the change in governance arrangements provides for.

(3) Subject to subsection (2) and section 9MB(2), the local authority may take steps for the purposes of preparing for the change or implementing it (including steps relating to transitional arrangements).

(4) If the local authority is not currently operating a mayor and cabinet executive and the change does not provide for the local authority to operate a mayor and cabinet executive, a 'relevant change time' for the purposes of subsection (2) is a time during –

(a) the first annual meeting of the local authority to be held after the resolution to make the change in governance arrangements is passed, or

(b) a later annual meeting of the local authority specified in that resolution.

(5) If the local authority is not currently operating a mayor and cabinet executive and the change provides for the local authority to operate a mayor and cabinet executive, a 'relevant change time' for the purposes of subsection (2) is –

(a) a time during the third day after the day of the declaration of the result of the poll at the first election of the mayor, or

(b) if a person is returned as the mayor at that first election without a poll being taken, a time during the third day after the day on which a poll would have been taken.

(6) If the local authority is currently operating a mayor and cabinet executive and the change provides for the local authority to cease to operate a mayor and cabinet executive, a 'relevant change time' for the purposes of subsection (2) is a time during the third day after the day on which the next ordinary election of a mayor was expected to be held when the resolution to make the change in governance arrangements was passed.

Referendums

9M Cases in which change is subject to approval in a referendum in accordance with sections 9MA and 9MB

(1) A change in governance arrangements which a local authority proposes to make by resolution is subject to approval in a referendum in either of the following cases.

(2) The first case is where –

(a) the proposed change in governance arrangements is of a kind set out in –

(i) section 9K (change from one form of governance to another), or

(ii) section 9KA (change to a different form of executive), and

(b) the implementation of the local authority's existing form of governance or existing form of executive was approved in a referendum under this Chapter.

(3) The second case is where the local authority resolves that a proposed change in governance arrangements is to be subject to approval in a referendum.

9MA Referendum: proposals by local authority

(1) This section applies to a local authority which wishes to make a change in governance arrangements that is subject to approval in a referendum under section 9M.

(2) The local authority must draw up proposals for the change.

(3) The proposals must include –

(a) a timetable with respect to the implementation of the proposals,

(b) details of any transitional arrangements which are necessary for the implementation of the proposals, and

(c) a statement that the change in governance arrangements is to be subject to approval in a referendum.

(4) Subsections (5) and (6) apply where the proposed change in governance arrangements is of the kind set out in –

(a) section 9K (change from one form of governance to another), or
(b) section 9KA (change to a different form of executive).

(5) If the proposed change in governance arrangements would result in the local authority having executive arrangements, the proposals must state the extent to which the functions specified in regulations under section 9D(3)(b) are to be the responsibility of the executive which will be operated if the proposals are implemented.
(6) The proposals (particularly any provision about timetables and transitional matters included in accordance with subsection (3)) must be such as to ensure that the proposed change can take effect (so far as required to) in accordance with section 9L(2).
(7) After drawing up the proposals, the local authority must –

(a) secure that copies of a document setting out the proposals are available at its principal office for inspection by members of the public at all reasonable times, and
(b) publish in one or more newspapers circulating in its area a notice which –

(i) states that the authority has drawn up the proposals,
(ii) describes the main features of the proposals,
(iii) states that copies of a document setting out the proposals are available at the authority's principal office for inspection by members of the public at such times as may be specified in the notice, and
(iv) specifies the address of the authority's principal office.

9MB Requirement to hold and give effect to referendum

(1) This section applies to a local authority which wishes to make a change in governance arrangements that is subject to approval in a referendum under section 9M.
(2) The local authority must, after complying with section 9MA(7), hold a referendum on its proposals before taking any steps to implement them.
(3) The local authority may not pass a resolution which makes the proposed change unless the result of the referendum is to approve the proposals.
(4) Any such resolution must be passed within the period of 28 days beginning with the day when the referendum is held.
(5) Any such resolution must be passed at a meeting which is specially convened for the purpose of deciding the resolution with notice of the object.

9MC Referendum following petition

(1) The Secretary of State may by regulations make provision for or in connection with requiring a local authority which receives a petition which complies with the provisions of the regulations to hold a referendum, in such circumstances as may be prescribed in the regulations, on whether the authority should have a relevant type of governance arrangement.
(2) Regulations under subsection (1) may, in particular, include provision –

(a) as to the form and content of petitions (including provision for petitions in electronic form),
(b) as to the minimum number of local government electors for a local authority's area who must support any petition presented to the authority during any period specified in the regulations,

(c) for or in connection with requiring an officer of a local authority to publish the number of local government electors for the authority's area who must support any petition presented to the authority,
(d) as to the way in which local government electors for a local authority's area are to support a petition (including provision enabling local government electors to support petitions by telephone or by electronic means),
(e) as to the action which may, may not or must be taken by a local authority in connection with any petition,
(f) as to the manner in which a petition is to be presented to a local authority,
(g) as to the verification of any petition,
(h) as to the date on which, or the time by which, a referendum must be held,
(i) as to the action which may, may not or must be taken by a local authority before or in connection with a referendum,
(j) as to the action which may, may not or must be taken by a local authority after a referendum, and
(k) for or in connection with enabling the Secretary of State, in the event of any failure by a local authority to take any action permitted or required by virtue of the regulations, to take that action.

(3) Provision made by virtue of subsection (2) may, in particular, apply or reproduce (with or without modifications) any provisions of, or made under, this Chapter.
(4) The number of local government electors mentioned in subsection (2)(b) is to be calculated at such times as may be provided by regulations under this section and (unless such regulations otherwise provide) is to be 5 per cent of the number of local government electors at each of those times.
(5) This section is subject to section 9NA (effect of order requiring, and giving effect to, referendum on change to mayor and cabinet executive).

9MD Referendum following direction

(1) The Secretary of State may by regulations make provision for or in connection with enabling the Secretary of State, in such circumstances as may be prescribed in the regulations, to direct a local authority to hold a referendum on whether it should have a relevant type of governance arrangements specified in the direction.
(2) Regulations under this section may, in particular, include provision –

(a) as to the date on which, or the time by which, a referendum must be held,
(b) as to the action which may, may not or must be taken by a local authority before or in connection with a referendum,
(c) as to the action which may, may not or must be taken by a local authority after a referendum, and
(d) for or in connection with enabling the Secretary of State, in the event of any failure by a local authority to take any action permitted or required by virtue of the regulations, to take that action.

(3) Provision made by virtue of subsection (2) may, in particular, apply or reproduce (with or without modifications) any provisions of, or made under, this Chapter.
(4) This section is subject to section 9NA (effect of order requiring, and giving effect to, referendum on change to mayor and cabinet executive).

9ME Referendum following order

(1) The Secretary of State may by order make provision requiring every local authority, or every local authority falling within a description of authority specified in the order, to hold a referendum on whether they should have a relevant type of governance arrangements specified in the order.

(2) An order under this section may, in particular, include provision –

- (a) as to the date on which, or the time by which, a referendum must be held,
- (b) as to the action which may, may not or must be taken by a local authority before or in connection with a referendum,
- (c) as to the action which may, may not or must be taken by a local authority after a referendum, and
- (d) for or in connection with enabling the Secretary of State, in the event of any failure by a local authority to take any action permitted or required by virtue of the order, to take that action.

(3) Provision made by virtue of subsection (2) may, in particular, apply or reproduce (with or without modifications) any provisions of, or made under, this Chapter.

(4) This section is subject to section 9NA (effect of order requiring, and giving effect to, referendum on change to mayor and cabinet executive).

9MF Further provision with respect to referendums

(1) If a local authority holds a referendum under this Chapter ('Referendum A') it may not hold, or be required to hold, another referendum under this Chapter ('Referendum B') within the period of ten years beginning with the date of Referendum A, unless subsection (2) or (3) applies.

(2) This subsection applies if –

- (a) Referendum A was held by the authority by virtue of an order under section 9N (power by order to require, and give effect to, referendum on change to mayor and cabinet executive), and
- (b) the proposal for the authority to operate a mayor and cabinet executive was rejected in Referendum A.

(3) This subsection applies if Referendum B is required to be held by virtue of an order made under section 9N.

(4) If the result of a referendum held by virtue of regulations, an order or a direction made under any provision of this Chapter is to approve the proposals to which the referendum relates, the local authority concerned must implement those proposals.

(5) If the result of a referendum held by virtue of regulations, an order or a direction made under any provision of this Chapter is to reject the proposals to which the referendum relates, the local authority concerned may not implement those proposals.

(6) Subsections (4) and (5) do not apply to a referendum held by virtue of section 9N (but see section 9N(2)(c)).

9MG Voting in and conduct of referendums

(1) The persons entitled to vote in a referendum held by a local authority under this Chapter are those who on the day of the referendum –

- (a) would be entitled to vote as electors at an election of councillors for an electoral area which is situated within the authority's area, and
- (b) are registered in the register of local government electors at an address within the authority's area.

(2) The Secretary of State may by regulations make provision as to the conduct of referendums under this Chapter.

(3) The Secretary of State may by regulations make provision for the combination of polls at referendums under this Chapter with polls at any elections.

(4) Regulations under subsection (2) or (3) may apply or incorporate, with or without modifications or exceptions, any provision of any enactment (whenever passed or made) relating to elections or referendums.

(5) Regulations under subsection (2) may, in particular, include provision –

(a) as to the question to be asked in a referendum,
(b) as to the publicity to be given in connection with a referendum (including the publicity to be given with respect to the consequences of the referendum),
(c) about the limitation of expenditure in connection with a referendum (and the creation of criminal offences in connection with the limitation of such expenditure),
(d) as to the conduct of the authority, members of the authority and officers of the authority in relation to a referendum,
(e) as to when, where and how voting in a referendum is to take place,
(f) as to how the votes cast in a referendum are to be counted, and
(g) for disregarding alterations in a register of electors.

(6) Before making any regulations under this section that include provision as to the question to be asked in a referendum, the Secretary of State must consult the Electoral Commission.

Further provisions as to mayor and cabinet executive

9N Requiring referendum on change to mayor and cabinet executive

(1) The Secretary of State may by order require a specified local authority to hold a referendum on whether the authority should operate a mayor and cabinet executive.

(2) An order under this section may include provision –

(a) as to the date on which, or the time by which, a referendum must be held,
(b) as to the action which may, may not or must be taken by a local authority before or in connection with a referendum,
(c) as to the effect of a referendum and the action which may, may not or must be taken by a local authority after a referendum,
(d) for or in connection with enabling the Secretary of State, in the event of any failure by a local authority to take any action permitted or required by virtue of the order, to take that action.

(3) Provision made by virtue of subsection (2) may, in particular, apply or reproduce (with or without modifications) any provisions of, or made under, this Chapter.

(4) In this section 'specified' means specified in an order made by the Secretary of State under this section.

9NA Effect of section 9N order

(1) Subject as follows, the provisions of this Chapter listed in subsection (2) do not apply to a local authority in relation to whom an order under section 9N has been made (and has not been revoked) unless the proposal for the authority to operate a mayor and cabinet executive has been rejected in the referendum held under the order.

(2) Those provisions are –

(a) section 9K (changing from one form of governance to another);
(b) section 9KA (executive arrangements: different form of executive);
(c) section 9MC (referendum following petition);
(d) section 9MD (referendum following direction);
(e) section 9ME (referendum following order).

9NB Variation of mayoral executive

(1) This section applies to a change in governance arrangements of the kind set out in section 9KB (variation of executive arrangements) if the local authority is operating a mayor and cabinet executive.
(2) The local authority may not resolve to make a change in governance arrangements unless the elected mayor has given written consent to the proposed change.

Miscellaneous

9O General

(1) A local authority may not –

(a) cease to operate a form of governance, or
(b) vary executive arrangements,

other than in accordance with this Chapter.
(2) In making a change in governance arrangements, the local authority must comply with any directions given by the Secretary of State in connection with the making of such a change.

9OA Interpretation

(1) This section applies for the purposes of this Chapter.
(2) References to a change in governance arrangements are references to any change of a kind set out in sections 9K to 9KB.
(3) References to a relevant type of governance arrangement are references to –

(a) a leader and cabinet executive (England);
(b) a mayor and cabinet executive;
(c) a committee system;
(d) any prescribed arrangements.

(4) References to a form of governance are references to –

(a) executive arrangements;
(b) a committee system;
(c) any prescribed arrangements.

CHAPTER 5 Supplementary

Local authority constitution

9P Local authority constitution

(1) A local authority must prepare and keep up to date a document (referred to in this section as its constitution) which contains –

(a) a copy of the authority's standing orders for the time being,
(b) a copy of the authority's code of conduct (if any) for the time being under section 28 of the Localism Act 2011,

(c) such information as the Secretary of State may direct, and
(d) such other information (if any) as the authority considers appropriate.

(2) In the case of a committee system local authority, the authority's constitution must also contain a statement as to whether the authority has resolved to have an overview and scrutiny committee under section 9JA.
(3) A local authority must ensure that copies of its constitution are available at its principal office for inspection by members of the public at all reasonable hours.
(4) A local authority must supply a copy of its constitution to any person who requests a copy and who pays to the authority such reasonable fee as the authority may determine.

Guidance

9Q Guidance

(1) A local authority must have regard to any guidance for the time being issued by the Secretary of State for the purposes of this Part.
(2) Guidance under this section may make different provision for different cases or descriptions of local authority.

Interpretation

9R Interpretation of Part 1A

(1) In this Part, unless the context otherwise requires –

'committee system' has the meaning given by section 9B,

'committee system local authority' has the meaning given by section 9J(3),

'elected mayor' has the meaning given by section 9H,

'electoral area' has the meaning given by section 203(1) of the Representation of the People Act 1983,

'enactment' includes an enactment contained in a local Act or comprised in subordinate legislation (within the meaning of the Interpretation Act 1978),

'executive', in relation to a local authority, is to be construed in accordance with section 9C,

'executive arrangements' has the meaning given by section 9B,

'executive leader' has the meaning given by section 9C(3)(a),

'first preference vote' has the meaning given by section 9HC,

'leader and cabinet executive (England)' has the meaning given by section 9C(3),

'local authority' means a county council in England, a district council or a London borough council,

'local government elector' has the meaning given by section 270(1) of the Local Government Act 1972,

'mayor and cabinet executive' has the meaning given by section 9C(2), 'ordinary day of election', in relation to a local authority, means the day of ordinary elections of councillors of the authority,

'the political balance requirements' means the provisions made by or under sections 15 to 17 of, and Schedule 1 to, the Local Government and Housing Act 1989,

'prescribed arrangements' has the meaning give by section 9B, and

'second preference vote' has the meaning given by section 9HC.

(2) In this Part 'relevant election years', in relation to a local authority, means the years specified in the second column of the following table in relation to that type of authority.

Type of local authority	Relevant election years
Metropolitan district	2014 and every fourth year afterwards
County	2013 and every fourth year afterwards
London borough	2014 and every fourth year afterwards
Non-metropolitan district	2011 and every fourth year afterwards

(3) Any reference in this Part to the chairman of a local authority –

(a) is a reference to that person whether or not the person is entitled to another style, and
(b) in the case of a London borough, is a reference to the person who (disregarding paragraphs 5B to 5I of Schedule 2 to the Local Government Act 1972) is referred to in Part 1 of that Schedule as the mayor of the borough.

(4) Any reference in this Part to the vice-chairman of a local authority –

(a) is a reference to that person whether or not the person is entitled to another style, and
(b) in the case of a London borough, is a reference to the person who (disregarding paragraphs 5B to 5I of Schedule 2 to the Local Government Act 1972) is referred to in Part 1 of that Schedule as the deputy mayor.

(5) Any reference in this Part to the discharge of any functions includes a reference to the doing of anything which is calculated to facilitate, or is conducive or incidental to, the discharge of those functions.
(6) Section 101 of the Local Government Act 1972 does not apply to the function of the passing of a resolution under any provision made by or under this Part.
(7) Any functions conferred on a local authority by virtue of this Part are not to be the responsibility of an executive of the authority under executive arrangements.
(8) Any directions given by the Secretary of State under any provision of this Part –

(a) may be varied or revoked by subsequent directions given by the Secretary of State under that provision, and

(b) may make different provision for different cases, different local authorities or different descriptions of local authority.'

PART 2 NEW SCHEDULE A1 TO THE LOCAL GOVERNMENT ACT 2000

2 Before Schedule 1 to the Local Government Act 2000 (executive arrangements: further provision) insert –

'SCHEDULE A1 **Executive arrangements in England: further provision**

Section 9GB

Mayor and cabinet executives

1 (1) This paragraph applies in relation to executive arrangements by a local authority which provide for a mayor and cabinet executive.

(2) Subject to section 9C(5), the executive arrangements must include provision which enables the elected mayor to determine the number of councillors who may be appointed to the executive under section 9C(2)(b).

(3) The executive arrangements must include provision which requires the elected mayor to appoint one of the members of the executive to be the elected mayor's deputy (referred to in this paragraph as the deputy mayor).

(4) Subject to sub-paragraph (5), the person who is appointed deputy mayor, unless the person resigns as deputy mayor or ceases to be a member of the authority, is to hold office until the end of the term of office of the elected mayor.

(5) The elected mayor may, if the elected mayor thinks fit, remove the deputy mayor from office.

(6) Where a vacancy occurs in the office of deputy mayor, the elected mayor must appoint another person to be deputy mayor.

(7) If for any reason the elected mayor is unable to act or the office of elected mayor is vacant, the deputy mayor must act in the elected mayor's place.

(8) If for any reason –

(a) the elected mayor is unable to act or the office of elected mayor is vacant, and

(b) the deputy mayor is unable to act or the office of deputy mayor is vacant,

the executive must act in the elected mayor's place or must arrange for a member of the executive to act in the elected mayor's place.

Leader and cabinet executives (England)

2 (1) This paragraph applies in relation to executive arrangements by a local authority which provide for a leader and cabinet executive (England).

(2) Subject to section 9C(5), the executive arrangements must include provision which enables the executive leader to determine the number of councillors who may be appointed to the executive under section 9C(3)(b).

(3) The executive arrangements must include provision which requires the executive leader to appoint one of the members of the executive to be the executive leader's deputy (referred to in this paragraph as the deputy executive leader).

(4) Subject to sub-paragraph (5), the person who is appointed deputy executive leader, unless the person resigns as deputy executive leader or ceases to be a member of the authority, is to hold office until the end of any term of office of the executive leader (where the executive arrangements provide for such a term).

(5) The executive leader may, if the executive leader thinks fit, remove the deputy executive leader from office.

(6) Where a vacancy occurs in the office of deputy executive leader, the executive leader must appoint another person to be deputy executive leader.

(7) If for any reason the executive leader is unable to act or the office of executive leader is vacant, the deputy executive leader must act in the executive leader's place.

(8) If for any reason –

(a) the executive leader is unable to act or the office of executive leader is vacant, and

(b) the deputy executive leader is unable to act or the office of deputy executive leader is vacant,

the executive must act in the executive leader's place or must arrange for a member of the executive to act in the executive leader's place.

Procedure

3 Executive arrangements by a local authority may include provision with respect to –

(a) the quorum, proceedings and location of meetings of the executive,

(b) the appointment of committees of the executive, and

(c) the quorum, proceedings and location of meetings of committees of the executive.

Meetings of executives and executive committees

4 A member of a local authority who is not a member of the authority's executive is entitled to attend, and speak at, a meeting of the executive, or of a committee of the executive, which is held in private only if invited to do so.

Mayor's assistant

5 (1) The Secretary of State may by regulations make provision for or in connection with the appointment of a person (an 'assistant') to provide assistance to an elected mayor.

(2) Regulations under this paragraph may, in particular, include provision with respect to the terms and conditions of appointment of an assistant.

Overview and scrutiny committees: education functions

6 (1) In paragraphs 7 and 8 'relevant authority' means a local authority which has education functions.

(2) Paragraphs 7 and 8 apply to an overview and scrutiny committee of a relevant authority if the committee's functions under section 9F relate wholly or partly to any education functions which are the responsibility of the authority's executive.

(3) Paragraph 7 and 8 also apply to a sub-committee of an overview and scrutiny committee of a relevant authority if the sub-committee's

functions under section 9FA relate wholly or partly to any education functions which are the responsibility of the authority's executive.

7 (1) In the case of a relevant authority that maintains one or more Church of England schools, an overview and scrutiny committee or sub-committee to which this paragraph applies must include at least one qualifying person.

(2) A person is a qualifying person for the purposes of sub-paragraph (1) if the person is nominated by the Diocesan Board of Education for any Church of England diocese which falls wholly or partly in the authority concerned's area.

(3) In the case of a relevant authority that maintains one or more Roman Catholic Church schools, an overview and scrutiny committee or sub-committee to which this paragraph applies must include at least one qualifying person.

(4) A person is a qualifying person for the purposes of sub-paragraph (3) if the person is nominated by the bishop of any Roman Catholic diocese which falls wholly or partly in the authority concerned's area.

(5) A member of an overview and scrutiny committee or sub-committee appointed by virtue of sub-paragraph (1) or (3) is to be entitled to vote at a meeting of the committee or sub-committee on any question –

(a) which relates to any education functions which are the responsibility of the authority concerned's executive, and
(b) which falls to be decided at the meeting.

(6) The Secretary of State may by directions to a relevant authority require any of the authority's overview and scrutiny committees or sub-committees to which this paragraph applies to include persons who are appointed, in accordance with the directions, as representatives of the persons who appoint foundation governors for the foundation or voluntary schools maintained by the authority which are not Church of England schools or Roman Catholic Church schools but which are specified in the directions.

(7) Directions under sub-paragraph (6) may make provision with respect to the voting rights of persons appointed in accordance with such directions.

8 (1) The Secretary of State may by regulations require an overview and scrutiny committee or sub-committee to which this paragraph applies to include one or more persons elected, in accordance with the regulations, as representatives of parent governors at maintained schools which are maintained by the relevant authority concerned.

(2) Regulations under this paragraph may make provision for –

(a) the number of persons who are to be elected in the case of any relevant authority,
(b) the procedure to be followed in connection with the election of such persons and the persons who are entitled to vote at such an election,
(c) the circumstances in which persons are qualified or disqualified for being so elected or for holding office once elected,
(d) the term of office of persons so elected and their voting rights,
(e) the application to any such committee or sub-committee, with or without any modification, of any enactment (whenever

passed or made) relating to committees or (as the case may be) sub-committees of a local authority,

(f) such other matters connected with such elections or persons so elected as the Secretary of State considers appropriate.

(3) Regulations under this paragraph may also make provision –

(a) enabling the Secretary of State to determine, where the Secretary of State considers it expedient to do so in view of the small number of maintained schools which are maintained by a relevant authority, that the requirement imposed on the committee or sub-committee by virtue of sub-paragraph (1) is to have effect as if it referred to representatives of parents of registered pupils (rather than representatives of parent governors) at those schools,

(b) for any regulations under this paragraph to have effect, where the Secretary of State makes any such determination, with such modifications as may be prescribed.

9 The following provisions of the Education Act 1996, namely –

(a) section 496 (powers of Secretary of State to require duties under that Act to be exercised reasonably), and

(b) section 497 (powers of Secretary of State where local authorities etc are in default),

are to apply to the performance of any duty imposed on a local authority by virtue of paragraphs 6 to 8 as they apply to the performance by a local authority of a duty imposed by that Act.

10 (1) Except for the expression 'local authority', expressions used in paragraphs 6 to 9 and the School Standards and Framework Act 1998 have the same meaning in those paragraphs as in that Act.

(2) In paragraphs 6 and 7 'education functions' has the meaning given by section 579(1) of the Education Act 1996.

Overview and scrutiny committees: voting rights of co-opted members

11 (1) A local authority may permit a co-opted member of an overview and scrutiny committee of the authority to vote at meetings of the committee.

(2) Permission under sub-paragraph (1) may only be given in accordance with a scheme made by the local authority.

(3) A scheme for the purposes of this paragraph may include –

(a) provision for a maximum or minimum in relation to the number of co-opted members of an overview and scrutiny committee entitled to vote at meetings of the committee, and

(b) provision for giving effect to any maximum or minimum established under paragraph (a).

(4) The power to make a scheme for the purposes of this paragraph includes power to vary or revoke such a scheme.

(5) In this paragraph, references to a co-opted member, in relation to an overview and scrutiny committee of a local authority, are to a member of the committee who is not a member of the authority.

12 (1) The Secretary of State may by regulations make provision about the exercise of the powers under paragraph 11.

(2) Regulations under sub-paragraph (1) may, in particular, require schemes for the purposes of paragraph 11 ('voting rights schemes') –

(a) to provide for permission to be given only by means of approving a proposal by the committee concerned;

(b) to provide for a proposal for the purposes of the scheme ('a scheme proposal') to specify –

(i) the person to whom the proposal relates,

(ii) the questions on which it is proposed the person should be entitled to vote, and

(iii) the proposed duration of the person's entitlement to vote,

and to include such other provision about the form and content of such a proposal as the regulations may provide;

(c) to provide for a scheme proposal to be made only in accordance with a published statement of the policy of the committee concerned about the making of such proposals;

(d) to include such provision about the procedure to be followed in relation to the approval of scheme proposals as the regulations may provide.

(3) Regulations under sub-paragraph (1) may include provision for the notification to the Secretary of State by local authorities of the making, variation or revocation of voting rights schemes.

(4) The Secretary of State may by direction require a local authority to vary a voting rights scheme.

13 (1) A local authority which makes a scheme for the purposes of paragraph 11 must, while the scheme is in force, make copies of it available at its principal office at all reasonable hours for inspection by members of the public.

(2) If a local authority makes a scheme for the purposes of paragraph 11, or varies or revokes such a scheme, it must as soon as reasonably practicable after doing so publish in one or more newspapers circulating in its area a notice which complies with this paragraph.

(3) In the case of the making of a scheme, the notice under sub-paragraph (2) must –

(a) record the making of the scheme,

(b) describe what it does,

(c) state that copies of it are available for inspection at the principal office of the local authority, and

(d) specify –

(i) the address of that office, and

(ii) the times when the scheme is available for inspection there.

(4) In the case of the variation of a scheme, the notice under sub-paragraph (2) must –

(a) record the variation,

(b) describe what it does,

(c) state that copies of the scheme as varied are available for inspection at the principal office of the local authority, and

(d) specify –

(i) the address of that office, and

(ii) the times when the scheme is available for inspection there.

(5) In the case of the revocation of a scheme, the notice under sub-paragraph (2) must record the revocation.'

ooo

SCHEDULE 4 CONDUCT OF LOCAL GOVERNMENT MEMBERS

Section 26

PART 1 AMENDMENTS OF EXISTING PROVISIONS

Parliamentary Commissioner Act 1967 (c. 13)

1 In Schedule 2 to the Parliamentary Commissioner Act 1967 (departments etc subject to investigation) omit the entry for the Standards Board for England.

House of Commons Disqualification Act 1975 (c. 24)

2 In Part 2 of Schedule 1 to the House of Commons Disqualification Act 1975 (bodies of which all members are disqualified) omit the entry for the Standards Board for England.

Northern Ireland Assembly Disqualification Act 1975 (c. 25)

3 In Part 2 of Schedule 1 to the Northern Ireland Assembly Disqualification Act 1975 (bodies of which all members are disqualified) omit the entry for the Standards Board for England.

Local Government and Housing Act 1989 (c. 42)

4 (1) Section 3A of the Local Government and Housing Act 1989 (grant and supervision of exemptions from political restriction: England) is amended as follows.

(2) In subsection (1) –

(a) for 'standards committee' substitute 'head of paid service',
(b) omit 'which is a relevant authority',
(c) in paragraph (a) for 'committee' substitute 'head of paid service', and
(d) in that paragraph and paragraph (b) omit 'relevant'.

(3) In subsection (2)(a) omit 'relevant'.

(4) In subsection (3) –

(a) for 'standards committee' substitute 'head of paid service',
(b) for 'committee' substitute 'head of paid service', and
(c) in paragraph (b) omit 'relevant'.

(5) In subsection (4) –

(a) for 'standards committee' substitute 'local authority's head of paid service',
(b) for 'committee' substitute 'head of paid service', and
(c) in paragraph (b)(i) omit 'relevant'.

(6) Omit subsection (5).

(7) In subsection (6) –

(a) omit 'which is a relevant authority', and
(b) in paragraph (a) –

(i) for 'standards committee' substitute 'head of paid service',
(ii) for 'committee' substitute 'head of paid service', and
(iii) omit 'its'.

(8) In subsection (7) –

(a) omit 'its', and
(b) for 'standards committee' substitute 'local authority's head of paid service'.

(9) After that subsection insert –

'(7A) In carrying out functions under this section a local authority's head of paid service must consult the monitoring officer of that authority (unless they are the same person).
(7B) The Secretary of State may by regulations make provision about the application of this section to a local authority that is not required to designate one of its officers as the head of its paid service.
(7C) Regulations under subsection (7B) may apply any provisions of this section (with or without modifications) to an authority to which they apply.'

(10) Omit subsections (8) to (10).

Audit Commission Act 1998 (c. 18)

5 In section 49(1)(de) of the Audit Commission Act 1998 (disclosure of information by Commission or auditor etc for purposes of functions of ethical standards officer or Public Services Ombudsman for Wales) omit 'an ethical standards officer or'.

Data Protection Act 1998 (c. 29)

6 In section 31 of the Data Protection Act 1998 (exemptions from subject information provisions for data processed in connection with certain regulatory functions) –

(a) in subsection (7) omit paragraph (b), and
(b) in subsection (8)(b) omit ', or to an ethical standards officer,'.

Local Government Act 2000 (c. 22)

7 The Local Government Act 2000 is amended as follows.

8 (1) Section 49 (principles governing conduct of members of relevant authorities) is amended as follows.
(2) Omit subsection (1).
(3) In subsection (2) omit 'in Wales (other than police authorities)'.
(4) Omit subsections (2C), (3) and (4).
(5) In subsection (5)(a) omit 'in Wales'.
(6) In subsection (6) –

(a) in paragraph (a) at the end insert 'in Wales',
(b) omit paragraphs (c) to (e),
(c) omit paragraphs (g) to (k),
(d) in paragraph (l) after 'authority' insert 'in Wales',
(e) omit paragraphs (m) to (o), and
(f) in paragraph (p) after 'authority' insert 'in Wales'.

9 (1) Section 50 (model code of conduct) is amended as follows.
(2) Omit subsection (1).
(3) In subsection (2) omit 'in Wales other than police authorities'.
(4) In subsection (3) omit '(1) or'.
(5) In subsection (4)(a) omit –

(a) '49(1) or', and
(b) '(as the case may be)'.

(6) Omit subsections (4C) and (4D).
(7) In subsection (5) omit 'the Secretary of State or'.
(8) Omit subsections (6) and (7).

10 (1) Section 51 (duty of relevant authorities to adopt codes of conduct) is amended as follows.
(2) In subsection (4C) omit the words from 'by a' to 'police authority'.
(3) In subsection (6)(c) –

(a) omit sub-paragraph (i), and
(b) in sub-paragraph (ii) omit the words from 'in the case' to 'in Wales,'.

11 In section 52(2) (power for prescribed form of declaration of acceptance of office to include undertaking to observe code of conduct) after '1972' insert 'in relation to a relevant authority'.

12 (1) Section 53 (standards committees) is amended as follows.
(2) In subsection (2) omit 'parish council or'.
(3) Omit subsections (3) to (10).
(4) In subsection (11) –

(a) in paragraph (a) omit 'in Wales other than police authorities', and
(b) in paragraph (k) omit 'in Wales (other than police authorities)'.

(5) In subsection (12) omit '(6)(c) to (f) or'.

13 (1) Section 54 (functions of standards committees) is amended as follows.
(2) Omit subsection (4).
(3) In subsection (5) omit 'in Wales (other than police authorities)'.
(4) Omit subsection (6).
(5) In subsection (7) omit 'in Wales (other than police authorities)'.

14 (1) Section 54A (sub-committees of standards committees) is amended as follows.
(2) In subsection (3) omit ', but this is subject to section 55(7)(b)'.
(3) Omit subsection (4).
(4) In subsection (5) omit 'in Wales other than a police authority'.
(5) In subsection (6) –

(a) omit 'section 55(5) and to', and
(b) for '53(6)(a) or (11)(a)' substitute '53(11)(a)'.

15 Omit section 55 (standards committees for parish councils).
16 Omit section 56A (joint committees of relevant authorities in England).
17 Omit section 57 (Standards Board for England).
18 Omit section 57A (written allegations: right to make, and initial assessment).
19 Omit section 57B (right to request review of decision not to act).
20 Omit section 57C (information to be given to subject of allegation).
21 Omit section 57D (power to suspend standards committee's functions).
22 Omit section 58 (allegations referred to Standards Board).
23 Omit section 59 (functions of ethical standards officers).
24 Omit section 60 (conduct of investigations).
25 Omit section 61 (procedure in respect of investigations).
26 Omit section 62 (investigations: further provisions).
27 Omit section 63 (restrictions on disclosure of information).
28 Omit section 64 (reports etc).
29 Omit section 65 (interim reports).
30 Omit section 65A (disclosure by monitoring officers of ethical standards officers' reports).

31 Omit section 66 (matters referred to monitoring officers).
32 Omit section 66A (references to First-tier Tribunal).
33 Omit section 66B (periodic returns).
34 Omit section 66C (information requests).
35 Omit section 67 (consultation with ombudsmen).
36 In section 68(2) (guidance by Public Services Ombudsman for Wales) –

(a) in paragraph (a) –

(i) omit 'in Wales (other than police authorities)', and
(ii) for 'such' substitute 'those', and

(b) in paragraph (b) omit 'in Wales (other than police authorities)'.

37 (1) Section 69 (investigations by the Public Services Ombudsman for Wales) is amended as follows.
(2) In subsection (1) omit 'in Wales' in both places.
(3) In subsection (5) omit 'in Wales'.

38 (1) Section 70 (investigations: further provisions) is amended as follows.
(2) In subsection (2)(a), after '63' insert 'as those sections had effect immediately before their repeal by the Localism Act 2011'.
(3) In subsection (5) omit 'in Wales'.

39 In section 71(4) (reports etc) omit 'in Wales'.
40 In section 72(6) (interim reports) omit 'in Wales'.
41 In section 73 (matters referred to monitoring officers) omit subsection (6).
42 In section 77(7) (offence of failure to comply with regulations about adjudications in Wales or equivalent provisions of Tribunal Procedure Rules) omit the words from ', or with' to 'First-tier Tribunal,'.

43 (1) Section 78 (decisions of the First-tier Tribunal or interim case tribunals) is amended as follows.
(2) In the heading omit 'the First-tier Tribunal or'.
(3) In subsection (1) –

(a) omit 'the First-tier Tribunal or', and
(b) in paragraph (a) omit '65(3) or'.

(4) In subsection (2) for 'the tribunal concerned' substitute 'the interim case tribunal'.
(5) In subsection (3) for 'the tribunal concerned' substitute 'the interim case tribunal'.
(6) Omit subsection (4).
(7) In subsection (6) omit '78A or'.
(8) In subsection (8A) –

(a) omit paragraph (a), and
(b) in paragraph (b) omit 'where the relevant authority concerned is in Wales,'.

(9) In subsection (9) omit –

(a) 'The First-tier Tribunal or (as the case may be)', and
(b) '59 or'.

(10) Omit subsections (9A) to (9D).

44 Omit section 78A (decisions of First-tier Tribunal).
45 Omit section 78B (section 78A: supplementary).
46 In section 79(13) (decisions of case tribunals: Wales) in subsection (13) omit 'in Wales'.

47 (1) Section 80 (recommendations by First-tier Tribunal or case tribunals) is amended as follows.

(2) In the heading omit 'First-tier Tribunal or'.
(3) In subsection (1) omit 'the First-tier Tribunal or'.
(4) In subsection (2) for 'The tribunal concerned' substitute 'A case tribunal'.
(5) In subsection (3) for 'relevant person' substitute 'Public Services Ombudsman for Wales'.
(6) In subsection (5) for 'relevant person' in both places substitute 'Public Services Ombudsman for Wales'.
(7) Omit subsection (6).

48 (1) Section 81 (disclosure and registration of members' interests) is amended as follows.
(2) In subsection (5) for 'Secretary of State' substitute 'Welsh Ministers'.
(3) In subsection (7) –

(a) omit paragraph (b), and
(b) in paragraph (c) omit 'if it is a relevant authority in Wales,'.

(4) Omit subsection (8).

49 (1) Section 82 (code of conduct for local government employees) is amended as follows.
(2) Omit subsection (1).
(3) In subsection (2) omit 'in Wales (other than police authorities)'.
(4) In subsection (3) omit '(1) or'.
(5) Omit subsections (4) and (5).
(6) In subsection (6)(a) –

(a) omit 'in Wales', and
(b) for 'such' substitute 'those'.

(7) In paragraph (9) omit –

(a) paragraph (a), and
(b) in paragraph (b) 'in relation to Wales,'.

50 In section 82A (monitoring officers: delegation of functions under Part 3), omit '57A, 60(2) or (3), 64(2) or (4),'.

51 (1) Section 83 (interpretation of Part 3) is amended as follows.
(2) In subsection (1) –

(a) omit the definitions of –

(i) 'the Audit Commission',
(ii) 'ethical standards officer', and
(iii) 'police authority', and

(b) in the definition of 'model code of conduct' omit '(1) and'.

(3) Omit subsections (4), (12), (15) and (16).

52 In section 105(6) (orders and regulations) omit ', 49, 63(1)(j)'.
53 Omit Schedule 4 (Standards Board for England).

Freedom of Information Act 2000 (c. 36)

54 In Part 6 of Schedule 1 to the Freedom of Information Act 2000 (public authorities) omit the entry for the Standards Board for England.

Local Government and Public Involvement in Health Act 2007 (c. 28)

55 (1) Section 183 of the Local Government and Public Involvement in Health Act 2007 (conduct of local authority members: codes of conduct) is amended as follows.

(2) In subsection (1) omit the subsections (2A) and (2B) to be inserted into section 49 of the Local Government Act 2000.
(3) In subsection (2) omit the subsections (4A) and (4B) to be inserted into section 50 of the Local Government Act 2000.
(4) In subsection (3) omit the subsections (4A) and (4B) to be inserted into section 51 of the Local Government Act 2000.
(5) In subsection (7)(b) omit 'in Wales other than a police authority'.

PART 2 PROVISION SUPPLEMENTARY TO PART 1

Codes of conduct under the Local Government Act 2000

56 (1) A code of conduct adopted by a relevant authority (within the meaning of this Chapter of this Part of this Act) ceases to have effect.
(2) An undertaking to comply with a code of conduct given by a person under section 52 of the Local Government Act 2000 or as part of a declaration of acceptance of office in a form prescribed by order under section 83 of the Local Government Act 1972 ceases to have effect when the code ceases to have effect.
(3) In this paragraph 'code of conduct' means a code of conduct under section 51 of the Local Government Act 2000 or a model code of conduct issued by order under section 50(1) of that Act.

Power to make provision in connection with the abolition of Standards Board for England

57 (1) The Secretary of State may by order make provision in connection with the abolition of the Standards Board for England ('the Board').
(2) An order under this paragraph may make provision that has effect on or before the abolition date.
(3) An order under this paragraph may, in particular, make provision about the property, rights and liabilities of the Board (including rights and liabilities relating to contracts of employment).
(4) This includes –

(a) provision for the transfer of property, rights and liabilities (including to the Secretary of State), and
(b) provision for the extinguishment of rights and liabilities.

(5) An order under this paragraph that makes provision for the transfer of property, rights and liabilities may –

(a) make provision for certificates issued by the Secretary of State to be conclusive evidence that property has been transferred;
(b) make provision about the transfer of property, rights and liabilities that could not otherwise be transferred;
(c) make provision about the continuation of things (including legal proceedings) in the process of being done by, on behalf of or in relation to the Board in respect of anything transferred;
(d) make provision for references to the Board in an instrument or document in respect of anything transferred to be treated as references to the transferee.

(6) An order under this paragraph may –

(a) make provision about the continuing effect of things done by or in relation to the Board before such date as the order may specify;

(b) make provision about the continuation of things (including legal proceedings) in the process of being done by, on behalf of or in relation to the Board on such a date;
(c) make provision for references to the Board in an instrument or document to be treated on and after such a date as references to such person as the order may specify;
(d) make provision for the payment of compensation by the Secretary of State to persons affected by the provisions it makes about the property, rights and liabilities of the Board.

Power to give directions in connection with the abolition of Standards Board for England

58 (1) The Secretary of State may direct the Board to take such steps as the Secretary of State may specify in connection with the abolition of the Board.
(2) The Secretary of State may, in particular, give directions to the Board about information held by the Board, including –
(a) directions requiring information to be transferred to another person (including to the Secretary of State);
(b) directions requiring information to be destroyed or made inaccessible.
(3) The Secretary of State may make available to the Board such facilities as the Board may reasonably require for exercising its functions by virtue of this Part of this Schedule.
(4) The Secretary of State may exercise a function of the Board for the purposes of taking steps in connection with its abolition (including functions by virtue of an order under paragraph 57).
(5) Sub-paragraph (4) does not prevent the exercise of the function by the Board.
(6) In the case of a duty of the Board, sub-paragraph (4) permits the Secretary of State to comply with that duty on behalf of the Board but does not oblige the Secretary of State to do so.

Final statement of accounts

59 (1) As soon as is reasonably practicable after the abolition date, the Secretary of State must prepare –
(a) a statement of the accounts of the Board for the last financial year to end before the abolition date, and
(b) a statement of the accounts of the Board for the period (if any) beginning immediately after the end of that financial year and ending immediately before the abolition date.
(2) The Secretary of State must, as soon as is reasonably practicable after preparing a statement under this paragraph, send a copy of it to the Comptroller and Auditor General.
(3) The Comptroller and Auditor General must –
(a) examine, certify and report on the statement, and
(b) lay a copy of the statement and the report before each House of Parliament.
(4) Sub-paragraph (1)(a) does not apply if the Board has already sent a copy of its statement of accounts for the year to the Comptroller and Auditor General.
(5) In such a case the repeal of paragraph 13(4B) of Schedule 4 to the Local Government Act 2000 does not remove the obligation of the Comptroller and Auditor General to take the steps specified in that provision in relation to the statement of accounts if the Comptroller has not already done so.

Disclosure of information

60 (1) Section 63 of the Local Government Act 2000 applies in relation to information obtained by a person who is exercising a function of the Board by virtue of paragraph 58(4) as it applies to information obtained by an ethical standards officer.

(2) That section has effect (in relation to information to which it applies apart from sub-paragraph (1) as well as to information to which it applies by virtue of that sub-paragraph) as if it permitted the disclosure of information for the purposes of the abolition of the Board.

(3) The repeal by Part 1 of that section, or of any provision by virtue of which it is applied to information obtained other than by ethical standards officers, does not affect its continuing effect in relation to information to which it applied before its repeal (including by virtue of this paragraph).

Interpretation

61 In this Part of this Schedule –

'the abolition date' means the date on which paragraphs 17 and 53 (repeal of section 57 of and Schedule 4 to the Local Government Act 2000) come fully into force;

'the Board' has the meaning given by paragraph 57(1);

'financial year' means the period of 12 months ending with 31 March in any year.

ooo

SCHEDULE 8 REGIONAL STRATEGIES: CONSEQUENTIAL AMENDMENTS

Section 109

Town and Country Planning Act 1990 (c. 8)

1 In Schedule 1 to the Town and Country Planning Act 1990 (local planning authorities: distribution of functions) in paragraph 7 –

(a) omit sub-paragraphs (2)(a), (3) and (5)(a),
(b) in sub-paragraph (7)(a) for the words from 'the responsible regional authorities' to '(the consulted body)' substitute 'the county planning authority',
(c) in sub-paragraphs (7)(b) and (8) for 'the consulted body' in each place substitute 'the county planning authority', and
(d) omit sub-paragraphs (9), (10)(b) and (11).

Regional Development Agencies Act 1998 (c. 45)

2 In the Regional Development Agencies Act 1998 omit section 7 (regional strategy).

Greater London Authority Act 1999 (c. 29)

3 The Greater London Authority Act 1999 is amended as follows.

4 In section 337(6)(a) (conflict between regional spatial strategy and spatial development strategy) omit 'or the regional spatial strategy for a region which adjoins Greater London'.

5 In section 342(1) (matters to which the Mayor is to have regard) –

(a) omit paragraph (a), and
(b) in paragraph (b) omit 'other'.

6 In Schedule 10 (Transport for London) in paragraph 2 –

(a) omit sub-paragraph (3A), and
(b) in sub-paragraph (8) omit the definition of 'regional planning body' and 'region'.

Planning and Compulsory Purchase Act 2004 (c. 5)

7 The Planning and Compulsory Purchase Act 2004 is amended as follows.
8 In section 15(3) (preparation of local development scheme) omit paragraph (c).
9 In section 19(2) (preparation of local development documents) omit paragraphs (b) and (d).

10 (1) Section 24 (conformity with regional strategy) is amended as follows.
(2) In the heading for 'regional strategy' substitute 'spatial development strategy'.
(3) In subsection (1) omit paragraph (a).

11 In section 28 (joint local development documents) omit subsection (4).
12 In section 37 (interpretation) omit subsections (6) and (6A).

13 (1) In section 38(3) (development plan for areas in England outside Greater London) in paragraph (a) after 'situated' insert '(if there is a regional strategy for that region)'.
(2) Omit section 38(3)(a).

14 (1) Section 45 (simplified planning zones) is amended as follows.
(2) Before subsection (1) insert –

'(A1) The principal Act is amended in relation to Wales as follows.'

(3) In subsection (1) for 'the principal Act' substitute 'that Act'.
(4) In the text to be inserted by subsection (2), in subsection (1A) –

(a) omit paragraph (a), and
(b) in paragraph (b) omit 'in Wales'.

(5) In the text to be inserted by subsection (3) –

(a) in subsection (2)(b) omit –

(i) 'the Secretary of State or', and
(ii) '(as the case may be)',

(b) in subsection (2A) omit paragraph (b), and
(c) omit subsection (2B).

(6) Omit subsection (4).
(7) In the text to be inserted by subsection (9) –

(a) in sub-paragraph (1A) –

(i) omit paragraph (a), and
(ii) in paragraph (b) omit 'in Wales',

(b) in sub-paragraph (1B) omit –

(i) 'the Secretary of State or', and
(ii) '(as the case may be)', and

(c) in sub-paragraph (1C) omit –

(i) 'Secretary of State or the', and
(ii) '(as the case may be)'.

15 In section 62(5) (preparation of local development plan) omit paragraph (c).
16 In section 78 (interpretation of Part 6) omit subsection (5).

17 (1) Section 113 (validity of strategies, plans and documents) is amended as follows.
(2) In subsection (1) –

(a) omit paragraph (a), and
(b) in the words following paragraph (g) for '(a)' substitute '(b)'.

(3) In subsection (9) omit paragraph (a).
(4) In subsection (11) omit paragraph (a).
(5) Omit subsection (12).

Local Democracy, Economic Development and Construction Act 2009 (c. 20)

18 In section 70(5) (which provides for how a regional strategy is to be interpreted) for 'the regional strategy' insert 'a regional strategy under this Part'.

19 In section 82(2) (during the interim period, a regional strategy does not include the regional economic strategy) for the words after 'For the purposes of that section,' substitute 'a regional strategy under this Part is to be regarded as consisting solely of the regional spatial strategy under section 1 of the Planning and Compulsory Purchase Act 2004 that subsisted for the region concerned immediately before 1 April 2010.'

Marine and Coastal Access Act 2009 (c. 23)

20 In Schedule 6 to the Marine and Coastal Access Act 2009, in paragraph 1 –

(a) in sub-paragraph (2) omit paragraph (e), and
(b) in sub-paragraph (3) omit the definition of 'responsible regional authorities'.

SCHEDULE 9 NEIGHBOURHOOD PLANNING

Section 116

PART 1 NEIGHBOURHOOD DEVELOPMENT ORDERS

1 The Town and Country Planning Act 1990 is amended as follows.
2 After section 61D insert –

'Neighbourhood development orders

61E Neighbourhood development orders

(1) Any qualifying body is entitled to initiate a process for the purpose of requiring a local planning authority in England to make a neighbourhood development order.

(2) A 'neighbourhood development order' is an order which grants planning permission in relation to a particular neighbourhood area specified in the order –

(a) for development specified in the order, or
(b) for development of any class specified in the order.

(3) Schedule 4B makes provision about the process for the making of neighbourhood development orders, including –

(a) provision for independent examination of orders proposed by qualifying bodies, and
(b) provision for the holding of referendums on orders proposed by those bodies.

(4) A local planning authority to whom a proposal for the making of a neighbourhood development order has been made –

(a) must make a neighbourhood development order to which the proposal relates if in each applicable referendum under that Schedule more than half of those voting have voted in favour of the order, and
(b) if paragraph (a) applies, must make the order as soon as reasonably practicable after the referendum is held.

(5) If–

(a) there are two applicable referendums under that Schedule (because the order relates to a neighbourhood area designated as a business area under section 61H), and
(b) in one of those referendums (but not the other) more than half of those voting have voted in favour of the order,

the authority may (but need not) make a neighbourhood development order to which the proposal relates.

(6) A 'qualifying body' means a parish council, or an organisation or body designated as a neighbourhood forum, authorised for the purposes of a neighbourhood development order to act in relation to a neighbourhood area as a result of section 61F.

(7) For the meaning of 'neighbourhood area', see sections 61G and 61I(1).

(8) The authority are not to be subject to the duty under subsection (4)(a) if they consider that the making of the order would breach, or would otherwise be incompatible with, any EU obligation or any of the Convention rights (within the meaning of the Human Rights Act 1998).

(9) Regulations may make provision as to the procedure to be followed by local planning authorities in cases where they act under subsection (8).

(10) The regulations may in particular make provision –

(a) for the holding of an examination,
(b) as to the payment by a local planning authority of remuneration and expenses of the examiner,
(c) as to the award of costs by the examiner,
(d) as to the giving of notice and publicity,
(e) as to the information and documents that are to be made available to the public,
(f) as to the making of reasonable charges for anything provided as a result of the regulations,
(g) as to consultation with and participation by the public, and
(h) as to the making and consideration of representations (including the time by which representations must be made).

(11) The authority must publish in such manner as may be prescribed –

(a) their decision to act under subsection (4) or (8),
(b) their reasons for making that decision, and
(c) such other matters relating to that decision as may be prescribed.

(12) The authority must send a copy of the matters required to be published to –

(a) the qualifying body that initiated the process for the making of the order, and
(b) such other persons as may be prescribed.

(13) A local planning authority must publish each neighbourhood development order that they make in such manner as may be prescribed.

61F Authorisation to act in relation to neighbourhood areas

(1) For the purposes of a neighbourhood development order, a parish council

are authorised to act in relation to a neighbourhood area if that area consists of or includes the whole or any part of the area of the council.

(2) If that neighbourhood area also includes the whole or any part of the area of another parish council, the parish council is authorised for those purposes to act in relation to that neighbourhood area only if the other parish council have given their consent.

(3) For the purposes of a neighbourhood development order, an organisation or body is authorised to act in relation to a neighbourhood area if it is designated by a local planning authority as a neighbourhood forum for that area.

(4) An organisation or body may be designated for a neighbourhood area only if that area does not consist of or include the whole or any part of the area of a parish council.

(5) A local planning authority may designate an organisation or body as a neighbourhood forum if the authority are satisfied that it meets the following conditions –

(a) it is established for the express purpose of promoting or improving the social, economic and environmental well-being of an area that consists of or includes the neighbourhood area concerned (whether or not it is also established for the express purpose of promoting the carrying on of trades, professions or other businesses in such an area),

(b) its membership is open to –

(i) individuals who live in the neighbourhood area concerned,

(ii) individuals who work there (whether for businesses carried on there or otherwise), and

(iii) individuals who are elected members of a county council, district council or London borough council any of whose area falls within the neighbourhood area concerned,

(c) its membership includes a minimum of 21 individuals each of whom –

(i) lives in the neighbourhood area concerned,

(ii) works there (whether for a business carried on there or otherwise), or

(iii) is an elected member of a county council, district council or London borough council any of whose area falls within the neighbourhood area concerned,

(d) it has a written constitution, and

(e) such other conditions as may be prescribed.

(6) A local planning authority may also designate an organisation or body as a neighbourhood forum if they are satisfied that the organisation or body meets prescribed conditions.

(7) A local planning authority –

(a) must, in determining under subsection (5) whether to designate an organisation or body as a neighbourhood forum for a neighbourhood area, have regard to the desirability of designating an organisation or body –

(i) which has secured (or taken reasonable steps to attempt to secure) that its membership includes at least one individual falling within each of sub-paragraphs (i) to (iii) of subsection (5)(b),

(ii) whose membership is drawn from different places in the neighbourhood area concerned and from different sections of the community in that area, and
(iii) whose purpose reflects (in general terms) the character of that area,

(b) may designate only one organisation or body as a neighbourhood forum for each neighbourhood area,
(c) may designate an organisation or body as a neighbourhood forum only if the organisation or body has made an application to be designated, and
(d) must give reasons to an organisation or body applying to be designated as a neighbourhood forum where the authority refuse the application.

(8) A designation –

(a) ceases to have effect at the end of the period of 5 years beginning with the day on which it is made but without affecting the validity of any proposal for a neighbourhood development order made before the end of that period, and
(b) in the case of the designation of an unincorporated association, is not to be affected merely because of a change in the membership of the association.

(9) A local planning authority may withdraw an organisation or body's designation as a neighbourhood forum if they consider that the organisation or body is no longer meeting –

(a) the conditions by reference to which it was designated, or
(b) any other criteria to which the authority were required to have regard in making the designation;

and, where an organisation or body's designation is withdrawn, the authority must give reasons to the organisation or body.

(10) A proposal for a neighbourhood development order by a parish council or neighbourhood forum may not be made at any time in relation to a neighbourhood area if there is at that time another proposal by the council or forum in relation to that area that is outstanding.

(11) Each local planning authority must make such arrangements as they consider appropriate for making people aware as to the times when organisations or bodies could make applications to be designated as neighbourhood forums for neighbourhood areas.

(12) Regulations –

(a) may make provision in connection with proposals made by qualifying bodies for neighbourhood development orders, and
(b) may make provision in connection with designations (or withdrawals of designations) of organisations or bodies as neighbourhood forums (including provision of a kind mentioned in section 61G(11)(a) to (g)).

(13) The regulations may in particular make provision –

(a) as to the consequences of the creation of a new parish council, or a change in the area of a parish council, on any proposal made for a neighbourhood development order,
(b) as to the consequences of the dissolution of a neighbourhood forum on any proposal for a neighbourhood development order made by it,

(c) suspending the operation of any duty of a local planning authority under paragraph 6 or 7 of Schedule 4B in cases where they are considering the withdrawal of the designation of an organisation or body as a neighbourhood forum,
(d) for determining when a proposal for a neighbourhood development order is to be regarded as outstanding, and
(e) requiring a local planning authority to have regard (in addition, where relevant, to the matters set out in subsection (7)(a)) to prescribed matters in determining whether to designate an organisation or body as a neighbourhood forum.

61G Meaning of 'neighbourhood area'

(1) A 'neighbourhood area' means an area within the area of a local planning authority in England which has been designated by the authority as a neighbourhood area; but that power to designate is exercisable only where –

(a) a relevant body has applied to the authority for an area specified in the application to be designated by the authority as a neighbourhood area, and
(b) the authority are determining the application (but see subsection (5)).

(2) A 'relevant body' means –

(a) a parish council, or
(b) an organisation or body which is, or is capable of being, designated as a neighbourhood forum (on the assumption that, for this purpose, the specified area is designated as a neighbourhood area).

(3) The specified area –

(a) in the case of an application by a parish council, must be one that consists of or includes the whole or any part of the area of the council, and
(b) in the case of an application by an organisation or body, must not be one that consists of or includes the whole or any part of the area of a parish council.

(4) In determining an application the authority must have regard to –

(a) the desirability of designating the whole of the area of a parish council as a neighbourhood area, and
(b) the desirability of maintaining the existing boundaries of areas already designated as neighbourhood areas.

(5) If –

(a) a valid application is made to the authority,
(b) some or all of the specified area has not been designated as a neighbourhood area, and
(c) the authority refuse the application because they consider that the specified area is not an appropriate area to be designated as a neighbourhood area,

the authority must exercise their power of designation so as to secure that some or all of the specified area forms part of one or more areas designated (or to be designated) as neighbourhood areas.

(6) The authority may, in determining any application, modify designations

already made; but if a modification relates to any extent to the area of a parish council, the modification may be made only with the council's consent.

(7) The areas designated as neighbourhood areas must not overlap with each other.

(8) A local planning authority must publish a map setting out the areas that are for the time being designated as neighbourhood areas.

(9) If the authority refuse an application, they must give reasons to the applicant for refusing the application.

(10) In this section 'specified', in relation to an application, means specified in the application.

(11) Regulations may make provision in connection with the designation of areas as neighbourhood areas; and the regulations may in particular make provision –

(a) as to the procedure to be followed in relation to designations,
(b) as to the giving of notice and publicity in connection with designations,
(c) as to consultation with and participation by the public in relation to designations,
(d) as to the making and consideration of representations about designations (including the time by which representations must be made),
(e) as to the form and content of applications for designations,
(f) requiring an application for a designation to be determined by a prescribed date,
(g) entitling or requiring a local planning authority in prescribed circumstances to decline to consider an application for a designation, and
(h) about the modification of designations (including provision about the consequences of modification on proposals for neighbourhood development orders, or on neighbourhood development orders, that have already been made).

61H Neighbourhood areas designated as business areas

(1) Whenever a local planning authority exercise their powers under section 61G to designate an area as a neighbourhood area, they must consider whether they should designate the area concerned as a business area.

(2) The reference here to the designation of an area as a neighbourhood area includes the modification under section 61G(6) of a designation already made.

(3) The power of a local planning authority to designate a neighbourhood area as a business area is exercisable by the authority only if, having regard to such matters as may be prescribed, they consider that the area is wholly or predominantly business in nature.

(4) The map published by a local planning authority under section 61G(8) must state which neighbourhood areas (if any) are for the time being designated as business areas.

61I Neighbourhood areas in areas of two or more local planning authorities

(1) The power to designate an area as a neighbourhood area under section 61G is exercisable by two or more local planning authorities in England if the area falls within the areas of those authorities.

(2) Regulations may make provision in connection with –

(a) the operation of subsection (1), and
(b) the operation of other provisions relating to neighbourhood development orders (including sections 61F to 61H) in cases where an area is designated as a neighbourhood area as a result of that subsection.

(3) The regulations may in particular make provision –

(a) modifying or supplementing the application of, or disapplying, any of the provisions mentioned in subsection (2)(b),
(b) applying (with or without modifications) any provision of Part 6 of the Local Government Act 1972 (discharge of functions) in cases where the provision would not otherwise apply,
(c) requiring local planning authorities to exercise, or not to exercise, any power conferred by any provision of that Part (including as applied by virtue of paragraph (b)), and
(d) conferring powers or imposing duties on local planning authorities.

61J Provision that may be made by neighbourhood development order

(1) A neighbourhood development order may make provision in relation to –

(a) all land in the neighbourhood area specified in the order,
(b) any part of that land, or
(c) a site in that area specified in the order.

(2) A neighbourhood development order may not provide for the granting of planning permission for any development that is excluded development.
(3) For the meaning of 'excluded development', see section 61K.
(4) A neighbourhood development order may not grant planning permission for any development in any particular case where planning permission is already granted for that development in that case.
(5) A neighbourhood development order may not relate to more than one neighbourhood area.
(6) A neighbourhood development order may make different provision for different cases or circumstances.

61K Meaning of 'excluded development'

The following development is excluded development for the purposes of section 61J –

(a) development that consists of a county matter within paragraph 1(1)(a) to (h) of Schedule 1,
(b) development that consists of the carrying out of any operation, or class of operation, prescribed under paragraph 1(j) of that Schedule (waste development) but that does not consist of development of a prescribed description,
(c) development that falls within Annex 1 to Council Directive 85/337/EEC on the assessment of the effects of certain public and private projects on the environment (as amended from time to time),
(d) development that consists (whether wholly or partly) of a nationally significant infrastructure project (within the meaning of the Planning Act 2008),
(e) prescribed development or development of a prescribed description, and
(f) development in a prescribed area or an area of a prescribed description.

61L Permission granted by neighbourhood development orders

(1) Planning permission granted by a neighbourhood development order may be granted –

(a) unconditionally, or
(b) subject to such conditions or limitations as are specified in the order.

(2) The conditions that may be specified include –

(a) obtaining the approval of the local planning authority who made the order but not of anyone else, and
(b) provision specifying the period within which applications must be

made to a local planning authority for the approval of the authority of any matter specified in the order.

(3) Regulations may make provision entitling a parish council in prescribed circumstances to require any application for approval under subsection (2) of a prescribed description to be determined by them instead of by a local planning authority.

(4) The regulations may in particular make provision –

(a) as to the procedure to be followed by parish councils in deciding whether to determine applications for approvals (including the time by which the decisions must be made),
(b) requiring parish councils in prescribed circumstances to cease determining applications for approvals,
(c) conferring powers or imposing duties on local planning authorities,
(d) treating parish councils as local planning authorities (instead of, or in addition to, the authorities) for the purposes of the determination of applications for approvals (subject to such exceptions or modifications in the application of any enactment as may be prescribed),
(e) applying any enactment relating to principal councils within the meaning of section 270 of the Local Government Act 1972 for those purposes (with or without modifications), and
(f) disapplying, or modifying the application of, any enactment relating to parish councils for those purposes.

(5) A neighbourhood development order may provide for the granting of planning permission to be subject to the condition that the development begins before the end of the period specified in the order.

(6) Regulations may make provision as to the periods that may be specified in neighbourhood development orders under subsection (5).

(7) If –

(a) planning permission granted by a neighbourhood development order for any development is withdrawn by the revocation of the order under section 61M, and
(b) the revocation is made after the development has begun but before it has been completed,

the development may, despite the withdrawal of the permission, be completed.

(8) But an order under section 61M revoking a neighbourhood development order may provide that subsection (7) is not to apply in relation to development specified in the order under that section.

61M Revocation or modification of neighbourhood development orders

(1) The Secretary of State may by order revoke a neighbourhood development order.

(2) A local planning authority may, with the consent of the Secretary of State, by order revoke a neighbourhood development order that they have made.

(3) If a neighbourhood development order is revoked, the person revoking the order must state the reasons for the revocation.

(4) A local planning authority may at any time by order modify a neighbourhood development order that they have made for the purpose of correcting errors.

(5) If the qualifying body that initiated the process for the making of that order is still authorised at that time to act for the purposes of a neighbourhood

development order in relation to the neighbourhood area concerned, the power under subsection (4) is exercisable only with that body's consent.

(6) A modification of a neighbourhood development order is to be done by replacing the order with a new one containing the modification.

(7) Regulations may make provision in connection with the revocation or modification of a neighbourhood development order.

(8) The regulations may in particular make provision –

- (a) for the holding of an examination in relation to a revocation proposed to be made by the authority,
- (b) as to the payment by a local planning authority of remuneration and expenses of the examiner,
- (c) as to the award of costs by the examiner,
- (d) as to the giving of notice and publicity in connection with a revocation or modification,
- (e) as to the information and documents relating to a revocation or modification that are to be made available to the public,
- (f) as to the making of reasonable charges for anything provided as a result of the regulations,
- (g) as to consultation with and participation by the public in relation to a revocation, and
- (h) as to the making and consideration of representations about a revocation (including the time by which representations must be made).

61N Legal challenges in relation to neighbourhood development orders

(1) A court may entertain proceedings for questioning a decision to act under section 61E(4) or (8) only if –

- (a) the proceedings are brought by a claim for judicial review, and
- (b) the claim form is filed before the end of the period of 6 weeks beginning with the day on which the decision is published.

(2) A court may entertain proceedings for questioning a decision under paragraph 12 of Schedule 4B (consideration by local planning authority of recommendations made by examiner etc) only if –

- (a) the proceedings are brought by a claim for judicial review, and
- (b) the claim form is filed before the end of the period of 6 weeks beginning with the day on which the decision is published.

(3) A court may entertain proceedings for questioning anything relating to a referendum under paragraph 14 or 15 of Schedule 4B only if –

- (a) the proceedings are brought by a claim for judicial review, and
- (b) the claim form is filed during the period of 6 weeks beginning with the day on which the result of the referendum is declared.

61O Guidance

Local planning authorities must have regard to any guidance issued by the Secretary of State in the exercise of any function under any provision relating to neighbourhood development orders (including any function under any of sections 61F to 61H).

61P Provision as to the making of certain decisions by local planning authorities

(1) Regulations may make provision regulating the arrangements of a local planning authority for the making of any prescribed decision under any provision relating to neighbourhood development orders (including under any of sections 61F to 61H).

(2) The provision made by the regulations is to have effect despite provision made by any enactment as to the arrangements of a local planning authority for the exercise of their functions (such as section 101 of the Local Government Act 1972 or section 13 of the Local Government Act 2000).

61Q Community right to build orders

Schedule 4C makes provision in relation to a particular type of neighbourhood development order (a community right to build order).'

3 In section 5(3) (provisions for the purposes of which the Broads Authority are the sole district planning authority) –

(a) after 'sections' insert '61E to 61Q,', and
(b) at the end insert 'and Schedules 4B and 4C'.

4 In Schedule 1 (local planning authorities: distribution of functions), after paragraph 6 insert –

'6A (1) This paragraph applies to the functions of local planning authorities under any of sections 61E to 61Q and Schedules 4B and 4C (neighbourhood development orders).

(2) Those functions are to be exercised by a district planning authority in any area of a non-metropolitan county.'

PART 2 NEIGHBOURHOOD DEVELOPMENT PLANS

5 The Planning and Compulsory Purchase Act 2004 is amended as follows.
6 In section 38 (development plan) –

(a) in subsection (2), omit the 'and' at the end of paragraph (a) and at the end of paragraph (b) insert ', and

(c) the neighbourhood development plans which have been made in relation to that area.',

(b) in subsection (3), at the end of paragraph (b) insert ', and

(c) the neighbourhood development plans which have been made in relation to that area.',

(c) in subsection (5), for 'to be adopted, approved or published (as the case may be)' substitute 'to become part of the development plan', and
(d) at the end insert –

'(10) Neighbourhood development plan must be construed in accordance with section 38A.'

7 After that section insert –

'38A Meaning of 'neighbourhood development plan'

(1) Any qualifying body is entitled to initiate a process for the purpose of requiring a local planning authority in England to make a neighbourhood development plan.
(2) A 'neighbourhood development plan' is a plan which sets out policies (however expressed) in relation to the development and use of land in the whole or any part of a particular neighbourhood area specified in the plan.
(3) Schedule 4B to the principal Act, which makes provision about the process for the making of neighbourhood development orders, including –

(a) provision for independent examination of orders proposed by qualifying bodies, and

(b) provision for the holding of referendums on orders proposed by those bodies,

is to apply in relation to neighbourhood development plans (subject to the modifications set out in section 38C(5) of this Act).

(4) A local planning authority to whom a proposal for the making of a neighbourhood development plan has been made –

(a) must make a neighbourhood development plan to which the proposal relates if in each applicable referendum under that Schedule (as so applied) more than half of those voting have voted in favour of the plan, and

(b) if paragraph (a) applies, must make the plan as soon as reasonably practicable after the referendum is held.

(5) If –

(a) there are two applicable referendums under that Schedule as so applied (because the plan relates to a neighbourhood area designated as a business area under section 61H of the principal Act), and

(b) in one of those referendums (but not the other) more than half of those voting have voted in favour of the plan,

the authority may (but need not) make a neighbourhood development plan to which the proposal relates.

(6) The authority are not to be subject to the duty under subsection (4)(a) if they consider that the making of the plan would breach, or would otherwise be incompatible with, any EU obligation or any of the Convention rights (within the meaning of the Human Rights Act 1998).

(7) Regulations made by the Secretary of State may make provision as to the procedure to be followed by local planning authorities in cases where they act under subsection (6).

(8) The regulations may in particular make provision –

(a) for the holding of an examination,

(b) as to the payment by a local planning authority of remuneration and expenses of the examiner,

(c) as to the award of costs by the examiner,

(d) as to the giving of notice and publicity,

(e) as to the information and documents that are to be made available to the public,

(f) as to the making of reasonable charges for anything provided as a result of the regulations,

(g) as to consultation with and participation by the public, and

(h) as to the making and consideration of representations (including the time by which representations must be made).

(9) The authority must publish in such manner as may be prescribed –

(a) their decision to act under subsection (4) or (6),

(b) their reasons for making that decision, and

(c) such other matters relating to that decision as may be prescribed.

(10) The authority must send a copy of the matters required to be published to –

(a) the qualifying body that initiated the process for the making of the plan, and

(b) such other persons as may be prescribed.

(11) If a neighbourhood development plan is in force in relation to a neighbourhood area –

(a) a qualifying body may make a proposal for the existing plan to be replaced by a new one, and
(b) the process for the making of the replacement plan is the same as the process for the making of the existing plan.

(12) For the purposes of this section –

'local planning authority' has the same meaning as it has in Part 2 (see section 37), but the Broads Authority are to be the only local planning authority for the Broads,

'neighbourhood area' has the meaning given by sections 61G and 61I(1) of the principal Act,

'prescribed' means prescribed by regulations made by the Secretary of State, and

'qualifying body' means a parish council, or an organisation or body designated as a neighbourhood forum, authorised for the purposes of a neighbourhood development plan to act in relation to a neighbourhood area as a result of section 61F of the principal Act, as applied by section 38C of this Act.

38B Provision that may be made by neighbourhood development plans

(1) A neighbourhood development plan –

(a) must specify the period for which it is to have effect,
(b) may not include provision about development that is excluded development, and
(c) may not relate to more than one neighbourhood area.

(2) Only one neighbourhood development plan may be made for each neighbourhood area.
(3) If to any extent a policy set out in a neighbourhood development plan conflicts with any other statement or information in the plan, the conflict must be resolved in favour of the policy.
(4) Regulations made by the Secretary of State may make provision –

(a) restricting the provision that may be included in neighbourhood development plans about the use of land,
(b) requiring neighbourhood development plans to include such matters as are prescribed in the regulations, and
(c) prescribing the form of neighbourhood development plans.

(5) A local planning authority must publish each neighbourhood development plan that they make in such manner as may be prescribed by regulations made by the Secretary of State.
(6) Section 61K of the principal Act (meaning of 'excluded development') is to apply for the purposes of subsection (1)(b).

38C Supplementary provisions

(1) The following provisions of the principal Act are to apply in relation to neighbourhood development plans.
(2) The provisions to be applied are –

(a) section 61F (authorisation to act in relation to neighbourhood areas),

(b) section 61I(2) and (3) (neighbourhood areas in areas of two or more local planning authorities),
(c) section 61M (revocation or modification of neighbourhood development orders),
(d) section 61N (legal challenges),
(e) section 61O (guidance), and
(f) section 61P (provision as to the making of certain decisions by local planning authorities).

(3) Section 61M of the principal Act is to apply in accordance with subsection (2) of this section as if the words 'by order' (wherever occurring) were omitted.
(4) Section 61N(1) of the principal Act is to apply in accordance with subsection (2) of this section as if the reference to section 61E(4) or (8) of that Act were a reference to section 38A(4) or (6) of this Act.
(5) Schedule 4B to the principal Act is to apply in accordance with 38A(3) of this Act with the following modifications –

(a) the reference to section 61E(8) of the principal Act is to be read as a reference to section 38A(6) of this Act,
(b) references to the provision made by or under sections 61E(2), 61J and 61L of the principal Act are to be read as references to the provision made by or under sections 38A and 38B of this Act,
(c) references to section 61L(2)(b) or (5) of the principal Act are to be disregarded, and
(d) paragraph 8 is to have effect as if sub-paragraphs (2)(b) and (c) and (3) to (5) were omitted.

(6) Regulations under section 61G(11) of the principal Act (designation of areas as neighbourhood areas) may include provision about the consequences of the modification of designations on proposals for neighbourhood development plans, or on neighbourhood development plans, that have already been made.
(7) The fact that the list of applied provisions includes section 61N(2) and (3) of the principal Act is not to affect the operation of section 20(2) of the Interpretation Act 1978 in relation to other references to enactments applied in accordance with this section.'

SCHEDULE 10 PROCESS FOR MAKING OF NEIGHBOURHOOD DEVELOPMENT ORDERS

Section 116

This is the Schedule to be inserted as Schedule 4B to the Town and Country Planning Act 1990 –

'SCHEDULE 4B Process for making of neighbourhood development orders

Section 61E

Proposals for neighbourhood development orders

1 (1) A qualifying body is entitled to submit a proposal to a local planning authority for the making of a neighbourhood development order by the authority in relation to a neighbourhood area within the area of the authority.
(2) The proposal must be accompanied by –

(a) a draft of the order, and

(b) a statement which contains a summary of the proposals and sets out the reasons why an order should be made in the proposed terms.

(3) The proposal must –

(a) be made in the prescribed form, and
(b) be accompanied by other documents and information of a prescribed description.

(4) The qualifying body must send to prescribed persons a copy of –

(a) the proposal,
(b) the draft neighbourhood development order, and
(c) such of the other documents and information accompanying the proposal as may be prescribed.

(5) The Secretary of State may publish a document setting standards for –

(a) the preparation of a draft neighbourhood development order and other documents accompanying the proposal,
(b) the coverage in any document accompanying the proposal of a matter falling to be dealt with in it, and
(c) all or any of the collection, sources, verification, processing and presentation of information accompanying the proposal.

(6) The documents and information accompanying the proposal (including the draft neighbourhood development order) must comply with those standards.

2 (1) A qualifying body may withdraw a proposal at any time before the local planning authority make a decision under paragraph 12.

(2) If –

(a) a proposal by a qualifying body is made by an organisation or body designated as a neighbourhood forum, and
(b) the designation is withdrawn at any time before the proposal is submitted for independent examination under paragraph 7,

the proposal is to be treated as withdrawn by the qualifying body at that time.

(3) If the withdrawal of the designation occurs after the proposal is submitted for independent examination under that paragraph, the withdrawal is not to affect the validity of the proposal.

Advice and assistance in connection with proposals

3 (1) A local planning authority must give such advice or assistance to qualifying bodies as, in all the circumstances, they consider appropriate for the purpose of, or in connection with, facilitating the making of proposals for neighbourhood development orders in relation to neighbourhood areas within their area.

(2) Nothing in this paragraph is to be read as requiring the giving of financial assistance.

Requirements to be complied with before proposals made or considered

4 (1) Regulations may make provision as to requirements that must be complied with before proposals for a neighbourhood development order may be submitted to a local planning authority or fall to be considered by a local planning authority.

(2) The regulations may in particular make provision –

(a) as to the giving of notice and publicity,
(b) as to the information and documents that are to be made available to the public,
(c) as to the making of reasonable charges for anything provided as a result of the regulations,
(d) as to consultation with and participation by the public,
(e) as to the making and consideration of representations (including the time by which they must be made),
(f) requiring prescribed steps to be taken before a proposal of a prescribed description falls to be considered by a local planning authority, and
(g) conferring powers or imposing duties on local planning authorities, the Secretary of State or other public authorities.

(3) The power to make regulations under this paragraph must be exercised to secure that –

(a) prescribed requirements as to consultation with and participation by the public must be complied with before a proposal for a neighbourhood development order may be submitted to a local planning authority, and
(b) a statement containing the following information in relation to that consultation and participation must accompany the proposal submitted to the authority –

(i) details of those consulted,
(ii) a summary of the main issues raised, and
(iii) any other information of a prescribed description.

Consideration of proposals by authority

5 (1) A local planning authority may decline to consider a proposal submitted to them if they consider that it is a repeat proposal.
(2) A proposal ('the proposal in question') is a 'repeat' proposal for the purposes of this paragraph if it meets conditions A and B.
(3) Condition A is that in the period of two years ending with the date on which the proposal in question is received –

(a) the authority have refused a proposal under paragraph 12 or section 61E(8) that is the same as or similar to the proposal in question, or
(b) a referendum on an order relating to a proposal under this Schedule that is the same as or similar to the proposal in question has been held under this Schedule and half or less than half of those voting voted in favour of the order.

(4) Condition B is that the local planning authority consider that there has been no significant change in relevant considerations since the refusal of the proposal or the holding of the referendum.
(5) For the purposes of this paragraph 'relevant considerations' means –

(a) national policies and advice contained in guidance issued by the Secretary of State that are relevant to the draft neighbourhood development order to which the proposal in question relates, and
(b) the strategic policies contained in the development plan for the area of the authority (or any part of that area).

(6) If the authority decline to consider the proposal, they must notify the qualifying body of that fact and of their reasons for declining to consider it.

6 (1) This paragraph applies if –

(a) a proposal has been made to a local planning authority, and
(b) the authority have not exercised their powers under paragraph 5 to decline to consider it.

(2) The authority must consider –

(a) whether the qualifying body is authorised for the purposes of a neighbourhood development order to act in relation to the neighbourhood area concerned as a result of section 61F,
(b) whether the proposal by the body complies with provision made by or under that section,
(c) whether the proposal and the documents and information accompanying it (including the draft neighbourhood development order) comply with provision made by or under paragraph 1, and
(d) whether the body has complied with the requirements of regulations made under paragraph 4 imposed on it in relation to the proposal.

(3) The authority must also consider whether the draft neighbourhood development order complies with the provision made by or under sections 61E(2), 61J and 61L.
(4) The authority must –

(a) notify the qualifying body as to whether or not they are satisfied that the matters mentioned in sub-paragraphs (2) and (3) have been met or complied with, and
(b) in any case where they are not so satisfied, refuse the proposal and notify the body of their reasons for refusing it.

Independent examination

7 (1) This paragraph applies if –

(a) a local planning authority have considered the matters mentioned in paragraph 6(2) and (3), and
(b) they are satisfied that the matters mentioned there have been met or complied with.

(2) The authority must submit for independent examination –

(a) the draft neighbourhood development order, and
(b) such other documents as may be prescribed.

(3) The authority must make such arrangements as they consider appropriate in connection with the holding of the examination.
(4) The authority may appoint a person to carry out the examination, but only if the qualifying body consents to the appointment.
(5) If –

(a) it appears to the Secretary of State that no person may be appointed under sub-paragraph (4), and
(b) the Secretary of State considers that it is expedient for an appointment to be made under this sub-paragraph,

the Secretary of State may appoint a person to carry out the examination.

(6) The person appointed must be someone who, in the opinion of the person making the appointment –

(a) is independent of the qualifying body and the authority,
(b) does not have an interest in any land that may be affected by the draft order, and
(c) has appropriate qualifications and experience.

(7) The Secretary of State or another local planning authority may enter into arrangements with the authority for the provision of the services of any of their employees as examiners.

(8) Those arrangements may include –

(a) provision requiring payments to be made by the authority to the Secretary of State or other local planning authority, and
(b) other provision in relation to those payments and other financial matters.

8 (1) The examiner must consider the following –

(a) whether the draft neighbourhood development order meets the basic conditions (see sub-paragraph (2)),
(b) whether the draft order complies with the provision made by or under sections 61E(2), 61J and 61L,
(c) whether any period specified under section 61L(2)(b) or (5) is appropriate,
(d) whether the area for any referendum should extend beyond the neighbourhood area to which the draft order relates, and
(e) such other matters as may be prescribed.

(2) A draft order meets the basic conditions if –

(a) having regard to national policies and advice contained in guidance issued by the Secretary of State, it is appropriate to make the order,
(b) having special regard to the desirability of preserving any listed building or its setting or any features of special architectural or historic interest that it possesses, it is appropriate to make the order,
(c) having special regard to the desirability of preserving or enhancing the character or appearance of any conservation area, it is appropriate to make the order,
(d) the making of the order contributes to the achievement of sustainable development,
(e) the making of the order is in general conformity with the strategic policies contained in the development plan for the area of the authority (or any part of that area),
(f) the making of the order does not breach, and is otherwise compatible with, EU obligations, and
(g) prescribed conditions are met in relation to the order and prescribed matters have been complied with in connection with the proposal for the order.

(3) Sub-paragraph (2)(b) applies in relation to a listed building only in so far as the order grants planning permission for development that affects the building or its setting.

(4) Sub-paragraph (2)(c) applies in relation to a conservation area only in so far as the order grants planning permission for development in relation to buildings or other land in the area.

(5) In this paragraph 'listed building' has the same meaning as in the Planning (Listed Buildings and Conservation Areas) Act 1990.

(6) The examiner is not to consider any matter that does not fall within sub-paragraph (1) (apart from considering whether the draft order is compatible with the Convention rights).

9 (1) The general rule is that the examination of the issues by the examiner is to take the form of the consideration of written representations.

(2) But the examiner must cause a hearing to be held for the purpose of receiving oral representations about a particular issue at the hearing –

(a) in any case where the examiner considers that the consideration of oral representations is necessary to ensure adequate examination of the issue or a person has a fair chance to put a case, or

(b) in such other cases as may be prescribed.

(3) The following persons are entitled to make oral representations about the issue at the hearing –

(a) the qualifying body,

(b) the local planning authority,

(c) where the hearing is held to give a person a fair chance to put a case, that person, and

(d) such other persons as may be prescribed.

(4) The hearing must be in public.

(5) It is for the examiner to decide how the hearing is to be conducted, including –

(a) whether a person making oral representations may be questioned by another person and, if so, the matters to which the questioning may relate, and

(b) the amount of time for the making of a person's oral representations or for any questioning by another person.

(6) In making decisions about the questioning of a person's oral representations by another, the examiner must apply the principle that the questioning should be done by the examiner except where the examiner considers that questioning by another is necessary to ensure –

(a) adequate examination of a particular issue, or

(b) a person has a fair chance to put a case.

(7) Sub-paragraph (5) is subject to regulations under paragraph 11.

10 (1) The examiner must make a report on the draft order containing recommendations in accordance with this paragraph (and no other recommendations).

(2) The report must recommend either –

(a) that the draft order is submitted to a referendum, or

(b) that modifications specified in the report are made to the draft order and that the draft order as modified is submitted to a referendum, or

(c) that the proposal for the order is refused.

(3) The only modifications that may be recommended are –

(a) modifications that the examiner considers need to be made to secure that the draft order meets the basic conditions mentioned in paragraph 8(2),
(b) modifications that the examiner considers need to be made to secure that the draft order is compatible with the Convention rights,
(c) modifications that the examiner considers need to be made to secure that the draft order complies with the provision made by or under sections 61E(2), 61J and 61L,
(d) modifications specifying a period under section 61L(2)(b) or (5), and
(e) modifications for the purpose of correcting errors.

(4) The report may not recommend that an order (with or without modifications) is submitted to a referendum if the examiner considers that the order does not –

(a) meet the basic conditions mentioned in paragraph 8(2), or
(b) comply with the provision made by or under sections 61E(2), 61J and 61L.

(5) If the report recommends that an order (with or without modifications) is submitted to a referendum, the report must also make –

(a) a recommendation as to whether the area for the referendum should extend beyond the neighbourhood area to which the order relates, and
(b) if a recommendation is made for an extended area, a recommendation as to what the extended area should be.

(6) The report must –

(a) give reasons for each of its recommendations, and
(b) contain a summary of its main findings.

(7) The examiner must send a copy of the report to the qualifying body and the local planning authority.
(8) The local planning authority must then arrange for the publication of the report in such manner as may be prescribed.

11 (1) Regulations may make provision in connection with examinations under paragraph 7.
(2) The regulations may in particular make provision as to –

(a) the giving of notice and publicity in connection with an examination,
(b) the information and documents relating to an examination that are to be made available to the public,
(c) the making of reasonable charges for anything provided as a result of the regulations,
(d) the making of written or oral representations in relation to draft neighbourhood development orders (including the time by which written representations must be made),
(e) the written representations which are to be, or which may be or may not be, considered at an examination,
(f) the refusal to allow oral representations of a prescribed description to be made at a hearing,
(g) the procedure to be followed at an examination (including the procedure to be followed at a hearing),

(h) the payment by a local planning authority of remuneration and expenses of the examiner, and
(i) the award of costs by the examiner.

Consideration by authority of recommendations made by examiner etc

12 (1) This paragraph applies if an examiner has made a report under paragraph 10.
(2) The local planning authority must –

(a) consider each of the recommendations made by the report (and the reasons for them), and
(b) decide what action to take in response to each recommendation.

(3) The authority must also consider such other matters as may be prescribed.
(4) If the authority are satisfied –

(a) that the draft order meets the basic conditions mentioned in paragraph 8(2), is compatible with the Convention rights and complies with the provision made by or under sections 61E(2), 61J and 61L, or
(b) that the draft order would meet those conditions, be compatible with those rights and comply with that provision if modifications were made to the draft order (whether or not recommended by the examiner),

a referendum in accordance with paragraph 14, and (if applicable) an additional referendum in accordance with paragraph 15, must be held on the making by the authority of a neighbourhood development order.
(5) The order on which the referendum is (or referendums are) to be held is the draft order subject to such modifications (if any) as the authority consider appropriate.
(6) The only modifications that the authority may make are –

(a) modifications that the authority consider need to be made to secure that the draft order meets the basic conditions mentioned in paragraph 8(2),
(b) modifications that the authority consider need to be made to secure that the draft order is compatible with the Convention rights,
(c) modifications that the authority consider need to be made to secure that the draft order complies with the provision made by or under sections 61E(2), 61J and 61L,
(d) modifications specifying a period under section 61L(2)(b) or (5), and
(e) modifications for the purpose of correcting errors.

(7) The area in which the referendum is (or referendums are) to take place must, as a minimum, be the neighbourhood area to which the proposed order relates.
(8) If the authority consider it appropriate to do so, they may extend the area in which the referendum is (or referendums are) to take place to include other areas (whether or not those areas fall wholly or partly outside the authority's area).

(9) If the authority decide to extend the area in which the referendum is (or referendums are) to take place, they must publish a map of that area.

(10) In any case where the authority are not satisfied as mentioned in sub-paragraph (4), they must refuse the proposal.

(11) The authority must publish in such manner as may be prescribed –

(a) the decisions they make under this paragraph,
(b) their reasons for making those decisions, and
(c) such other matters relating to those decisions as may be prescribed.

(12) The authority must send a copy of the matters required to be published to –

(a) the qualifying body, and
(b) such other persons as may be prescribed.

13 (1) If –

(a) the local planning authority propose to make a decision which differs from that recommended by the examiner, and
(b) the reason for the difference is (wholly or partly) as a result of new evidence or a new fact or a different view taken by the authority as to a particular fact,

the authority must notify prescribed persons of their proposed decision (and the reason for it) and invite representations.

(2) If the authority consider it appropriate to do so, they may refer the issue to independent examination.

(3) Regulations may make provision about examinations under this paragraph (and the regulations may include any provision of a kind mentioned in paragraph 11(2)).

(4) This paragraph does not apply in relation to recommendations in relation to the area in which a referendum is to take place.

Referendum

14 (1) This paragraph makes provision in relation to a referendum that, as a result of paragraph 12(4), must be held on the making of a neighbourhood development order.

(2) A relevant council must make arrangements for the referendum to take place in so much of their area as falls within the area ('the referendum area') in which the referendum is to take place (as determined under paragraph 12(7) and (8)).

This sub-paragraph is subject to regulations under paragraph 16(2)(b).

(3) A 'relevant council' means –

(a) a district council,
(b) a London borough council,
(c) a metropolitan district council, or
(d) a county council in relation to any area in England for which there is no district council.

(4) A person is entitled to vote in the referendum if on the prescribed date –

(a) the person is entitled to vote in an election of any councillors of a relevant council any of whose area is in the referendum area, and

(b) the person's qualifying address for the election is in the referendum area.

(5) Sub-paragraph (4) does not apply in relation to so much of the referendum area as falls within the City of London.

(6) In that case a person is entitled to vote in the referendum if on the prescribed date –

(a) the person is entitled to vote in an Authority election, and

(b) the person's qualifying address for the election is in the City of London.

(7) For the purposes of this paragraph –

(a) 'Authority election' has the same meaning as in the Representation of the People Act 1983 (see section 203(1)),

(b) the Inner Temple and the Middle Temple are to be treated as forming part of the City of London, and

(c) 'qualifying address' has the same meaning as in the Representation of the People Act 1983 (see section 9).

15 (1) The additional referendum mentioned in paragraph 12(4) must be held on the making of a neighbourhood development order if the draft order relates to a neighbourhood area that has been designated as a business area under section 61H.

(2) Sub-paragraph (2) of paragraph 14 is to apply in relation to the additional referendum as it applies in relation to a referendum under that paragraph.

(3) A person is entitled to vote in the additional referendum if on the prescribed date –

(a) the person is a non-domestic ratepayer in the referendum area, or

(b) the person meets such other conditions as may be prescribed.

(4) 'Non-domestic ratepayer' has the same meaning as in Part 4 of the Local Government Act 2003 (see section 59(1)).

(5) Regulations may make provision for excluding a person's entitlement to vote in the additional referendum.

16 (1) Regulations may make provision about referendums held under paragraph 14 or 15.

(2) The regulations may in particular make provision –

(a) dealing with any case where there are two or more relevant councils any of whose areas fall within the referendum area,

(b) for only one relevant council to be subject to the duty to make arrangements for the referendum in a case within paragraph (a),

(c) prescribing a date by which the referendum must be held or before which it cannot be held,

(d) as to the question to be asked in the referendum and any explanatory material in relation to that question (including provision conferring power on a local planning authority to set the question and provide that material),

(e) as to the publicity to be given in connection with the referendum,
(f) about the limitation of expenditure in connection with the referendum,
(g) as to the conduct of the referendum,
(h) as to when, where and how voting in the referendum is to take place,
(i) as to how the votes cast are to be counted,
(j) about certification as to the number of persons voting in the referendum and as to the number of those persons voting in favour of a neighbourhood development order, and
(k) about the combination of polls at a referendum held under paragraph 14 or 15 with polls at another referendum or at any election.

(3) The regulations may apply or incorporate, with or without modifications, any provision made by or under any enactment relating to elections or referendums.
(4) But where the regulations apply or incorporate (with or without modifications) any provision that creates an offence, the regulations may not impose a penalty greater than is provided for in respect of that provision.
(5) Before making the regulations, the Secretary of State must consult the Electoral Commission.
(6) In this paragraph 'enactment' means an enactment, whenever passed or made.

Interpretation

17 In this Schedule –

'the Convention rights' has the same meaning as in the Human Rights Act 1998, and

'development plan' –

(a) includes a development plan for the purposes of paragraph 1 of Schedule 8 to the Planning and Compulsory Purchase Act 2004 (transitional provisions), but
(b) does not include so much of a development plan as consists of a neighbourhood development plan under section 38A of that Act.'

SCHEDULE 11 NEIGHBOURHOOD PLANNING: COMMUNITY RIGHT TO BUILD ORDERS

Section 116

This is the Schedule to be inserted as Schedule 4C to the Town and Country Planning Act 1990 –

'SCHEDULE 4C Community right to build orders

Section 61Q

Introduction

1 (1) This Schedule makes special provision about a particular type of neighbourhood development order, which is to be known as a 'community right to build order'.

(2) In their application to community right to build orders, the provisions of this Act relating to neighbourhood development orders have effect subject to the provision made by or under this Schedule.

(3) In its application to community organisations, section 61G (meaning of 'neighbourhood area') has effect subject to the provision made by this Schedule.

Meaning of 'community right to build order'

2 (1) A neighbourhood development order is a community right to build order if –

(a) the order is made pursuant to a proposal made by a community organisation,

(b) the order grants planning permission for specified development in relation to a specified site in the specified neighbourhood area, and

(c) the specified development does not exceed prescribed limits.

(2) Regulations under sub-paragraph (1)(c) may prescribe a limit by reference to –

(a) the area in which the development is to take place,

(b) the number or type of operations or uses of land constituting the development, or

(c) any other factor.

(3) In this paragraph 'specified' means specified in the community right to build order.

Meaning of 'community organisation'

3 (1) For the purposes of this Schedule a 'community organisation' is a body corporate –

(a) which is established for the express purpose of furthering the social, economic and environmental well-being of individuals living, or wanting to live, in a particular area, and

(b) which meets such other conditions in relation to its establishment or constitution as may be prescribed.

(2) Regulations under sub-paragraph (1)(b) may make provision in relation to –

(a) the distribution of profits made by the body to its members,

(b) the distribution of the assets of the body (in the event of its winding up or in any other circumstances),

(c) the membership of the body, and

(d) the control of the body (whether by the exercise of voting rights or otherwise).

Proposals by community organisations for community right to build orders

4 (1) A community organisation is authorised for the purposes of a community right to build order to act in relation to a neighbourhood area (whether or not any part of the neighbourhood area falls within the area of a parish council) if –

(a) the area mentioned in paragraph 3(1)(a) consists of or includes the neighbourhood area, and

(b) at the time the proposal for the order is made more than half of the members of the organisation live in the neighbourhood area.

(2) Accordingly, the community organisation is in that case to be regarded as a qualifying body for the purposes of section 61E.

(3) Nothing in section 61F is to apply in relation to community right to build orders except subsections (12)(a) and (13)(d) of that section.

(4) In particular, the reference in section 61F(10) to a neighbourhood development order is not to include a reference to a community right to build order (in a case where a community organisation is also a neighbourhood forum).

(5) But a local planning authority may decline to consider a proposal for a community right to build order or other neighbourhood development order if –

(a) another proposal has been made for a community right to build order or other neighbourhood development order,

(b) the other proposal is outstanding, and

(c) the authority consider that the development and site to which the proposals relate are the same or substantially the same.

(6) If the authority decline to consider the proposal, they must notify the person making the proposal of that fact and of their reasons for declining to consider it.

(7) A proposal for a community right to build order must state that the proposal is for such an order.

5 (1) A community organisation is to be regarded as a relevant body for the purposes of section 61G if –

(a) the area specified in the application made by the organisation consists of or includes the area mentioned in paragraph 3(1)(a), and

(b) at the time the application is made more than half of the members of the organisation live in the area specified in the application.

(2) The application made by the community organisation may specify any area within the local planning authority's area, irrespective of whether or not any part of the specified area falls within the area of a parish council.

(3) This paragraph applies only if the application by the community organisation under section 61G is made in connection with a proposal (or an anticipated proposal) for a community right to build order.

Development likely to have significant effects on environment etc

6 (1) A local planning authority must decline to consider a proposal for a community right to build order if they consider that –

(a) the specified development falls within Annex 2 to the EIA directive and is likely to have significant effects on the environment by virtue of factors such as its nature, size or location, or

(b) the specified development is likely to have significant effects on a qualifying European site (whether alone or in combination with other plans or projects) and is not directly connected with or necessary to the management of that site.

(2) In determining whether or not the specified development is within sub-paragraph (1)(a), the authority must take into account any relevant criteria mentioned in Annex 3 to the EIA directive.

(3) If the authority decline to consider the proposal as a result of sub-paragraph (1), they must notify the community organisation making the proposal of that fact and of their reasons for declining to consider it.

(4) Regulations may make provision requiring the publication of any decisions made by a local planning authority under this paragraph.

(5) In this paragraph –

'the EIA directive' means Council Directive 85/337/EEC on the assessment of the effects of certain public and private projects on the environment (as amended from time to time),

'qualifying European site' means –

(a) a European offshore marine site within the meaning of the Offshore Marine Conservation (Natural Habitats, &c.) Regulations 2007, or

(b) a European site within the meaning of the Conservation of Habitats and Species Regulations 2010, and

'specified' means specified in the community right to build order.

Examination of proposals for community right to build orders etc

7 The provisions of Schedule 4B have effect in relation to community right to build orders with the following modifications.

8 Any reference in that Schedule to section 61E(2) includes a reference to paragraph 2 of this Schedule.

9 Any reference in that Schedule to section 61F includes a reference to paragraph 4 of this Schedule.

10 (1) The provision made by sub-paragraphs (2) to (5) of this paragraph is to have effect instead of paragraph 12(4) to (6) and (10) of that Schedule.

(2) If the examiner's report recommends that the draft order is refused, the authority must refuse the proposal.

(3) If the examiner's report recommends that the draft order is submitted to a referendum (with or without modifications), a referendum in accordance with paragraph 14 of that Schedule must be held on the making by the authority of a community right to build order.

(4) The order on which the referendum is to be held is the order that the examiner's report recommended be submitted to a referendum subject to such modifications (if any) as the authority consider appropriate.

(5) The only modifications that the authority may make are –

(a) modifications that the authority consider need to be made to secure that the order does not breach, and is otherwise compatible with, EU obligations,

(b) modifications that the authority consider need to be made to secure that the order is compatible with the Convention rights (within the meaning of the Human Rights Act 1998), and

(c) modifications for the purpose of correcting errors.

(6) In consequence of the provision made by sub-paragraphs (2) to (5) of this paragraph –

(a) paragraph 12(7) to (9) of Schedule 4B have effect as if the words '(or referendums are)' were omitted, and
(b) that Schedule has effect as if paragraph 15 (and references to that paragraph) were omitted.

(7) Any reference in this Act or any other enactment to paragraph 12 of Schedule 4B includes a reference to that paragraph as modified in accordance with this paragraph.

Use of land

11 (1) Regulations may make provision for securing that in prescribed circumstances –

(a) an enfranchisement right is not exercisable in relation to land the development of which is authorised by a community right to build order, or
(b) the exercise of an enfranchisement right in relation to that land is subject to modifications provided for by the regulations.

(2) Each of the following is an 'enfranchisement right' –

(a) the right under Part 1 of the Leasehold Reform Act 1967 to acquire the freehold of a house (enfranchisement),
(b) the right under Chapter 1 of Part 1 of the Leasehold Reform, Housing and Urban Development Act 1993 (collective enfranchisement in case of tenants of flats), and
(c) the right under section 180 of the Housing and Regeneration Act 2008 (right to acquire social housing).

(3) The regulations may –

(a) confer discretionary powers on the Secretary of State, a community organisation or any other specified person, and
(b) require notice to be given in any case where, as a result of the regulations, an enfranchisement right is not exercisable or is exercisable subject to modifications.

Different provision made by regulations for community right to build orders

12 (1) The provision that may be made by regulations under any provision of this Act relating to neighbourhood development orders includes different provision in relation to community right to build orders.
(2) Sub-paragraph (1) is not to be read as limiting in any way the generality of section 333(2A) (which provides that regulations may make different provision for different purposes).'

SCHEDULE 12 NEIGHBOURHOOD PLANNING: CONSEQUENTIAL AMENDMENTS

Section 121

Town and Country Planning Act 1990

1 The Town and Country Planning Act 1990 is amended as follows.
2 In section 56(3) (time when development begun) –

(a) after 'sections' insert '61L(5) and (7),', and
(b) for 'and 94' substitute ', 94 and 108(3E)(c)(i)'.

3 In section 57(3) (extent of permission granted by development order), for 'or a local development order' substitute ', a local development order or a neighbourhood development order'.

4 In section 58(1)(a) (grant of planning permission by development order), for 'or a local development order' substitute ', a local development order or a neighbourhood development order'.

5 In section 62 (applications for planning permission), after subsection (2) insert –

'(2A) In subsections (1) and (2) references to applications for planning permission include references to applications for approval under section 61L(2).'

6 In section 65 (notice etc of applications for planning permission), after subsection (3) insert –

'(3A) In subsections (1) and (3) references to any application for planning permission or any applicant for such permission include references to any application for approval under section 61L(2) or any applicant for such approval.'

7 (1) Section 69 (register of applications etc) is amended as follows.

(2) In subsection (1), after paragraph (c) insert –

'(ca) neighbourhood planning matters;'.

(3) In subsection (2)(b), after 'order' insert ', neighbourhood planning matter'.

(4) After subsection (2) insert –

'(2A) For the purposes of subsections (1) and (2) 'neighbourhood planning matters' means –

(a) neighbourhood development orders;
(b) neighbourhood development plans (made under section 38A of the Planning and Compulsory Purchase Act 2004); and
(c) proposals for such orders or plans.'

8 (1) Section 71 (consultations in connection with determinations under s.70) is amended as follows.

(2) After subsection (2) insert –

'(2ZA)In subsections (1) and (2) references to an application for planning permission include references to an application for approval under section 61L(2).'

(3) After subsection (3) insert –

'(3A) Subsection (3) does not apply in relation to planning permission granted by a neighbourhood development order.'

9 In section 74 (directions etc as to method of dealing with applications), after subsection (1) insert –

'(1ZA) In subsection (1) –

(a) in paragraph (c) the reference to planning permission for any development includes a reference to an approval under section 61L(2), and
(b) in paragraph (f) references to applications for planning permission include references to applications for approvals under section 61L(2).'

10 In section 77(1) (certain applications to be referred to the Secretary of State), for 'or a local development order' substitute ', a local development order or a neighbourhood development order'.

11 In section 78(1)(c) (right of appeal in relation to certain planning directions), for 'or a local development order' substitute ', a local development order or a neighbourhood development order'.

12 In section 88(9) (grant of planning permission in enterprise zone), for 'or a local development order' substitute ', a local development order or a neighbourhood development order'.

13 In section 91(4)(a) (no limit to duration of planning permission granted by development order), for 'or a local development order' substitute ', a local development order or a neighbourhood development order'.

14 In section 94(1) (termination of planning permission by reference to time limit: completion notices), at the end of paragraph (c) insert '; or

(d) a planning permission under a neighbourhood development order is subject to a condition that the development to which the permission relates must be begun before the expiration of a particular period, that development has been begun within that period, but that period has elapsed without the development having been completed.'

15 (1) Section 108 (compensation for refusal or conditional grant of planning permission formerly granted by development order or local development order) is amended as follows.

(2) In subsection (1) –

(a) in paragraph (a), for 'or a local development order' substitute ', a local development order or a neighbourhood development order', and

(b) in the words after paragraph (b), for 'or a local development order' substitute ', the local development order or the neighbourhood development order'.

(3) In subsection (2), for 'or a local development order' substitute ', a local development order or a neighbourhood development order'.

(4) In subsection (3B), at the end insert –

'(c) in the case of planning permission granted by a neighbourhood development order, the condition in subsection (3E) is met.'

(5) After subsection (3D) insert –

'(3E) The condition referred to in subsection (3B)(c) is that –

(a) the planning permission is withdrawn by the revocation of the neighbourhood development order,

(b) notice of the revocation was published in the prescribed manner not less than 12 months or more than the prescribed period before the revocation took effect, and

(c) either –

(i) the development authorised by the neighbourhood development order had not begun before the notice was published, or

(ii) section 61L(7) applies in relation to the development.'

(6) In the title, for 'or a local development order' substitute ', local development order or neighbourhood development order'.

16 In section 109(6) (apportionment of compensation for depreciation), in the definition of 'relevant planning permission', for 'or a local development order' substitute ', the local development order or the neighbourhood development order'.

17 In section 171H(1)(a) (temporary stop notice: compensation), for 'a development order or local development order' substitute 'by a development order, a local development order or a neighbourhood development order'.

18 In section 197 (planning permission to include appropriate provision for preservation and planting of trees), at the end insert –

'Nothing in this section applies in relation to neighbourhood development orders.'

19 In section 253(2)(c) (cases in which certain procedures may be carried out in anticipation of planning permission), for 'or a local development order' substitute ', a local development order or a neighbourhood development order'.

20 In section 264(5) (land treated not as operational land) –

(a) in paragraph (b), omit 'or a local development order', and

(b) after paragraph (c) (but before the 'or' at the end of the paragraph) insert –

'(ca) granted by a local development order or a neighbourhood development order;'.

21 (1) Section 324 (rights of entry) is amended as follows.

(2) In subsection (1), after paragraph (a) insert –

'(aa) the preparation, making, modification or revocation of a neighbourhood development plan under Part 3 of that Act;'.

(3) After that subsection insert –

'(1A) For the purposes of subsection (1)(c) the reference to a proposal by the local planning authority to make any order under Part 3 includes a reference to a proposal submitted (or to be submitted) to the authority for the making by them of a neighbourhood development order.'

22 (1) Section 333 (regulations and orders) is amended as follows.

(2) In subsection (3) (regulations to be subject to annulment) after 'except regulations under section 88' insert 'or paragraph 15(5) or 16 of Schedule 4B'.

(3) After that subsection insert –

'(3A) No regulations may be made under paragraph 15(5) or 16 of Schedule 4B unless a draft of the instrument containing the regulations has been laid before, and approved by a resolution of, each House of Parliament.'

23 In paragraph 1A of Schedule 13 (blighted land: land allocated for public authority functions in development plans etc) –

(a) after 'for the area in which the land is situated' insert 'or by a neighbourhood development plan for the area in which the land is situated',

(b) after Note (2) insert –

'(2A) For the purposes of this paragraph a neighbourhood development plan includes a draft of a neighbourhood development plan which has been submitted for examination under paragraph 7(2) of Schedule 4B (as applied by section 38A(3) of the 2004 Act).', and

(c) after Note (5) insert –

'(6) Note (2A) does not apply if the proposal for the draft plan is withdrawn under paragraph 2 of Schedule 4B (as applied by section 38A(3) of the 2004 Act) at any time after the draft plan has been submitted for examination.'

Planning (Listed Buildings and Conservation Areas) Act 1990

24 The Planning (Listed Buildings and Conservation Areas) Act 1990 is amended as follows.

25 In section 66 (general duty as respects listed buildings in exercise of planning functions), at the end insert –

'(4) Nothing in this section applies in relation to neighbourhood development orders.'

26 In section 72 (general duty as respects conservation areas in exercise of planning functions), at the end insert –

'(4) Nothing in this section applies in relation to neighbourhood development orders.'

Planning and Compulsory Purchase Act 2004

27 The Planning and Compulsory Purchase Act 2004 is amended as follows.
28 In section 18 (statement of community involvement), after subsection (2) insert –

'(2A) The reference in subsection (2) to functions under Part 3 of the principal Act does not include functions under any provision of that Act relating to neighbourhood development orders (including any function under any of sections 61F to 61H of that Act).'

29 In section 40(2) (local development orders), omit paragraphs (b) to (k).
30 In section 116(2)(b) (Isles of Scilly), after 'Part 2' insert 'or 3'.

Housing and Regeneration Act 2008

31 In section 13(5) of the Housing and Regeneration Act 2008 (power of Secretary of State to make designation orders) –

(a) in paragraph (a) of the definition of 'local planning authority', after 'Part 2' insert 'or 3', and
(b) in paragraph (c) of the definition of 'permitted purposes', after 'Part 2' insert 'or 3'.

SCHEDULE 13 INFRASTRUCTURE PLANNING COMMISSION: TRANSFER OF FUNCTIONS TO SECRETARY OF STATE

Section 128

PART 1 AMENDMENTS OF THE PLANNING ACT 2008

Introductory

1 The Planning Act 2008 is amended as follows.

Abolition of Infrastructure Planning Commission

2 Omit sections 1 to 3 and Schedule 1 (establishment and governance of Commission and conduct and interests of Commissioners).

Fees

3 (1) Amend section 4 (regulations setting fees for performance of Commission's functions) as follows.
(2) In subsection (1) for 'charging of fees by the Commission in connection with the performance of any of its functions' substitute 'charging of fees by the Secretary of State in connection with the performance of any of the Secretary of State's major-infrastructure functions'.
(3) In subsection (3) (power to set fees calculated by reference to costs incurred) –

(a) for 'incurred by the Commission' substitute 'incurred by the Secretary of State', and

(b) for 'its functions' (in both places) substitute 'the Secretary of State's major-infrastructure functions'.

(4) After subsection (3) insert –

'(4) In this section 'the Secretary of State's major-infrastructure functions' means –

(a) the Secretary of State's functions under Parts 2 to 8 and under Part 12 so far as applying for the purposes of those Parts,
(b) the giving of advice to which section 51 applies, and
(c) the Secretary of State's functions, in relation to proposed applications for orders granting development consent, under statutory provisions implementing –

(i) Council Directive 85/337/EC on the assessment of the effects of certain public and private projects on the environment, as amended from time to time, or
(ii) provisions of an EU instrument which from time to time replace provisions of that Directive.

(5) In subsection (4)(c) 'statutory provision' means a provision of an Act or of an instrument made under an Act.'

(5) In the heading of Part 1 for 'The Infrastructure Planning Commission' substitute 'Infrastructure planning: fees'.

Directions referring applications for other consents to Commission

4 In section 35(6) (relevant authority must refer application to Commission) for 'Commission' substitute 'Secretary of State'.

Applications for orders granting development consent

5 (1) Amend section 37 (applications to be made to Commission, which may give guidance about their contents and set standards for them) as follows.
(2) For 'Commission' (in each place) substitute 'Secretary of State'.
(3) In subsection (6) for 'it' substitute 'the Secretary of State'.

Model provisions for incorporation in draft orders

6 Omit section 38 (Secretary of State may prescribe non-compulsory model provisions).

Register of applications

7 (1) Amend section 39 (Commission to maintain and give access to register of applications) as follows.
(2) For 'Commission' (in each place) substitute 'Secretary of State'.
(3) In subsections (1) and (2) for 'it' substitute 'the Secretary of State'.

Notification of proposed application

8 (1) Amend section 46 (duty to notify Commission of proposed application) as follows.
(2) In subsection (1) for 'Commission' (in each place) substitute 'Secretary of State'.
(3) In the heading for 'Commission' substitute 'Secretary of State'.

Guidance about pre-application procedure

9 In section 50(2) (guidance may be issued by Commission or Secretary of State) omit 'the Commission or'.

Advice for potential applicants and others

10 (1) Section 51 (giving of advice by Commission and disclosure of advice and requests for advice) is amended as follows.

(2) In subsection (1) for 'The Commission may give advice to an applicant or potential applicant, or to others,' substitute 'This section applies to advice'.

(3) For subsections (2) to (4) substitute –

'(3) The Secretary of State may by regulations make provision about the giving of advice to which this section applies.

(4) In particular, regulations under subsection (3) may make provision that has the effect that –

(a) a request for advice made by an applicant, potential applicant or other person, or

(b) advice given to an applicant, potential applicant or other person,

must be, or may be, disclosed by the Secretary of State to other persons or to the public generally.'

Information about, and entry onto, land

11 In section 52(2) and (4) (authorisation by Commission to serve notice requiring names and addresses of persons with interests in land) for 'Commission' substitute 'Secretary of State'.

12 (1) Amend section 53 (rights of entry) as follows.

(2) In subsections (1) and (2) (Commission may authorise entry) for 'Commission' (in each place) substitute 'Secretary of State'.

(3) In subsection (4)(c) for 'Commission's' substitute 'Secretary of State's'.

Acceptance of applications

13 (1) Amend section 55 (acceptance by Commission of applications) as follows.

(2) For 'Commission' (in each place) substitute 'Secretary of State'.

(3) In subsections (2), (4) and (6) for 'it' (in each place) substitute 'the Secretary of State'.

(4) In subsection (7) –

(a) for 'it cannot accept the application, it' substitute 'the application cannot be accepted, the Secretary of State', and

(b) in paragraph (b) for 'its' substitute 'the Secretary of State's'.

14 In section 56 (if Commission accepts application, applicant to notify deadline for receipt by Commission of representations) for 'Commission' (in each place) substitute 'Secretary of State'.

15 In section 58(1) and (2) (applicant must certify to Commission that section 56 has been complied with) for 'Commission' substitute 'Secretary of State'.

16 In section 59(1) and (2) (applicant must notify Commission of persons affected by any request to authorise compulsory acquisition) for 'Commission' substitute 'Secretary of State'.

17 (1) Amend section 60 (Commission's duty to seek local impact reports) as follows.

(2) For 'Commission' (in each place) substitute 'Secretary of State'.

(3) In subsection (2) for 'to it' substitute 'to the Secretary of State'.

Deciding how application is to be handled

18 (1) Amend section 61 (initial choice of Panel or single Commissioner) as follows.

(2) In subsection (1) (which refers to acceptance of an application by the Commission) for 'Commission' substitute 'Secretary of State'.

(3) For subsections (2) to (5) (person appointed to chair Commission must make initial choice after consultation within the Commission and having regard to Secretary of State's guidance) substitute –

'(2) The Secretary of State must decide whether the application –

(a) is to be handled by a Panel under Chapter 2, or

(b) is to be handled by a single appointed person under Chapter 3.

(3) The Secretary of State must publish the criteria that are to be applied in making decisions under subsection (2).'

(4) In the heading for 'Commissioner' substitute 'appointed person'.

19 (1) Amend section 62 (switching from single Commissioner to Panel) as follows.

(2) In subsection (1), and in the heading, for 'Commissioner' substitute 'appointed person'.

(3) For subsections (2) to (5) (person appointed to chair Commission may make switch after consultation within the Commission and having regard to the Secretary of State's guidance) substitute –

'(2) The Secretary of State may decide that the application should instead be handled by a Panel under Chapter 2.

(3) The Secretary of State must publish the criteria that are to be applied in making decisions under subsection (2).'

Delegation of functions conferred on person appointed to chair Commission

20 Omit section 63 (power for Commission's chair to delegate functions under Part 6 to a deputy).

Handling of applications by a Panel

21 In section 64(1)(a) (which refers to an application accepted by the Commission) for 'Commission' substitute 'Secretary of State'.

22 (1) Amend section 65 (appointment of members, and lead member, of Panel) as follows.

(2) For subsection (1) (Commission chair must appoint Panel and Panel chair) substitute –

'(1) The Secretary of State must appoint –

(a) three, four or five persons to be members of the Panel, and

(b) one of those persons to chair the Panel.'

(3) Omit subsections (3) to (5) (self-appointments, and duty to consult within the Commission before making appointments).

23 (1) Amend section 66 (ceasing to be member, or lead member, of Panel) as follows.

(2) Omit subsection (1) (generally, person ceases to be Panel member on ceasing to be a Commissioner).

(3) In subsections (3) and (4) (member, or lead member, may resign by notice to Commission) for 'Commission' substitute 'Secretary of State'.

(4) In subsection (5) (Commission chair may remove Panel member or lead member) –

(a) for 'person appointed to chair the Commission ('the chair')' substitute 'Secretary of State', and

(b) in paragraphs (a) and (b) for 'chair' substitute 'Secretary of State'.

24 Omit section 67 (Panel member continuing though ceasing to be Commissioner).

25 (1) Amend section 68 (additional appointments to Panel) as follows.
(2) For subsection (2) (Commission chair may appoint additional Panel member) substitute –

'(2) The Secretary of State may appoint a person to be a member of the Panel, but this power may not be exercised so as to cause the Panel to have more than five members.'

(3) In subsection (3) (Commission chair must ensure Panel continues to have at least three members) for 'person appointed to chair the Commission' substitute 'Secretary of State
(4) Omit subsection (5) (self-appointments).

26 (1) Amend section 69 (replacement of lead member of Panel) as follows.
(2) In subsection (2) (Commission chair must make appointment to fill vacancy in office of lead member) for 'person appointed to chair the Commission' substitute 'Secretary of State'.
(3) Omit subsection (4) (self-appointments).

27 Omit section 70 (membership of Panel where application relates to land in Wales).

28 (1) Amend section 71 (supplementary provision where Panel replaces single Commissioner) as follows.
(2) In subsection (2) (single Commissioner may be appointed member, or member and lead member, of Panel) for 'A Commissioner who has handled the application under Chapter 3' substitute 'An appointed person'.
(3) In subsection (3) (power to treat things done by or to single Commissioner as done by or to Panel) for 'a Commissioner' substitute 'an appointed person'.
(4) After subsection (4) insert –

'(5) In this section 'appointed person' means a person appointed to handle the application under Chapter 3.'

(5) In the heading for 'Commissioner' substitute 'appointed person'.

29 (1) Amend section 74 (Panel to decide, or make recommendations in respect of, application) as follows.
(2) Omit subsection (1) (cases in which Panel has function of deciding application).
(3) In subsection (2) (cases in which Panel has function of examining application and reporting on it to the Secretary of State) for 'In any other case, the Panel' substitute 'The Panel'.
(4) Omit subsection (4) (duty of Commission staff to give support to Panel).

Single-Commissioner procedure to become single-appointed-person procedure

30 (1) Amend section 78 (single Commissioner to handle application) as follows.
(2) In subsection (1)(a) (which refers to an application accepted by the Commission) for 'Commission' substitute 'Secretary of State'.
(3) In subsection (1)(b) (which refers to decision that application be handled by a single Commissioner) for 'Commissioner' substitute 'appointed person'.
(4) In subsection (2) (meaning of 'the single Commissioner') for 'Commissioner' substitute 'appointed person'.
(5) In the heading, and in the italic heading immediately preceding the section, for 'Commissioner' substitute 'appointed person'.
(6) In the heading of Chapter 3 of Part 6 for 'single-Commissioner' substitute 'single-appointed-person'.

31 For section 79 (Commission chair must appoint single Commissioner) substitute –

'79 Appointment of single appointed person

The Secretary of State must appoint a person to handle the application.'

32 (1) Amend section 80 (person ceasing to be single Commissioner) as follows.
(2) Omit subsection (1) (generally, person ceases to be single Commissioner on ceasing to be a Commissioner).
(3) In subsection (2) (single Commissioner may resign by notice to Commission) –

(a) for 'Commissioner' substitute 'appointed person', and
(b) for 'Commission' substitute 'Secretary of State'.

(4) In subsection (3) (Commission chair may remove single Commissioner) –

(a) for 'person appointed to chair the Commission ('the chair')' substitute 'Secretary of State',
(b) for 'Commissioner' (in both places) substitute 'appointed person', and
(c) for 'if the chair' substitute 'if the Secretary of State'.

(5) In the heading for 'Commissioner' substitute 'appointed person'.

33 Omit section 81 (single Commissioner continuing though ceasing to be Commissioner).
34 In section 82 (appointment of replacement single Commissioner) for 'Commissioner' (in each place, including in the heading) substitute 'appointed person'.

35 (1) Amend section 83 (single Commissioner to examine and report on application) as follows.
(2) In subsections (1) and (3), in the heading, and in the italic heading immediately preceding the section, for 'Commissioner' (in each place, including in the word 'Commissioner's') substitute 'appointed person'.
(3) In subsection (1)(b) (duty to make report) after 'making a report' insert 'to the Secretary of State'.
(4) Omit subsection (2) (report to be made to the Commission in some cases and to the Secretary in other cases).
(5) Omit subsection (4) (duty of Commission staff to support single Commissioner).

36 Omit sections 84 and 85 (procedure where single Commissioner's report made to Commission) and the italic heading immediately preceding section 84.

Examination of applications

37 In section 86 (Chapter applies to examination by Panel or single Commissioner), and in its heading, for 'Commissioner' (in each place) substitute 'appointed person'.
38 Omit section 87(2)(b) (Examining authority to have regard to guidance given by Secretary of State or Commission).
39 In section 92 (notifying Commission that compulsory acquisition hearing wanted) for 'Commission' (in each place) substitute 'Secretary of State'.
40 In section 93 (notifying Commission that open-floor hearing wanted) for 'Commission' (in both places) substitute 'Secretary of State'.
41 In section 94(2)(b) (Panel member or single Commissioner to preside over hearing) for 'Commissioner' substitute 'appointed person'.
42 After section 95 insert –

'95A Hearings: defence and national security

(1) Subsection (2) applies if the Secretary of State is satisfied that if all or part of the Examining Authority's examination of the application takes the form of a meeting or hearing –

(a) the making of particular oral representations at such a meeting or hearing would be likely to result in the disclosure of information as to defence or national security, and
(b) the public disclosure of that information would be contrary to the national interest.

(2) The Secretary of State may direct that representations of a description specified in the direction may be made only to persons of a description so specified (instead of being made in public).
(3) If the Secretary of State gives a direction under subsection (2), the Attorney General or (where the representations are to be made in Scotland) the Advocate General for Scotland may appoint a person (an 'appointed representative') to represent the interests of an interested party who (by virtue of the direction) is prevented from being present when the representations are made.
(4) Rules under section 97 may (in particular) make provision as to the functions of an appointed representative.
(5) The Secretary of State may direct a person (a 'responsible person') to pay the fees and expenses of an appointed representative if the Secretary of State thinks that the responsible person is interested in a meeting or hearing in relation to any representations that are the subject of a direction under subsection (2).
(6) Subsections (7) and (8) apply if the Secretary of State gives a direction under subsection (5).
(7) If the appointed representative and the responsible person are unable to agree the amount of the fees and expenses, the amount must be determined by the Secretary of State.
(8) The Secretary of State must cause the amount agreed between the appointed representative and the responsible person, or determined by the Secretary of State, to be certified.
(9) An amount so certified is recoverable from the responsible person as a civil debt.
(10) In this section 'representations' includes evidence.'

43 In section 96(1)(c) (which refers to representations received by the Commission) for 'Commission' substitute 'Secretary of State'.

44 (1) Amend section 98 (timetable for examining, and reporting on, application) as follows.
(2) In subsection (3) (deadline for making report to Secretary of State) for the words from the beginning to 'its report' substitute 'The Examining authority is under a duty to make its report under section 74(2)(b) or 83(1)(b)'.
(3) In subsection (4) (Commission chair may extend deadlines under the section) for 'person appointed to chair the Commission' substitute 'Secretary of State'.
(4) For subsection (6) (extensions of deadlines to be reported to Secretary of State and in Commission's annual report) substitute –

'(6) Subsections (7) and (8) apply where the power under subsection (4) is exercised.
(7) The Secretary of State must –

(a) notify each interested party of the new deadline, and
(b) publicise the new deadline in such manner as the Secretary of State thinks appropriate.

(8) The Secretary of State exercising the power must make a statement, to the House of Parliament of which that Secretary of State is a member, announcing the new deadline.

(9) A statement under subsection (8) may be written or oral.'

45 (1) Amend section 100 (Commission chair may appoint assessors at request of Examining authority) as follows.
(2) In subsection (1) for 'person appointed to chair the Commission ('the chair')' substitute 'Secretary of State'.
(3) In subsection (2) for 'chair' substitute 'Secretary of State'.

46 In section 101(1) (Commission chair may appoint lawyer to assist Examining authority) for 'person appointed to chair the Commission' substitute 'Secretary of State'.

47 In section 102(4) (meaning of 'relevant representation') for 'Commission' (in each place) substitute 'Secretary of State'.

Decisions on applications

48 (1) Amend section 103 as follows.
(2) In subsection (1) (cases where Secretary of State is the decision-maker) omit the words after 'consent'.
(3) Omit subsection (2) (meaning in Act of 'decision-maker').
(4) For the heading substitute 'Secretary of State is to decide applications'.

49 (1) Amend section 104 (decisions of Panel and Council) as follows.
(2) In subsection (1) for 'the decision-maker is a Panel or the Council' substitute 'a national policy statement has effect in relation to development of the description to which the application relates'.
(3) In subsection (2) –

(a) for 'Panel or Council' (in both places) substitute 'Secretary of State',
(b) in paragraph (b) for 'Commission' substitute 'Secretary of State', and
(c) in paragraph (d) for 'its' substitute 'the Secretary of State's'.

(4) In subsections (3) and (4) for 'Panel or Council' substitute 'Secretary of State'.
(5) In subsection (5) –

(a) for 'Panel or Council is' substitute 'Secretary of State is', and
(b) for 'Panel or Council, or the Commission, being in breach of any duty imposed on it' substitute 'Secretary of State being in breach of any duty imposed on the Secretary of State'.

(6) In subsections (6), (7) and (8) for 'Panel or Council' substitute 'Secretary of State'.
(7) For the heading substitute 'Decisions in cases where national policy statement has effect '

50 (1) Amend section 105 (decisions of Secretary of State) as follows.
(2) In subsection (1) for 'if the decision-maker is the Secretary of State' substitute 'if section 104 does not apply in relation to the application'.
(3) In subsection (2)(a) (which refers to reports submitted to the Commission) for 'Commission' substitute 'Secretary of State'.
(4) For the heading substitute 'Decisions in cases where no national policy statement has effect'.

51 In section 106(1) (representations which decision-maker may disregard) for 'decision-maker' (in both places) substitute 'Secretary of State'.

52 (1) Section 107 (timetable for decisions) is amended as follows.
(2) In subsection (1) (deadline for deciding application) –

(a) for 'decision-maker' substitute 'Secretary of State', and
(b) for 'day after the start day' substitute 'deadline under section 98(3)'.

(3) Omit subsection (2) (meaning of 'the start day').

(4) In subsection (3) (extension of deadline) for 'appropriate authority' substitute 'Secretary of State'.
(5) Omit subsection (4) (meaning of 'appropriate authority').
(6) For subsections (6) to (9) (publicising deadline extensions) substitute –

'(6) Subsection (7) applies where the power under subsection (3) is exercised.
(7) The Secretary of State exercising the power must make a statement, to the House of Parliament of which that Secretary of State is a member, announcing the new deadline.
(8) A statement under subsection (7) must be published in such form and manner as the Secretary of State considers appropriate.
(8A) A statement under subsection (7) may be written or oral.'

Suspension of decision-making process

53 In section 108(2) (suspension of proceedings on application) for the words from 'the following' to the end substitute 'examination of the application by a Panel under Chapter 2, or a single appointed person under Chapter 3, is suspended (if not already completed).'

Intervention by Secretary of State

54 In Part 6, omit Chapter 7 (which consists of sections 109 to 113 and Schedule 3).

Grant or refusal

55 (1) Section 114 (decision-maker to grant or refuse consent) is amended as follows.
(2) In subsection (1) –

(a) for 'it' substitute 'the Secretary of State', and
(b) for 'decision-maker' substitute 'Secretary of State'.

(3) In subsection (2) for 'decision-maker' substitute 'Secretary of State'.

56 Omit section 115(6) (Panel or Council to have regard to Secretary of State's guidance in deciding whether development is associated).

57 (1) Amend section 116 (reasons) as follows.
(2) In subsection (1) –

(a) for 'decision-maker' substitute 'Secretary of State', and
(b) for 'its' substitute 'the Secretary of State's'.

(3) In subsection (2) for 'appropriate authority' substitute 'Secretary of State'.
(4) In subsection (3) –

(a) for 'appropriate authority' substitute 'Secretary of State', and
(b) for 'the authority' substitute 'the Secretary of State'.

(5) Omit subsection (4) (meaning of 'appropriate authority').

58 (1) Amend section 117 (orders granting consent: formalities) as follows.
(2) Omit subsections (2) and (5) (orders made by Panel or Council).
(3) In subsection (3) (duty to publish order) –

(a) for 'appropriate authority' substitute 'Secretary of State', and
(b) for 'the authority' substitute 'the Secretary of State'.

(4) For subsection (4) (order exercising powers under section 120(5)(a) or (b) must be in statutory instrument) substitute –

'(4) If the order includes provision –

(a) made under section 120(3) for or relating to any of the matters listed in paragraphs 32A and 32B of Schedule 5, or
(b) made in the exercise of any of the powers conferred by section 120(5)(a) or (b),

the order must be contained in a statutory instrument.'

(5) In subsection (6) for 'is made, the appropriate authority' substitute 'containing the order is made, the Secretary of State'.
(6) Omit subsection (7) (meaning of 'appropriate authority').

59 (1) Amend section 118 (legal challenges) as follows.
(2) In subsection (3) (challenges to Commission decision not to accept application) for 'Commission' (in both places) substitute 'Secretary of State'.
(3) In subsection (7) (other challenges to things done by Secretary of State or Commission) omit 'or the Commission'.

Orders granting development consent

60 (1) Amend section 120 (what may be contained in order) as follows.
(2) In subsection (5)(b) and (c) (order may contain provision that appears necessary or expedient to decision-maker) for 'decision-maker' substitute 'Secretary of State'.
(3) For subsection (8) (order may not create offences or make byelaws or confer or amend power to do so) substitute –

'(8) With the exception of provision made under subsection (3) for or relating to any of the matters listed in paragraph 32B of Schedule 5, an order granting development consent may not include –

(a) provision creating offences,
(b) provision conferring power to create offences, or
(c) provision changing an existing power to create offences.'

61 Omit section 121 (Secretary of State's control of exercise of legislative powers by Panel or Council).
62 In sections 122(1) and 123(1) (compulsory acquisition may be authorised only if decision-maker satisfied conditions met) for 'decision-maker' substitute 'Secretary of State'.
63 Omit section 124 (guidance to Panels and Council about authorising compulsory acquisition).

64 (1) Amend section 127 (statutory undertakers' land) as follows.
(2) In subsection (1)(c) (decision-maker must be satisfied as to use of land) for 'decision-maker' substitute 'Secretary of State'.
(3) Omit subsection (7)(b) (Secretary of State to notify Commission).

65 Omit sections 131(10)(b) and 132(10)(b) (Secretary of State to notify Commission).

66 (1) Amend section 136 (public rights of way) as follows.
(2) In subsection (1) (decision-maker must be satisfied) for 'decision-maker' substitute 'Secretary of State'.
(3) In subsections (4)(b) and (5) (revival of right extinguished in connection with abandoned acquisition proposal) for 'appropriate authority' substitute 'Secretary of State'.
(4) Omit subsection (6) (meaning of 'appropriate authority').

67 In section 138(4)(a) (decision-maker must be satisfied) for 'decision-maker' substitute 'Secretary of State'.

68 (1) Amend section 147 (Green Belt land) as follows.

(2) In subsection (2) (decision-maker's duty to notify) for 'decision-maker' substitute 'Secretary of State'.

(3) Omit subsection (3) (cases where Secretary of State not decision-maker).

69 In section 235(1) (interpretation of Act) omit the definitions of –

'the Commission',

'Commissioner',

'the Council', and

'decision-maker'.

70 (1) Amend Schedule 4 (corrections of errors in development consent decisions) as follows.

(2) In paragraph 1(1)(a) for 'decision-maker' substitute 'Secretary of State'.

(3) In paragraph 1(4), (5) and (7) for 'appropriate authority' (in each place) substitute 'Secretary of State'.

(4) Omit paragraph 1(9) (instruments made by the Commission).

(5) In paragraph 1(10) for 'is made, the appropriate authority' substitute 'containing the order is made, the Secretary of State'.

(6) In paragraph 2 for 'appropriate authority' (in each place) substitute 'Secretary of State'.

(7) In paragraph 2(4) (Secretary of State may specify other persons to whom correction notice is to be given) for the words after 'may' substitute 'give the correction notice to persons other than those to whom sub-paragraph (3) requires it to be given.'

(8) In paragraph 4 omit the definition of 'the appropriate authority'.

71 (1) Amend Schedule 5 (provisions relating to, or to matters ancillary to, development) as follows.

(2) In paragraph 18 (order granting development consent may make provision for or relating to charging tolls, fares and other charges) after 'fares' insert '(including penalty fares)'.

(3) After paragraph 32 insert –

'32A The making of byelaws by any person and their enforcement.

32B (1) The creation of offences within sub-paragraph (2) in connection with –

(a) non-payment of tolls, fares or other charges,

(b) a person's failure to give the person's name or address in accordance with provision relating to penalty fares,

(c) enforcement of byelaws, or

(d) construction, improvement, maintenance or management of a harbour.

(2) An offence is within this sub-paragraph if –

(a) it is triable only summarily,

(b) a person guilty of the offence is not liable to imprisonment, and

(c) any fine to which a person guilty of the offence may be liable cannot be higher than level 3 on the standard scale.'

72 (1) Amend Schedule 6 (changes to, and revocation of, orders) as follows.

(2) Omit paragraph 1(4) (meaning of 'appropriate authority').

(3) Except in paragraphs 3(6) and (7) and 6(2), for 'appropriate authority' (in each place) substitute 'Secretary of State'.

(4) In paragraph 2(1) for 'it' substitute 'the Secretary of State'.

(5) In paragraph 2(4) for 'Commission' substitute 'Secretary of State'.
(6) Omit paragraph 2(10) (instruments made by Commission).
(7) In paragraph 2(11) after 'instrument' insert 'containing the order'.
(8) Omit paragraph 3(6) (cases where Commission is appropriate authority).
(9) In paragraph 3(7) for 'Where the appropriate authority is the Secretary of State, the' substitute 'The'.
(10) Omit paragraph 4(8) (instruments made by Commission).
(11) In paragraph 4(9) after 'instrument' insert 'containing the order'.
(12) In paragraph 6(2) for the words after 'payable to the person' substitute 'by the Secretary of State.'

73 In Schedule 12 (application of Act to Scotland: modifications) in paragraph 27 (application of Part 1 of Schedule 5) after '32' insert ', 32B(1)(a), (b) and (d)'.

PART 2 OTHER AMENDMENTS

Parliamentary Commissioner Act 1967 (c. 13)

74 In Schedule 2 to the Parliamentary Commissioner Act 1967 (departments etc subject to investigation) omit the entry for the Infrastructure Planning Commission.

House of Commons Disqualification Act 1975 (c. 24)

75 In Part 2 of Schedule 1 to the House of Commons Disqualification Act 1975 (bodies of which all members are disqualified) omit the entry for the Infrastructure Planning Commission.

Northern Ireland Assembly Disqualification Act 1975 (c. 25)

76 In Part 2 of Schedule 1 to the Northern Ireland Assembly Disqualification Act 1975 (bodies of which all members are disqualified) omit the entry for the Infrastructure Planning Commission.

Town and Country Planning Act 1990 (c. 8)

77 (1) The Town and Country Planning Act 1990 is amended as follows.
(2) In section 106A(11) (modification and discharge of planning obligations: meaning of 'appropriate authority') –

(a) in paragraph (aa) (Secretary of State is appropriate authority in certain development consent cases) omit the words after 'any development consent obligation', and
(b) omit paragraph (ab) (Commission is appropriate authority in all other development consent cases).

(3) In section 106B(1) (planning obligation appeals otherwise than from Secretary of State or Commission) omit 'or the Infrastructure Planning Commission'.
(4) In section 106C (development consent obligations: legal challenges) omit 'or the Infrastructure Planning Commission' (in both places).

Freedom of Information Act 2000 (c. 36)

78 In Part 6 of Schedule 1 to the Freedom of Information Act 2000 (other public bodies and offices: general) omit the entry for the Infrastructure Planning Commission.

Government of Wales Act 2006 (c. 32)

79 In Part 1 of Schedule 7 to the Government of Wales Act 2006 (subjects to which provisions of Acts of the Assembly may relate) in the exception to paragraph 18 (Town

and Country Planning) for 'Functions of the Infrastructure Planning Commission or any of its members under the Planning Act 2008' substitute 'Development consent under the Planning Act 2008'.

○○○

SCHEDULE 20 ABOLITION OF LONDON DEVELOPMENT AGENCY: CONSEQUENTIAL AMENDMENTS

Section 195

Local Authorities (Goods and Services) Act 1970 (c. 39)

1 In section 1(4) of the Local Authorities (Goods and Services) Act 1970, in the definition of 'local authority' for ', Transport for London and the London Development Agency' substitute 'and Transport for London'.

Local Government Finance Act 1988 (c. 41)

2 In section 115(4A) of the Local Government Finance Act 1988 (duties as regards reports under section 114) –

(a) omit 'the London Development Agency or', and
(b) for the words from 'neither' to 'shall' substitute 'paragraph 7 of Schedule 10 to the 1999 Act (delegation by Transport for London) shall not'.

Audit Commission Act 1998 (c. 18)

3 In section 11(8A) of the Audit Commission Act 1998 (which prevents delegation of duties under the section as regards reports etc) –

(a) omit 'the London Development Agency or', and
(b) for the words from 'neither' to 'shall' substitute 'paragraph 7 of Schedule 10 to the Greater London Authority Act 1999 (delegation by Transport for London) shall not'.

Greater London Authority Act 1999 (c. 29)

4 The Greater London Authority Act 1999 is amended as follows.
5 In section 38(8) (application of section 101 of the Local Government Act 1972) after paragraph (a) insert 'or'.
6 In section 127(4) ('officers' in section 127(2)(b) includes, in the case of Transport for London or the London Development Agency, its members) for the words after 'in the case of Transport for London' substitute ', includes a reference to its members.'
7 In section 362(3)(b) (air quality strategy to contain information about measures to be taken by the Authority, Transport for London and the London Development Agency) for ', Transport for London and the London Development Agency' substitute 'and Transport for London'.
8 In section 380(10) (application of section 101 of the Local Government Act 1972) after paragraph (a) insert 'or'.

London Olympic Games and Paralympic Games Act 2006 (c. 12)

9 In section 10(4) of the London Olympic Games and Paralympic Games Act 2006 (matters to which regard to be had when Olympic Transport Plan being prepared or revised) for paragraph (c) (the London Development Agency's strategy) substitute –

'(c) the Economic development strategy for London prepared in accordance with section 333F of that Act.'

ooo

SCHEDULE 25 REPEALS AND REVOCATIONS

Section 237

PART 1 GENERAL POWER OF COMPETENCE

Reference	Extent of repeal
Local Government Act 2000 (c. 22)	Section 2(3) and (3A).
	Section 3(7).
	Section 4A(2) and (3).
Local Government and Public Involvement in Health Act 2007 (c. 28)	Section 78(2).
	Section 115(2).
Local Government (Wales) Measure 2009 (nawm 2)	In Schedule 2, paragraph 2(a).

PART 2 FIRE AND RESCUE AUTHORITIES

Reference	Extent of repeal
Fire and Rescue Services Act 2004 (c. 21)	Section 5.
	Section 19.
	Section 62(3).

PART 3 OTHER AUTHORITIES

Reference	Extent of repeal
Transport Act 1968 (c. 73)	In section 10(1)(xxviii), the words 'so far as not required for the purposes of their business'.
Local Government Act 2003 (c. 26)	In section 93(7)(b), the 'and' at the end.

PART 4 LOCAL AUTHORITY GOVERNANCE

Reference	Extent of repeal or revocation
Local Government Act 1972 (c. 70)	In section 2(2A) the words 'or a mayor and council manager executive'.
	In section 245(1A) and (4A)(a) the words 'or a mayor and council manager executive'.
Local Government Act 2000 (c. 22)	In section 11 –
	(a) subsections (2A) and (9A),
	(b) in subsection (9) the words 'in relation to Wales', and
	(c) in subsection (10) the words '(2A)(a) or'.
	In section 13(9)(b) the words from 'or section 236' to 'England)'.
	Section 14(7).
	In section 18 –
	(a) subsections (4) and (5), and
	(b) in subsection (6) the words 'in Wales'.
	In section 19(1) the words '(within the meaning of this Part)' in the first place they appear.
	In section 21 –
	(a) in subsection (2)(f) the words 'section 244 of the National Health Service Act 2006 or',
	(b) in subsection (2ZA) the words 'in Wales',
	(c) subsection (2A)(a) and (b),
	(d) in subsection (4) the words from 'or any functions' to the end,
	(e) in subsection (10) the words ', unless permitted to do so under paragraph 12 of that Schedule',
	(f) in subsection (10A) the words 'in Wales',
	(g) in subsection (13)(aa) the words from 'by virtue of' to 'England) or',
	(h) in subsection (13)(c) the words from the beginning to 'in Wales',
	(i) in subsection (16), paragraph (a) and the word 'and' immediately following that paragraph, and

(j) in subsection (16)(b) the words 'in Wales'.

Section 21ZA.

In section 21A –

(a) in subsection (3) the words from '(in the case of a local authority in England' to 'Wales)',

(b) in subsection (6)(a) the words from 'section 236' to '2007 or',

(c) subsections (10) and (11), and

(d) in subsection (12) the words 'in Wales'.

Section 21C.

In section 21D –

(a) in subsection (1)(b), sub-paragraph (ii) and the word 'or' immediately preceding that sub-paragraph,

(b) in subsection (2) the words 'or providing a copy of the document to a relevant partner authority',

(c) in subsection (6) in the definition of 'exempt information' the words 'section 246 of the National Health Service Act 2006 or', and

(d) in that subsection the definition of 'relevant partner authority' and the word 'and' immediately preceding that definition.

Section 21E.

In section 21F (as inserted by the Local Government (Wales) Measure 2011 (nawm 4)), in subsection (1) the words 'in Wales'.

Section 21F (as inserted by the Flood and Water Management Act 2010).

In section 22(12A)(a) the words from ', or under' to 'section 21B,'.

Section 22A.

Section 31.

Section 32.

In section 33ZA the words 'in Wales,'.

Section 33A.

Section 33B.

Section 33C.

Section 33D.

Section 33E.

Section 33F.

Section 33G.

Section 33H.

Section 33I.

Section 33J (and the italic heading immediately preceding it).

Section 33K.

Section 33L.

Section 33M.

Section 33N.

Section 33O (and the italic heading immediately preceding it).

In section 34(3) the words 'or of any of sections 33A to 33O'.

In section 35(3) the words 'or of any of sections 33A to 33O'.

In section 36(3) the words 'or of any of sections 33A to 33O'.

In section 39 –

(a) subsection (2),

(b) in subsection (3) the words 'in Wales', and

(c) subsection (6).

Section 44A (and the italic heading immediately preceding it).

Section 44B.

Section 44C.

Section 44D.

Section 44E.

Section 44F.

Section 44G.

Section 44H.

In section 45(9) the words 'or 33K'.

In section 47 –

(a) in subsection (4) the words '(including changes of the kinds set out in sections 33A to 33D)', and

(b) subsection (6)(b).

In section 48 –

(a) in subsection (1) the definition of 'ordinary day of election',

(b) subsection (1A),

	(c) in subsection (2), paragraph (b) and the word 'and' immediately preceding that paragraph, and (d) in subsection (3), paragraph (b) and the word 'and' immediately preceding that paragraph. Section 106(1)(a). In Schedule 1 – (a) paragraphs 1A, 7 and 12 to 14 (and the italic headings immediately preceding paragraphs 1A and 12), (b) in paragraph 8 – (a) in sub-paragraph (1) the words 'Welsh' and 'in Wales', and (b) in sub-paragraphs (2), (3) and (7) the word 'Welsh', and (c) in paragraph 10 the word '7,'.
Local Government Act 2003 (c. 26)	Section 115. In Schedule 7, paragraph 80 (and the italic heading immediately preceding it).
National Health Service Act 2006 (c. 41)	Section 245(3)(b)(ia) and (ib). Section 247(3)(b) to (d).
Police and Justice Act 2006 (c. 48)	In section 19(9) the words '(within the meaning of Part 2 of the Local Government Act 2000 (c. 22))'.
Local Government and Public Involvement in Health Act 2007 (c. 28)	Section 33(4), (6) and (7). Section 34(5) and (6). Section 38(4), (6) and (7). Section 40(4), (6) and (7). Section 62(4), (8)(c) and (9). Section 63(8). Section 64. Section 65(4) to (6). Section 67. Section 69(3). Section 70(3) and (4). Section 121(1). Section 124. In section 127 – (a) subsection (1)(c)(ii) (and the word 'and' immediately following it), (b) subsection (2), and (c) subsection (3)(b) (and the word 'and' immediately preceding it).

	Section 236(9).
	In Schedule 3, paragraph 28.
Local Democracy, Economic Development and Construction Act 2009 (c. 20)	Section 31.
Flood and Water Management Act 2010 (c. 29)	In Schedule 2, paragraph 54 (and the italic heading immediately preceding it).
Local Education Authorities and Children's Services Authorities (Integration of Functions) Order 2010 (S.I. 2010/1158)	In paragraph 47(2) of Schedule 2, the word '7(1),'.
Local Government (Wales) Measure 2011 (nawm 4)	Section 36(1)(b) and (c).

PART 5 STANDARDS

Reference	Extent of repeal or revocation
Parliamentary Commissioner Act 1967 (c. 13)	In Schedule 2, the entry for the Standards Board for England.
Local Government Act 1972 (c. 70)	In section 85(3A), the words '66A,' and ', 78A'.
	In section 86(1)(b), the words '66A, 78A or'.
	In section 87(1)(ee), the words '66A, 78A or'.
House of Commons Disqualification Act 1975 (c. 24)	In Schedule 1, in Part 2, the entry for the Standards Board for England.
Northern Ireland Assembly Disqualification Act 1975 (c. 25)	In Schedule 1, in Part 2, the entry for the Standards Board for England.
Local Government and Housing Act 1989 (c. 42)	In section 3A –
	(a) in subsection (1), the words 'which is a relevant authority' and, in paragraphs (a) and (b), the word 'relevant',
	(b) in subsection (2)(a), the word 'relevant',
	(c) in subsection (3)(b), the word 'relevant',
	(d) in subsection (4)(b)(i), the word relevant,
	(e) subsection (5),
	(f) in subsection (6), the words 'which is a relevant authority' and, in paragraph (a), the word 'its',
	(g) in subsection (7), the word 'its', and

	(h) subsections (8) to (10).
Audit Commission Act 1998 (c. 18)	In section 49(1)(de), the words 'an ethical standards officer or'.
Data Protection Act 1998 (c. 29)	In section 31 – (a) in subsection (7), paragraph (b) (but not the word 'or' at the end of that paragraph), and (b) in subsection (8)(b), the words ', or to an ethical standards officer,'.
Greater London Authority Act 1999 (c. 29)	In section 6(5), the words '66A,' and ', 78A'. In section 13(2), the words '66A,' and ', 78A'.
Local Government Act 2000 (c. 22)	In section 49 – (a) subsection (1), (b) in subsection (2) the words 'in Wales (other than police authorities)', (c) subsections (2C), (3) and (4), (d) in subsection (5)(a) the words 'in Wales', and (e) in subsection (6), paragraphs (c) to (e), (g) to (k) and (m) to (o) (but not the word 'or' at the end of paragraph (o)). In section 50 – (a) subsection (1), (b) in subsection (2) the words 'in Wales other than police authorities', (c) in subsection (3) the words '(1) or', (d) in subsection (4)(a) the words '49(1) or' and the words '(as the case may be)', (e) subsections (4C) and (4D), (f) in subsection (5) the words 'the Secretary of State or', and (g) subsections (6) and (7). In section 51 – (a) in subsection (4C) the words from 'by a' to 'police authority', and (b) in subsection (6)(c), sub-paragraph (i) and in sub-paragraph (ii) the words from 'in the case' to 'in Wales,'. In section 53 – (a) in subsection (2) the words 'parish council or', (b) subsections (3) to (10),

(c) in subsection (11), in paragraph (a) the words 'in Wales other than police authorities' and in paragraph (k) the words 'in Wales (other than police authorities)', and

(d) in subsection (12) the words '(6)(c) to (f) or'.

In section 54 –

(a) subsection (4),

(b) in subsection (5) the words 'in Wales (other than police authorities)',

(c) subsection (6), and

(d) in subsection (7) the words 'in Wales (other than police authorities)'.

In section 54A –

(a) in subsection (3) the words 'but this is subject to section 55(7)(b)',

(b) subsection (4),

(c) in subsection (5) the words 'in Wales other than a police authority', and

(d) in subsection (6) the words 'section 55(5) and to'.

Section 55.

Sections 56A to 67.

In section 68(2), in each of paragraphs (a) and (b), the words 'in Wales (other than police authorities)'.

In section 69 –

(a) in subsection (1), the words 'in Wales' in both places, and

(b) in subsection (5), the words 'in Wales'.

In section 70(5), the words 'in Wales'.

In section 71(4), the words 'in Wales'.

In section 72(6), the words 'in Wales'.

Section 73(6).

In section 77(7), the words from ', or with' to 'First-tier Tribunal,'.

In section 78 –

(a) in the heading, the words 'the First-tier Tribunal or',

(b) in subsection (1), the words 'the First-tier Tribunal or' and, in paragraph (a), the words '65(3) or',

(c) subsection (4),

(d) in subsection (6), the words '78A or',

	(e) in subsection (8A), paragraph (a) and, in paragraph (b), the words 'where the relevant authority concerned is in Wales,', (f) in subsection (9), the words 'The First-tier Tribunal or (as the case may be)' and the words '59 or', and (g) subsections (9A) to (9D). Sections 78A and 78B. In section 79(13), the words 'in Wales'. In section 80 – (a) in the heading, the words 'First-tier Tribunal or', (b) in subsection (1), the words 'the First-tier Tribunal or', and (c) subsection (6). In section 81 – (a) in subsection (7), paragraph (b) and, in paragraph (c), the words 'if it is a relevant authority in Wales,', and (b) subsection (8). In section 82 – (a) subsection (1), (b) in subsection (2), the words 'in Wales (other than police authorities)', (c) in subsection (3), the words '(1) or', (d) subsections (4) and (5), (e) in subsection (6)(a), the words 'in Wales', and (f) in subsection (9), paragraph (a), the word 'and' immediately preceding paragraph (b) and, in that paragraph, the words 'in relation to Wales,'. In section 82A(4), the words '57A, 60(2) or (3), 64(2) or (4),'. In section 83 – (a) in subsection (1), the definitions of 'the Audit Commission', 'ethical standards officer' and 'police authority' and, in the definition of 'model code of conduct', the words '(1) and', and (b) subsections (4), (12), (15) and (16). In section 105(6), the words ', 49, 63(1)(j)'. Schedule 4.
Freedom of Information Act 2000 (c. 36)	In Schedule 1, in Part 6, the entry for the Standards Board for England.

Local Government Act 2003 (c. 26)	Section 112.
Government Resources and Accounts Act 2000 (Audit of Public Bodies) Order 2003 (S.I. 2003/1326)	Article 20.
Public Audit (Wales) Act 2004 (c. 23)	In Schedule 2 – (a) paragraph 53(2), (b) paragraph 54, and (c) paragraph 55(2).
Public Services Ombudsman (Wales) Act 2005 (c. 10)	In Schedule 4 – (a) paragraph 2(a), (b) paragraphs 5 to 8, (c) paragraph 21, (d) paragraph 22(a), and (e) in paragraph 23, the words '(5)(b) and'.
Local Government and Public Involvement in Health Act 2007 (c. 28)	In section 183 – (a) in subsection (1), the subsections (2A) and (2B) to be inserted into section 49 of the Local Government Act 2000 and the subsection (2C) inserted into that section, (b) in subsection (2), the subsections (4A) and (4B) to be inserted into section 50 of the Local Government Act 2000 and the subsections (4C) and (4D) inserted into that section, (c) in subsection (3), the subsections (4A) and (4B) to be inserted into section 51 of the Local Government Act 2000, and (d) in subsection (7)(b), the words 'in Wales other than a police authority'. Sections 185 to 187. In section 188 – (a) in subsection (1), paragraphs (b) and (c), and (b) subsection (2). Sections 189 to 193. In section 194, subsections (1) to (7). Sections 195 and 196. Section 198. Section 201(4)(b) and (c). In Schedule 12, paragraph 17.
Local Democracy, Economic Development and Construction Act 2009 (c. 20)	In Schedule 6, paragraph 93.

Transfer of Tribunal Functions Order 2010 (S.I. 2010/22)	In Schedule 2 – (a) paragraphs 51 to 55, (b) paragraph 59(b), (c) paragraph 60(a) and (c) to (f), (d) paragraphs 61 and 62, (e) paragraph 63(a) and (c), and (f) paragraph 65.
Localism Act 2011 (c. 20)	In section 27(6), paragraphs (f) and (k).

PART 6 DUTY TO PROMOTE DEMOCRACY

Reference	**Extent of repeal**
Local Democracy, Economic Development and Construction Act 2009 (c. 20)	Chapter 1 of Part 1. Section 148(1)(a).

PART 7 PETITIONS

Reference	**Extent of repeal**
Local Democracy, Economic Development and Construction Act 2009 (c. 20)	Chapter 2 of Part 1. Section 148(1)(a).

PART 8 WASTE REDUCTION SCHEMES

Reference	**Extent of repeal**
Climate Change Act 2008 (c. 27)	Sections 71 to 75. In section 98, the entry for 'the waste reduction provisions'. Schedule 5.

PART 9 BUSINESS RATE SUPPLEMENTS

Reference	Extent of repeal
Business Rate Supplements Act 2009 (c. 7)	Section 7(1), (2) and (5). In section 10 –

	(a) in subsection (2)(c) the words from the beginning to 'subsection (7),', and (b) subsections (7) to (9).

PART 10 NON-DOMESTIC RATES: DISCRETIONARY RELIEF

Reference	Extent of repeal
Local Government Finance Act 1988 (c. 41)	In section 47 – (a) subsection (2), (b) in subsection (3), the word 'second', and (c) subsections (3A) to (3D). In section 48(1), the words from '(but' to the end.
Local Government and Rating Act 1997 (c. 29)	In Schedule 1, paragraphs 3 and 4.
Rating (Former Agricultural Premises and Rural Shops) Act 2001 (c. 14)	Section 2.
Local Government Act 2003 (c. 26)	Section 61(6) and (7). Section 63(3). Section 64(3).
Corporation Tax Act 2010 (c. 4)	In Schedule 1, paragraph 208.

PART 11 SMALL BUSINESS RATE RELIEF

Reference	Extent of repeal
Local Government Finance Act 1988 (c. 41)	In section 43 – (a) subsection (4B)(a)(i) and (iii), and (b) subsection (4C).

PART 12 COUNCIL TAX REFERENDUMS

Reference	Extent of repeal or revocation
Local Government Finance Act 1992 (c. 14)	Section 52F(6). In section 52J –

	(a) in subsection (1), paragraph (a) and the word 'or' at the end of that paragraph and, in paragraph (b), the words '(in any other case)', (b) subsection (3), (c) subsection (6), and (d) subsections (8) to (10). In section 52K – (a) in subsection (1), paragraph (a) and the word 'or' at the end of that paragraph and, in paragraph (b), the words '(in any other case)', and (b) in subsection (4)(b) the words '52I or'. Section 52Q(5). In section 52U – (a) in subsection (2), paragraph (a) and the word 'or' at the end of that paragraph and, in paragraph (b), the words '(in any other case)', (b) subsection (3), (c) in subsection (4), the words 'is not the Greater London Authority and it', (d) in subsection (5), the words '(3) or', (e) subsection (6), (f) subsection (9), and (g) subsections (11) to (13). In section 52V(5)(b), the words '52T or'. In section 52W – (a) in subsection (1), the words 'other than the Greater London Authority', and (b) subsection (2). Section 52Z. In section 113(3)(a), the words '52F(4), 52H(2), 52Q(2), 52S(2), 52X(6),'.
Local Government Act 1999 (c. 27)	In Schedule 1, paragraph 9(b).
Greater London Authority Act 1999 (c. 29)	Section 136(2). Schedule 9.

Government of Wales Act 2006 (Consequential Modifications and Transitional Provisions) Order 2007 (S.I. 2007/1388)	In Schedule 1, paragraphs 41 to 44.

PART 13 COUNCIL TAX

Reference	Extent of repeal or revocation
Local Government Finance Act 1992 (c. 14)	In section 32 – (a) in subsection (2), the paragraph (a) inserted in relation to authorities in England by the Local Authorities (Alteration of Requisite Calculations) (England) Regulations 2005 (S.I. 2005/190), and paragraph (e) and the word 'and' immediately preceding it, (b) in subsection (3), the words 'general fund (or as the case may be)', the words from 'BID levy' to '2003,', the words 'or (in the case of the Common Council only) police grant' and paragraph (b) (but not the 'and' at the end of that paragraph), (c) in subsection (3A), the words 'In the case of any billing authority in Wales,', (d) in subsection (7)(a), in sub-paragraph (i), the words 'general fund or (as the case may be)', and sub-paragraph (ii) and the word 'and' at the end of that sub-paragraph, (e) subsections (8) to (8B), (f) in subsection (12), the definition of 'police grant' and the word 'and' at the end of that definition, and (g) subsection (13). In section 33 – (a) in subsection (1), in the definition of item P, the words 'general fund or (as the case may be)' and the words 'or (in the case of the Common Council only) police grant', (b) subsections (3) and (3A),

	(c) in subsection (3B), the words 'In the case of a Welsh county council or county borough council,', and (d) in subsection (4), the words 'or subsection (3) above'. In section 43 – (a) in subsection (2)(a), the words from ', other than' to '1988 Act', (b) in subsection (3)(a), sub-paragraph (iii) and the word 'or' immediately preceding that sub-paragraph (but not the word 'and' at the end of that sub-paragraph), and (c) subsection (5). In section 44 – (a) subsection (3), and (b) in subsection (4), the words 'or subsection (3) above'. In section 49 – (a) in subsection (3A), the words 'P1 or' and the words 'item P2 or', and (b) subsections (4A) to (4C). Section 69(2A).
Local Government (Wales) Act 1994 (c. 19)	In Schedule 12 – (a) paragraph 4(5), and (b) paragraph 5(3).
The Local Authorities (Alteration of Requisite Calculations and Funds) Regulations 1994 (S.I. 1994/246)	Regulation 3(1). Regulation 4(2).
The Local Authorities (Alteration of Requisite Calculations and Funds) Regulations 1995 (S.I. 1995/234)	Regulation 4(2).
Greater London Authority Act 1999 (c. 29)	Section 85(9). Section 86(6). Section 88(3) to (5). Section 89(5) and (6). Section 94(5). In section 95 –

	(a) in subsection (8), the words 'P1 or' and the words 'item P2 or', and
	(b) subsections (9) to (11).
	In section 99, the definitions of 'police grant' and 'relevant special grant'.
	Section 102(2)(c).
The Local Authorities (Alteration of Requisite Calculations) (Wales) Regulations 1999 (S.I. 1999/296)	Regulation 3.
The Local Authorities (Alteration of Requisite Calculations) (Wales) Regulations 2000 (S.I. 2000/717 (W.24))	Regulation 3.
Local Government Act 2003 (c. 26)	In Schedule 7, paragraphs 51(3) and 70.
The Local Authorities (Alteration of Requisite Calculations) (England) Regulations 2005 (S.I. 2005/190)	In regulation 2 –
	(a) paragraph (a),
	(b) paragraph (b)(i), and
	(c) paragraph (d).

PART 14 COUNCIL TAX REVALUATIONS IN WALES

Reference	Extent of repeal
Local Government Act 2003	In Schedule 7, paragraph 52(3).

PART 15 REGIONAL STRATEGIES (COMMENCEMENT ON PASSING)

Reference	Extent of repeal
Town and Country Planning Act 1990 (c. 8)	In Schedule 1 –
	(a) paragraph 7(2)(a), (3), (5)(a), (9) and (11), and
	(b) in paragraph 7(10), paragraph (b) and the 'or' immediately preceding it.
Local Democracy, Economic Development and Construction Act 2009 (c. 20)	Sections 70(1) to (4) and (6) to (8) and 71 to 81.
	Section 82(3).
	Section 84.
	Section 85(2) to (6).
	Sections 86 and 87.

	In section 147(1)(b), the words '85(2) to (6),'.

PART 16 REGIONAL STRATEGIES (COMMENCEMENT BY ORDER)

Reference	Extent of repeal
Town and Country Planning Act 1990	Section 83(5).
Regional Development Agencies Act 1998 (c. 45)	Section 7.
Greater London Authority Act 1999 (c. 29)	In section 337(6)(a), the words 'or the regional spatial strategy for a region which adjoins Greater London'.
	In section 342(1) –
	(a) paragraph (a), and
	(b) in paragraph (b), the word 'other'.
	In Schedule 10, in paragraph 2 –
	(a) sub-paragraph (3A), and
	(b) in sub-paragraph (8), the definition of 'regional planning body' and 'region' and the word 'and' immediately preceding it.
Planning and Compulsory Purchase Act 2004 (c. 5)	Section 15(3)(c).
	Section 19(2)(b) and (d).
	Section 24(1)(a).
	Section 28(4).
	Section 37(6) and (6A).
	In section 38(3) –
	(a) paragraph (a), and
	(b) the word 'and' immediately preceding paragraph (b).
	In section 45 –
	(a) in the text to be inserted by subsection (2), in subsection (1A), paragraph (a) and, in paragraph (b), the words 'in Wales',
	(b) in the text to be inserted by subsection (3), in subsection (2)(b), the words 'the Secretary of State or' and the words '(as the case may be)', subsection (2A)(b) and subsection (2B),
	(c) subsection (4), and

	(d) in the text to be inserted by subsection (9), in sub-paragraph (1A), paragraph (a) and the word 'or' at the end of that paragraph and, in paragraph (b), the words 'in Wales', in sub-paragraph (1B), the words 'the Secretary of State or' and the words '(as the case may be)' and, in sub-paragraph (1C), the words 'Secretary of State or the' and the words '(as the case may be)'.
	Section 62(5)(c).
	Section 78(5).
	In section 113 –
	(a) subsection (1)(a),
	(b) subsection (9)(a),
	(c) subsection (11)(a), and
	(d) subsection (12).
	In Schedule 7, paragraph 22(2)(a) and (3).
Railways Act 2005 (c. 14)	Section 17(5).
Greater London Authority Act 2007 (c. 24)	Section 30(2).
Local Democracy, Economic Development and Construction Act 2009 (c. 20)	Sections 70(5), 82(1) and (2) and 83.
	In Schedule 5, paragraphs 2 to 4, 9 to 11, 14, 15(2), 16, 17 and 19.
Marine and Coastal Access Act 2009 (c. 23)	In Schedule 6, in paragraph 1 –
	(a) sub-paragraph (2)(e), and
	(b) in sub-paragraph (3), the definition of 'responsible regional authorities'.
Localism Act 2011 (c. 20)	In Schedule 8, paragraphs 13(1), 18 and 19.

PART 17 LOCAL DEVELOPMENT SCHEMES AND DOCUMENTS

Reference	**Extent of repeal**
Planning and Compulsory Purchase Act 2004 (c. 5)	Section 15(3).
	Section 22(2).
	Section 35(1).
Greater London Authority Act 2007	Section 30(2) and (3).

PART 18 NEIGHBOURHOOD PLANNING

Reference	Extent of repeal
Town and Country Planning Act 1990 (c. 8)	Section 69(1)(b).
	In section 264(5)(b), the words 'or a local development order'.
Planning and Compulsory Purchase Act 2004	In section 38(2), the word 'and' at the end of paragraph (a).
	Section 40(2)(b) to (k).

PART 19 UNAUTHORISED ADVERTISEMENTS AND DEFACEMENT OF PREMISES

Reference	Extent of repeal or revocation
London Local Authorities Act 1995 (c. x)	Sections 11 to 13.
Transport for London (Consequential Provisions) Order 2003 (S.I. 2003/1615)	In Schedule 1, paragraph 36.
London Local Authorities Act 2004 (c. i)	Sections 12 to 14.
London Local Authorities Act 2007 (c. ii)	Section 7.
	Section 18.
Companies Act 2006 (Consequential Amendments, Transitional Provisions and Savings) Order 2009 (S.I. 2009/1941)	In Schedule 1, paragraph 157.
Postal Services Act 2011 (c. 5)	In Schedule 12, paragraph 171.

PART 20 ABOLITION OF INFRASTRUCTURE PLANNING COMMISSION

Reference	Extent of repeal
Parliamentary Commissioner Act 1967 (c. 13)	In Schedule 2, the entry for the Infrastructure Planning Commission.
House of Commons Disqualification Act 1975 (c. 24)	In Schedule 1, in Part 2, the entry for the Infrastructure Planning Commission.
Northern Ireland Assembly Disqualification Act 1975 (c. 25)	In Schedule 1, in Part 2, the entry for the Infrastructure Planning Commission.
Town and Country Planning Act 1990 (c. 8)	In section 106A(11) –
	(a) in paragraph (aa), the words after 'any development consent obligation', and
	(b) paragraph (ab).

	In section 106B(1), the words 'or the Infrastructure Planning Commission'.
	In section 106C, the words 'or the Infrastructure Planning Commission' (in both places).
Freedom of Information Act 2000 (c. 36)	In Schedule 1, in Part 6, the entry for the Infrastructure Planning Commission.
Planning Act 2008 (c. 29)	Sections 1 to 3.
	In section 5(9), paragraph (b) and the 'and' preceding that paragraph.
	Section 12.
	Section 38.
	In section 50(2), the words 'the Commission or'.
	Section 53(2)(b) and (c).
	Section 63.
	Section 65(3) to (5).
	Section 66(1).
	Section 67.
	Section 68(5).
	Section 69(4).
	Section 70.
	Section 74(1) and (4).
	Section 80(1).
	Section 81.
	Section 83(2) and (4).
	Sections 84 and 85 (including the italic heading immediately preceding section 84).
	Section 87(2)(b).
	In section 103(1), the words after 'consent'.
	Section 103(2).
	Section 107(2) and (4).
	Sections 109 to 113.
	Section 115(6).
	Section 116(4).
	Section 117(2), (5) and (7).
	In section 118(7), the words 'or the Commission'.
	Section 121.
	Section 124.

	In section 127(7), paragraph (b) and the 'and' preceding that paragraph. In section 131(10), paragraph (b) and the 'and' preceding that paragraph. In section 132(10), paragraph (b) and the 'and' preceding that paragraph. Section 136(6). Section 147(3). In section 235(1), the definitions of 'the Commission', 'Commissioner', 'the Council' and 'decision-maker'. Schedule 1. Schedule 3. In Schedule 4 – (a) paragraph 1(9), and (b) in paragraph 4, the definition of 'the appropriate authority'. In Schedule 6 – (a) paragraphs 1(4), 2(10), 3(6) and 4(8), and (b) ', (6)' in paragraph 6(1)(b). In Schedule 12, the 'and' at the end of paragraph 6(b).

PART 21 NATIONALLY SIGNIFICANT INFRASTRUCTURE PROJECTS

Reference	**Extent of repeal**
Planning Act 2008 (c. 29)	In section 35 – (a) subsection (1)(a), and (b) in subsection (1)(b) the word 'the'. Section 55(3)(b) and (d). In section 88(3) the word 'and' at the end of paragraph (a). Section 102(3) and (5) to (7). In section 134 – (a) in subsection (3)(a) the words 'and a copy of the order', and (b) subsection (8). In Schedule 12, the word 'and' at the end of paragraph 4(a).

PART 22 HOMELESSNESS

Reference	Extent of repeal
Housing Act 1996 (c. 52)	In section 193 –
	(a) subsection (3A),
	(b) in subsection (7AA), the words 'In a restricted case',
	(c) subsections (7B) to (7E), and
	(d) in subsection (7F), paragraph (b) and the word 'or' immediately preceding that paragraph.
	Section 195(3A).
Homelessness Act 2002 (c. 7)	Section 7(5).
	In section 8(1), the words '(5) and'.

PART 23 HOUSING TENURE

Reference	Extent of repeal
Housing Act 1988 (c. 50)	In section 17(1), paragraph (c) and the 'and' immediately preceding that paragraph.
	In Part 1 of Schedule 2, in Ground 7, in the second unnumbered paragraph, the word 'periodic'.
Housing and Regeneration Act 2008 (c. 17)	In section 180(2)(a), the words 'an assured shorthold tenancy or'.

PART 24 HOUSING FINANCE

Reference	Extent of repeal
Local Government and Housing Act 1989 (c. 42)	Sections 82 to 84.
	In section 85 –
	(a) in subsection (1), the words 'or 83', and
	(b) in subsection (3), the words 'or 83'.
	In section 86(1), the words 'or residual debt subsidy'.
	In section 88 –
	(a) subsection (2),

	(b) in subsection (3), the words 'Subject to subsection (2) above,', and (c) subsections (4) and (5).
Local Government Act 2003 (c. 26)	Section 89(4).

PART 25 MUTUAL EXCHANGE

Reference	Extent of repeal
Housing and Regeneration Act 2008 (c. 17)	In section 197(2), the word 'or' at the end of paragraph (b).

PART 26 OFFICE FOR TENANTS AND SOCIAL LANDLORDS

Reference	Extent of repeal
Public Records Act 1958 (c. 51)	In Schedule 1, in Part 2 of the Table at the end of paragraph 3, the entry for the Office for Tenants and Social Landlords.
Parliamentary Commissioner Act 1967 (c. 13)	In Schedule 2, the entry for the Office for Tenants and Social Landlords.
House of Commons Disqualification Act 1975 (c. 24)	In Schedule 1, in Part 2, the entry for the Office for Tenants and Social Landlords.
Freedom of Information Act 2000 (c. 36)	In Schedule 1, in Part 6, the entry for the Office for Tenants and Social Landlords.
Housing and Regeneration Act 2008 (c. 17)	In section 31 – (a) subsections (9) and (10), (b) in subsection (11), the words 'or low cost home ownership accommodation' and the words 'or (as the case may be) low cost home ownership accommodation', and (c) in subsection (12), the definition of 'low cost home ownership accommodation'. Section 32(11). In section 34(2) – (a) paragraph (a), and the word 'and' at the end of it, and (b) in paragraph (b), the word 'other'. Section 37. Section 78. Sections 81 to 92.

Section 99.

Sections 101 to 106.

Section 112(4)(a).

Section 145(4).

In section 146 –

(a) in subsection (4), paragraph (c) and the word 'and' at the end of paragraph (b), and

(b) subsection (8).

In section 147(4), paragraph (c) and the word 'and' at the end of paragraph (b).

Section 174(5)(a).

Section 196(1)(f) (but not the word 'and' at the end of that paragraph).

Section 197(4)(b).

Section 216(e).

In section 222, paragraph (a) and the word 'and' at the end of that paragraph.

In section 230(2), paragraph (a) and the word 'and' at the end of that paragraph.

Section 232.

In section 242(3), paragraph (a) and the word 'and' at the end of that paragraph.

In section 248 –

(a) subsection (4)(a),

(b) subsection (7)(c), and

(c) in subsection (8), paragraph (a) and the word 'and' at the end of that paragraph.

In section 250 –

(a) subsection (4)(a),

(b) subsection (7)(c), and

(c) in subsection (8), paragraph (a) and the word 'and' at the end of that paragraph.

In section 252 –

(a) in subsection (4), paragraph (a) and the word 'and' at the end of that paragraph, and

(b) subsection (7).

In section 276, in the Table, the entry for 'Appointed member'.

In Schedule 9 –

(a) paragraph 1,

	(b) paragraph 2(2), (c) paragraph 3(2), and (d) paragraph 28(2).
Equality Act 2010 (c. 15)	In Schedule 19, the entry for the Office for Tenants and Social Landlords.

PART 27 REGULATION OF SOCIAL HOUSING

Reference	Extent of repeal
Housing and Regeneration Act 2008 (c. 17)	Section 193(2)(c). In section 194(1), the words 'the management of'. Section 198(1). Section 201(3), (6) and (8). In section 202 – (a) in subsection (6), paragraph (c) (but not the word 'and' at the end of that paragraph), and (b) in subsection (7), paragraph (c) and word 'and' immediately preceding that paragraph. Section 204. Section 205. Section 216(d). Section 218(2)(b) and (c)

PART 28 HOUSING OMBUDSMAN

Reference	Extent of repeal
Housing and Regeneration Act 2008 (c. 17)	Section 239(2).

PART 29 HOME INFORMATION PACKS

Reference	Extent of repeal
Terrorism Act 2000 (c. 11)	In Schedule 3A, in paragraph 2(1), paragraph (f) and the word 'or' immediately preceding it.
Proceeds of Crime Act 2002 (c. 29)	In Schedule 9, in paragraph 2(1), paragraph (f) and the word 'or' immediately preceding it.
Housing Act 2004 (c. 34)	Part 5.
	Section 250(3).
	In section 262(6), the words 'does not apply for the purposes of Part 5 and'.
	In section 270 –
	(a) in subsection (2)(a), the words '161 to 164, 176,',
	(b) subsection (6), and
	(c) in subsection (8) the word ', (6)'.
	Schedule 8.
Consumers, Estate Agents and Redress Act 2007 (c. 17)	In Schedule 7, paragraph 23.
Housing and Regeneration Act 2008 (c. 17)	In section 290(2)(e), the words 'made by virtue of Part 5 of the Housing Act 2004 (c. 34) (home information packs) or'.

PART 30 TENANTS' DEPOSITS

Reference	Extent of repeal
Housing Act 2004 (c. 34)	In section 214(4), the word 'also'.

PART 31 LONDON (HOUSING AND REGENERATION)

Reference	Extent of repeal
Housing Act 1985 (c. 68)	In Schedule 5 to the Housing Act 1985, in paragraph 3, in the entry in the list for section 19 of the Housing and Regeneration Act 2008, the words from '(and' to 'Act)'.
Housing Act 1996 (c. 52)	In section 51(3)(a) –

	(a) in the entry in the list for section 19 of the Housing and Regeneration Act 2008 the words from '(and' to 'Act)', and (b) the word '; or' immediately after the entry in that list for section 50 of the Housing Act 1988 etc.
Greater London Authority Act 1999 (c. 29)	Section 31(3)(a) and (4).
Housing and Regeneration Act 2008 (c. 17)	In section 13(6), the words from ', a London' to the end of the subsection. In section 14(7), in paragraph (a) of the definition of 'relevant functions', the words from ', a London' to 'of London,'. In section 148(1), in each of paragraphs (a) and (b), the words 'may not'. In Schedule 8 – (a) paragraph 62(b), (b) paragraph 73(2) and (3), and (c) paragraph 74(a).

PART 32 LONDON DEVELOPMENT AGENCY ETC

Reference	**Extent of repeal or revocation**
Parliamentary Commissioner Act 1967 (c. 13)	In Schedule 2, in the entry relating to regional development agencies, the words '(other than the London Development Agency)'.
Superannuation Act 1972 (c. 11)	In Schedule 1 – (a) in the entry for a development agency established under section 1 of the Regional Development Agencies Act 1998, the words '(other than the London Development Agency (for which there is a separate entry))', and (b) the entry for the London Development Agency.
Local Government Act 1974 (c. 7)	Section 25(1)(bbb).
Local Government Finance Act 1988 (c. 41)	Section 114(3B). In section 115 – (a) subsection (3A), and (b) in subsection (4A), the words 'the London Development Agency or'.
Local Government (Overseas Assistance) Act 1993 (c. 25)	Section 1(6A).

Audit Commission Act 1998 (c. 18)	Section 11(7A)(b).
	In section 11(8A), the words 'the London Development Agency or'.
Crime and Disorder Act 1998 (c. 37)	In section 17(2), the entry for the London Development Agency.
Regional Development Agencies Act 1998 (c. 45)	Section 2(6) to (11).
	Section 5(4).
	Section 6(7).
	Section 6A.
	Section 7(3).
	Sections 7A and 7B.
	Section 9(5).
	In section 10(1) the words 'other than the London Development Agency'.
	Section 10(2) and (3).
	Section 11(8).
	Section 12(5).
	Section 13(6).
	Section 14(7).
	Section 15(4) and (5).
	In section 16 the words 'other than the London Development Agency'.
	Section 17(4) to (7).
	Section 18(5).
	Section 20(3A).
	Section 25(7A).
	Section 26(2A) and (3A).
	Section 26A.
	Section 27(1A).
	Section 30A.
	In section 41, the definition of 'the London Development Agency'.
	In Schedule 1, the entry for the London region.
	In Schedule 2 –
	(a) paragraphs 1(4) and (5), 2(2) and (3), 3A and 4(5), and
	(b) in paragraph 5(1) the words from 'other than the London Development Agency' to the end.
	Schedule 6A.
Local Government Act 1999 (c. 27)	Section 1(1)(j).

Greater London Authority Act 1999 (c. 29)	Section 31(2). In section 38 – (a) subsections (2)(d) and (7)(b), and (b) in subsection (8), paragraph (c) and the 'or' preceding it. In section 46(2)(a) the words 'or under section 7A(2) of the Regional Development Agencies Act 1998'. In section 58(4) the words 'or the London Development Agency'. In section 60A(3), the entry for chairman, or deputy chairman, of the London Development Agency. In section 68 – (a) subsection (2)(c), (b) in subsection (3) the words 'or the London Development Agency', (c) in subsection (6), paragraph (b) and the 'and' preceding it, (d) in subsection (6) the words 'or, as the case may be, the London Development Agency', and (e) subsection (7). In section 73(6), in the substituted subsection (2), in the definition of 'GLA body or person ' (a) paragraph (c), (b) in paragraph (g), the words 'or the London Development Agency,' and the words '(or in the case of the London Development Agency section 380)', and (c) in paragraph (m), the words 'or the London Development Agency,' and the words '(or, in the case of a member or member of staff of the London Development Agency, section 380)'. Sections 304 to 309. Section 361B(6)(d)(iii). In section 380 – (a) subsections (2)(d) and (9)(b), and (b) in subsection (10), paragraph (c) and the 'or' preceding it. Section 389(1)(c), (5)(c) and (6). Section 394(2) and (6). Section 400(2). Section 408(5).

	Section 409(4).
	In section 424(1), paragraph (b) of the definition of 'functional body'.
	In Schedule 25, paragraphs 2 to 5, 6(3) and 7 to 21.
Freedom of Information Act 2000 (c. 36)	In Schedule 1 –
	(a) paragraph 35, and
	(b) in Part 6, in the entry for regional development agencies, the words ', other than the London Development Agency'.
Greater London Authority (Miscellaneous Amendments) Order 2000 (S.I. 2000/1435)	In the Schedule, paragraph 5(2).
Local Government Act 2003 (c. 26)	In section 95(7), in paragraph (a) of the definition of 'relevant authority', the words 'or the London Development Agency'.
London Development Agency Act 2003 (c. i)	The whole Act.
London Olympic Games and Paralympic Games Act 2006 (c. 12)	Section 8(3)(b), but not the 'and' at the end.
	Section 34(5).
Greater London Authority Act 2007 (c. 24)	Section 20.
Crossrail Act 2008 (c. 18)	In section 36, the words ', the London Development Agency'.
	In Schedule 12, in the heading of Part 2 and in paragraph 2(1)(a) and (b), the words ', the London Development Agency'.
Local Democracy, Economic Development and Construction Act 2009 (c. 20)	Section 35(2)(q).
	In Schedule 5, paragraph 6.
Equality Act 2010 (c. 15)	In Part 1 of Schedule 19 –
	(a) the entry for the London Development Agency, and
	(b) in the entry for other regional development agencies, the words '(other than the London Development Agency)'.

PART 33 GREATER LONDON AUTHORITY GOVERNANCE

Reference	Extent of repeal
Greater London Authority Act 1999 (c. 29)	Section 41(1)(d) to (g), (10) and (11). Section 42(5). Section 42A. Section 335(1) to (1B). Section 351. Section 352(1), (3), (4)(b) (with the preceding 'and'), (5) and (6). Section 353(1), (4)(b) (with the preceding 'and') and (5) to (7). Section 354(2)(a). In section 355(7), in the words after paragraph (c), the words 'of the strategy'. Section 360(5). In section 361B, subsections (1), (7) and (9) to (11) and, in subsection (12), the definition of 'prescribed'. Section 361C. Section 361D(1) and (3) to (5). Section 361E. Section 362(1) and (5) to (7). Section 363(2)(a). Section 370(1) and (6) to (8).

PART 34 COMPENSATION FOR COMPULSORY ACQUISITION

Reference	Extent of repeal or revocation
Land Compensation Act 1961 (c. 33)	In section 20 – (a) in the opening words, the words 'and appeals under section eighteen of this Act' and the word 'respectively', and (b) paragraphs (b) and (d). Section 21.
Local Government, Planning and Land Act 1980 (c. 65)	Section 121(1). In section 121(2) – (a) the words 'Section 17 of the Land Compensation Act 1961 and', and (b) the word 'each'. In Schedule 24, Part 1.

	In Schedule 33 – (a) in paragraph 5(1), the words '2(2), 15(5) and', and (b) paragraph 5(2) and(3).
Norfolk and Suffolk Broads Act 1988 (c. 4)	In Schedule 3, paragraph 3.
Planning and Compensation Act 1991 (c. 34)	Sections 64 and 65. In Schedule 6, paragraph 1(1)(a). In Schedule 15 – (a) in paragraph 15(1), the words 'section 14(1) of' and the words after '1961', and (b) paragraphs 15(2) and 16(a).
Tribunals and Inquiries Act 1992 (c. 53)	In Schedule 3, paragraph 1.
Transfer of Tribunal Functions (Lands Tribunal and Miscellaneous Amendments) Order 2009 (S.I. 2009/1307)	In Schedule 1, paragraph 42.

Appendix B
NATIONAL PLANNING POLICY FRAMEWORK

March 2012, Department for Communities and Local Government

MINISTERIAL FOREWORD

The purpose of planning is to help achieve sustainable development.

Sustainable means ensuring that better lives for ourselves don't mean worse lives for future generations.

Development means growth. We must accommodate the new ways by which we will earn our living in a competitive world.

We must house a rising population, which is living longer and wants to make new choices. We must respond to the changes that new technologies offer us. Our lives, and the places in which we live them, can be better, but they will certainly be worse if things stagnate.

Sustainable development is about change for the better, and not only in our built environment.

Our natural environment is essential to our wellbeing, and it can be better looked after than it has been. Habitats that have been degraded can be restored. Species that have been isolated can be reconnected. Green Belt land that has been depleted of diversity can be refilled by nature – and opened to people to experience it, to the benefit of body and soul.

Our historic environment – buildings, landscapes, towns and villages – can better be cherished if their spirit of place thrives, rather than withers.

Our standards of design can be so much higher. We are a nation renowned worldwide for creative excellence, yet, at home, confidence in development itself has been eroded by the too frequent experience of mediocrity.

So sustainable development is about positive growth – making economic, environmental and social progress for this and future generations.

The planning system is about helping to make this happen.

Development that is sustainable should go ahead, without delay – a presumption in favour of sustainable development that is the basis for every plan, and every decision. This framework sets out clearly what could make a proposed plan or development unsustainable.

In order to fulfil its purpose of helping achieve sustainable development, planning must not simply be about scrutiny. Planning must be a creative exercise in finding ways to enhance and improve the places in which we live our lives.

This should be a collective enterprise. Yet, in recent years, planning has tended to exclude, rather than to include, people and communities. In part, this has been a result of targets being imposed, and decisions taken, by bodies remote from them. Dismantling the unaccountable regional apparatus and introducing neighbourhood planning addresses this.

In part, people have been put off from getting involved because planning policy itself has become so elaborate and forbidding – the preserve of specialists, rather than people in communities.

This National Planning Policy Framework changes that. By replacing over a thousand pages of national policy with around fifty, written simply and clearly, we are allowing people and communities back into planning.

Rt Hon Greg Clark MP, Minister for Planning

INTRODUCTION

1. The National Planning Policy Framework sets out the Government's planning policies for England and how these are expected to be applied.[1] It sets out the Government's requirements for the planning system only to the extent that it is relevant, proportionate and necessary to do so. It provides a framework within which local people and their accountable councils can produce their own distinctive local and neighbourhood plans, which reflect the needs and priorities of their communities.

2. Planning law requires that applications for planning permission must be determined in accordance with the development plan,[2] unless material considerations indicate otherwise.[3] The National Planning Policy Framework must be taken into account in the preparation of local and neighbourhood plans, and is a material consideration in planning decisions.[4] Planning policies and decisions must reflect and where appropriate promote relevant EU obligations and statutory requirements.

3. This Framework does not contain specific policies for nationally significant infrastructure projects for which particular considerations apply. These are determined in accordance with the decision-making framework set out in the Planning Act 2008 and relevant national policy statements for major infrastructure, as well as any other matters that are considered both important and relevant (which may include the National Planning Policy Framework). National policy statements form part of the overall framework of national planning policy, and are a material consideration in decisions on planning applications.

4. This Framework should be read in conjunction with the Government's planning policy for traveller sites. Local planning authorities preparing plans for and taking decisions on travellers sites should also have regard to the policies in this Framework so far as relevant.

5. This Framework does not contain specific waste policies, since national waste planning policy will be published as part of the National Waste Management Plan for England.[5] However, local authorities preparing waste plans and taking decisions on waste applications should have regard to policies in this Framework so far as relevant.

ACHIEVING SUSTAINABLE DEVELOPMENT

International and national bodies have set out broad principles of sustainable development. Resolution 42/187 of the United Nations General Assembly defined sustainable development as meeting the needs of the present without compromising the ability of future generations to meet their own needs. The UK Sustainable Development *Strategy Securing the Future* set out five 'guiding principles' of sustainable development: living within the planet's environmental limits; ensuring a strong, healthy and just society; achieving a sustainable economy; promoting good governance; and using sound science responsibly.

6. The purpose of the planning system is to contribute to the achievement of sustainable development. The policies in paragraphs 18 to 219, taken as a whole, constitute the Government's view of what sustainable development in England means in practice for the planning system.

7. There are three dimensions to sustainable development: economic, social and environmental. These dimensions give rise to the need for the planning system to perform a number of roles:

- **an economic role** – contributing to building a strong, responsive and competitive economy, by ensuring that sufficient land of the right type is available in the right places and at the right time to support growth and innovation; and by identifying and coordinating development requirements, including the provision of infrastructure;
- **a social role** – supporting strong, vibrant and healthy communities, by providing the supply of housing required to meet the needs of present and future generations; and by creating a high quality built environment, with accessible local services that reflect the community's needs and support its health, social and cultural well-being; and
- **an environmental role** – contributing to protecting and enhancing our natural, built and historic environment; and, as part of this, helping to improve biodiversity, use natural resources prudently, minimise waste and pollution, and mitigate and adapt to climate change including moving to a low carbon economy.

8. These roles should not be undertaken in isolation, because they are mutually dependent. Economic growth can secure higher social and environmental standards, and well-designed buildings and places can improve the lives of people and communities. Therefore, to achieve sustainable development, economic, social and environmental gains should be sought jointly and simultaneously through the planning system. The planning system should play an active role in guiding development to sustainable solutions.

9. Pursuing sustainable development involves seeking positive improvements in the quality of the built, natural and historic environment, as well as in people's quality of life, including (but not limited to):

- making it easier for jobs to be created in cities, towns and villages;
- moving from a net loss of bio-diversity to achieving net gains for nature;[6]
- replacing poor design with better design;
- improving the conditions in which people live, work, travel and take leisure; and
- widening the choice of high quality homes.

10. Plans and decisions need to take local circumstances into account, so that they respond to the different opportunities for achieving sustainable development in different areas.

The presumption in favour of sustainable development

11. Planning law requires that applications for planning permission must be determined in accordance with the development plan unless material considerations indicate otherwise.[7]

12. This National Planning Policy Framework does not change the statutory status of the development plan as the starting point for decision making. Proposed development that accords with an up-to-date Local Plan should be approved, and proposed development that conflicts should be refused unless other material considerations indicate otherwise. It is highly desirable that local planning authorities should have an up-to-date plan in place.

13. The National Planning Policy Framework constitutes guidance[8] for local planning authorities and decision-takers both in drawing up plans and as a material consideration in determining applications.

14. At the heart of the National Planning Policy Framework is a **presumption in favour of sustainable development**, which should be seen as a golden thread running through both plan-making and decision-taking.

For **plan-making** this means that:

- local planning authorities should positively seek opportunities to meet the development needs of their area;

- Local Plans should meet objectively assessed needs, with sufficient flexibility to adapt to rapid change, unless:
  - any adverse impacts of doing so would significantly and demonstrably outweigh the benefits, when assessed against the policies in this Framework taken as a whole; or
  - specific policies in this Framework indicate development should be restricted.[9]

For **decision-taking** this means:[10]

- approving development proposals that accord with the development plan without delay; and
- where the development plan is absent, silent or relevant policies are out-of-date, granting permission unless:
  - any adverse impacts of doing so would significantly and demonstrably outweigh the benefits, when assessed against the policies in this Framework taken as a whole; or
  - specific policies in this Framework indicate development should be restricted.[9]

15. Policies in Local Plans should follow the approach of the presumption in favour of sustainable development so that it is clear that development which is sustainable can be approved without delay. All plans should be based upon and reflect the presumption in favour of sustainable development, with clear policies that will guide how the presumption should be applied locally.

16. The application of the presumption will have implications for how communities engage in neighbourhood planning. Critically, it will mean that neighbourhoods should:

- develop plans that support the strategic development needs set out in Local Plans, including policies for housing and economic development;
- plan positively to support local development, shaping and directing development in their area that is outside the strategic elements of the Local Plan; and
- identify opportunities to use Neighbourhood Development Orders to enable developments that are consistent with their neighbourhood plan to proceed.

Core planning principles

17. Within the overarching roles that the planning system ought to play, a set of core land-use planning principles should underpin both plan-making and decision-taking. These 12 principles are that planning should:

- be genuinely plan-led, empowering local people to shape their surroundings, with succinct local and neighbourhood plans setting out a positive vision for the future of the area. Plans should be kept up-to-date, and be based on joint working and co-operation to address larger than local issues. They should provide a practical framework within which decisions on planning applications can be made with a high degree of predictability and efficiency;
- not simply be about scrutiny, but instead be a creative exercise in finding ways to enhance and improve the places in which people live their lives;
- proactively drive and support sustainable economic development to deliver the homes, business and industrial units, infrastructure and thriving local places that the country needs. Every effort should be made objectively to identify and then meet the housing, business and other development needs of an area, and respond positively to wider opportunities for growth. Plans should take account of market signals, such as land prices and housing affordability, and set out a clear strategy for allocating sufficient land which is suitable for development in their area, taking account of the needs of the residential and business communities;

- always seek to secure high quality design and a good standard of amenity for all existing and future occupants of land and buildings;
- take account of the different roles and character of different areas, promoting the vitality of our main urban areas, protecting the Green Belts around them, recognising the intrinsic character and beauty of the countryside and supporting thriving rural communities within it;
- support the transition to a low carbon future in a changing climate, taking full account of flood risk and coastal change, and encourage the reuse of existing resources, including conversion of existing buildings, and encourage the use of renewable resources (for example, by the development of renewable energy);
- contribute to conserving and enhancing the natural environment and reducing pollution. Allocations of land for development should prefer land of lesser environmental value, where consistent with other policies in this Framework;
- encourage the effective use of land by reusing land that has been previously developed (brownfield land), provided that it is not of high environmental value;
- promote mixed use developments, and encourage multiple benefits from the use of land in urban and rural areas, recognising that some open land can perform many functions (such as for wildlife, recreation, flood risk mitigation, carbon storage, or food production);
- conserve heritage assets in a manner appropriate to their significance, so that they can be enjoyed for their contribution to the quality of life of this and future generations;
- actively manage patterns of growth to make the fullest possible use of public transport, walking and cycling, and focus significant development in locations which are or can be made sustainable; and
- take account of and support local strategies to improve health, social and cultural wellbeing for all, and deliver sufficient community and cultural facilities and services to meet local needs.

DELIVERING SUSTAINABLE DEVELOPMENT

1. Building a strong, competitive economy

18. The Government is committed to securing economic growth in order to create jobs and prosperity, building on the country's inherent strengths, and to meeting the twin challenges of global competition and of a low carbon future.

19. The Government is committed to ensuring that the planning system does everything it can to support sustainable economic growth. Planning should operate to encourage and not act as an impediment to sustainable growth. Therefore significant weight should be placed on the need to support economic growth through the planning system.

20. To help achieve economic growth, local planning authorities should plan proactively to meet the development needs of business and support an economy fit for the 21st century.

21. Investment in business should not be over-burdened by the combined requirements of planning policy expectations. Planning policies should recognise and seek to address potential barriers to investment, including a poor environment or any lack of infrastructure, services or housing. In drawing up Local Plans, local planning authorities should:

- set out a clear economic vision and strategy for their area which positively and proactively encourages sustainable economic growth;
- set criteria, or identify strategic sites, for local and inward investment to match the strategy and to meet anticipated needs over the plan period;
- support existing business sectors, taking account of whether they are expanding or contracting and, where possible, identify and plan for new or emerging sectors likely to locate in their area. Policies should be flexible enough to accommodate needs not anticipated in the plan and to allow a rapid response to changes in economic circumstances;

- plan positively for the location, promotion and expansion of clusters or networks of knowledge driven, creative or high technology industries;
- identify priority areas for economic regeneration, infrastructure provision and environmental enhancement; and
- facilitate flexible working practices such as the integration of residential and commercial uses within the same unit.

22. Planning policies should avoid the long term protection of sites allocated for employment use where there is no reasonable prospect of a site being used for that purpose. Land allocations should be regularly reviewed. Where there is no reasonable prospect of a site being used for the allocated employment use, applications for alternative uses of land or buildings should be treated on their merits having regard to market signals and the relative need for different land uses to support sustainable local communities.

2. Ensuring the vitality of town centres

23. Planning policies should be positive, promote competitive town centre environments and set out policies for the management and growth of centres over the plan period. In drawing up Local Plans, local planning authorities should:

- recognise town centres as the heart of their communities and pursue policies to support their viability and vitality;
- define a network and hierarchy of centres that is resilient to anticipated future economic changes;
- define the extent of town centres and primary shopping areas, based on a clear definition of primary and secondary frontages in designated centres, and set policies that make clear which uses will be permitted in such locations;
- promote competitive town centres that provide customer choice and a diverse retail offer and which reflect the individuality of town centres;
- retain and enhance existing markets and, where appropriate, re-introduce or create new ones, ensuring that markets remain attractive and competitive;
- allocate a range of suitable sites to meet the scale and type of retail, leisure, commercial, office, tourism, cultural, community and residential development needed in town centres. It is important that needs for retail, leisure, office and other main town centre uses are met in full and are not compromised by limited site availability. Local planning authorities should therefore undertake an assessment of the need to expand town centres to ensure a sufficient supply of suitable sites;
- allocate appropriate edge of centre sites for main town centre uses that are well connected to the town centre where suitable and viable town centre sites are not available. If sufficient edge of centre sites cannot be identified, set policies for meeting the identified needs in other accessible locations that are well connected to the town centre;
- set policies for the consideration of proposals for main town centre uses which cannot be accommodated in or adjacent to town centres;
- recognise that residential development can play an important role in ensuring the vitality of centres and set out policies to encourage residential development on appropriate sites; and
- where town centres are in decline, local planning authorities should plan positively for their future to encourage economic activity.

24. Local planning authorities should apply a sequential test to planning applications for main town centre uses that are not in an existing centre and are not in accordance with an up-to-date Local Plan. They should require applications for main town centre uses to be located in town centres, then in edge of centre locations and only if suitable sites are not available should out of centre sites be considered. When considering edge of centre and out of centre proposals, preference should be given to accessible sites that are well connected to

the town centre. Applicants and local planning authorities should demonstrate flexibility on issues such as format and scale.

25. This sequential approach should not be applied to applications for small scale rural offices or other small scale rural development.

26. When assessing applications for retail, leisure and office development outside of town centres, which are not in accordance with an up-to-date Local Plan, local planning authorities should require an impact assessment if the development is over a proportionate, locally set floorspace threshold (if there is no locally set threshold, the default threshold is 2,500 sq m).This should include assessment of:

- the impact of the proposal on existing, committed and planned public and private investment in a centre or centres in the catchment area of the proposal; and
- the impact of the proposal on town centre vitality and viability, including local consumer choice and trade in the town centre and wider area, up to five years from the time the application is made. For major schemes where the full impact will not be realised in five years, the impact should also be assessed up to ten years from the time the application is made.

27. Where an application fails to satisfy the sequential test or is likely to have significant adverse impact on one or more of the above factors, it should be refused.

3. Supporting a prosperous rural economy

28. Planning policies should support economic growth in rural areas in order to create jobs and prosperity by taking a positive approach to sustainable new development. To promote a strong rural economy, local and neighbourhood plans should:

- support the sustainable growth and expansion of all types of business and enterprise in rural areas, both through conversion of existing buildings and well designed new buildings;
- promote the development and diversification of agricultural and other land-based rural businesses;
- support sustainable rural tourism and leisure developments that benefit businesses in rural areas, communities and visitors, and which respect the character of the countryside. This should include supporting the provision and expansion of tourist and visitor facilities in appropriate locations where identified needs are not met by existing facilities in rural service centres; and
- promote the retention and development of local services and community facilities in villages, such as local shops, meeting places, sports venues, cultural buildings, public houses and places of worship.

4. Promoting sustainable transport

29. Transport policies have an important role to play in facilitating sustainable development but also in contributing to wider sustainability and health objectives. Smarter use of technologies can reduce the need to travel. The transport system needs to be balanced in favour of sustainable transport modes, giving people a real choice about how they travel. However, the Government recognises that different policies and measures will be required in different communities and opportunities to maximise sustainable transport solutions will vary from urban to rural areas.

30. Encouragement should be given to solutions which support reductions in greenhouse gas emissions and reduce congestion. In preparing Local Plans, local planning authorities should therefore support a pattern of development which, where reasonable to do so, facilitates the use of sustainable modes of transport.

31. Local authorities should work with neighbouring authorities and transport providers to develop strategies for the provision of viable infrastructure necessary to support sustainable

development, including large scale facilities such as rail freight interchanges, roadside facilities for motorists or transport investment necessary to support strategies for the growth of ports, airports or other major generators of travel demand in their areas. The primary function of roadside facilities for motorists should be to support the safety and welfare of the road user.

32. All developments that generate significant amounts of movement should be supported by a Transport Statement or Transport Assessment. Plans and decisions should take account of whether:

- the opportunities for sustainable transport modes have been taken up depending on the nature and location of the site, to reduce the need for major transport infrastructure;
- safe and suitable access to the site can be achieved for all people; and
- improvements can be undertaken within the transport network that cost effectively limit the significant impacts of the development. Development should only be prevented or refused on transport grounds where the residual cumulative impacts of development are severe.

33. When planning for ports, airports and airfields that are not subject to a separate national policy statement, plans should take account of their growth and role in serving business, leisure, training and emergency service needs. Plans should take account of this Framework as well as the principles set out in the relevant national policy statements and the Government Framework for UK Aviation.

34. Plans and decisions should ensure developments that generate significant movement are located where the need to travel will be minimised and the use of sustainable transport modes can be maximised. However this needs to take account of policies set out elsewhere in this Framework, particularly in rural areas.

35. Plans should protect and exploit opportunities for the use of sustainable transport modes for the movement of goods or people. Therefore, developments should be located and designed where practical to

- accommodate the efficient delivery of goods and supplies;
- give priority to pedestrian and cycle movements, and have access to high quality public transport facilities;
- create safe and secure layouts which minimise conflicts between traffic and cyclists or pedestrians, avoiding street clutter and where appropriate establishing home zones;
- incorporate facilities for charging plug-in and other ultra-low emission vehicles; and
- consider the needs of people with disabilities by all modes of transport.

36. A key tool to facilitate this will be a Travel Plan. All developments which generate significant amounts of movement should be required to provide a Travel Plan.

37. Planning policies should aim for a balance of land uses within their area so that people can be encouraged to minimise journey lengths for employment, shopping, leisure, education and other activities.

38. For larger scale residential developments in particular, planning policies should promote a mix of uses in order to provide opportunities to undertake day-to-day activities including work on site. Where practical, particularly within large-scale developments, key facilities such as primary schools and local shops should be located within walking distance of most properties.

39. If setting local parking standards for residential and non-residential development, local planning authorities should take into account:

- the accessibility of the development;
- the type, mix and use of development;
- the availability of and opportunities for public transport;

- local car ownership levels; and
- an overall need to reduce the use of high-emission vehicles.

40. Local authorities should seek to improve the quality of parking in town centres so that it is convenient, safe and secure, including appropriate provision for motorcycles. They should set appropriate parking charges that do not undermine the vitality of town centres. Parking enforcement should be proportionate.

41. Local planning authorities should identify and protect, where there is robust evidence, sites and routes which could be critical in developing infrastructure to widen transport choice.

5. Supporting high quality communications infrastructure

42. Advanced, high quality communications infrastructure is essential for sustainable economic growth. The development of high speed broadband technology and other communications networks also plays a vital role in enhancing the provision of local community facilities and services.

43. In preparing Local Plans, local planning authorities should support the expansion of electronic communications networks, including telecommunications and high speed broadband. They should aim to keep the numbers of radio and telecommunications masts and the sites for such installations to a minimum consistent with the efficient operation of the network. Existing masts, buildings and other structures should be used, unless the need for a new site has been justified. Where new sites are required, equipment should be sympathetically designed and camouflaged where appropriate.

44. Local planning authorities should not impose a ban on new telecommunications development in certain areas, impose blanket Article 4 directions over a wide area or a wide range of telecommunications development or insist on minimum distances between new telecommunications development and existing development. They should ensure that:

- they have evidence to demonstrate that telecommunications infrastructure will not cause significant and irremediable interference with other electrical equipment, air traffic services or instrumentation operated in the national interest; and
- they have considered the possibility of the construction of new buildings or other structures interfering with broadcast and telecommunications services.

45. Applications for telecommunications development (including for prior approval under Part 24 of the General Permitted Development Order) should be supported by the necessary evidence to justify the proposed development. This should include:

- the outcome of consultations with organisations with an interest in the proposed development, in particular with the relevant body where a mast is to be installed near a school or college or within a statutory safeguarding zone surrounding an aerodrome or technical site; and
- for an addition to an existing mast or base station, a statement that self-certifies that the cumulative exposure, when operational, will not exceed International Commission on non-ionising radiation protection guidelines; or
- for a new mast or base station, evidence that the applicant has explored the possibility of erecting antennas on an existing building, mast or other structure and a statement that self-certifies that, when operational, International Commission guidelines will be met.

46. Local planning authorities must determine applications on planning grounds. They should not seek to prevent competition between different operators, question the need for the telecommunications system, or determine health safeguards if the proposal meets International Commission guidelines for public exposure.

6. Delivering a wide choice of high quality homes

47. To boost significantly the supply of housing, local planning authorities should:

- use their evidence base to ensure that their Local Plan meets the full, objectively assessed needs for market and affordable housing in the housing market area, as far as is consistent with the policies set out in this Framework, including identifying key sites which are critical to the delivery of the housing strategy over the plan period;
- identify and update annually a supply of specific deliverable[11] sites sufficient to provide five years worth of housing against their housing requirements with an additional buffer of 5% (moved forward from later in the plan period) to ensure choice and competition in the market for land. Where there has been a record of persistent under delivery of housing, local planning authorities should increase the buffer to 20% (moved forward from later in the plan period) to provide a realistic prospect of achieving the planned supply and to ensure choice and competition in the market for land;
- identify a supply of specific, developable[12] sites or broad locations for growth, for years 6-10 and, where possible, for years 11-15;
- for market and affordable housing, illustrate the expected rate of housing delivery through a housing trajectory for the plan period and set out a housing implementation strategy for the full range of housing describing how they will maintain delivery of a five-year supply of housing land to meet their housing target; and
- set out their own approach to housing density to reflect local circumstances.

48. Local planning authorities may make an allowance for windfall sites in the five-year supply if they have compelling evidence that such sites have consistently become available in the local area and will continue to provide a reliable source of supply. Any allowance should be realistic having regard to the Strategic Housing Land Availability Assessment, historic windfall delivery rates and expected future trends, and should not include residential gardens.

49. Housing applications should be considered in the context of the presumption in favour of sustainable development. Relevant policies for the supply of housing should not be considered up-to-date if the local planning authority cannot demonstrate a five-year supply of deliverable housing sites.

50. To deliver a wide choice of high quality homes, widen opportunities for home ownership and create sustainable, inclusive and mixed communities, local planning authorities should:

- plan for a mix of housing based on current and future demographic trends, market trends and the needs of different groups in the community (such as, but not limited to, families with children, older people, people with disabilities, service families and people wishing to build their own homes);
- identify the size, type, tenure and range of housing that is required in particular locations, reflecting local demand; and
- where they have identified that affordable housing is needed, set policies for meeting this need on site, unless off-site provision or a financial contribution of broadly equivalent value can be robustly justified (for example to improve or make more effective use of the existing housing stock) and the agreed approach contributes to the objective of creating mixed and balanced communities. Such policies should be sufficiently flexible to take account of changing market conditions over time.

51. Local planning authorities should identify and bring back into residential use empty housing and buildings in line with local housing and empty homes strategies and, where appropriate, acquire properties under compulsory purchase powers. They should normally approve planning applications for change to residential use and any associated development from commercial buildings (currently in the B use classes) where there is an identified need for additional housing in that area, provided that there are not strong economic reasons why such development would be inappropriate.

52. The supply of new homes can sometimes be best achieved through planning for larger scale development, such as new settlements or extensions to existing villages and towns that follow the principles of Garden Cities. Working with the support of their communities, local

planning authorities should consider whether such opportunities provide the best way of achieving sustainable development. In doing so, they should consider whether it is appropriate to establish Green Belt around or adjoining any such new development.

53. Local planning authorities should consider the case for setting out policies to resist inappropriate development of residential gardens, for example where development would cause harm to the local area.

54. In rural areas, exercising the duty to cooperate with neighbouring authorities, local planning authorities should be responsive to local circumstances and plan housing development to reflect local needs, particularly for affordable housing, including through rural exception sites where appropriate. Local planning authorities should in particular consider whether allowing some market housing would facilitate the provision of significant additional affordable housing to meet local needs.

55. To promote sustainable development in rural areas, housing should be located where it will enhance or maintain the vitality of rural communities. For example, where there are groups of smaller settlements, development in one village may support services in a village nearby. Local planning authorities should avoid new isolated homes in the countryside unless there are special circumstances such as:

- the essential need for a rural worker to live permanently at or near their place of work in the countryside; or
- where such development would represent the optimal viable use of a heritage asset or would be appropriate enabling development to secure the future of heritage assets; or
- where the development would re-use redundant or disused buildings and lead to an enhancement to the immediate setting; or
- the exceptional quality or innovative nature of the design of the dwelling. Such a design should:
  - be truly outstanding or innovative, helping to raise standards of design more generally in rural areas;
  - reflect the highest standards in architecture;
  - significantly enhance its immediate setting; and
  - be sensitive to the defining characteristics of the local area.

7. Requiring good design

56. The Government attaches great importance to the design of the built environment. Good design is a key aspect of sustainable development, is indivisible from good planning, and should contribute positively to making places better for people.

57. It is important to plan positively for the achievement of high quality and inclusive design for all development, including individual buildings, public and private spaces and wider area development schemes.

58. Local and neighbourhood plans should develop robust and comprehensive policies that set out the quality of development that will be expected for the area. Such policies should be based on stated objectives for the future of the area and an understanding and evaluation of its defining characteristics. Planning policies and decisions should aim to ensure that developments:

- will function well and add to the overall quality of the area, not just for the short term but over the lifetime of the development;
- establish a strong sense of place, using streetscapes and buildings to create attractive and comfortable places to live, work and visit;
- optimise the potential of the site to accommodate development, create and sustain an appropriate mix of uses (including incorporation of green and other public space as part of developments) and support local facilities and transport networks;

- respond to local character and history, and reflect the identity of local surroundings and materials, while not preventing or discouraging appropriate innovation;
- create safe and accessible environments where crime and disorder, and the fear of crime, do not undermine quality of life or community cohesion; and
- are visually attractive as a result of good architecture and appropriate landscaping.

59. Local planning authorities should consider using design codes where they could help deliver high quality outcomes. However, design policies should avoid unnecessary prescription or detail and should concentrate on guiding the overall scale, density, massing, height, landscape, layout, materials and access of new development in relation to neighbouring buildings and the local area more generally.

60. Planning policies and decisions should not attempt to impose architectural styles or particular tastes and they should not stifle innovation, originality or initiative through unsubstantiated requirements to conform to certain development forms or styles. It is, however, proper to seek to promote or reinforce local distinctiveness.

61. Although visual appearance and the architecture of individual buildings are very important factors, securing high quality and inclusive design goes beyond aesthetic considerations. Therefore, planning policies and decisions should address the connections between people and places and the integration of new development into the natural, built and historic environment.

62. Local planning authorities should have local design review arrangements in place to provide assessment and support to ensure high standards of design. They should also when appropriate refer major projects for a national design review.[13] In general, early engagement on design produces the greatest benefits. In assessing applications, local planning authorities should have regard to the recommendations from the design review panel.

63. In determining applications, great weight should be given to outstanding or innovative designs which help raise the standard of design more generally in the area.

64. Permission should be refused for development of poor design that fails to take the opportunities available for improving the character and quality of an area and the way it functions.

65. Local planning authorities should not refuse planning permission for buildings or infrastructure which promote high levels of sustainability because of concerns about incompatibility with an existing townscape, if those concerns have been mitigated by good design (unless the concern relates to a designated heritage asset and the impact would cause material harm to the asset or its setting which is not outweighed by the proposal's economic, social and environmental benefits).

66. Applicants will be expected to work closely with those directly affected by their proposals to evolve designs that take account of the views of the community. Proposals that can demonstrate this in developing the design of the new development should be looked on more favourably.

67. Poorly placed advertisements can have a negative impact on the appearance of the built and natural environment. Control over outdoor advertisements should be efficient, effective and simple in concept and operation. Only those advertisements which will clearly have an appreciable impact on a building or on their surroundings should be subject to the local planning authority's detailed assessment. Advertisements should be subject to control only in the interests of amenity and public safety, taking account of cumulative impacts.

68. Where an area justifies a degree of special protection on the grounds of amenity, an Area of Special Control Order[14] may be approved. Before formally proposing an Area of Special Control, the local planning authority is expected to consult local trade and amenity organisations about the proposal. Before a direction to remove deemed planning consent is

made for specific advertisements,[15] local planning authorities will be expected to demonstrate that the direction would improve visual amenity and there is no other way of effectively controlling the display of that particular class of advertisement. The comments of organisations, and individuals, whose interests would be affected by the direction should be sought as part of the process.

8. Promoting healthy communities

69. The planning system can play an important role in facilitating social interaction and creating healthy, inclusive communities. Local planning authorities should create a shared vision with communities of the residential environment and facilities they wish to see. To support this, local planning authorities should aim to involve all sections of the community in the development of Local Plans and in planning decisions, and should facilitate neighbourhood planning. Planning policies and decisions, in turn, should aim to achieve places which promote:

- opportunities for meetings between members of the community who might not otherwise come into contact with each other, including through mixed-use developments, strong neighbourhood centres and active street frontages which bring together those who work, live and play in the vicinity;
- safe and accessible environments where crime and disorder, and the fear of crime, do not undermine quality of life or community cohesion; and
- safe and accessible developments, containing clear and legible pedestrian routes, and high quality public space, which encourage the active and continual use of public areas.

70. To deliver the social, recreational and cultural facilities and services the community needs, planning policies and decisions should:

- plan positively for the provision and use of shared space, community facilities (such as local shops, meeting places, sports venues, cultural buildings, public houses and places of worship) and other local services to enhance the sustainability of communities and residential environments;
- guard against the unnecessary loss of valued facilities and services, particularly where this would reduce the community's ability to meet its day-to-day needs;
- ensure that established shops, facilities and services are able to develop and modernise in a way that is sustainable, and retained for the benefit of the community; and
- ensure an integrated approach to considering the location of housing, economic uses and community facilities and services.

71. Local planning authorities should take a positive and collaborative approach to enable development to be brought forward under a Community Right to Build Order, including working with communities to identify and resolve key issues before applications are submitted.

72. The Government attaches great importance to ensuring that a sufficient choice of school places is available to meet the needs of existing and new communities. Local planning authorities should take a proactive, positive and collaborative approach to meeting this requirement, and to development that will widen choice in education. They should:

- give great weight to the need to create, expand or alter schools; and
- work with schools promoters to identify and resolve key planning issues before applications are submitted.

73. Access to high quality open spaces and opportunities for sport and recreation can make an important contribution to the health and well-being of communities. Planning policies should be based on robust and up-to-date assessments of the needs for open space, sports and recreation facilities and opportunities for new provision. The assessments should identify specific needs and quantitative or qualitative deficits or surpluses of open space, sports and

recreational facilities in the local area. Information gained from the assessments should be used to determine what open space, sports and recreational provision is required.

74. Existing open space, sports and recreational buildings and land, including playing fields, should not be built on unless:

- an assessment has been undertaken which has clearly shown the open space, buildings or land to be surplus to requirements; or
- the loss resulting from the proposed development would be replaced by equivalent or better provision in terms of quantity and quality in a suitable location; or
- the development is for alternative sports and recreational provision, the needs for which clearly outweigh the loss.

75. Planning policies should protect and enhance public rights of way and access. Local authorities should seek opportunities to provide better facilities for users, for example by adding links to existing rights of way networks including National Trails.

76. Local communities through local and neighbourhood plans should be able to identify for special protection green areas of particular importance to them. By designating land as Local Green Space local communities will be able to rule out new development other than in very special circumstances. Identifying land as Local Green Space should therefore be consistent with the local planning of sustainable development and complement investment in sufficient homes, jobs and other essential services. Local Green Spaces should only be designated when a plan is prepared or reviewed, and be capable of enduring beyond the end of the plan period.

77. The Local Green Space designation will not be appropriate for most green areas or open space. The designation should only be used:

- where the green space is in reasonably close proximity to the community it serves;
- where the green area is demonstrably special to a local community and holds a particular local significance, for example because of its beauty, historic significance, recreational value (including as a playing field), tranquillity or richness of its wildlife; and
- where the green area concerned is local in character and is not an extensive tract of land.

78. Local policy for managing development within a Local Green Space should be consistent with policy for Green Belts.

9. Protecting Green Belt land

79. The Government attaches great importance to Green Belts. The fundamental aim of Green Belt policy is to prevent urban sprawl by keeping land permanently open; the essential characteristics of Green Belts are their openness and their permanence.

80. Green Belt serves five purposes:

- to check the unrestricted sprawl of large built-up areas;
- to prevent neighbouring towns merging into one another;
- to assist in safeguarding the countryside from encroachment;
- to preserve the setting and special character of historic towns; and
- to assist in urban regeneration, by encouraging the recycling of derelict and other urban land.

81. Once Green Belts have been defined, local planning authorities should plan positively to enhance the beneficial use of the Green Belt, such as looking for opportunities to provide access; to provide opportunities for outdoor sport and recreation; to retain and enhance landscapes, visual amenity and biodiversity; or to improve damaged and derelict land.

82. The general extent of Green Belts across the country is already established. New Green Belts should only be established in exceptional circumstances, for example when planning

for larger scale development such as new settlements or major urban extensions. If proposing a new Green Belt, local planning authorities should:

- demonstrate why normal planning and development management policies would not be adequate;
- set out whether any major changes in circumstances have made the adoption of this exceptional measure necessary;
- show what the consequences of the proposal would be for sustainable development;
- demonstrate the necessity for the Green Belt and its consistency with Local Plans for adjoining areas; and
- show how the Green Belt would meet the other objectives of the Framework.

83. Local planning authorities with Green Belts in their area should establish Green Belt boundaries in their Local Plans which set the framework for Green Belt and settlement policy. Once established, Green Belt boundaries should only be altered in exceptional circumstances, through the preparation or review of the Local Plan. At that time, authorities should consider the Green Belt boundaries having regard to their intended permanence in the long term, so that they should be capable of enduring beyond the plan period.

84. When drawing up or reviewing Green Belt boundaries local planning authorities should take account of the need to promote sustainable patterns of development. They should consider the consequences for sustainable development of channelling development towards urban areas inside the Green Belt boundary, towards towns and villages inset within the Green Belt or towards locations beyond the outer Green Belt boundary.

85. When defining boundaries, local planning authorities should:

- ensure consistency with the Local Plan strategy for meeting identified requirements for sustainable development;
- not include land which it is unnecessary to keep permanently open;
- where necessary, identify in their plans areas of 'safeguarded land' between the urban area and the Green Belt, in order to meet longer-term development needs stretching well beyond the plan period;
- make clear that the safeguarded land is not allocated for development at the present time. Planning permission for the permanent development of safeguarded land should only be granted following a Local Plan review which proposes the development;
- satisfy themselves that Green Belt boundaries will not need to be altered at the end of the development plan period; and
- define boundaries clearly, using physical features that are readily recognisable and likely to be permanent.

86. If it is necessary to prevent development in a village primarily because of the important contribution which the open character of the village makes to the openness of the Green Belt, the village should be included in the Green Belt. If, however, the character of the village needs to be protected for other reasons, other means should be used, such as conservation area or normal development management policies, and the village should be excluded from the Green Belt.

87. As with previous Green Belt policy, inappropriate development is, by definition, harmful to the Green Belt and should not be approved except in very special circumstances.

88. When considering any planning application, local planning authorities should ensure that substantial weight is given to any harm to the Green Belt. 'Very special circumstances' will not exist unless the potential harm to the Green Belt by reason of inappropriateness, and any other harm, is clearly outweighed by other considerations.

89. A local planning authority should regard the construction of new buildings as inappropriate in Green Belt. Exceptions to this are:

- buildings for agriculture and forestry;

- provision of appropriate facilities for outdoor sport, outdoor recreation and for cemeteries, as long as it preserves the openness of the Green Belt and does not conflict with the purposes of including land within it;
- the extension or alteration of a building provided that it does not result in disproportionate additions over and above the size of the original building;
- the replacement of a building, provided the new building is in the same use and not materially larger than the one it replaces;
- limited infilling in villages, and limited affordable housing for local community needs under policies set out in the Local Plan; or
- limited infilling or the partial or complete redevelopment of previously developed sites (brownfield land), whether redundant or in continuing use (excluding temporary buildings), which would not have a greater impact on the openness of the Green Belt and the purpose of including land within it than the existing development.

90. Certain other forms of development are also not inappropriate in Green Belt provided they preserve the openness of the Green Belt and do not conflict with the purposes of including land in Green Belt. These are:

- mineral extraction;
- engineering operations;
- local transport infrastructure which can demonstrate a requirement for a Green Belt location;
- the re-use of buildings provided that the buildings are of permanent and substantial construction; and
- development brought forward under a Community Right to Build Order.

91. When located in the Green Belt, elements of many renewable energy projects will comprise inappropriate development. In such cases developers will need to demonstrate very special circumstances if projects are to proceed. Such very special circumstances may include the wider environmental benefits associated with increased production of energy from renewable sources.

92. Community Forests offer valuable opportunities for improving the environment around towns, by upgrading the landscape and providing for recreation and wildlife. An approved Community Forest plan may be a material consideration in preparing development plans and in deciding planning applications. Any development proposals within Community Forests in the Green Belt should be subject to the normal policies controlling development in Green Belts.

10. Meeting the challenge of climate change, flooding and coastal change

93. Planning plays a key role in helping shape places to secure radical reductions in greenhouse gas emissions, minimising vulnerability and providing resilience to the impacts of climate change, and supporting the delivery of renewable and low carbon energy and associated infrastructure. This is central to the economic, social and environmental dimensions of sustainable development.

94. Local planning authorities should adopt proactive strategies to mitigate and adapt to climate change,[16] taking full account of flood risk, coastal change and water supply and demand considerations.

95. To support the move to a low carbon future, local planning authorities should:

- plan for new development in locations and ways which reduce greenhouse gas emissions;
- actively support energy efficiency improvements to existing buildings; and
- when setting any local requirement for a building's sustainability, do so in a way consistent with the Government's zero carbon buildings policy and adopt nationally described standards.

96. In determining planning applications, local planning authorities should expect new development to:

- comply with adopted Local Plan policies on local requirements for decentralised energy supply unless it can be demonstrated by the applicant, having regard to the type of development involved and its design, that this is not feasible or viable; and
- take account of landform, layout, building orientation, massing and landscaping to minimise energy consumption.

97. To help increase the use and supply of renewable and low carbon energy, local planning authorities should recognise the responsibility on all communities to contribute to energy generation from renewable or low carbon sources. They should:

- have a positive strategy to promote energy from renewable and low carbon sources;
- design their policies to maximise renewable and low carbon energy development while ensuring that adverse impacts are addressed satisfactorily, including cumulative landscape and visual impacts;
- consider identifying suitable areas for renewable and low carbon energy sources, and supporting infrastructure, where this would help secure the development of such sources;[17]
- support community-led initiatives for renewable and low carbon energy, including developments outside such areas being taken forward through neighbourhood planning; and
- identify opportunities where development can draw its energy supply from decentralised, renewable or low carbon energy supply systems and for co-locating potential heat customers and suppliers.

98. When determining planning applications, local planning authorities should:

- not require applicants for energy development to demonstrate the overall need for renewable or low carbon energy and also recognise that even small-scale projects provide a valuable contribution to cutting greenhouse gas emissions; and
- approve the application[18] if its impacts are (or can be made) acceptable. Once suitable areas for renewable and low carbon energy have been identified in plans, local planning authorities should also expect subsequent applications for commercial scale projects outside these areas to demonstrate that the proposed location meets the criteria used in identifying suitable areas.

99. Local Plans should take account of climate change over the longer term, including factors such as flood risk, coastal change, water supply and changes to biodiversity and landscape. New development should be planned to avoid increased vulnerability to the range of impacts arising from climate change. When new development is brought forward in areas which are vulnerable, care should be taken to ensure that risks can be managed through suitable adaptation measures, including through the planning of green infrastructure.

100. Inappropriate development in areas at risk of flooding should be avoided by directing development away from areas at highest risk, but where development is necessary, making it safe without increasing flood risk elsewhere.[19] Local Plans should be supported by Strategic Flood Risk Assessment and develop policies to manage flood risk from all sources, taking account of advice from the Environment Agency and other relevant flood risk management bodies, such as lead local flood authorities and internal drainage boards. Local Plans should apply a sequential, risk-based approach to the location of development to avoid where possible flood risk to people and property and manage any residual risk, taking account of the impacts of climate change, by:

- applying the Sequential Test;
- if necessary, applying the Exception Test;
- safeguarding land from development that is required for current and future flood management;

- using opportunities offered by new development to reduce the causes and impacts of flooding; and
- where climate change is expected to increase flood risk so that some existing development may not be sustainable in the long-term, seeking opportunities to facilitate the relocation of development, including housing, to more sustainable locations.

101. The aim of the Sequential Test is to steer new development to areas with the lowest probability of flooding. Development should not be allocated or permitted if there are reasonably available sites appropriate for the proposed development in areas with a lower probability of flooding. The Strategic Flood Risk Assessment will provide the basis for applying this test. A sequential approach should be used in areas known to be at risk from any form of flooding.

102. If, following application of the Sequential Test, it is not possible, consistent with wider sustainability objectives, for the development to be located in zones with a lower probability of flooding, the Exception Test can be applied if appropriate. For the Exception Test to be passed:

- it must be demonstrated that the development provides wider sustainability benefits to the community that outweigh flood risk, informed by a Strategic Flood Risk Assessment where one has been prepared; and
- a site-specific flood risk assessment must demonstrate that the development will be safe for its lifetime taking account of the vulnerability of its users, without increasing flood risk elsewhere, and, where possible, will reduce flood risk overall.

Both elements of the test will have to be passed for development to be allocated or permitted.

103. When determining planning applications, local planning authorities should ensure flood risk is not increased elsewhere and only consider development appropriate in areas at risk of flooding where, informed by a site-specific flood risk assessment[20] following the Sequential Test, and if required the Exception Test, it can be demonstrated that:

- within the site, the most vulnerable development is located in areas of lowest flood risk unless there are overriding reasons to prefer a different location; and
- development is appropriately flood resilient and resistant, including safe access and escape routes where required, and that any residual risk can be safely managed, including by emergency planning; and it gives priority to the use of sustainable drainage systems.[21]

104. For individual developments on sites allocated in development plans through the Sequential Test, applicants need not apply the Sequential Test. Applications for minor development and changes of use should not be subject to the Sequential or Exception Tests[22] but should still meet the requirements for site-specific flood risk assessments.

105. In coastal areas, local planning authorities should take account of the UK Marine Policy Statement and marine plans and apply Integrated Coastal Zone Management across local authority and land/sea boundaries, ensuring integration of the terrestrial and marine planning regimes.

106. Local planning authorities should reduce risk from coastal change by avoiding inappropriate development in vulnerable areas or adding to the impacts of physical changes to the coast. They should identify as a Coastal Change Management Area any area likely to be affected by physical changes to the coast, and:

- be clear as to what development will be appropriate in such areas and in what circumstances; and
- make provision for development and infrastructure that needs to be relocated away from Coastal Change Management Areas.

107. When assessing applications, authorities should consider development in a Coastal Change Management Area appropriate where it is demonstrated that:

- it will be safe over its planned lifetime and will not have an unacceptable impact on coastal change;
- the character of the coast including designations is not compromised;
- the development provides wider sustainability benefits; and
- the development does not hinder the creation and maintenance of a continuous signed and managed route around the coast.[23]

108. Local planning authorities should also ensure appropriate development in a Coastal Change Management Area is not impacted by coastal change by limiting the planned life-time of the proposed development through temporary permission and restoration conditions where necessary to reduce the risk to people and the development.

11. Conserving and enhancing the natural environment

109. The planning system should contribute to and enhance the natural and local environment by:

- protecting and enhancing valued landscapes, geological conservation interests and soils;
- recognising the wider benefits of ecosystem services;
- minimising impacts on biodiversity and providing net gains in biodiversity where possible, contributing to the Government's commitment to halt the overall decline in biodiversity, including by establishing coherent ecological networks that are more resilient to current and future pressures;
- preventing both new and existing development from contributing to or being put at unacceptable risk from, or being adversely affected by unacceptable levels of soil, air, water or noise pollution or land instability; and
- remediating and mitigating despoiled, degraded, derelict, contaminated and unstable land, where appropriate.

110. In preparing plans to meet development needs, the aim should be to minimise pollution and other adverse effects on the local and natural environment. Plans should allocate land with the least environmental or amenity value, where consistent with other policies in this Framework.

111. Planning policies and decisions should encourage the effective use of land by re-using land that has been previously developed (brownfield land), provided that it is not of high environmental value. Local planning authorities may continue to consider the case for setting a locally appropriate target for the use of brownfield land.

112. Local planning authorities should take into account the economic and other benefits of the best and most versatile agricultural land. Where significant development of agricultural land is demonstrated to be necessary, local planning authorities should seek to use areas of poorer quality land in preference to that of a higher quality.

113. Local planning authorities should set criteria based policies against which proposals for any development on or affecting protected wildlife or geodiversity sites or landscape areas will be judged. Distinctions should be made between the hierarchy of international, national and locally designated sites,[24] so that protection is commensurate with their status and gives appropriate weight to their importance and the contribution that they make to wider ecological networks.

114. Local planning authorities should:

- set out a strategic approach in their Local Plans, planning positively for the creation, protection, enhancement and management of networks of biodiversity and green infrastructure; and

- maintain the character of the undeveloped coast, protecting and enhancing its distinctive landscapes, particularly in areas defined as Heritage Coast, and improve public access to and enjoyment of the coast.

115. Great weight should be given to conserving landscape and scenic beauty in National Parks, the Broads and Areas of Outstanding Natural Beauty, which have the highest status of protection in relation to landscape and scenic beauty. The conservation of wildlife and cultural heritage are important considerations in all these areas, and should be given great weight in National Parks and the Broads.[25]

116. Planning permission should be refused for major developments in these designated areas except in exceptional circumstances and where it can be demonstrated they are in the public interest. Consideration of such applications should include an assessment of:

- the need for the development, including in terms of any national considerations, and the impact of permitting it, or refusing it, upon the local economy;
- the cost of, and scope for, developing elsewhere outside the designated area, or meeting the need for it in some other way; and
- any detrimental effect on the environment, the landscape and recreational opportunities, and the extent to which that could be moderated.

117. To minimise impacts on biodiversity and geodiversity, planning policies should:

- plan for biodiversity at a landscape-scale across local authority boundaries;
- identify and map components of the local ecological networks, including the hierarchy of international, national and locally designated sites of importance for biodiversity, wildlife corridors and stepping stones that connect them and areas identified by local partnerships for habitat restoration or creation;
- promote the preservation, restoration and re-creation of priority habitats, ecological networks and the protection and recovery of priority species populations, linked to national and local targets, and identify suitable indicators for monitoring biodiversity in the plan;
- aim to prevent harm to geological conservation interests; and
- where Nature Improvement Areas are identified in Local Plans, consider specifying the types of development that may be appropriate in these Areas.

118. When determining planning applications, local planning authorities should aim to conserve and enhance biodiversity by applying the following principles:

- if significant harm resulting from a development cannot be avoided (through locating on an alternative site with less harmful impacts), adequately mitigated, or, as a last resort, compensated for, then planning permission should be refused;
- proposed development on land within or outside a Site of Special Scientific Interest likely to have an adverse effect on a Site of Special Scientific Interest (either individually or in combination with other developments) should not normally be permitted. Where an adverse effect on the site's notified special interest features is likely, an exception should only be made where the benefits of the development, at this site, clearly outweigh both the impacts that it is likely to have on the features of the site that make it of special scientific interest and any broader impacts on the national network of Sites of Special Scientific Interest;
- development proposals where the primary objective is to conserve or enhance biodiversity should be permitted;
- opportunities to incorporate biodiversity in and around developments should be encouraged;
- planning permission should be refused for development resulting in the loss or deterioration of irreplaceable habitats, including ancient woodland and the loss of aged or veteran trees found outside ancient woodland, unless the need for, and benefits of, the development in that location clearly outweigh the loss; and

- the following wildlife sites should be given the same protection as European sites:
  - potential Special Protection Areas and possible Special Areas of Conservation;
  - listed or proposed Ramsar sites;[26] and
  - sites identified, or required, as compensatory measures for adverse effects on European sites, potential Special Protection Areas, possible Special Areas of Conservation, and listed or proposed Ramsar sites.

119. The presumption in favour of sustainable development (paragraph 14) does not apply where development requiring appropriate assessment under the Birds or Habitats Directives is being considered, planned or determined.

120. To prevent unacceptable risks from pollution and land instability, planning policies and decisions should ensure that new development is appropriate for its location. The effects (including cumulative effects) of pollution on health, the natural environment or general amenity, and the potential sensitivity of the area or proposed development to adverse effects from pollution, should be taken into account. Where a site is affected by contamination or land stability issues, responsibility for securing a safe development rests with the developer and/or landowner.

121. Planning policies and decisions should also ensure that:

- the site is suitable for its new use taking account of ground conditions and land instability, including from natural hazards or former activities such as mining, pollution arising from previous uses and any proposals for mitigation including land remediation or impacts on the natural environment arising from that remediation;
- after remediation, as a minimum, land should not be capable of being determined as contaminated land under Part IIA of the Environmental Protection Act 1990; and
- adequate site investigation information, prepared by a competent person, is presented.

122. In doing so, local planning authorities should focus on whether the development itself is an acceptable use of the land, and the impact of the use, rather than the control of processes or emissions themselves where these are subject to approval under pollution control regimes. Local planning authorities should assume that these regimes will operate effectively. Equally, where a planning decision has been made on a particular development, the planning issues should not be revisited through the permitting regimes operated by pollution control authorities.

123. Planning policies and decisions should aim to:

- avoid noise from giving rise to significant adverse impacts[27] on health and quality of life as a result of new development;
- mitigate and reduce to a minimum other adverse impacts[27] on health and quality of life arising from noise from new development, including through the use of conditions;
- recognise that development will often create some noise and existing businesses wanting to develop in continuance of their business should not have unreasonable restrictions put on them because of changes in nearby land uses since they were established;[28] and
- identify and protect areas of tranquillity which have remained relatively undisturbed by noise and are prized for their recreational and amenity value for this reason.

124. Planning policies should sustain compliance with and contribute towards EU limit values or national objectives for pollutants, taking into account the presence of Air Quality Management Areas and the cumulative impacts on air quality from individual sites in local areas. Planning decisions should ensure that any new development in Air Quality Management Areas is consistent with the local air quality action plan.

125. By encouraging good design, planning policies and decisions should limit the impact of light pollution from artificial light on local amenity, intrinsically dark landscapes and nature conservation.

12. Conserving and enhancing the historic environment

126. Local planning authorities should set out in their Local Plan a positive strategy for the conservation and enjoyment of the historic environment,[29] including heritage assets most at risk through neglect, decay or other threats. In doing so, they should recognise that heritage assets are an irreplaceable resource and conserve them in a manner appropriate to their significance. In developing this strategy, local planning authorities should take into account:

- the desirability of sustaining and enhancing the significance of heritage assets and putting them to viable uses consistent with their conservation;
- the wider social, cultural, economic and environmental benefits that conservation of the historic environment can bring;
- the desirability of new development making a positive contribution to local character and distinctiveness; and
- opportunities to draw on the contribution made by the historic environment to the character of a place.

127. When considering the designation of conservation areas, local planning authorities should ensure that an area justifies such status because of its special architectural or historic interest, and that the concept of conservation is not devalued through the designation of areas that lack special interest.

128. In determining applications, local planning authorities should require an applicant to describe the significance of any heritage assets affected, including any contribution made by their setting. The level of detail should be proportionate to the assets' importance and no more than is sufficient to understand the potential impact of the proposal on their significance. As a minimum the relevant historic environment record should have been consulted and the heritage assets assessed using appropriate expertise where necessary. Where a site on which development is proposed includes or has the potential to include heritage assets with archaeological interest, local planning authorities should require developers to submit an appropriate desk-based assessment and, where necessary, a field evaluation.

129. Local planning authorities should identify and assess the particular significance of any heritage asset that may be affected by a proposal (including by development affecting the setting of a heritage asset) taking account of the available evidence and any necessary expertise. They should take this assessment into account when considering the impact of a proposal on a heritage asset, to avoid or minimise conflict between the heritage asset's conservation and any aspect of the proposal.

130. Where there is evidence of deliberate neglect of or damage to a heritage asset the deteriorated state of the heritage asset should not be taken into account in any decision.

131. In determining planning applications, local planning authorities should take account of:

- the desirability of sustaining and enhancing the significance of heritage assets and putting them to viable uses consistent with their conservation;
- the positive contribution that conservation of heritage assets can make to sustainable communities including their economic vitality; and
- the desirability of new development making a positive contribution to local character and distinctiveness.

132. When considering the impact of a proposed development on the significance of a designated heritage asset, great weight should be given to the asset's conservation. The more important the asset, the greater the weight should be. Significance can be harmed or lost through alteration or destruction of the heritage asset or development within its setting. As heritage assets are irreplaceable, any harm or loss should require clear and convincing justification. Substantial harm to or loss of a grade II listed building, park or garden should be

exceptional. Substantial harm to or loss of designated heritage assets of the highest significance, notably scheduled monuments, protected wreck sites, battlefields, grade I and II° listed buildings, grade I and II° registered parks and gardens, and World Heritage Sites, should be wholly exceptional.

133. Where a proposed development will lead to substantial harm to or total loss of significance of a designated heritage asset, local planning authorities should refuse consent, unless it can be demonstrated that the substantial harm or loss is necessary to achieve substantial public benefits that outweigh that harm or loss, or all of the following apply:

- the nature of the heritage asset prevents all reasonable uses of the site; and
- no viable use of the heritage asset itself can be found in the medium term through appropriate marketing that will enable its conservation; and
- conservation by grant-funding or some form of charitable or public ownership is demonstrably not possible; and
- the harm or loss is outweighed by the benefit of bringing the site back into use.

134. Where a development proposal will lead to less than substantial harm to the significance of a designated heritage asset, this harm should be weighed against the public benefits of the proposal, including securing its optimum viable use.

135. The effect of an application on the significance of a non-designated heritage asset should be taken into account in determining the application. In weighing applications that affect directly or indirectly non designated heritage assets, a balanced judgement will be required having regard to the scale of any harm or loss and the significance of the heritage asset.

136. Local planning authorities should not permit loss of the whole or part of a heritage asset without taking all reasonable steps to ensure the new development will proceed after the loss has occurred.

137. Local planning authorities should look for opportunities for new development within Conservation Areas and World Heritage Sites and within the setting of heritage assets to enhance or better reveal their significance. Proposals that preserve those elements of the setting that make a positive contribution to or better reveal the significance of the asset should be treated favourably.

138. Not all elements of a World Heritage Site or Conservation Area will necessarily contribute to its significance. Loss of a building (or other element) which makes a positive contribution to the significance of the Conservation Area or World Heritage Site should be treated either as substantial harm under paragraph 133 or less than substantial harm under paragraph 134, as appropriate, taking into account the relative significance of the element affected and its contribution to the significance of the Conservation Area or World Heritage Site as a whole.

139. Non-designated heritage assets of archaeological interest that are demonstrably of equivalent significance to scheduled monuments, should be considered subject to the policies for designated heritage assets.

140. Local planning authorities should assess whether the benefits of a proposal for enabling development, which would otherwise conflict with planning policies but which would secure the future conservation of a heritage asset, outweigh the disbenefits of departing from those policies.

141. Local planning authorities should make information about the significance of the historic environment gathered as part of plan-making or development management publicly accessible. They should also require developers to record and advance understanding of the significance of any heritage assets to be lost (wholly or in part) in a manner proportionate to their importance and the impact, and to make this evidence (and any archive generated)

publicly accessible.[30] However, the ability to record evidence of our past should not be a factor in deciding whether such loss should be permitted.

13. Facilitating the sustainable use of minerals

142. Minerals are essential to support sustainable economic growth and our quality of life. It is therefore important that there is a sufficient supply of material to provide the infrastructure, buildings, energy and goods that the country needs. However, since minerals are a finite natural resource, and can only be worked where they are found, it is important to make best use of them to secure their long-term conservation.

143. In preparing Local Plans, local planning authorities should:

- identify and include policies for extraction of mineral resource of local and national importance in their area, but should not identify new sites or extensions to existing sites for peat extraction;
- so far as practicable, take account of the contribution that substitute or secondary and recycled materials and minerals waste would make to the supply of materials, before considering extraction of primary materials, whilst aiming to source minerals supplies indigenously;
- define Minerals Safeguarding Areas and adopt appropriate policies in order that known locations of specific minerals resources of local and national importance are not needlessly sterilised by non-mineral development, whilst not creating a presumption that resources defined will be worked; and define Minerals Consultation Areas based on these Minerals Safeguarding Areas;
- safeguard:
  - existing, planned and potential rail heads, rail links to quarries, wharfage and associated storage, handling and processing facilities for the bulk transport by rail, sea or inland waterways of minerals, including recycled, secondary and marine-dredged materials; and
  - existing, planned and potential sites for concrete batching, the manufacture of coated materials, other concrete products and the handling, processing and distribution of substitute, recycled and secondary aggregate material.
- set out policies to encourage the prior extraction of minerals, where practicable and environmentally feasible, if it is necessary for non-mineral development to take place;
- set out environmental criteria, in line with the policies in this Framework, against which planning applications will be assessed so as to ensure that permitted operations do not have unacceptable adverse impacts on the natural and historic environment or human health, including from noise, dust, visual intrusion, traffic, tip- and quarry-slope stability, differential settlement of quarry backfill, mining subsidence, increased flood risk, impacts on the flow and quantity of surface and groundwater and migration of contamination from the site; and take into account the cumulative effects of multiple impacts from individual sites and/or a number of sites in a locality;
- when developing noise limits, recognise that some noisy short-term activities, which may otherwise be regarded as unacceptable, are unavoidable to facilitate minerals extraction; and
- put in place policies to ensure worked land is reclaimed at the earliest opportunity, taking account of aviation safety, and that high quality restoration and aftercare of mineral sites takes place, including for agriculture (safeguarding the long term potential of best and most versatile agricultural land and conserving soil resources), geodiversity, biodiversity, native woodland, the historic environment and recreation.

144. When determining planning applications, local planning authorities should:

- give great weight to the benefits of the mineral extraction, including to the economy;
- as far as is practical, provide for the maintenance of landbanks of non-energy minerals

from outside National Parks, the Broads, Areas of Outstanding Natural Beauty and World Heritage sites, Scheduled Monuments and Conservation Areas;

- ensure, in granting planning permission for mineral development, that there are no unacceptable adverse impacts on the natural and historic environment, human health or aviation safety, and take into account the cumulative effect of multiple impacts from individual sites and/or from a number of sites in a locality;
- ensure that any unavoidable noise, dust and particle emissions and any blasting vibrations are controlled, mitigated or removed at source,[31] and establish appropriate noise limits for extraction in proximity to noise sensitive properties;
- not grant planning permission for peat extraction from new or extended sites;
- provide for restoration and aftercare at the earliest opportunity to be carried out to high environmental standards, through the application of appropriate conditions, where necessary. Bonds or other financial guarantees to underpin planning conditions should only be sought in exceptional circumstances;
- not normally permit other development proposals in mineral safeguarding areas where they might constrain potential future use for these purposes;
- consider how to meet any demand for small-scale extraction of building stone at, or close to, relic quarries needed for the repair of heritage assets, taking account of the need to protect designated sites; and
- recognise the small-scale nature and impact of building and roofing stone quarries, and the need for a flexible approach to the potentially long duration of planning permissions reflecting the intermittent or low rate of working at many sites.

145. Minerals planning authorities should plan for a steady and adequate supply of aggregates by:

- preparing an annual Local Aggregate Assessment, either individually or jointly by agreement with another or other mineral planning authorities, based on a rolling average of 10 years sales data and other relevant local information, and an assessment of all supply options (including marine dredged, secondary and recycled sources);
- participating in the operation of an Aggregate Working Party and taking the advice of that Party into account when preparing their Local Aggregate Assessment;
- making provision for the land-won and other elements of their Local Aggregate Assessment in their mineral plans taking account of the advice of the Aggregate Working Parties and the National Aggregate Co-ordinating Group as appropriate. Such provision should take the form of specific sites, preferred areas and/or areas of search and locational criteria as appropriate;
- taking account of published National and Sub National Guidelines on future provision which should be used as a guideline when planning for the future demand for and supply of aggregates;
- using landbanks of aggregate minerals reserves principally as an indicator of the security of aggregate minerals supply, and to indicate the additional provision that needs to be made for new aggregate extraction and alternative supplies in mineral plans;
- making provision for the maintenance of landbanks of at least 7 years for sand and gravel and at least 10 years for crushed rock, whilst ensuring that the capacity of operations to supply a wide range of materials is not compromised. Longer periods may be appropriate to take account of the need to supply a range of types of aggregates, locations of permitted reserves relative to markets, and productive capacity of permitted sites;
- ensuring that large landbanks bound up in very few sites do not stifle competition; and
- calculating and maintaining separate landbanks for any aggregate materials of a specific type or quality which have a distinct and separate market.

146. Minerals planning authorities should plan for a steady and adequate supply of industrial minerals by:

- co-operating with neighbouring and more distant authorities to co-ordinate the planning of industrial minerals to ensure adequate provision is made to support their likely use in industrial and manufacturing processes;
- encouraging safeguarding or stockpiling so that important minerals remain available for use;
- providing a stock of permitted reserves to support the level of actual and proposed investment required for new or existing plant and the maintenance and improvement of existing plant and equipment, as follows:
  - at least 10 years for individual silica sand sites;
  - at least 15 years for cement primary (chalk and limestone) and secondary (clay and shale) materials to maintain an existing plant, and for silica sand sites where significant new capital is required; and
  - at least 25 years for brick clay, and for cement primary and secondary materials to support a new kiln.
- taking account of the need for provision of brick clay from a number of different sources to enable appropriate blends to be made.

147. Minerals planning authorities should also:

- when planning for on-shore oil and gas development, including unconventional hydrocarbons, clearly distinguish between the three phases of development (exploration, appraisal and production) and address constraints on production and processing within areas that are licensed for oil and gas exploration or production;
- encourage underground gas and carbon storage and associated infrastructure if local geological circumstances indicate its feasibility;
- indicate any areas where coal extraction and the disposal of colliery spoil may be acceptable;
- encourage capture and use of methane from coal mines in active and abandoned coalfield areas; and
- provide for coal producers to extract separately, and if necessary stockpile, fireclay so that it remains available for use.

148. When determining planning applications, minerals planning authorities should ensure that the integrity and safety of underground storage facilities are appropriate, taking into account the maintenance of gas pressure, prevention of leakage of gas and the avoidance of pollution.

149. Permission should not be given for the extraction of coal unless the proposal is environmentally acceptable, or can be made so by planning conditions or obligations; or if not, it provides national, local or community benefits which clearly outweigh the likely impacts to justify the grant of planning permission.

PLAN-MAKING

Local Plans

150. Local Plans are the key to delivering sustainable development that reflects the vision and aspirations of local communities. Planning decisions must be taken in accordance with the development plan unless material considerations indicate otherwise.[32]

151. Local Plans must be prepared with the objective of contributing to the achievement of sustainable development.[33] To this end, they should be consistent with the principles and policies set out in this Framework, including the presumption in favour of sustainable development.

152. Local planning authorities should seek opportunities to achieve each of the economic, social and environmental dimensions of sustainable development, and net gains across all

three. Significant adverse impacts on any of these dimensions should be avoided and, wherever possible, alternative options which reduce or eliminate such impacts should be pursued. Where adverse impacts are unavoidable, measures to mitigate the impact should be considered. Where adequate mitigation measures are not possible, compensatory measures may be appropriate.

153. Each local planning authority should produce a Local Plan for its area. This can be reviewed in whole or in part to respond flexibly to changing circumstances. Any additional development plan documents should only be used where clearly justified. Supplementary planning documents should be used where they can help applicants make successful applications or aid infrastructure delivery, and should not be used to add unnecessarily to the financial burdens on development.

154. Local Plans should be aspirational but realistic. They should address the spatial implications of economic, social and environmental change. Local Plans should set out the opportunities for development and clear policies on what will or will not be permitted and where. Only policies that provide a clear indication of how a decision maker should react to a development proposal should be included in the plan.

155. Early and meaningful engagement and collaboration with neighbourhoods, local organisations and businesses is essential. A wide section of the community should be proactively engaged, so that Local Plans, as far as possible, reflect a collective vision and a set of agreed priorities for the sustainable development of the area, including those contained in any neighbourhood plans that have been made.

156. Local planning authorities should set out the **strategic priorities** for the area in the Local Plan. This should include strategic policies to deliver:

- the homes and jobs needed in the area;
- the provision of retail, leisure and other commercial development;
- the provision of infrastructure for transport, telecommunications, waste management, water supply, wastewater, flood risk and coastal change management, and the provision of minerals and energy (including heat);
- the provision of health, security, community and cultural infrastructure and other local facilities; and
- climate change mitigation and adaptation, conservation and enhancement of the natural and historic environment, including landscape.

157. Crucially, Local Plans should:

- plan positively for the development and infrastructure required in the area to meet the objectives, principles and policies of this Framework;
- be drawn up over an appropriate time scale, preferably a 15-year time horizon, take account of longer term requirements, and be kept up to date;
- be based on co-operation with neighbouring authorities, public, voluntary and private sector organisations;
- indicate broad locations for strategic development on a key diagram and land-use designations on a proposals map;
- allocate sites to promote development and flexible use of land, bringing forward new land where necessary, and provide detail on form, scale, access and quantum of development where appropriate;
- identify areas where it may be necessary to limit freedom to change the uses of buildings, and support such restrictions with a clear explanation;
- identify land where development would be inappropriate, for instance because of its environmental or historic significance; and
- contain a clear strategy for enhancing the natural, built and historic environment, and supporting Nature Improvement Areas where they have been identified.

Using a proportionate evidence base

158. Each local planning authority should ensure that the Local Plan is based on adequate, up-to-date and relevant evidence about the economic, social and environmental characteristics and prospects of the area. Local planning authorities should ensure that their assessment of and strategies for housing, employment and other uses are integrated, and that they take full account of relevant market and economic signals.

Housing

159. Local planning authorities should have a clear understanding of housing needs in their area. They should:

- prepare a Strategic Housing Market Assessment to assess their full housing needs, working with neighbouring authorities where housing market areas cross administrative boundaries. The Strategic Housing Market Assessment should identify the scale and mix of housing and the range of tenures that the local population is likely to need over the plan period which:
  - meets household and population projections, taking account of migration and demographic change;
  - addresses the need for all types of housing, including affordable housing and the needs of different groups in the community (such as, but not limited to, families with children, older people, people with disabilities, service families and people wishing to build their own homes);[34] and
  - caters for housing demand and the scale of housing supply necessary to meet this demand;
- prepare a Strategic Housing Land Availability Assessment to establish realistic assumptions about the availability, suitability and the likely economic viability of land to meet the identified need for housing over the plan period.

Business

160. Local planning authorities should have a clear understanding of business needs within the economic markets operating in and across their area. To achieve this, they should:

- work together with county and neighbouring authorities and with Local Enterprise Partnerships to prepare and maintain a robust evidence base to understand both existing business needs and likely changes in the market; and
- work closely with the business community to understand their changing needs and identify and address barriers to investment, including a lack of housing, infrastructure or viability.

161. Local planning authorities should use this evidence base to assess:

- the needs for land or floorspace for economic development, including both the quantitative and qualitative needs for all foreseeable types of economic activity over the plan period, including for retail and leisure development;
- the existing and future supply of land available for economic development and its sufficiency and suitability to meet the identified needs. Reviews of land available for economic development should be undertaken at the same time as, or combined with, Strategic Housing Land Availability Assessments and should include a reappraisal of the suitability of previously allocated land;
- the role and function of town centres and the relationship between them, including any trends in the performance of centres;
- the capacity of existing centres to accommodate new town centre development;
- locations of deprivation which may benefit from planned remedial action; and
- the needs of the food production industry and any barriers to investment that planning can resolve.

Infrastructure

162. Local planning authorities should work with other authorities and providers to:

- assess the quality and capacity of infrastructure for transport, water supply, wastewater and its treatment, energy (including heat), telecommunications, utilities, waste, health, social care, education, flood risk and coastal change management, and its ability to meet forecast demands; and
- take account of the need for strategic infrastructure including nationally significant infrastructure within their areas.

Minerals

163. Minerals planning authorities should work with other relevant organisations to use the best available information to:

- develop and maintain an understanding of the extent and location of mineral resource in their areas; and
- assess the projected demand for their use, taking full account of opportunities to use materials from secondary and other sources which could provide suitable alternatives to primary materials.

Defence, national security, counter-terrorism and resilience

164. Local planning authorities should:

- work with the Ministry of Defence's Strategic Planning Team to ensure that they have and take into account the most up-to-date information about defence and security needs in their area; and
- work with local advisors and others to ensure that they have and take into account the most up-to-date information about higher risk sites in their area for malicious threats and natural hazards, including steps that can be taken to reduce vulnerability and increase resilience.

Environment

165. Planning policies and decisions should be based on up-to-date information about the natural environment and other characteristics of the area including drawing, for example, from River Basin Management Plans. Working with Local Nature Partnerships where appropriate, this should include an assessment of existing and potential components of ecological networks. A sustainability appraisal which meets the requirements of the European Directive on strategic environmental assessment should be an integral part of the plan preparation process, and should consider all the likely significant effects on the environment, economic and social factors.

166. Local Plans may require a variety of other environmental assessments, including under the Habitats Regulations where there is a likely significant effect on a European wildlife site (which may not necessarily be within the same local authority area), Strategic Flood Risk Assessment and assessments of the physical constraints on land use.[35] Wherever possible, assessments should share the same evidence base and be conducted over similar timescales, but local authorities should take care to ensure that the purposes and statutory requirements of different assessment processes are respected.

167. Assessments should be proportionate, and should not repeat policy assessment that has already been undertaken. Wherever possible the local planning authority should consider how the preparation of any assessment will contribute to the plan's evidence base. The process should be started early in the plan-making process and key stakeholders should be consulted in identifying the issues that the assessment must cover.

168. Shoreline Management Plans should inform the evidence base for planning in coastal areas. The prediction of future impacts should include the longer term nature and inherent uncertainty of coastal processes (including coastal landslip), and take account of climate change.

Historic environment

169. Local planning authorities should have up-to-date evidence about the historic environment in their area and use it to assess the significance of heritage assets and the contribution they make to their environment. They should also use it to predict the likelihood that currently unidentified heritage assets, particularly sites of historic and archaeological interest, will be discovered in the future. Local planning authorities should either maintain or have access to a historic environment record.

170. Where appropriate, landscape character assessments should also be prepared, integrated with assessment of historic landscape character, and for areas where there are major expansion options assessments of landscape sensitivity.

Health and well-being

171. Local planning authorities should work with public health leads and health organisations to understand and take account of the health status and needs of the local population (such as for sports, recreation and places of worship), including expected future changes, and any information about relevant barriers to improving health and well-being.

Public safety from major accidents

172. Planning policies should be based on up-to-date information on the location of major hazards and on the mitigation of the consequences of major accidents.

Ensuring viability and deliverability

173. Pursuing sustainable development requires careful attention to viability and costs in plan-making and decision-taking. Plans should be deliverable. Therefore, the sites and the scale of development identified in the plan should not be subject to such a scale of obligations and policy burdens that their ability to be developed viably is threatened. To ensure viability, the costs of any requirements likely to be applied to development, such as requirements for affordable housing, standards, infrastructure contributions or other requirements should, when taking account of the normal cost of development and mitigation, provide competitive returns to a willing land owner and willing developer to enable the development to be deliverable.

174. Local planning authorities should set out their policy on local standards in the Local Plan, including requirements for affordable housing. They should assess the likely cumulative impacts on development in their area of all existing and proposed local standards, supplementary planning documents and policies that support the development plan, when added to nationally required standards. In order to be appropriate, the cumulative impact of these standards and policies should not put implementation of the plan at serious risk, and should facilitate development throughout the economic cycle. Evidence supporting the assessment should be proportionate, using only appropriate available evidence.

175. Where practical, Community Infrastructure Levy charges should be worked up and tested alongside the Local Plan. The Community Infrastructure Levy should support and incentivise new development, particularly by placing control over a meaningful proportion of the funds raised with the neighbourhoods where development takes place.

176. Where safeguards are necessary to make a particular development acceptable in planning terms (such as environmental mitigation or compensation), the development should not be approved if the measures required cannot be secured through appropriate

conditions or agreements. The need for such safeguards should be clearly justified through discussions with the applicant, and the options for keeping such costs to a minimum fully explored, so that development is not inhibited unnecessarily.

177. It is equally important to ensure that there is a reasonable prospect that planned infrastructure is deliverable in a timely fashion. To facilitate this, it is important that local planning authorities understand district-wide development costs at the time Local Plans are drawn up. For this reason, infrastructure and development policies should be planned at the same time, in the Local Plan. Any affordable housing or local standards requirements that may be applied to development should be assessed at the plan-making stage, where possible, and kept under review.

Planning strategically across local boundaries

178. Public bodies have a duty to cooperate on planning issues that cross administrative boundaries, particularly those which relate to the **strategic priorities** set out in paragraph 156. The Government expects joint working on areas of common interest to be diligently undertaken for the mutual benefit of neighbouring authorities.

179. Local planning authorities should work collaboratively with other bodies to ensure that strategic priorities across local boundaries are properly co-ordinated and clearly reflected in individual Local Plans.[36] Joint working should enable local planning authorities to work together to meet development requirements which cannot wholly be met within their own areas – for instance, because of a lack of physical capacity or because to do so would cause significant harm to the principles and policies of this Framework. As part of this process, they should consider producing joint planning policies on strategic matters and informal strategies such as joint infrastructure and investment plans.

180. Local planning authorities should take account of different geographic areas, including travel-to-work areas. In two tier areas, county and district authorities should cooperate with each other on relevant issues. Local planning authorities should work collaboratively on strategic planning priorities to enable delivery of sustainable development in consultation with Local Enterprise Partnerships and Local Nature Partnerships. Local planning authorities should also work collaboratively with private sector bodies, utility and infrastructure providers.

181. Local planning authorities will be expected to demonstrate evidence of having effectively cooperated to plan for issues with cross-boundary impacts when their Local Plans are submitted for examination. This could be by way of plans or policies prepared as part of a joint committee, a memorandum of understanding or a jointly prepared strategy which is presented as evidence of an agreed position. Cooperation should be a continuous process of engagement from initial thinking through to implementation, resulting in a final position where plans are in place to provide the land and infrastructure necessary to support current and projected future levels of development.

Examining Local Plans

182. The Local Plan will be examined by an independent inspector whose role is to assess whether the plan has been prepared in accordance with the Duty to Cooperate, legal and procedural requirements, and whether it is sound. A local planning authority should submit a plan for examination which it considers is 'sound' – namely that it is:

- **Positively prepared** – the plan should be prepared based on a strategy which seeks to meet objectively assessed development and infrastructure requirements, including unmet requirements from neighbouring authorities where it is reasonable to do so and consistent with achieving sustainable development;
- **Justified** – the plan should be the most appropriate strategy, when considered against the reasonable alternatives, based on proportionate evidence;

- **Effective** – the plan should be deliverable over its period and based on effective joint working on cross-boundary strategic priorities; and
- **Consistent with national policy** – the plan should enable the delivery of sustainable development in accordance with the policies in the Framework.

Neighbourhood plans

183. Neighbourhood planning gives communities direct power to develop a shared vision for their neighbourhood and deliver the sustainable development they need. Parishes and neighbourhood forums can use neighbourhood planning to:

- set planning policies through neighbourhood plans to determine decisions on planning applications; and
- grant planning permission through Neighbourhood Development Orders and Community Right to Build Orders for specific development which complies with the order.

184. Neighbourhood planning provides a powerful set of tools for local people to ensure that they get the right types of development for their community. The ambition of the neighbourhood should be aligned with the strategic needs and priorities of the wider local area. Neighbourhood plans must be in general conformity with the strategic policies of the Local Plan. To facilitate this, local planning authorities should set out clearly their strategic policies for the area and ensure that an up-to-date Local Plan is in place as quickly as possible. Neighbourhood plans should reflect these policies and neighbourhoods should plan positively to support them. Neighbourhood plans and orders should not promote less development than set out in the Local Plan or undermine its strategic policies.

185. Outside these strategic elements, neighbourhood plans will be able to shape and direct sustainable development in their area. Once a neighbourhood plan has demonstrated its general conformity with the strategic policies of the Local Plan and is brought into force, the policies it contains take precedence over existing non-strategic policies in the Local Plan for that neighbourhood, where they are in conflict. Local planning authorities should avoid duplicating planning processes for non-strategic policies where a neighbourhood plan is in preparation.

DECISION-TAKING

186. Local planning authorities should approach decision-taking in a positive way to foster the delivery of sustainable development. The relationship between decision-taking and plan-making should be seamless, translating plans into high quality development on the ground.

187. Local planning authorities should look for solutions rather than problems, and decision-takers at every level should seek to approve applications for sustainable development where possible. Local planning authorities should work proactively with applicants to secure developments that improve the economic, social and environmental conditions of the area.

Pre-application engagement and front loading

188. Early engagement has significant potential to improve the efficiency and effectiveness of the planning application system for all parties. Good quality pre-application discussion enables better coordination between public and private resources and improved outcomes for the community.

189. Local planning authorities have a key role to play in encouraging other parties to take maximum advantage of the pre-application stage. They cannot require that a developer engages with them before submitting a planning application, but they should encourage take-up of any pre-application services they do offer. They should also, where they think this

would be beneficial, encourage any applicants who are not already required to do so by law to engage with the local community before submitting their applications.

190. The more issues that can be resolved at pre-application stage, the greater the benefits. For their role in the planning system to be effective and positive, statutory planning consultees will need to take the same early, pro-active approach, and provide advice in a timely manner throughout the development process. This assists local planning authorities in issuing timely decisions, helping to ensure that applicants do not experience unnecessary delays and costs.

191. The participation of other consenting bodies in pre-application discussions should enable early consideration of all the fundamental issues relating to whether a particular development will be acceptable in principle, even where other consents relating to how a development is built or operated are needed at a later stage. Wherever possible, parallel processing of other consents should be encouraged to help speed up the process and resolve any issues as early as possible.

192. The right information is crucial to good decision-taking, particularly where formal assessments are required (such as Environmental Impact Assessment, Habitats Regulations Assessment and Flood Risk Assessment). To avoid delay, applicants should discuss what information is needed with the local planning authority and expert bodies as early as possible.

193. Local planning authorities should publish a list of their information requirements for applications, which should be proportionate to the nature and scale of development proposals and reviewed on a frequent basis. Local planning authorities should only request supporting information that is relevant, necessary and material to the application in question.

194. Local planning authorities should consult the appropriate bodies when planning, or determining applications, for development around major hazards.

195. Applicants and local planning authorities should consider the potential of entering into planning performance agreements, where this might achieve a faster and more effective application process.

Determining applications

196. The planning system is plan-led. Planning law requires that applications for planning permission must be determined in accordance with the development plan,[37] unless material considerations indicate otherwise.[38] This Framework is a material consideration in planning decisions.

197. In assessing and determining development proposals, local planning authorities should apply the presumption in favour of sustainable development.

198. Where a Neighbourhood Development Order has been made, a planning application is not required for development that is within the terms of the order. Where a planning application conflicts with a neighbourhood plan that has been brought into force, planning permission should not normally be granted.

Tailoring planning controls to local circumstances

199. Local planning authorities should consider using Local Development Orders to relax planning controls for particular areas or categories of development, where the impacts would be acceptable, and in particular where this would promote economic, social or environmental gains for the area, such as boosting enterprise.

200. The use of Article 4 directions to remove national permitted development rights should be limited to situations where this is necessary to protect local amenity or the wellbeing of the

area (this could include the use of Article 4 directions to require planning permission for the demolition of local facilities). Similarly, planning conditions should not be used to restrict national permitted development rights unless there is clear justification to do so.

201. Communities can use Neighbourhood Development Orders and Community Right to Build Orders to grant planning permission. Where such an order is in place, no further planning permission is required for development which falls within its scope.

202. Neighbourhood Development Orders and Community Right to Build Orders require the support of the local community through a referendum. Therefore, local planning authorities should take a proactive and positive approach to proposals, working collaboratively with community organisations to resolve any issues before draft orders are submitted for examination. Policies in this Framework that relate to decision-taking should be read as applying to the consideration of proposed Neighbourhood Development Orders, wherever this is appropriate given the context and relevant legislation.

Planning conditions and obligations

203. Local planning authorities should consider whether otherwise unacceptable development could be made acceptable through the use of conditions or planning obligations. Planning obligations should only be used where it is not possible to address unacceptable impacts through a planning condition.

204. Planning obligations should only be sought where they meet all of the following tests:

- necessary to make the development acceptable in planning terms;
- directly related to the development; and
- fairly and reasonably related in scale and kind to the development.

205. Where obligations are being sought or revised, local planning authorities should take account of changes in market conditions over time and, wherever appropriate, be sufficiently flexible to prevent planned development being stalled.

206. Planning conditions should only be imposed where they are necessary, relevant to planning and to the development to be permitted, enforceable, precise and reasonable in all other respects.

Enforcement

207. Effective enforcement is important as a means of maintaining public confidence in the planning system. Enforcement action is discretionary, and local planning authorities should act proportionately in responding to suspected breaches of planning control. Local planning authorities should consider publishing a local enforcement plan to manage enforcement proactively, in a way that is appropriate to their area. This should set out how they will monitor the implementation of planning permissions, investigate alleged cases of unauthorised development and take action where it is appropriate to do so.

ANNEX 1: IMPLEMENTATION

208. The policies in this Framework apply from the day of publication.

209. The National Planning Policy Framework aims to strengthen local decision making and reinforce the importance of up-to-date plans.

210. Planning law requires that applications for planning permission must be determined in accordance with the development plan unless material considerations indicate otherwise.

211. For the purposes of decision-taking, the policies in the Local Plan (and the London Plan) should not be considered out-of-date simply because they were adopted prior to the publication of this Framework.

212. However, the policies contained in this Framework are material considerations which local planning authorities should take into account from the day of its publication. The Framework must also be taken into account in the preparation of plans.

213. Plans may, therefore, need to be revised to take into account the policies in this Framework. This should be progressed as quickly as possible, either through a partial review or by preparing a new plan.

214. For 12 months from the day of publication, decision-takers may continue to give full weight to relevant policies adopted since 2004[39] even if there is a limited degree of conflict with this Framework.

215. In other cases and following this 12-month period, due weight should be given to relevant policies in existing plans according to their degree of consistency with this framework (the closer the policies in the plan to the policies in the Framework, the greater the weight that may be given).

216. From the day of publication, decision-takers may also give weight[40] to relevant policies in emerging plans according to:

- the stage of preparation of the emerging plan (the more advanced the preparation, the greater the weight that may be given);
- the extent to which there are unresolved objections to relevant policies (the less significant the unresolved objections, the greater the weight that may be given); and
- the degree of consistency of the relevant policies in the emerging plan to the policies in this Framework (the closer the policies in the emerging plan to the policies in the Framework, the greater the weight that may be given).

217. Advice will be available immediately and free of charge from a support service provided by the Local Government Association, the Planning Inspectorate and the Department for Communities and Local Government. This will assist local planning authorities in considering the need to update their Local Plan and taking forward efficient and effective reviews.

218. Where it would be appropriate and assist the process of preparing or amending Local Plans, regional strategy[41] policies can be reflected in Local Plans by undertaking a partial review focusing on the specific issues involved. Local planning authorities may also continue to draw on evidence that informed the preparation of regional strategies to support Local Plan policies, supplemented as needed by up-to-date, robust local evidence.

219. This Framework has been drafted to reflect the law following the implementation of the Localism Act 2011, so, where appropriate, policies will apply only when the relevant legislation is in force.

ANNEX 2: GLOSSARY

Affordable housing: Social rented, affordable rented and intermediate housing, provided to eligible households whose needs are not met by the market. Eligibility is determined with regard to local incomes and local house prices. Affordable housing should include provisions to remain at an affordable price for future eligible households or for the subsidy to be recycled for alternative affordable housing provision.

Social rented housing is owned by local authorities and private registered providers (as defined in section 80 of the Housing and Regeneration Act 2008), for which guideline target rents are determined through the national rent regime. It may also be owned by other persons and provided under equivalent rental arrangements to the above, as agreed with the local authority or with the Homes and Communities Agency.

Affordable rented housing is let by local authorities or private registered providers of social housing to households who are eligible for social rented housing. Affordable Rent is subject to rent controls that require a rent of no more than 80% of the local market rent (including service charges, where applicable).

Intermediate housing is homes for sale and rent provided at a cost above social rent, but below market levels subject to the criteria in the Affordable Housing definition above. These can include shared equity (shared ownership and equity loans), other low cost homes for sale and intermediate rent, but not affordable rented housing.

Homes that do not meet the above definition of affordable housing, such as 'low cost market' housing, may not be considered as affordable housing for planning purposes.

Aged or veteran tree: A tree which, because of its great age, size or condition is of exceptional value for wildlife, in the landscape, or culturally.

Air Quality Management Areas: Areas designated by local authorities because they are not likely to achieve national air quality objectives by the relevant deadlines.

Ancient woodland: An area that has been wooded continuously since at least 1600 AD.

Archaeological interest: There will be archaeological interest in a heritage asset if it holds, or potentially may hold, evidence of past human activity worthy of expert investigation at some point. Heritage assets with archaeological interest are the primary source of evidence about the substance and evolution of places, and of the people and cultures that made them.

Article 4 direction: A direction which withdraws automatic planning permission granted by the General Permitted Development Order.

Best and most versatile agricultural land: Land in grades 1, 2 and 3a of the Agricultural Land Classification.

Birds and Habitats Directives: European Directives to conserve natural habitats and wild fauna and flora.

Climate change adaptation: Adjustments to natural or human systems in response to actual or expected climatic factors or their effects, including from changes in rainfall and rising temperatures, which moderate harm or exploit beneficial opportunity.

Climate change mitigation: Action to reduce the impact of human activity on the climate system, primarily through reducing greenhouse gas emissions.

Coastal Change Management Area: An area identified in Local Plans as likely to be affected by coastal change (physical change to the shoreline through erosion, coastal landslip, permanent inundation or coastal accretion).

Conservation (for heritage policy): The process of maintaining and managing change to a heritage asset in a way that sustains and, where appropriate, enhances its significance.

Community Forest: An area identified through the England Community Forest Programme to revitalise countryside and green space in and around major conurbations.

Community Infrastructure Levy: A levy allowing local authorities to raise funds from owners or developers of land undertaking new building projects in their area.

Community Right to Build Order: An Order made by the local planning authority (under the Town and Country Planning Act 1990) that grants planning permission for a site-specific development proposal or classes of development.

Competent person (to prepare site investigation information): A person with a recognised relevant qualification, sufficient experience in dealing with the type(s) of pollution or land instability, and membership of a relevant professional organisation.

Decentralised energy: Local renewable energy and local low-carbon energy usually but not always on a relatively small scale encompassing a diverse range of technologies.

Designated heritage asset: A World Heritage Site, Scheduled Monument, Listed Building, Protected Wreck Site, Registered Park and Garden, Registered Battlefield or Conservation Area designated under the relevant legislation.

Development plan: This includes adopted Local Plans, neighbourhood plans and the London Plan, and is defined in section 38 of the Planning and Compulsory Purchase Act 2004. (Regional strategies remain part of the development plan until they are abolished by Order using powers taken in the Localism Act. It is the government's clear policy intention to revoke the regional strategies outside of London, subject to the outcome of the environmental assessments that are currently being undertaken.)

Economic development: Development, including those within the B Use Classes, public and community uses and main town centre uses (but excluding housing development).

Ecological networks: These link sites of biodiversity importance.

Ecosystem services: The benefits people obtain from ecosystems such as, food, water, flood and disease control and recreation.

Edge of centre: For retail purposes, a location that is well connected and up to 300 metres of the primary shopping area. For all other main town centre uses, a location within 300 metres of a town centre boundary. For office development, this includes locations outside the town centre but within 500 metres of a public transport interchange. In determining whether a site falls within the definition of edge of centre, account should be taken of local circumstances.

Environmental Impact Assessment: A procedure to be followed for certain types of project to ensure that decisions are made in full knowledge of any likely significant effects on the environment.

European site: This includes candidate Special Areas of Conservation, Sites of Community Importance, Special Areas of Conservation and Special Protection Areas, and is defined in regulation 8 of the Conservation of Habitats and Species Regulations 2010.

Geodiversity: The range of rocks, minerals, fossils, soils and landforms.

Green infrastructure: A network of multi-functional green space, urban and rural, which is capable of delivering a wide range of environmental and quality of life benefits for local communities.

Heritage asset: A building, monument, site, place, area or landscape identified as having a degree of significance meriting consideration in planning decisions, because of its heritage interest. Heritage asset includes designated heritage assets and assets identified by the local planning authority (including local listing).

Heritage Coast: Areas of undeveloped coastline which are managed to conserve their natural beauty and, where appropriate, to improve accessibility for visitors.

Historic environment: All aspects of the environment resulting from the interaction between people and places through time, including all surviving physical remains of past human activity, whether visible, buried or submerged, and landscaped and planted or managed flora.

Historic environment record: Information services that seek to provide access to comprehensive and dynamic resources relating to the historic environment of a defined geographic area for public benefit and use.

Inclusive design: Designing the built environment, including buildings and their surrounding spaces, to ensure that they can be accessed and used by everyone.

Instrumentation operated in the national interest: Includes meteorological and climate monitoring installations, satellite and radio communication, defence and national security sites and magnetic calibration facilities operated by or on behalf of the Government, delegated authorities or for defence purposes.

International, national and locally designated sites of importance for biodiversity: All international sites (Special Areas of Conservation, Special Protection Areas, and Ramsar sites), national sites (Sites of Special Scientific Interest) and locally designated sites including Local Wildlife Sites.

Local Development Order: An Order made by a local planning authority (under the Town and Country Planning Act 1990) that grants planning permission for a specific development proposal or classes of development.

Local Enterprise Partnership: A body, designated by the Secretary of State for Communities and Local Government, established for the purpose of creating or improving the conditions for economic growth in an area.

Local Nature Partnership: A body, designated by the Secretary of State for Environment, Food and Rural Affairs, established for the purpose of protecting and improving the natural environment in an area and the benefits derived from it.

Local planning authority: The public authority whose duty it is to carry out specific planning functions for a particular area. All references to local planning authority apply to the district council, London borough council, county council, Broads Authority, National Park Authority and the Greater London Authority, to the extent appropriate to their responsibilities.

Local Plan: The plan for the future development of the local area, drawn up by the local planning authority in consultation with the community. In law this is described as the development plan documents adopted under the Planning and Compulsory Purchase Act 2004. Current core strategies or other planning policies, which under the regulations would be considered to be development plan documents, form part of the Local Plan. The term includes old policies which have been saved under the 2004 Act.

Main town centre uses: Retail development (including warehouse clubs and factory outlet centres); leisure, entertainment facilities the more intensive sport and recreation uses (including cinemas, restaurants, drive-through restaurants, bars and pubs, night-clubs, casinos, health and fitness centres, indoor bowling centres, and bingo halls); offices; and arts, culture and tourism development (including theatres, museums, galleries and concert halls, hotels and conference facilities).

Major Hazards: Major hazard installations and pipelines, licensed explosive sites and nuclear installations, around which Health and Safety Executive (and Office for Nuclear Regulation) consultation distances to mitigate the consequences to public safety of major accidents may apply.

Minerals of local and national importance: Minerals which are necessary to meet society's needs, including aggregates, brickclay (especially Etruria Marl and fireclay), silica sand (including high grade silica sands), cement raw materials, gypsum, salt, fluorspar, shallow and deep-mined coal, oil and gas (including hydrocarbons), tungsten, kaolin, ball clay, potash and local minerals of importance to heritage assets and local distinctiveness.

Mineral Safeguarding Area: An area designated by Minerals Planning Authorities which covers known deposits of minerals which are desired to be kept safeguarded from unnecessary sterilisation by non-mineral development.

National Trails: Long distance routes for walking, cycling and horse riding.

Nature Improvement Areas: Inter-connected networks of wildlife habitats intended to re-establish thriving wildlife populations and help species respond to the challenges of climate change.

Neighbourhood Development Order: An Order made by a local planning authority (under the Town and Country Planning Act 1990) through which Parish Councils and neighbourhood forums can grant planning permission for a specific development proposal or classes of development.

Neighbourhood plans: A plan prepared by a Parish Council or Neighbourhood Forum for a particular neighbourhood area (made under the Planning and Compulsory Purchase Act 2004).

Older people: People over retirement age, including the active, newly-retired through to the very frail elderly, whose housing needs can encompass accessible, adaptable general needs housing for those looking to downsize from family housing and the full range of retirement and specialised housing for those with support or care needs.

Open space: All open space of public value, including not just land, but also areas of water (such as rivers, canals, lakes and reservoirs) which offer important opportunities for sport and recreation and can act as a visual amenity.

Original building: A building as it existed on 1 July 1948 or, if constructed after 1 July 1948, as it was built originally.

Out of centre: A location which is not in or on the edge of a centre but not necessarily outside the urban area.

Out of town: A location out of centre that is outside the existing urban area.

People with disabilities: People have a disability if they have a physical or mental impairment, and that impairment has a substantial and long-term adverse effect on their ability to carry out normal day-to-day activities. These persons include, but are not limited to, people with ambulatory difficulties, blindness, learning difficulties, autism and mental health needs.

Planning condition: A condition imposed on a grant of planning permission (in accordance with the Town and Country Planning Act 1990) or a condition included in a Local Development Order or Neighbourhood Development Order.

Planning obligation: A legally enforceable obligation entered into under section 106 of the Town and Country Planning Act 1990 to mitigate the impacts of a development proposal.

Playing field: The whole of a site which encompasses at least one playing pitch as defined in the Town and Country Planning (Development Management Procedure) (England) Order 2010.

Pollution: Anything that affects the quality of land, air, water or soils, which might lead to an adverse impact on human health, the natural environment or general amenity. Pollution can arise from a range of emissions, including smoke, fumes, gases, dust, steam, odour, noise and light.

Previously developed land: Land which is or was occupied by a permanent structure, including the curtilage of the developed land (although it should not be assumed that the whole of the curtilage should be developed) and any associated fixed surface infrastructure. This excludes: land that is or has been occupied by agricultural or forestry buildings; land that has been developed for minerals extraction or waste disposal by landfill purposes where provision for restoration has been made through development control procedures; land in built-up areas such as private residential gardens, parks, recreation grounds and allotments; and land that was previously-developed but where the remains of the permanent structure or fixed surface structure have blended into the landscape in the process of time.

Primary shopping area: Defined area where retail development is concentrated (generally comprising the primary and those secondary frontages which are adjoining and closely related to the primary shopping frontage).

Primary and secondary frontages: Primary frontages are likely to include a high proportion of retail uses which may include food, drinks, clothing and household goods. Secondary frontages provide greater opportunities for a diversity of uses such as restaurants, cinemas and businesses.

Priority habitats and species: Species and Habitats of Principle Importance included in the England Biodiversity List published by the Secretary of State under section 41 of the Natural Environment and Rural Communities Act 2006.

Ramsar sites: Wetlands of international importance, designated under the 1971 Ramsar Convention.

Renewable and low carbon energy: Includes energy for heating and cooling as well as generating electricity. Renewable energy covers those energy flows that occur naturally and repeatedly in the environment – from the wind, the fall of water, the movement of the oceans, from the sun and also from biomass and deep geothermal heat. Low carbon technologies are those that can help reduce emissions (compared to conventional use of fossil fuels).

Rural exception sites: Small sites used for affordable housing in perpetuity where sites would not normally be used for housing. Rural exception sites seek to address the needs of the local community by accommodating households who are either current residents or have an existing family or employment connection. Small numbers of market homes may be allowed at the local authority's discretion, for example where essential to enable the delivery of affordable units without grant funding.

Safeguarding zone: An area defined in Circular 01/03: Safeguarding aerodromes, technical sites and military explosives storage areas, to safeguard such sites.

Setting of a heritage asset: The surroundings in which a heritage asset is experienced. Its extent is not fixed and may change as the asset and its surroundings evolve. Elements of a setting may make a positive or negative contribution to the significance of an asset, may affect the ability to appreciate that significance or may be neutral.

Shoreline Management Plans: A plan providing a large-scale assessment of the risk to people and to the developed, historic and natural environment associated with coastal processes.

Significance (for heritage policy): The value of a heritage asset to this and future generations because of its heritage interest. That interest may be archaeological, architectural, artistic or historic. Significance derives not only from a heritage asset's physical presence, but also from its setting.

Special Areas of Conservation: Areas given special protection under the European Union's Habitats Directive, which is transposed into UK law by the Habitats and Conservation of Species Regulations 2010.

Special Protection Areas: Areas which have been identified as being of international importance for the breeding, feeding, wintering or the migration of rare and vulnerable species of birds found within European Union countries. They are European designated sites, classified under the Birds Directive.

Site investigation information: Includes a risk assessment of land potentially affected by contamination, or ground stability and slope stability reports, as appropriate. All investigations of land potentially affected by contamination should be carried out in accordance with established procedures (such as BS10175 (2001) Code of Practice for the Investigation of Potentially Contaminated Sites). The minimum information that should be provided by an applicant is the report of a desk study and site reconnaissance.

Site of Special Scientific Interest: Sites designated by Natural England under the Wildlife and Countryside Act 1981.

Stepping stones: Pockets of habitat that, while not necessarily connected, facilitate the movement of species across otherwise inhospitable landscapes.

Strategic Environmental Assessment: A procedure (set out in the Environmental Assessment of Plans and Programmes Regulations 2004) which requires the formal environmental assessment of certain plans and programmes which are likely to have significant effects on the environment.

Supplementary planning documents: Documents which add further detail to the policies in the Local Plan. They can be used to provide further guidance for development on specific sites, or on particular issues, such as design. Supplementary planning documents are capable of being a material consideration in planning decisions but are not part of the development plan.

Sustainable transport modes: Any efficient, safe and accessible means of transport with overall low impact on the environment, including walking and cycling, low and ultra low emission vehicles, car sharing and public transport.

Town centre: Area defined on the local authority's proposal map, including the primary shopping area and areas predominantly occupied by main town centre uses within or adjacent to the primary shopping area. References to town centres or centres apply to city centres, town centres, district centres and local centres but exclude small parades of shops of purely neighbourhood significance. Unless they are identified as centres in Local Plans, existing out-of-centre developments, comprising or including main town centre uses, do not constitute town centres.

Transport assessment: A comprehensive and systematic process that sets out transport issues relating to a proposed development. It identifies what measures will be required to improve accessibility and safety for all modes of travel, particularly for alternatives to the car such as walking, cycling and public transport and what measures will need to be taken to deal with the anticipated transport impacts of the development.

Transport statement: A simplified version of a transport assessment where it is agreed the transport issues arising out of development proposals are limited and a full transport assessment is not required.

Travel plan: A long-term management strategy for an organisation or site that seeks to deliver sustainable transport objectives through action and is articulated in a document that is regularly reviewed.

Wildlife corridor: Areas of habitat connecting wildlife populations.

Windfall sites: Sites which have not been specifically identified as available in the Local Plan process. They normally comprise previously-developed sites that have unexpectedly become available.

ANNEX 3: DOCUMENTS REPLACED BY THIS FRAMEWORK

1. Planning Policy Statement: *Delivering Sustainable Development* (31 January 2005)
2. Planning Policy Statement: *Planning and Climate Change – Supplement to Planning Policy Statement 1* (17 December 2007)
3. Planning Policy Guidance 2: *Green Belts* (24 January 1995)
4. Planning Policy Statement 3: *Housing* (9 June 2011)
5. Planning Policy Statement 4: *Planning for Sustainable Economic Growth* (29 December 2009)
6. Planning Policy Statement 5: *Planning for the Historic Environment* (23 March 2010)
7. Planning Policy Statement 7: *Sustainable Development in Rural Areas* (3 August 2004)
8. Planning Policy Guidance 8: *Telecommunications* (23 August 2001)
9. Planning Policy Statement 9: *Biodiversity and Geological Conservation* (16 August 2005)
10. Planning Policy Statement 12: *Local Spatial Planning* (4 June 2008)
11. Planning Policy Guidance 13: *Transport* (3 January 2011)
12. Planning Policy Guidance 14: *Development on Unstable Land* (30 April 1990)
13. Planning Policy Guidance 17: *Planning for Open Space, Sport and Recreation* (24 July 2002)
14. Planning Policy Guidance 18: *Enforcing Planning Control* (20 December 1991)
15. Planning Policy Guidance 19: *Outdoor Advertisement Control* (23 March 1992)
16. Planning Policy Guidance 20: *Coastal Planning* (1 October 1992)

17. Planning Policy Statement 22: *Renewable Energy* (10 August 2004)
18. Planning Policy Statement 23: *Planning and Pollution Control* (3 November 2004)
19. Planning Policy Guidance 24: *Planning and Noise* (3 October 1994)
20. Planning Policy Statement 25: *Development and Flood Risk* (29 March 2010)
21. Planning Policy Statement 25 Supplement: *Development and Coastal Change* (9 March 2010)
22. Minerals Policy Statement 1: *Planning and Minerals* (13 November 2006)
23. Minerals Policy Statement 2: *Controlling and Mitigating the Environmental Effects of Minerals Extraction In England*. This includes its Annex 1: *Dust* and Annex 2: *Noise* (23 March 2005 – Annex 1: 23 March 2005 and Annex 2: 23 May 2005)
24. Minerals Planning Guidance 2: *Applications, permissions and conditions* (10 July 1998)
25. Minerals Planning Guidance 3: *Coal Mining and Colliery Spoil Disposal* (30 March 1999)
26. Minerals Planning Guidance 5: *Stability in surface mineral workings and tips* (28 January 2000)
27. Minerals Planning Guidance 7: *Reclamation of minerals workings* (29 November 1996)
28. Minerals Planning Guidance 10: *Provision of raw material for the cement industry* (20 November 1991)
29. Minerals Planning Guidance 13: *Guidance for peat provision in England* (13 July 1995)
30. Minerals Planning Guidance 15: *Provision of silica sand in England* (23 September 1996)
31. Circular 05/2005: *Planning Obligations* (18 July 2005)
32. Government Office London Circular 1/2008: *Strategic Planning in London* (4 April 2008)
33. Letter to Chief Planning Officers: *Town and Country Planning (Electronic Communications) (England) Order 2003* (2 April 2003)
34. Letter to Chief Planning Officers: *Planning Obligations and Planning Registers* (3 April 2002)
35. Letter to Chief Planning Officers: *Model Planning Conditions for development on land affected by contamination* (30 May 2008)
36. Letter to Chief Planning Officers: *Planning for Housing and Economic Recovery* (12 May 2009)
37. Letter to Chief Planning Officers: *Development and Flood Risk – Update to the Practice Guide to Planning Policy Statement 25* (14 December 2009)
38. Letter to Chief Planning Officers: *Implementation of Planning Policy Statement 25 (PPS25) – Development and Flood Risk* (7 May 2009)
39. Letter to Chief Planning Officers: *The Planning Bill – delivering well designed homes and high quality places* (23 February 2009)
40. Letter to Chief Planning Officers: *Planning and Climate Change – Update* (20 January 2009)
41. Letter to Chief Planning Officers: *New powers for local authorities to stop 'garden-grabbing'* (15 June 2010)
42. Letter to Chief Planning Officer: *Area Based Grant: Climate Change New Burdens* (14 January 2010)
43. Letter to Chief Planning Officers: *The Localism Bill* (15 December 2010)
44. Letter to Chief Planning Officers: *Planning policy on residential parking standards, parking charges, and electric vehicle charging infrastructure* (14 January 2011)

---

1 A list of the documents revoked and replaced by this Framework is at Annex 3.

2 This includes the Local Plan and neighbourhood plans which have been made in relation to the area (see glossary for full definition).

3 Section 38(6) of the Planning and Compulsory Purchase Act 2004 and section 70(2) of the Town and Country Planning Act 1990.

4 Sections 19(2)(a) and 38(6) of the Planning and Compulsory Purchase Act 2004 and section 70(2) of the Town and Country Planning Act 1990. In relation to neighbourhood plans, under section 38B and C and paragraph 8(2) of new Schedule 4B to the 2004 Act (inserted by the

Localism Act 2011 section 116 and Schedules 9 and 10) the independent examiner will consider whether having regard to national policy it is appropriate to make the plan.

5 The Waste Planning Policy Statement will remain in place until the National Waste Management Plan is published.

6 Natural Environment White Paper, *The Natural Choice: Securing the Value of Nature*, 2011.

7 Section 38(6) of the Planning and Compulsory Purchase Act 2004 and section 70(2) of the Town and Country Planning Act 1990.

8 A list of the documents revoked and replaced by this Framework is at Annex 3. Section 19(2)(a) of the Planning and Compulsory Purchase Act 2004 states, in relation to plan-making, that the local planning authority must have regard to national policies and advice contained in guidance issued by the Secretary of State.

9 For example, those policies relating to sites protected under the Birds and Habitats Directives (see paragraph 119) and/or designated as Sites of Special Scientific Interest; land designated as Green Belt, Local Green Space, an Area of Outstanding Natural Beauty, Heritage Coast or within a National Park (or the Broads Authority); designated heritage assets; and locations at risk of flooding or coastal erosion.

10 Unless material considerations indicate otherwise.

11 To be considered deliverable, sites should be available now, offer a suitable location for development now, and be achievable with a realistic prospect that housing will be delivered on the site within five years and in particular that development of the site is viable. Sites with planning permission should be considered deliverable until permission expires, unless there is clear evidence that schemes will not be implemented within five years, for example they will not be viable, there is no longer a demand for the type of units or sites have long term phasing plans.

12 To be considered developable, sites should be in a suitable location for housing development and there should be a reasonable prospect that the site is available and could be viably developed at the point envisaged.

13 Currently provided by Design Council Cabe.

14 Regulation 20, The Town and Country Planning (Control of Advertisements) (England) Regulations 2007.

15 Regulation 7, The Town and Country Planning (Control of Advertisements) (England) Regulations 2007.

16 In line with the objectives and provisions of the Climate Change Act 2008.

17 In assessing the likely impacts of potential wind energy development when identifying suitable areas, and in determining planning applications for such development, planning authorities should follow the approach set out in the National Policy Statement for Renewable Energy Infrastructure (read with the relevant sections of the Overarching National Policy Statement for Energy Infrastructure, including that on aviation impacts). Where plans identify areas as suitable for renewable and low-carbon energy development, they should make clear what criteria have determined their selection, including for what size of development the areas are considered suitable.

18 Unless material considerations indicate otherwise.

19 Technical guidance on flood risk published alongside this Framework sets out how this policy should be implemented.

20 A site-specific flood risk assessment is required for proposals of 1 hectare or greater in Flood Zone 1; all proposals for new development (including minor development and change of use) in Flood Zones 2 and 3, or in an area within Flood Zone 1 which has critical drainage problems (as notified to the local planning authority by the Environment Agency); and where proposed development or a change of use to a more vulnerable class may be subject to other sources of flooding.

21 The Floods and Water Management Act 2010 establishes a Sustainable Drainage Systems Approving Body in unitary or county councils. This body must approve drainage systems in new developments and re-developments before construction begins.

22 Except for any proposal involving a change of use to a caravan, camping or chalet site, or to a mobile home or park home site, where the Sequential and Exception Tests should be applied as appropriate.

23 As required by the Marine and Coastal Access Act 2009.

24 Circular 06/2005 provides further guidance in respect of statutory obligations for biodiversity and geological conservation and their impact within the planning system.

25 *English National Parks and the Broads: UK Government Vision and Circular 2010* provides further guidance and information about their statutory purposes, management and other matters.

26 Potential Special Protection Areas, possible Special Areas of Conservation and proposed Ramsar sites are sites on which Government has initiated public consultation on the scientific case for designation as a Special Protection Area, candidate Special Area of Conservation or Ramsar site.
27 See Explanatory Note to the Noise Policy Statement for England (Department for the Environment, Food and Rural Affairs).
28 Subject to the provisions of the Environmental Protection Act 1990 and other relevant law.
29 The principles and policies set out in this section apply to the heritage-related consent regimes for which local planning authorities are responsible under the Planning (Listed Buildings and Conservation Areas) Act 1990, as well as to plan-making and decision-taking.
30 Copies of evidence should be deposited with the relevant Historic Environment Record, and any archives with a local museum or other public depository.
31 Technical guidance on minerals published alongside this Framework sets out how these policies should be implemented.
32 Section 38(6) of the Planning and Compulsory Purchase Act 2004.
33 Under section 39(2) of the Planning and Compulsory Purchase Act 2004 a local authority exercising their plan making functions must do so with the objective of contributing to the achievement of sustainable development.
34 The planning policy for traveller sites sets out how travellers' accommodation needs should also be assessed.
35 Such as land instability, contamination and subsidence.
36 In marine areas, local planning authorities should collaborate with the Marine Management Organisation to ensure that policies across the land/sea boundary are integrated.
37 Section 38(1) of the Planning and Compulsory Purchase Act 2004: this includes adopted or approved development plan documents i.e. the Local Plan and neighbourhood plans which have been made in relation to the area (and the London Plan).
38 Section 38(6) of the Planning and Compulsory Purchase Act 2004 and section 70(2) of the Town and Country Planning Act 1990.
39 In development plan documents adopted in accordance with the Planning and Compulsory Purchase Act 2004 or published in the London Plan.
40 Unless other material considerations indicate otherwise.
41 Regional strategies remain part of the development plan until they are abolished by Order using powers taken in the Localism Act. It is the government's clear policy intention to revoke the regional strategies outside of London, subject to the outcome of the environmental assessments that are currently being undertaken.

Appendix C
SECONDARY LEGISLATION

The following statutory instruments related to the Localism Act 2011 are in force as at 20 April 2012:

- City of Birmingham (Mayoral Referendum) Order 2012, SI 2012/324
- City of Bradford (Mayoral Referendum) Order 2012, SI 2012/325
- City of Bristol (Mayoral Referendum) Order 2012, SI 2012/326
- City of Coventry (Mayoral Referendum) Order 2012, SI 2012/327
- City of Leeds (Mayoral Referendum) Order 2012, SI 2012/328
- City of Manchester (Mayoral Referendum) Order 2012, SI 2012/329
- City of Newcastle-upon-Tyne (Mayoral Referendum) Order 2012, SI 2012/330
- City of Nottingham (Mayoral Referendum) Order 2012, SI 2012/331
- City of Sheffield (Mayoral Referendum) Order 2012, SI 2012/332
- City of Wakefield (Mayoral Referendum) Order 2012, SI 2012/333
- Council Tax (Administration and Enforcement) (Amendment) (England) Regulations 2012, SI 2012/672
- Council Tax and Non-Domestic Rating (Demand Notices) (England) (Amendment) Regulations 2012, SI 2012/538
- Council Tax (Demand Notices) (England) Regulations 2011, SI 2011/3038
- Flexible Tenancies (Review Procedures) Regulations 2012, SI 2012/695
- Land Compensation Development (England) Order 2012, SI 2012/634
- Local Authorities (Conduct of Referendums) (Council Tax Increases) (England) Regulations 2011, SI 2012/444
- Local Authorities (Conduct of Referendums) (England) Regulations 2012, SI 2012/323
- Local Authorities (Elected Mayors) (Elections, Terms of Office and Casual Vacancies) (England) Regulations 2012, SI 2012/336
- Local Authorities (Referendums) (Petitions) (England) Regulations 2011, SI 2011/2914
- Local Authority (Referendums Relating to Council Tax Increases) Regulations 2012, SI 2012/460
- Local Government (Structural Changes) (Finance) (Amendment) Regulations 2011, SI 2012/20
- Localism Act 2011 (Commencement No. 1 and Transitional Provisions) Order 2011, SI 2011/2896
- Localism Act 2011 (Commencement No. 2 and Transitional and Saving Provision) Order 2012, SI 2012/57
- Localism Act 2011 (Commencement No. 3) Order 2012, SI 2012/411
- Localism Act 2011 (Commencement No. 4 and Transitional, Transitory and Saving Provisions) Order 2012, SI 2012/628
- Localism Act 2011 (Commencement No. 5 and Transitional, Savings and Transitory Provisions) Order 2012, SI 2012/1008
- Localism Act 2011 (Consequential Provisions) Order 2012, SI 2012/961
- Localism Act 2011 (Housing and Regeneration Functions in Greater London) (Consequential, Transitional and Saving Provisions) (No. 2) Order 2012, SI 2012/702
- Localism Act 2011 (Housing and Regeneration Functions in Greater London) (Consequential, Transitory, Transitional and Saving Provisions) Order 2012, SI 2012/666

- Localism Act 2011 (Infrastructure Planning) (Consequential Amendments) Regulations 2012, SI 2012/635
- Localism Act 2011 (Regulation of Social Housing) (Consequential Provisions) Order 2012, SI 2012/641
- Neighbourhood Planning (General) Regulations 2012, SI 2012/637
- Non-Domestic Rating (Cancellation of Backdated Liabilities) Regulations 2012, SI 2012/537
- Non-Domestic Rating Contributions (England) (Amendment) Regulations 2011, SI 2011/2993
- Non-Domestic Rating (Small Business Rate Relief) (England) Order 2012, SI 2012/148
- Parish Councils (General Power of Competence) (Prescribed Conditions) Order 2012, SI 2012/965
- Standards Board for England (Abolition) Order 2012, SI 2012/668
- Town and Country Planning (Development Management Procedure) (England) (Amendment) Order 2012, SI 2012/636
- Town and Country Planning (Local Planning) (England) Regulations 2012, SI 2012/767
- Town and Country Planning (Tree Preservation) (England) Regulations 2012, SI 2012/605
- Transfer of Tenancies and Right to Acquire (Exclusion) Regulations 2012, SI 2012/696

Appendix D
COMMENCEMENT

The table below provides the dates that each section and Schedule in the Localism Act 2011 came into force as at 20 April 2012. Sections and Schedules that are not in force at that date are in italics. The relevant commencement orders are:

- Localism Act 2011 (Commencement No. 1 and Transitional Provisions) Order 2011, SI 2011/2896
- Localism Act 2011 (Commencement No. 2 and Transitional and Saving Provision) Order 2012, SI 2012/57
- Localism Act 2011 (Commencement No. 1) (Wales) Order 2012, SI 2012/193
- Localism Act 2011 (Commencement No. 3) Order 2012, SI 2012/411
- Localism Act 2011 (Commencement No. 4 and Transitional, Transitory and Saving Provisions) Order 2012, SI 2012/628
- Localism Act 2011 (Commencement No. 2 and Saving Provision) (Wales) Order 2012, SI 2012/887
- Localism Act 2011 (Commencement No. 5 and Transitional, Savings and Transitory Provisions) Order 2012, SI 2012/1008

Provision	Date of commencement	Commencement provision or order
s.1 partially	18 February 2012	SI 2012/411
s.1 otherwise	4 April 2012	SI 2012/1008
ss.2–7	18 February 2012	SI 2012/411
s.8 partially	3 December 2011	SI 2011/2896
s.8 otherwise	18 February 2012	SI 2012/411
ss.9, 10 partially	18 February 2012	SI 2012/411
ss.9, 10 otherwise	1 April 2012	SI 2012/887
ss.11–14	18 February 2012	SI 2012/411
s.15	3 December 2011	SI 2011/2896
s.16–18	15 January 2012	SI 2012/57
s.19	3 December 2011	SI 2011/2896
s.20 partially	3 December 2011	SI 2011/2896
s.20 otherwise	15 January 2012	SI 2012/57
s.21 partially	3 December 2011	SI 2011/2896
s.21 partially	15 January 2012	SI 2012/57
s.21 partially	9 March 2012	SI 2012/628

Provision	Date of commencement	Commencement provision or order
s.21 otherwise	*4 May 2012*	*SI 2012/1008*
s.22 partially	15 January 2012	SI 2012/57
s.22 partially	9 March 2012	SI 2012/628
s.22 otherwise	*4 May 2012*	*SI 2012/1008*
s.23	15 November 2011	s.240(5)(a)
s.24	15 January 2012	SI 2012/57
s.25	15 January 2012	s.240(1)(a)
s.26 partially	15 November 2011	s.240(5)(b)
s.26 partially	31 January 2012	SI 2012/57
s.26 partially	1 April 2012	SI 2012/628
s.26 otherwise	*Not yet in force*	
ss.27–29	*Not yet in force*	
s.30 partially	31 January 2012	SI 2012/57
s.30 otherwise	*Not yet in force*	
ss.31–35	*Not yet in force*	
s.36 partially	15 January 2012	SI 2012/57
s.36 otherwise	*Not yet in force*	
s.37	15 November 2011	s.240(5)(c)
ss.38–43 as to England	15 January 2012	s.240(1)(b)
ss.38–43 as to Wales	31 January 2012	SI 2012/193
s.44	15 January 2012	s.240(1)(c)
s.45	15 January 2012	s.240(1)(d)
s.46 as to England	1 April 2012	SI 2012/628
s.46 as to Wales	1 April 2012	SI 2012/887
s.47	15 January 2012	s.240(1)(e)
ss.48–57	*31 May 2012*	*SI 2012/1008*
ss.58–67	*Not yet in force*	
s.68 as to England	15 January 2012	SI 2012/57
s.68 as to Wales	*Not yet in force*	
s.69 partially	3 December 2011	SI 2011/2896
s.69 partially as to England	15 January 2012	SI 2011/57

Provision	Date of commencement	Commencement provision or order
s.69 otherwise as to Wales	31 January 2012	SI 2012/193
s.69 otherwise as to England	1 April 2012	SI 2012/628
s.70	15 January 2012	SI 2012/57
s.71	15 January 2012	s.240(1)(f)
ss.72–79	3 December 2011	SI 2011/2896
s.80	15 January 2012	s.240(1)(g)
ss.81–85 partially	15 November 2011	s.240(5)(d)
ss.81–85 otherwise	*Not yet in force*	
s.86	15 November 2011	s.240(5)(e)
ss.87–102 partially	15 November 2011	s.240(5)(f)
ss.87–102 otherwise	*Not yet in force*	
ss.103, 104	15 November 2011	s.240(5)(g)
ss.105–108 partially	15 November 2011	s.240(5)(f)
ss.105–108 otherwise	*Not yet in force*	
s.109 partially	15 November 2011	s.240(5)(h)
s.109 otherwise	*Not yet in force*	
s.110	15 November 2011	s.240(5)(i)
s.111–113	15 January 2012	s.240(1)(h)
s.114	16 November 2011	s.240(6)
s.115	15 January 2012	SI 2012/57
s.116 partially	15 November 2011	s.240(5)(j)
s.116 partially	15 January 2012	SI 2012/57
s.116 partially	6 April 2012	SI 2012/628
s.116 otherwise	*Not yet in force*	
ss.117–120	15 November 2011	s.240(5)(k)
s.121 partially	15 November 2011	s.240(5)(j)
s.121 partially	15 January 2012	SI 2012/57
s.121 otherwise	6 April 2012	SI 2012/628
s.122 partially	15 November 2011	s.240(5)(l)
s.122 otherwise	*Not yet in force*	
s.123	6 April 2012	SI 2012/628

Provision	Date of commencement	Commencement provision or order
s.124 partially	15 January 2012	SI 2012/57
s.124 otherwise	6 April 2012	SI 2012/628
ss.125–127	6 April 2012	SI 2012/628
s.128 partially	15 January 2012	SI 2012/57
s.128 otherwise	1 April 2012	SI 2012/628
s.129 partially	15 January 2012	SI 2012/57
s.129 otherwise	1 April 2012	SI 2012/628
ss.130–137	1 April 2012	SI 2012/628
s.138 partially	15 January 2012	SI 2012/57
s.138 otherwise	1 April 2012	SI 2012/628
ss.139–141	1 April 2012	SI 2012/628
s.142 partially	15 January 2012	SI 2012/57
s.142 otherwise	1 April 2012	SI 2012/628
s.143	15 January 2012	s.240(1)(i)
s.144	15 November 2011	s.240(5)(m)
s.145 partially	15 January 2012	SI 2012/57
s.145 otherwise	*Not yet in force*	
s.146 partially	15 January 2012	SI 2012/57
s.146 otherwise	*Not yet in force*	
s.147 partially	15 January 2012	SI 2012/57
s.147 otherwise	*Not yet in force*	
ss.148, 149	*Not yet in force*	
s.150 partially	15 January 2012	SI 2012/57
s.150 otherwise	*15 January 2013*	*SI 2012/1008*
ss.151, 152	15 January 2012	SI 2012/57
s.153 partially	15 January 2012	SI 2012/57
s.153 otherwise	*Not yet in force*	
s.154 partially	15 January 2012	SI 2012/57
s.154 otherwise	1 April 2012	SI 2012/628
ss.155–157	1 April 2012	SI 2012/628
s.158 partially	15 January 2012	SI 2012/57

Provision	**Date of commencement**	**Commencement provision or order**
s.158 otherwise	1 April 2012	SI 2012/628
ss.159–161	1 April 2012	SI 2012/628
s.162 partially	1 April 2012	SI 2012/628
s.162 otherwise	1 April 2012	SI 2012/887
ss.163, 164	1 April 2012	SI 2012/628
s.165 partially	15 January 2012	SI 2012/57
s.165 otherwise	1 April 2012	SI 2012/628
s.166	1 April 2012	SI 2012/628
s.167	*Not yet in force*	
ss.168–175	15 November 2011	s.240(5)(n)
s.176	15 January 2012	SI 2012/57
s.177	15 January 2012	s.240(1)(j)
s.178 partially	15 January 2012	SI 2012/57
s.178 otherwise	1 April 2012	SI 2012/628
s.179	1 April 2012	SI 2012/628
ss.180–182	*Not yet in force*	
s.183	15 January 2012	s.240(1)(k)
s.184	6 April 2012	SI 2012/628
s.185	1 April 2012	SI 2012/628
s.186 partially	15 January 2012	SI 2012/57
s.186 otherwise	1 April 2012	SI 2012/628
s.187 partially	15 January 2012	SI 2012/57
s.187 otherwise	1 April 2012	SI 2012/628
s.188	*3 May 2012*	*SI 2012/1008*
s.189	1 April 2012	SI 2012/628
s.190	15 January 2012	SI 2012/57
s.191 partially	15 January 2012	SI 2012/57
s.191 otherwise	31 March 2012	SI 2012/628
s.192	*3 May 2012*	*SI 2012/1008*
ss.193, 194	15 January 2012	SI 2012/57
s.195 partially	15 January 2012	SI 2012/57

Provision	**Date of commencement**	**Commencement provision or order**
s.195 partially	31 March 2012	SI 2012/628
s.195 otherwise	1 April 2012	SI 2012/628
s.196	15 January 2012	s.240(1)(l)
s.197 partially	15 January 2012	s.240(1)(l)
s.197 otherwise	15 January 2012	SI 2012/57
ss.198–222	15 January 2012	s.240(1)(l)
ss.223, 224	15 January 2012	SI 2012/57
ss.225–229	*3 May 2012*	*SI 2012/1008*
s.230	15 January 2012	SI 2012/57
s.231	*3 May 2012*	*SI 2012/1008*
s.232	6 April 2012	SI 2012/628
s.233 partially	15 November 2011	s.240(5)(o)
s.233 otherwise as to England and Wales	30 March 2012	SI 2012/628
s.233 otherwise as to Scotland and Northern Ireland	*Not yet in force*	
s.234	15 November 2011	s.240(5)(p)
ss.235, 236	15 November 2011	s.240(5)(p)
s.237 so far as relating to Sched.25, Part 1	4 April 2012	SI 2012/1008
s.237 so far as relating to Sched.25, Part 2 (partially)	18 February 2012	SI 2012/411
s.237 so far as relating to Sched.25, Part 3	18 February 2012	SI 2012/411
s.237 so far as relating to Sched.25, Part 4 (partially)	15 January 2012	SI 2012/57
s.237 so far as relating to Sched.25, Part 4 (partially)	9 March 2012	SI 2012/628
s.237 so far as relating to Sched.25, Part 4 (otherwise)	*4 May 2012*	*SI 2012/1008*

Provision	Date of commencement	Commencement provision or order
s.237 so far as relating to Sched.25, Part 5 (partially)	31 January 2012	SI 2012/57
s.237 so far as relating to Sched.25, Part 6	15 January 2012	s.240(1)(m)
s.237 so far as relating to Sched.25, Part 8	15 January 2012	s.240(1)(m)
s.237 so far as relating to Sched.25, Part 7 as to England	1 April 2012	SI 2012/628
s.237 so far as relating to Sched.25, Part 7 as to Wales	1 April 2012	SI 2012/887
s.237 so far as relating to Sched.25, Part 9 as to England	15 January 2012	SI 2012/57
s.237 so far as relating to Sched.25, Part 10 as to England	1 April 2012	SI 2012/628
s.237 so far as relating to Sched.25, Part 10 as to Wales	1 April 2012	SI 2012/887
s.237 so far as relating to Sched.25, Parts 11–13	15 January 2012	SI 2012/57
s.237 so far as relating to Sched.25, Part 14	15 January 2012	s.240(1)(m)
s.237 so far as relating to Sched.25, Part 15	15 November 2011	s.240(5)(q)
s.237 so far as relating to Sched.25, Part 17	15 January 2012	s.240(1)(m)
s.237 so far as relating to Sched.25, Part 18, 19	6 April 2012	SI 2012/628
s.237 so far as relating to Sched.25, Parts 20, 21	1 April 2012	SI 2012/628
s.237 so far as relating to Sched.25, Part 25	15 January 2012	SI 2012/57
s.237 so far as relating to Sched.25, Parts 26, 27	1 April 2012	SI 2012/628
s.237 so far as relating to Sched.25, Part 29	15 January 2012	s.240(1)(m)

Provision	**Date of commencement**	**Commencement provision or order**
s.237 so far as relating to Sched.25, Part 30	6 April 2012	SI 2012/628
s.237 so far as relating to Sched.25, Part 31 (partially)	1 April 2012	SI 2012/628
s.237 so far as relating to Sched.25, Part 32	31 March 2012	SI 2012/628
s.237 so far as relating to Sched.25, Part 33	*3 May 2012*	*SI 2012/1008*
s.237 so far as relating to Sched.25, Part 34	6 April 2012	SI 2012/628
s.237 otherwise	*Not yet in force*	
ss.238–241	15 November 2011	s.240(5)(p)
Sched.1	4 April 2012	SI 2012/1008
Sched.2 partially	3 December 2011	SI 2011/2896
Sched.2 partially	15 January 2012	SI 2012/57
Sched.2 partially	9 March 2012	SI 2012/628
Sched.2 otherwise	*4 May 2012*	*SI 2012/1008*
Sched.3 partially	15 January 2012	SI 2012/57
Sched.3 partially	9 March 2012	SI 2012/628
Sched.3 otherwise	*4 May 2012*	*SI 2012/1008*
Sched.4 partially	15 November 2011	s.240(5)(b)
Sched.4 partially	31 January 2012	SI 2012/57
Sched.4 partially	1 April 2012	SI 2012/628
Sched.4 otherwise	*Not yet in force*	
Scheds.5–7	3 December 2011	SI 2011/2896
Sched.8 partially	15 November 2011	s.240(5)(h)
Sched.8 otherwise	*Not yet in force*	
Sched.9 partially	15 November 2011	s.240(5)(j)
Sched.9 otherwise	6 April 2012	SI 2012/628
Sched.10 partially	15 November 2011	s.240(5)(j)
Sched.10 partially	15 January 2012	SI 2012/57
Sched.10 partially	6 April 2012	SI 2012/628
Sched.10 otherwise	*Not yet in force*	

Provision	Date of commencement	Commencement provision or order
Sched.11 partially	15 November 2011	s.240(5)(j)
Sched.11 partially	15 January 2012	SI 2012/57
Sched.11 otherwise	6 April 2012	SI 2012/628
Sched.12 partially	15 November 2011	s.240(5)(j)
Sched.12 partially	15 January 2012	SI 2012/57
Sched.12 otherwise	6 April 2012	SI 2012/628
Sched.13 partially	15 January 2012	SI 2012/57
Sched.13 otherwise	1 April 2012	SI 2012/628
Sched.14	4 April 2012	SI 2012/1008
Sched.15	*Not yet in force*	
Sched.16 partially	15 January 2012	SI 2012/57
Sched.16 otherwise	1 April 2012	SI 2012/628
Sched.17	1 April 2012	SI 2012/628
Sched.18	15 January 2012	s.240(1)(k)
Sched.19 partially	15 January 2012	SI 2012/57
Sched.19 otherwise	1 April 2012	SI 2012/628
Sched.20	31 March 2012	SI 2012/628
Sched.21	15 January 2012	240(1)(l)
Sched.22	15 January 2012	240(1)(l)
Sched.23	*3 May 2012*	*SI 2012/1008*
Sched.24 partially	15 November 2011	s.240(5)(o)
Sched.24 otherwise as to England and Wales	30 March 2012	SI 2012/628
Sched.24 otherwise as to Scotland and Northern Ireland	*Not yet in force*	
Sched.25, Part 1	4 April 2012	SI 2012/1008
Sched.25, Part 2 partially	18 February 2012	SI 2012/411
Sched.25, Part 2 otherwise	1 April 2012	SI 2012/887
Sched.25, Part 3	18 February 2012	SI 2012/411
Sched.25, Part 4 partially	15 January 2012	SI 2012/57
Sched.25, Part 4 partially	9 March 2012	SI 2012/628
Sched.25, Part 4 otherwise	*4 May 2012*	*SI 2012/1008*

Provision	Date of commencement	Commencement provision or order
Sched.25, Part 5 partially	31 January 2012	SI 2012/57
Sched.25, Part 5 otherwise	*Not yet in force*	
Sched.25, Part 6	15 January 2012	s.240(1)(m)
Sched.25, Part 7 as to England	1 April 2012	SI 2012/628
Sched.25, Part 7 as to Wales	1 April 2012	SI 2012/887
Sched.25, Part 8	15 January 2012	s.240(1)(m)
Sched.25, Part 9 as to England	15 January 2012	SI 2012/57
Sched.25, Part 10 as to England	1 April 2012	SI 2012/628
Sched.25, Part 10 as to Wales	1 April 2012	SI 2012/628
Sched.25, Parts 11–13	15 January 2012	SI 2012/57
Sched.25, Part 14	15 January 2012	s.240(1)(m)
Sched.25, Part 15	15 November 2011	s.240(5)(q)
Sched.25, Part 16	*Not yet in force*	
Sched.25, Part 17	15 January 2012	s.240(1)(m)
Sched.25, Parts 18, 19	6 April 2012	SI 2012/628
Sched.25, Parts 20, 21	1 April 2012	SI 2012/628
Sched.25, Parts 22–24	*Not yet in force*	
Sched.25, Part 25	15 January 2012	SI 2012/57
Sched.25, Parts 26, 27	1 April 2012	SI 2012/628
Sched.25, Part 29	15 January 2012	s.240(1)(m)
Sched.25, Part 30	6 April 2012	SI 2012/628
Sched.25, Part 31 partially	1 April 2012	SI 2012/628
Sched.25, Part 31 otherwise	*Not yet in force*	
Sched.25, Part 32	31 March 2012	SI 2012/628
Sched.25, Part 33	*3 May 2012*	*SI 2012/1008*
Sched.25, Part 34	6 April 2012	SI 2012/628

INDEX